Shojo Beat

DRAGON GIRL

VOLUME ONE

Story & Art by **Natsumi Matsumoto**

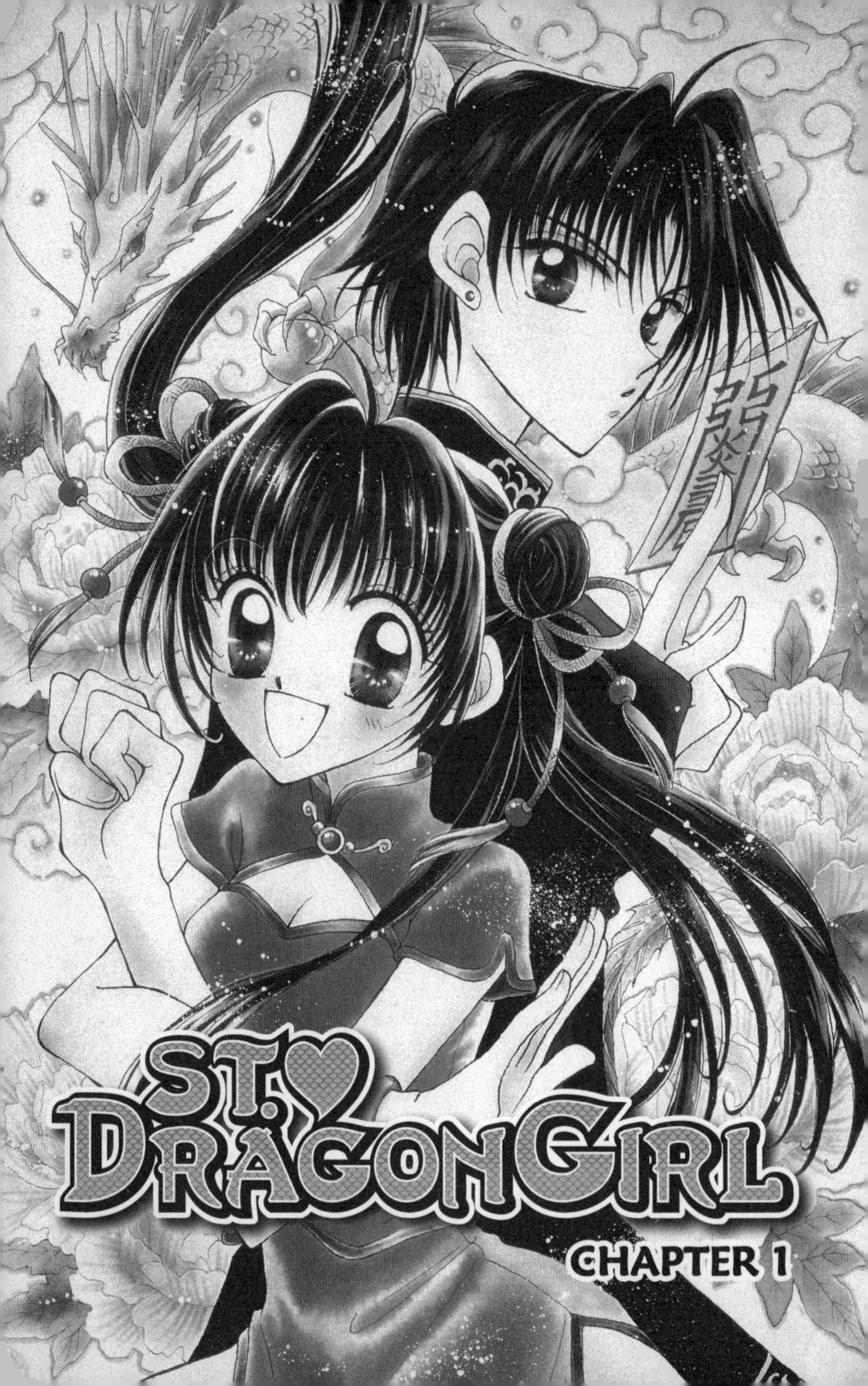
ST.♥ DRAGON GIRL
CHAPTER 1

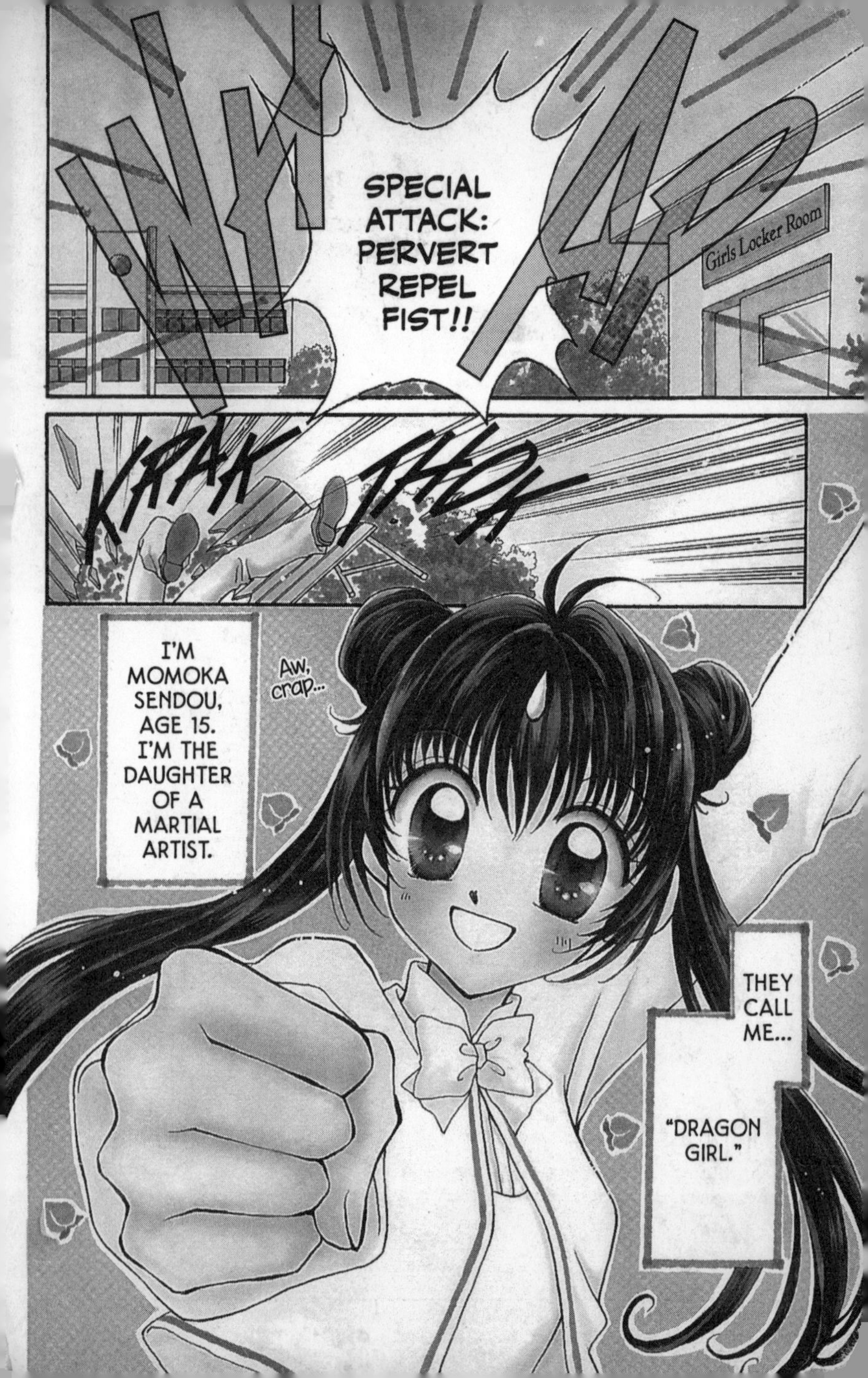
SPECIAL ATTACK: PERVERT REPEL FIST!!
Girls Locker Room
THOK
KRAK
Aw, crap...
I'M MOMOKA SENDOU, AGE 15. I'M THE DAUGHTER OF A MARTIAL ARTIST.
THEY CALL ME...
"DRAGON GIRL."

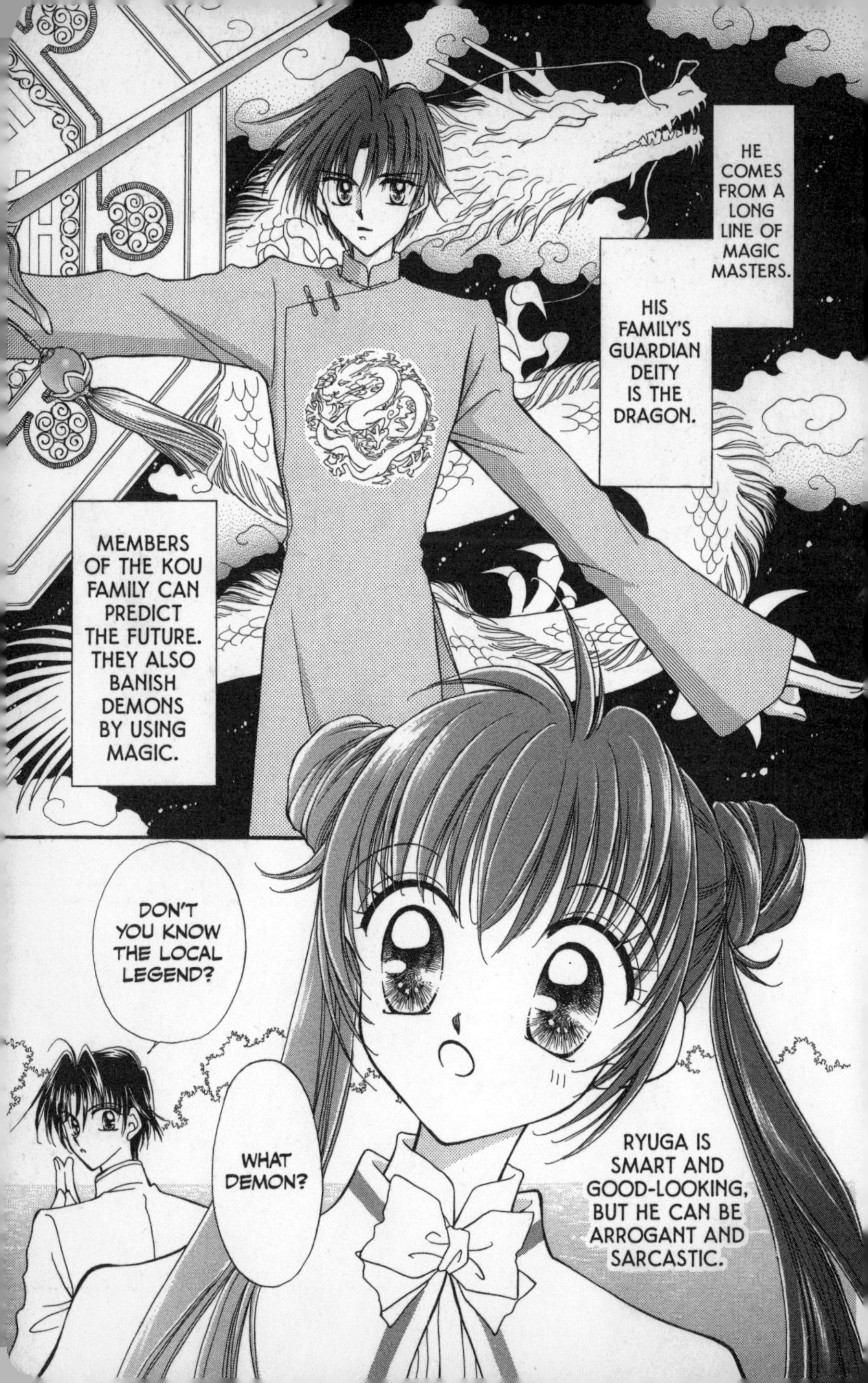
HE COMES FROM A LONG LINE OF MAGIC MASTERS.
HIS FAMILY'S GUARDIAN DEITY IS THE DRAGON.
MEMBERS OF THE KOU FAMILY CAN PREDICT THE FUTURE. THEY ALSO BANISH DEMONS BY USING MAGIC.
RYUGA IS SMART AND GOOD-LOOKING, BUT HE CAN BE ARROGANT AND SARCASTIC.
DON'T YOU KNOW THE LOCAL LEGEND?
WHAT DEMON?

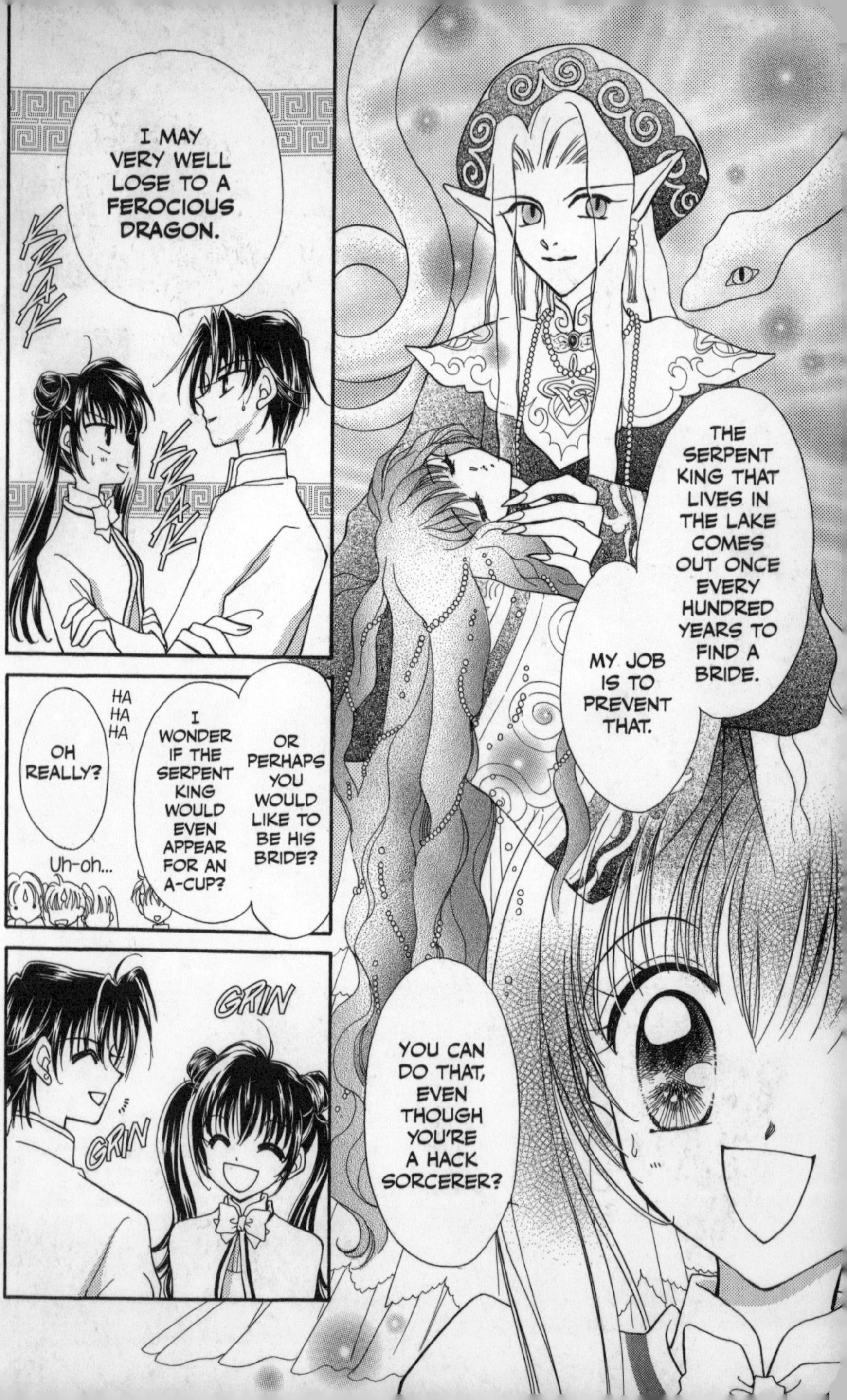
THE SERPENT KING THAT LIVES IN THE LAKE COMES OUT ONCE EVERY HUNDRED YEARS TO FIND A BRIDE.
MY JOB IS TO PREVENT THAT.
YOU CAN DO THAT, EVEN THOUGH YOU'RE A HACK SORCERER?
I MAY VERY WELL LOSE TO A FEROCIOUS DRAGON.
KNAK
KNAK
I WONDER IF THE SERPENT KING WOULD EVEN APPEAR FOR AN A-CUP?
OR PERHAPS YOU WOULD LIKE TO BE HIS BRIDE?
HA HA HA
OH REALLY?
Uh-oh...
GRIN
GRIN

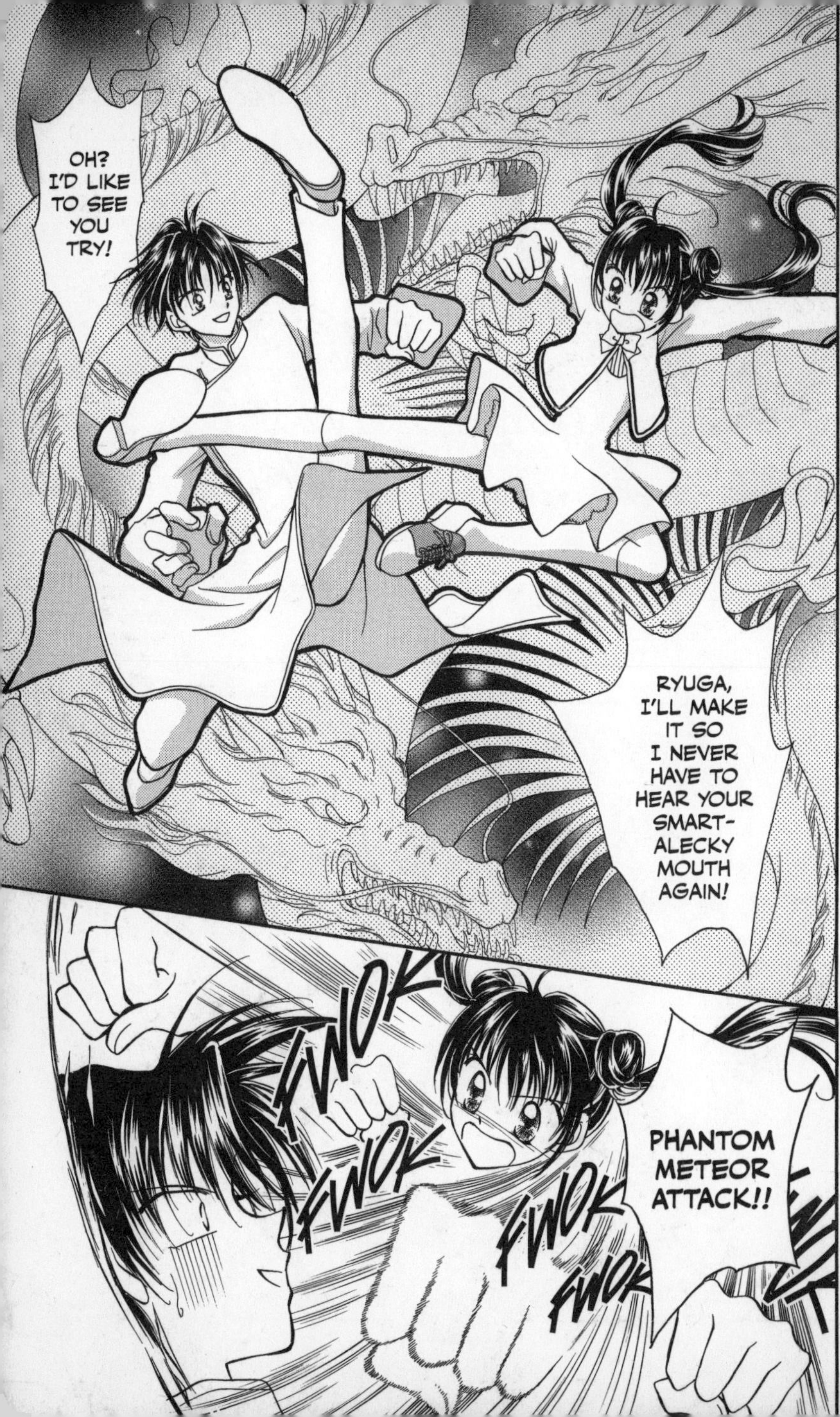
OH? I'D LIKE TO SEE YOU TRY!
RYUGA, I'LL MAKE IT SO I NEVER HAVE TO HEAR YOUR SMART-ALECKY MOUTH AGAIN!
PHANTOM METEOR ATTACK!!
FWOK
FWOK
FWOK
FWOK
FWOK

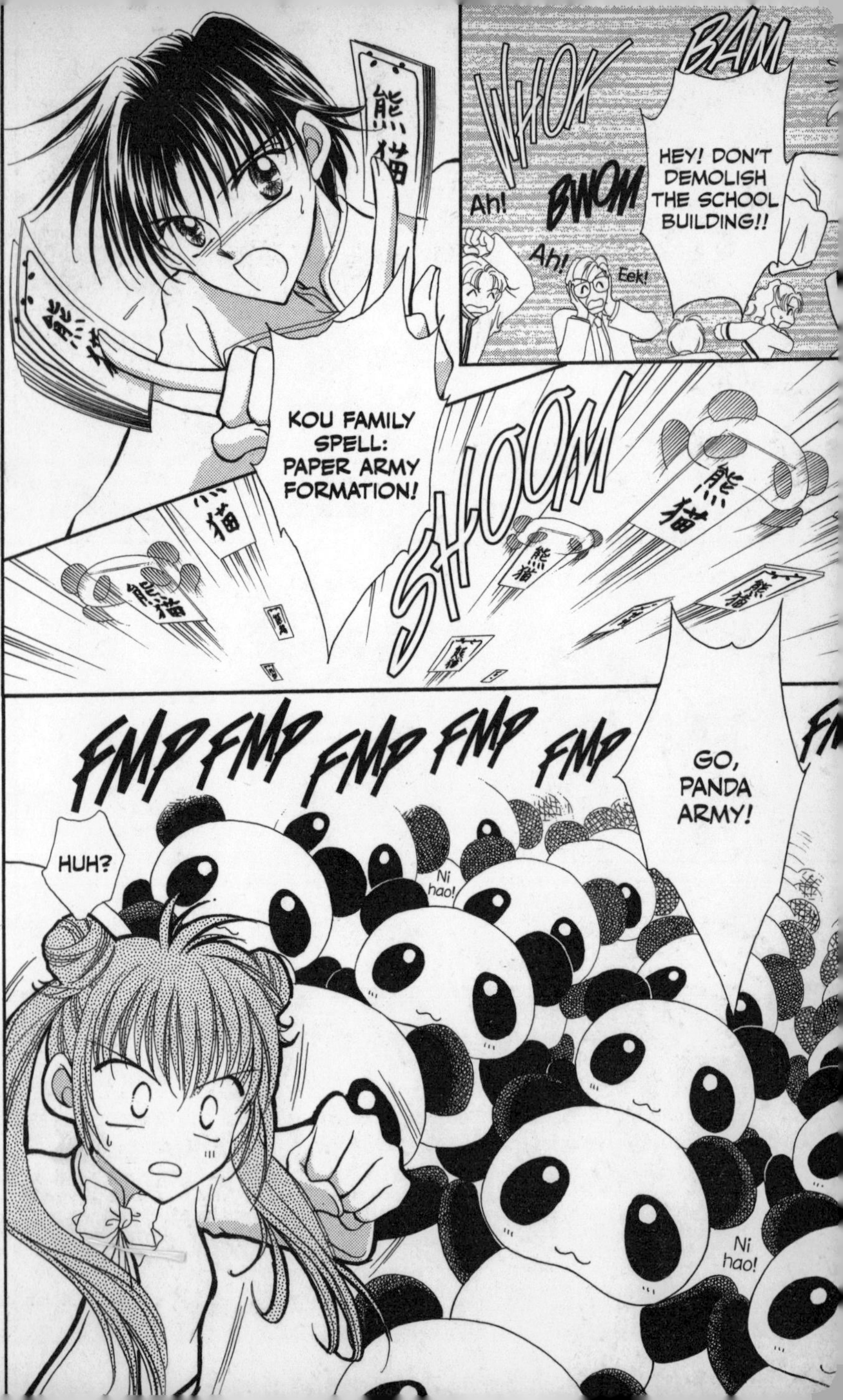
BAM
WHOK
HEY! DON'T DEMOLISH THE SCHOOL BUILDING!!
BWOM
Ah!
Ah!
Eek!
熊猫
KOU FAMILY SPELL: PAPER ARMY FORMATION!
SHOOM
FMP
GO, PANDA ARMY!
FMP FMP FMP FMP FMP
Ni hao!
HUH?
Ni hao!

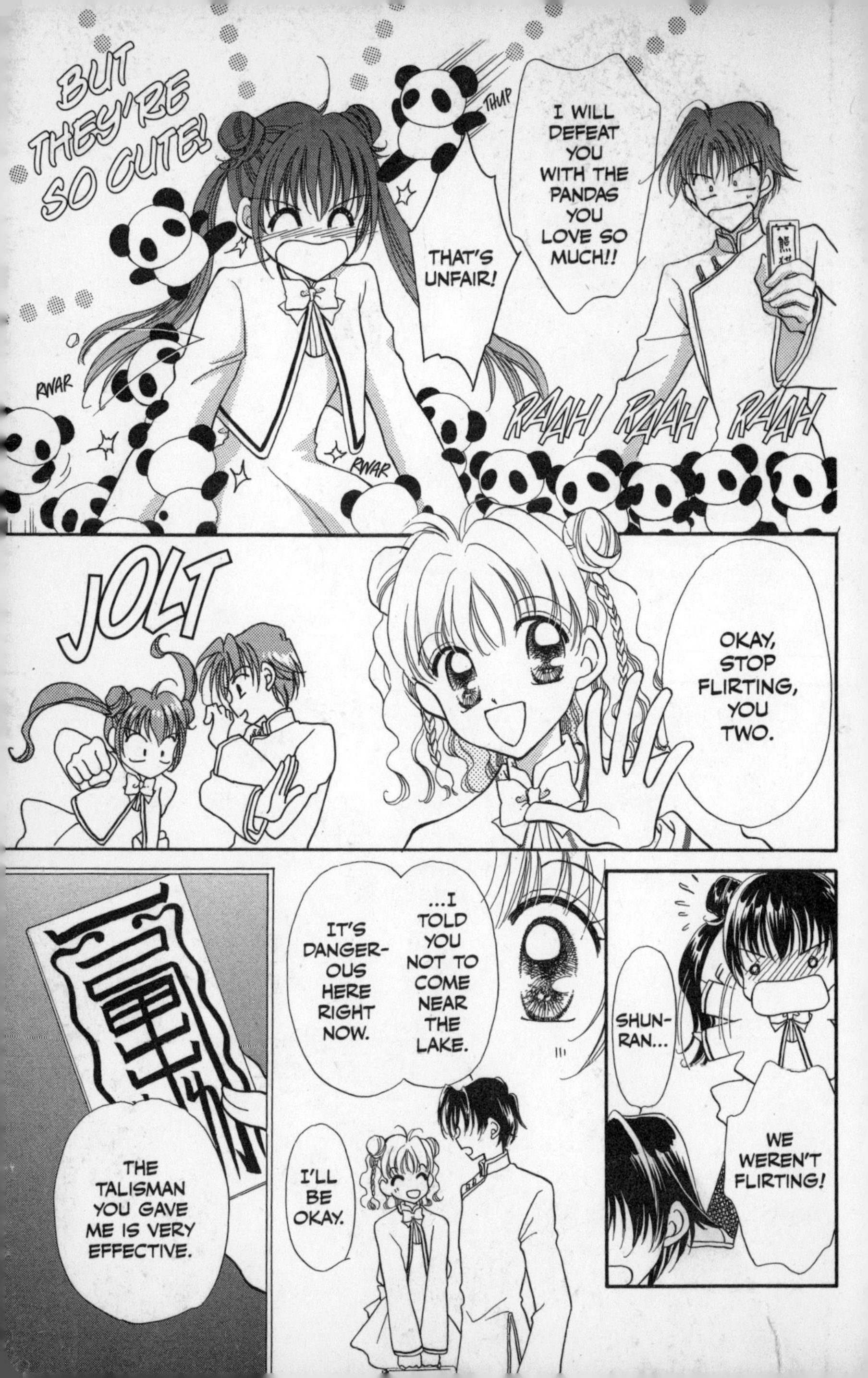
I WILL DEFEAT YOU WITH THE PANDAS YOU LOVE SO MUCH!!
THUP
THAT'S UNFAIR!
BUT THEY'RE SO CUTE!
RAAH RAAH RAAH
RWAR
RWAR
OKAY, STOP FLIRTING, YOU TWO.
JOLT
SHUN-RAN...
WE WEREN'T FLIRTING!
...I TOLD YOU NOT TO COME NEAR THE LAKE.
IT'S DANGER-OUS HERE RIGHT NOW.
I'LL BE OKAY.
THE TALISMAN YOU GAVE ME IS VERY EFFECTIVE.

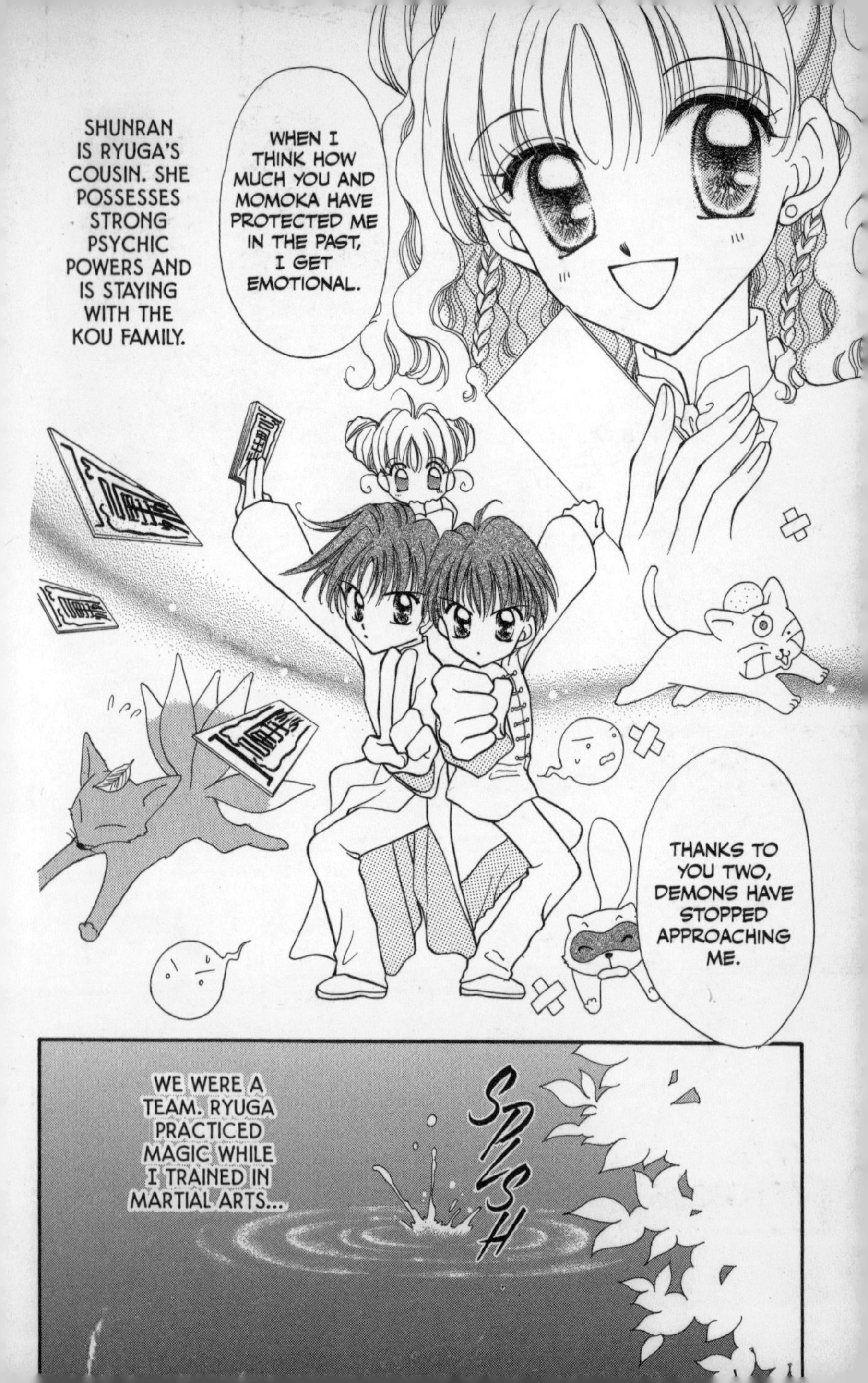
WHEN I THINK HOW MUCH YOU AND MOMOKA HAVE PROTECTED ME IN THE PAST, I GET EMOTIONAL.
SHUNRAN IS RYUGA'S COUSIN. SHE POSSESSES STRONG PSYCHIC POWERS AND IS STAYING WITH THE KOU FAMILY.
THANKS TO YOU TWO, DEMONS HAVE STOPPED APPROACHING ME.
SPLISH
WE WERE A TEAM. RYUGA PRACTICED MAGIC WHILE I TRAINED IN MARTIAL ARTS...

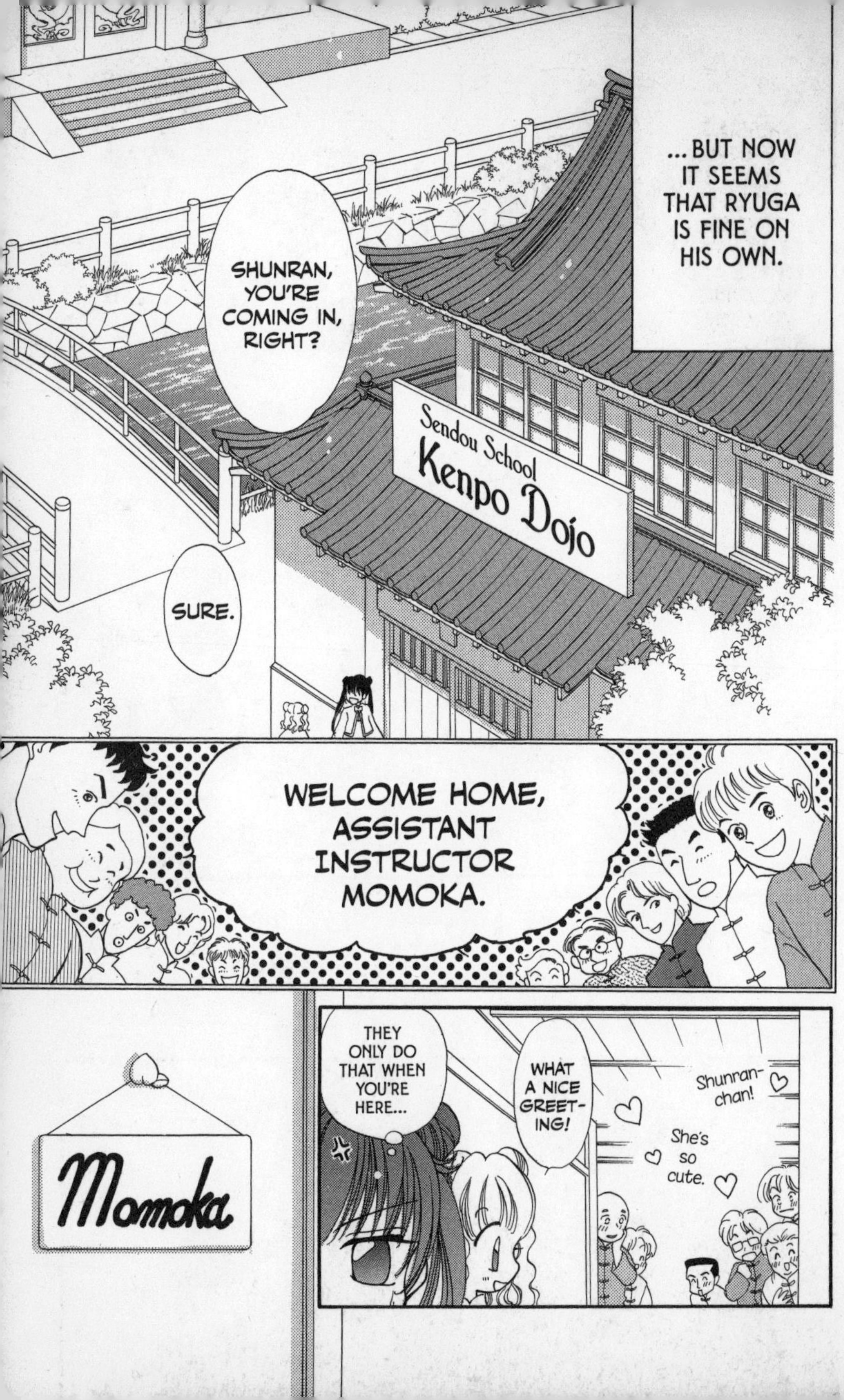
...BUT NOW IT SEEMS THAT RYUGA IS FINE ON HIS OWN.
Sendou School Kenpo Dojo
SHUNRAN, YOU'RE COMING IN, RIGHT?
SURE.
WELCOME HOME, ASSISTANT INSTRUCTOR MOMOKA.
Shunran-chan!
She's so cute.
WHAT A NICE GREETING!
THEY ONLY DO THAT WHEN YOU'RE HERE...
Momoka

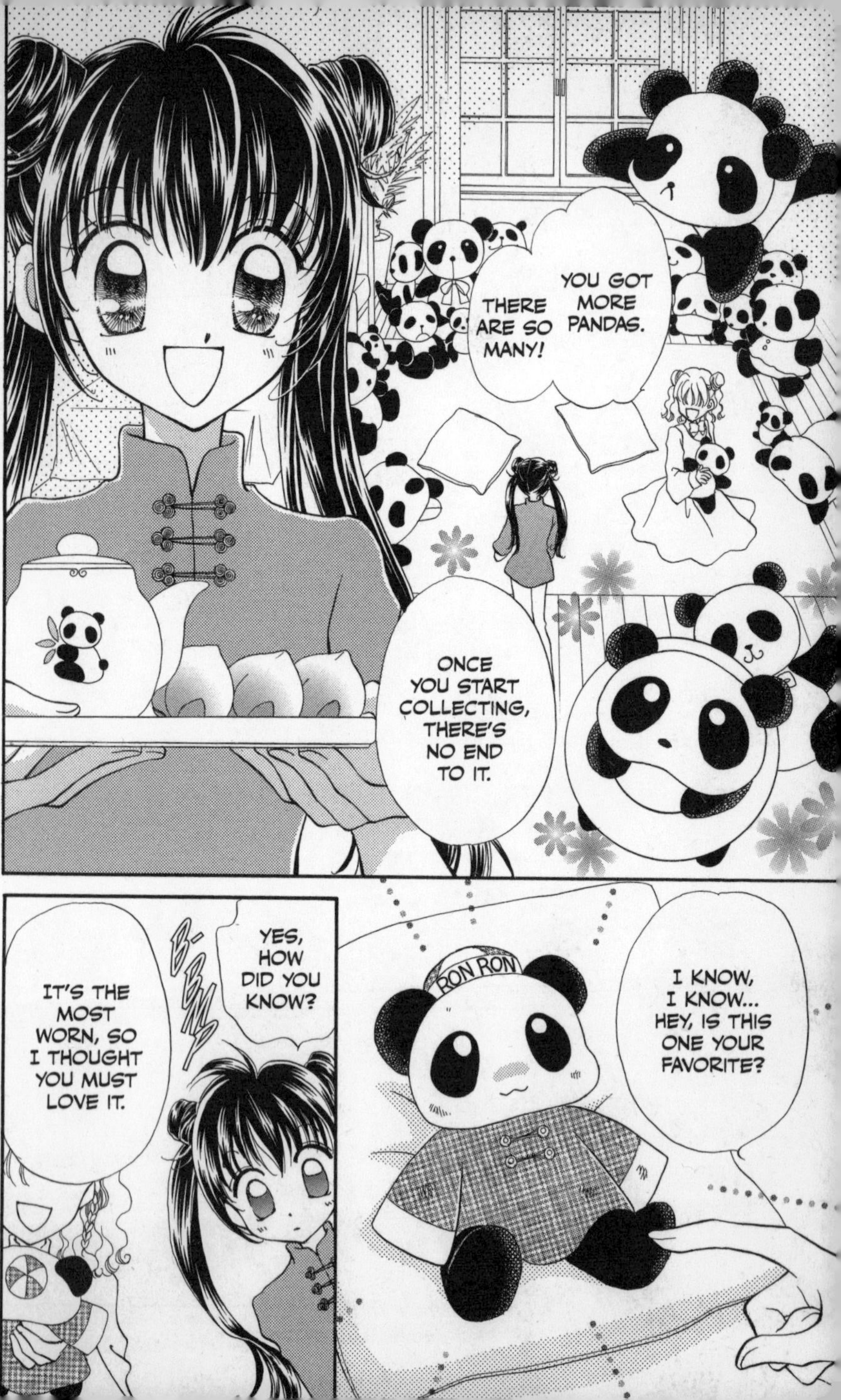
YOU GOT MORE PANDAS.
THERE ARE SO MANY!
ONCE YOU START COLLECTING, THERE'S NO END TO IT.
RON RON
I KNOW, I KNOW... HEY, IS THIS ONE YOUR FAVORITE?
YES, HOW DID YOU KNOW?
B-BMP
IT'S THE MOST WORN, SO I THOUGHT YOU MUST LOVE IT.

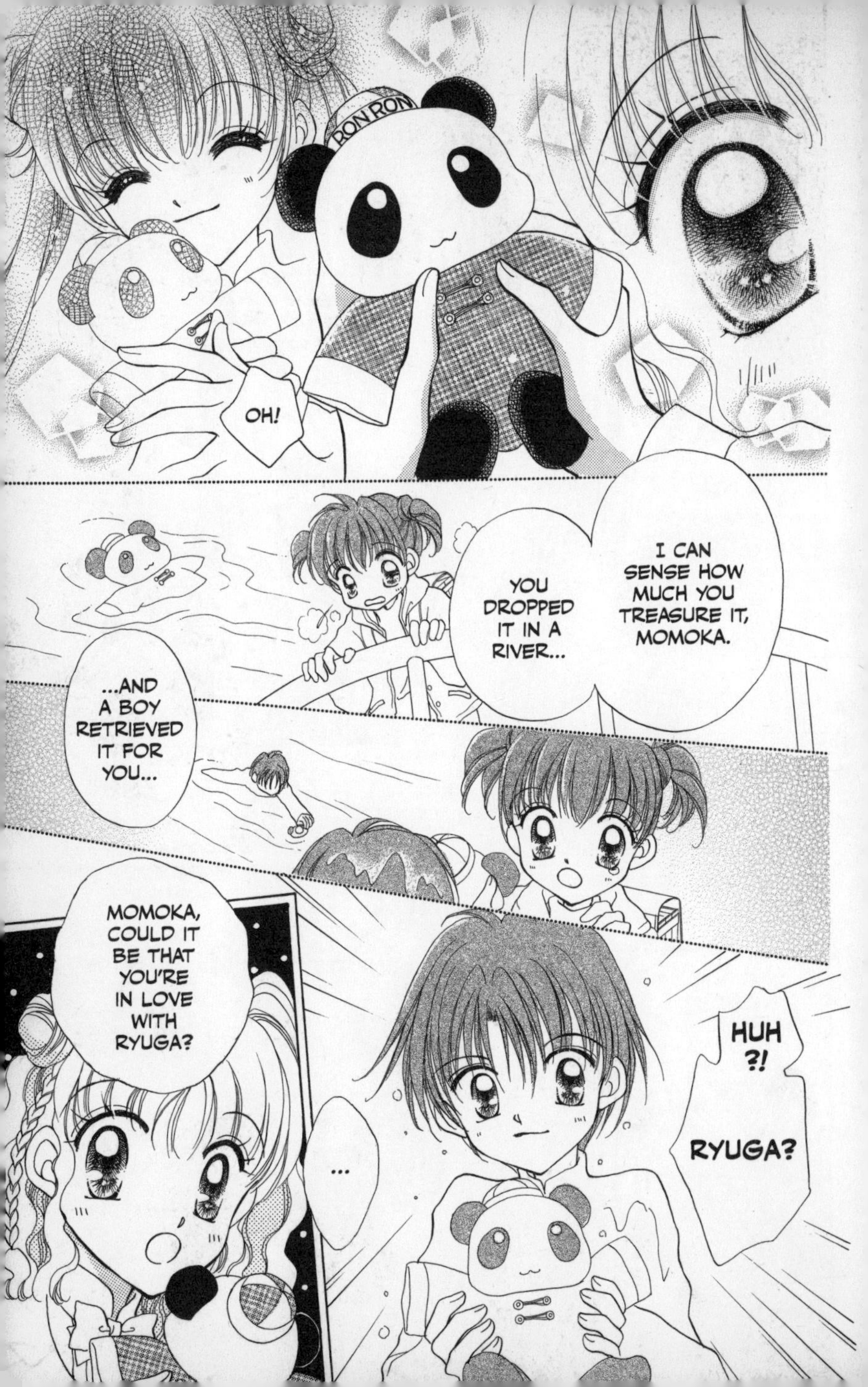
OH!
I CAN SENSE HOW MUCH YOU TREASURE IT, MOMOKA.
YOU DROPPED IT IN A RIVER...
...AND A BOY RETRIEVED IT FOR YOU...
HUH ?!
RYUGA?
...
MOMOKA, COULD IT BE THAT YOU'RE IN LOVE WITH RYUGA?

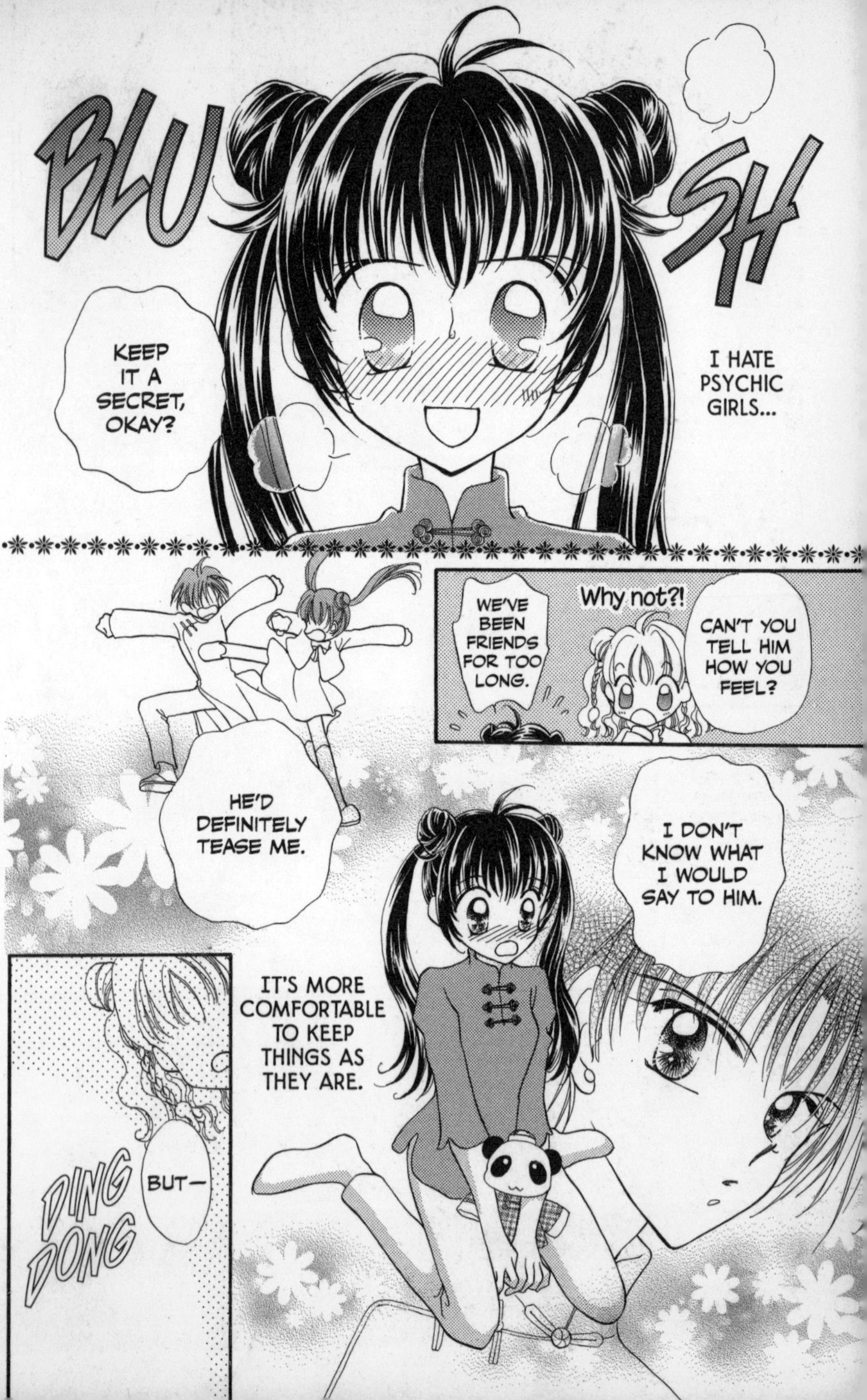
BLUSH
I HATE PSYCHIC GIRLS...
KEEP IT A SECRET, OKAY?
CAN'T YOU TELL HIM HOW YOU FEEL?
Why not?!
WE'VE BEEN FRIENDS FOR TOO LONG.
I DON'T KNOW WHAT I WOULD SAY TO HIM.
HE'D DEFINITELY TEASE ME.
IT'S MORE COMFORTABLE TO KEEP THINGS AS THEY ARE.
BUT—
DING DONG

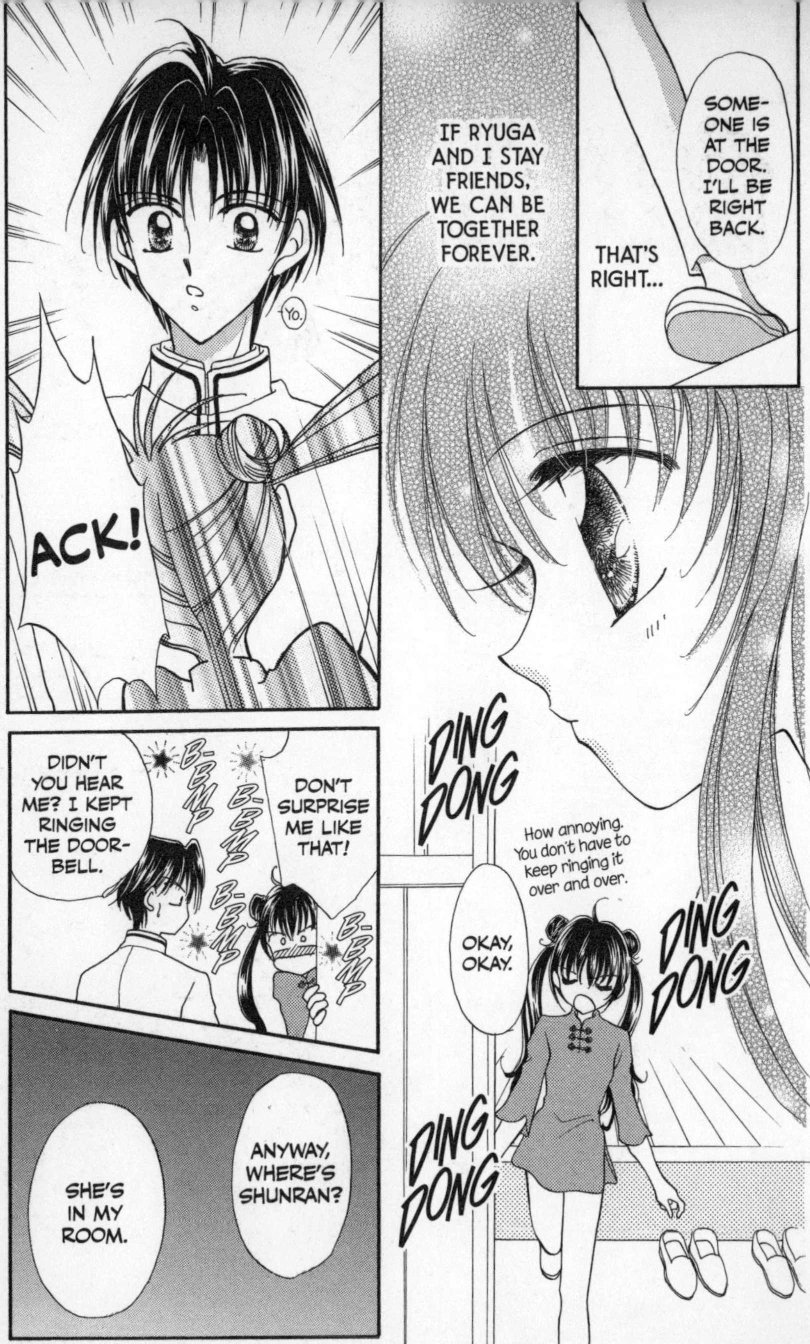
SOME-ONE IS AT THE DOOR. I'LL BE RIGHT BACK.
THAT'S RIGHT...
IF RYUGA AND I STAY FRIENDS, WE CAN BE TOGETHER FOREVER.
DING DONG
DING DONG
How annoying. You don't have to keep ringing it over and over.
OKAY, OKAY.
DING DONG
Yo.
ACK!
DON'T SURPRISE ME LIKE THAT!
B-BMP B-BMP B-BMP B-BMP
DIDN'T YOU HEAR ME? I KEPT RINGING THE DOOR-BELL.
ANYWAY, WHERE'S SHUNRAN?
SHE'S IN MY ROOM.

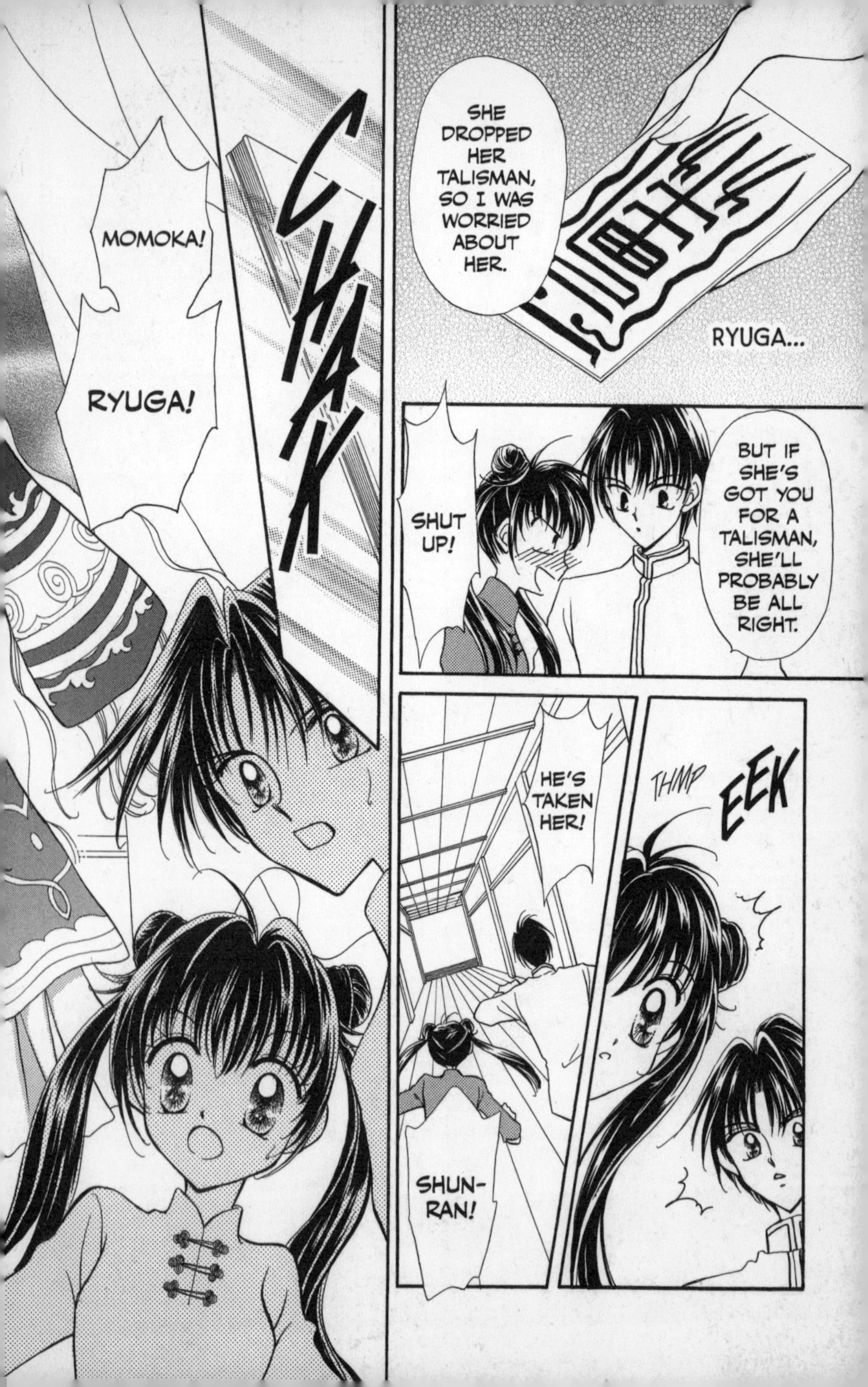
SHE DROPPED HER TALISMAN, SO I WAS WORRIED ABOUT HER.
RYUGA...
BUT IF SHE'S GOT YOU FOR A TALISMAN, SHE'LL PROBABLY BE ALL RIGHT.
SHUT UP!
EEK
THMP
HE'S TAKEN HER!
SHUN-RAN!
CHAKK
MOMOKA!
RYUGA!

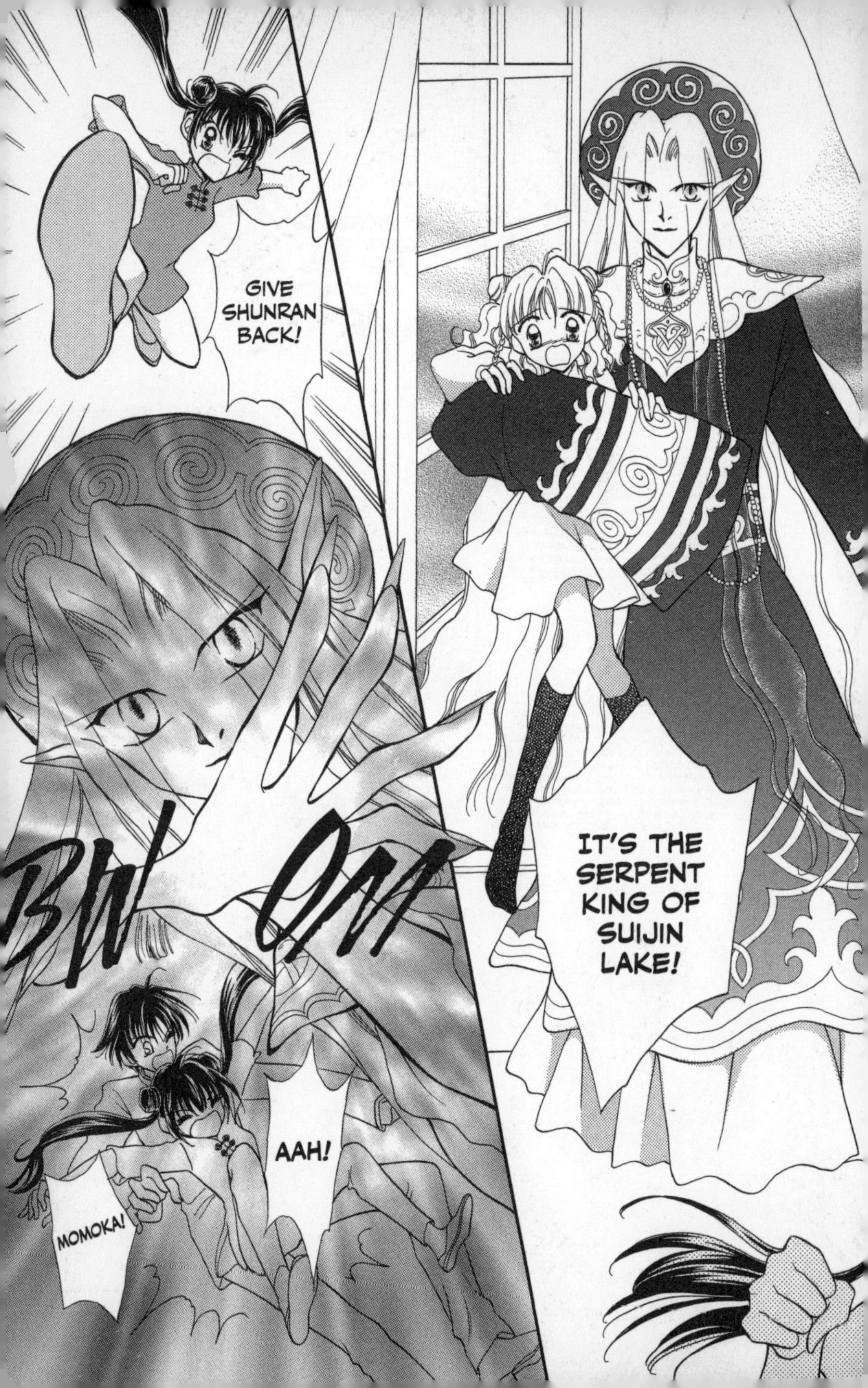
IT'S THE SERPENT KING OF SUIJIN LAKE!
GIVE SHUNRAN BACK!
BWOM
AAH!
MOMOKA!

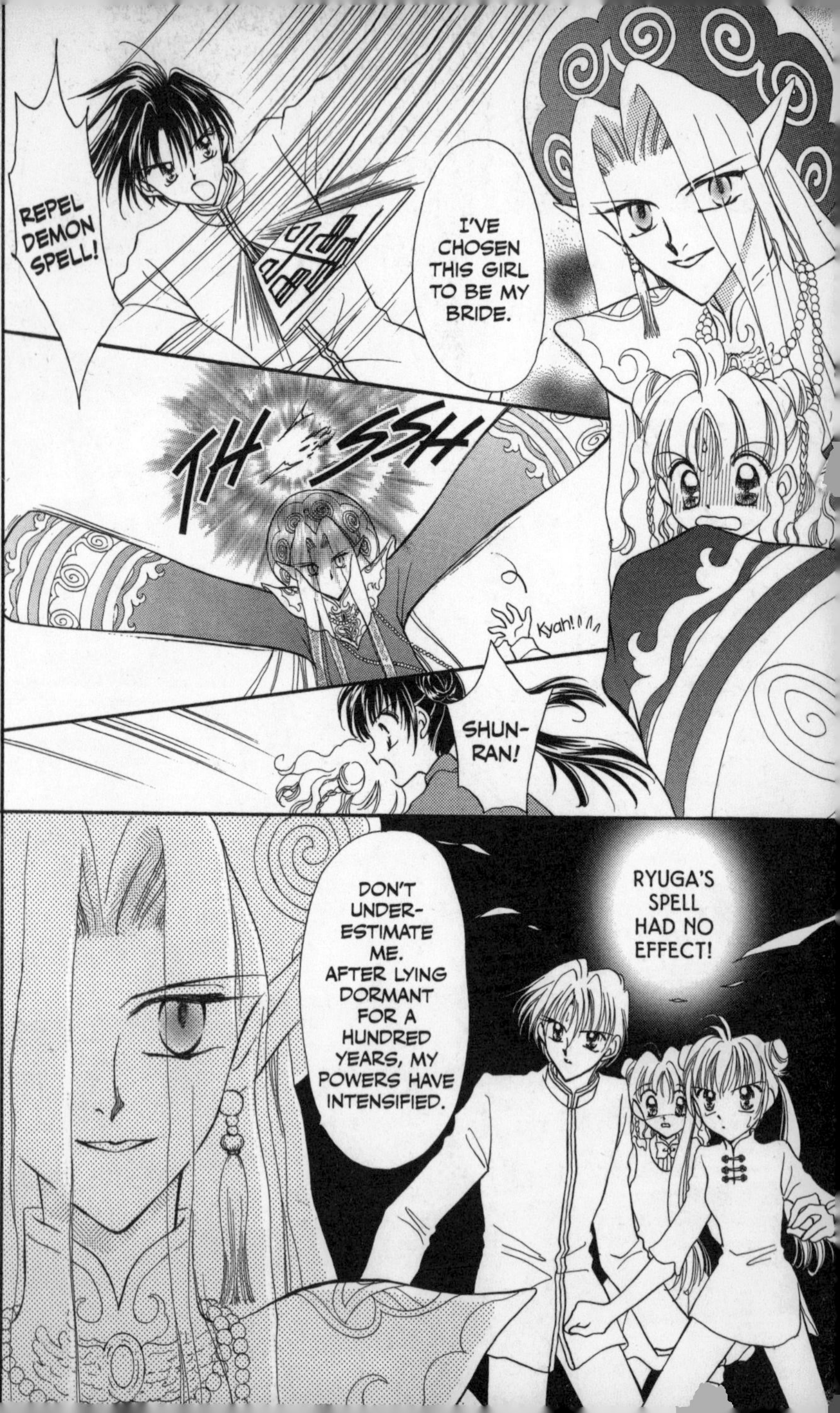
I'VE CHOSEN THIS GIRL TO BE MY BRIDE.
REPEL DEMON SPELL!
THSSH
Kyah!
SHUN-RAN!
RYUGA'S SPELL HAD NO EFFECT!
DON'T UNDER-ESTIMATE ME. AFTER LYING DORMANT FOR A HUNDRED YEARS, MY POWERS HAVE INTENSIFIED.

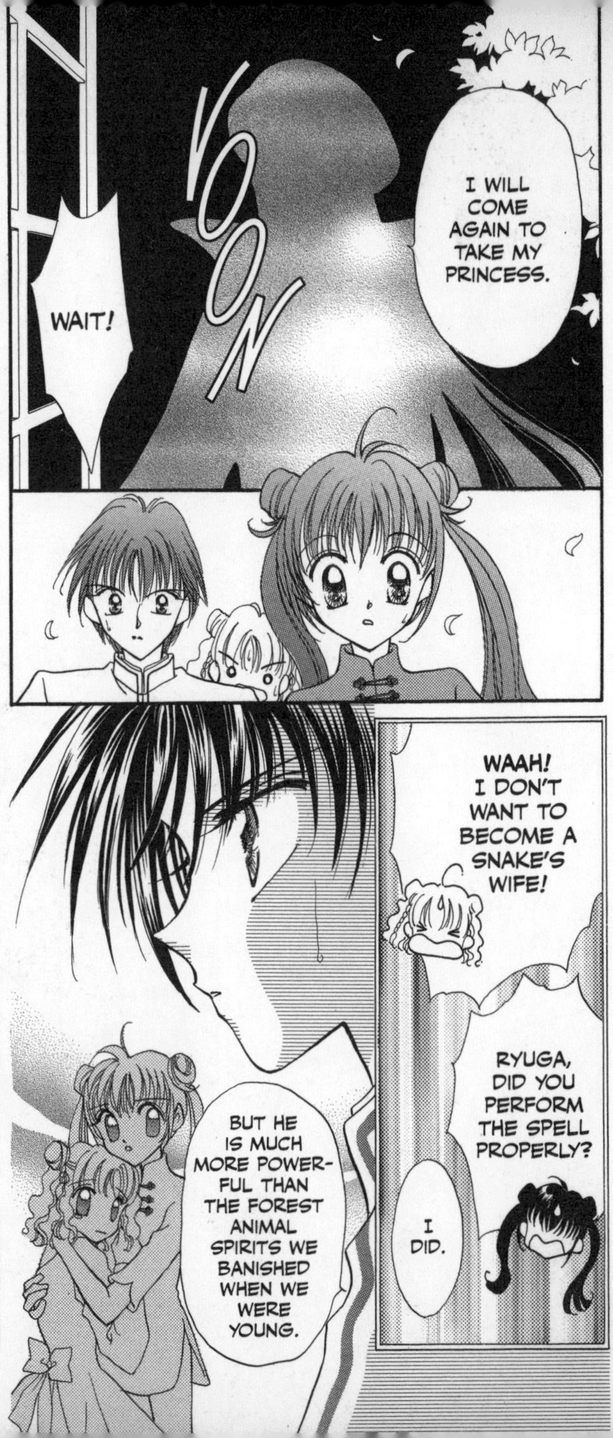
I WILL COME AGAIN TO TAKE MY PRINCESS.
VOON
WAIT!
WAAH! I DON'T WANT TO BECOME A SNAKE'S WIFE!
RYUGA, DID YOU PERFORM THE SPELL PROPERLY?
I DID.
BUT HE IS MUCH MORE POWER-FUL THAN THE FOREST ANIMAL SPIRITS WE BANISHED WHEN WE WERE YOUNG.

1

Hello!

I'm Natsumi Matsumoto.

St. ♥ *Dragon Girl* vol. 1 is finally out! ♥ I've been waiting for this, and after eight volumes, it's finally here. (tears) It looks like it will become a work with many memories.

Now it's time for the manga's inside story. *St.* ♥ *Dragon Girl* is an amazing title... I wanted to write about a girl who was good at kenpo, so that is how this manga started. I wanted the story to be about banishing the baddies. I thought it might be interesting for a boy and a girl to work together to finish them off, so I made Momoka a martial artist and Ryuga a Chinese magic master.

The year 2000 is the year of the dragon, so I wanted lots of dragons in it and lots of action scenes! I love dragon scenes, but am I the only one who feels like I'm reading a manga about demons?

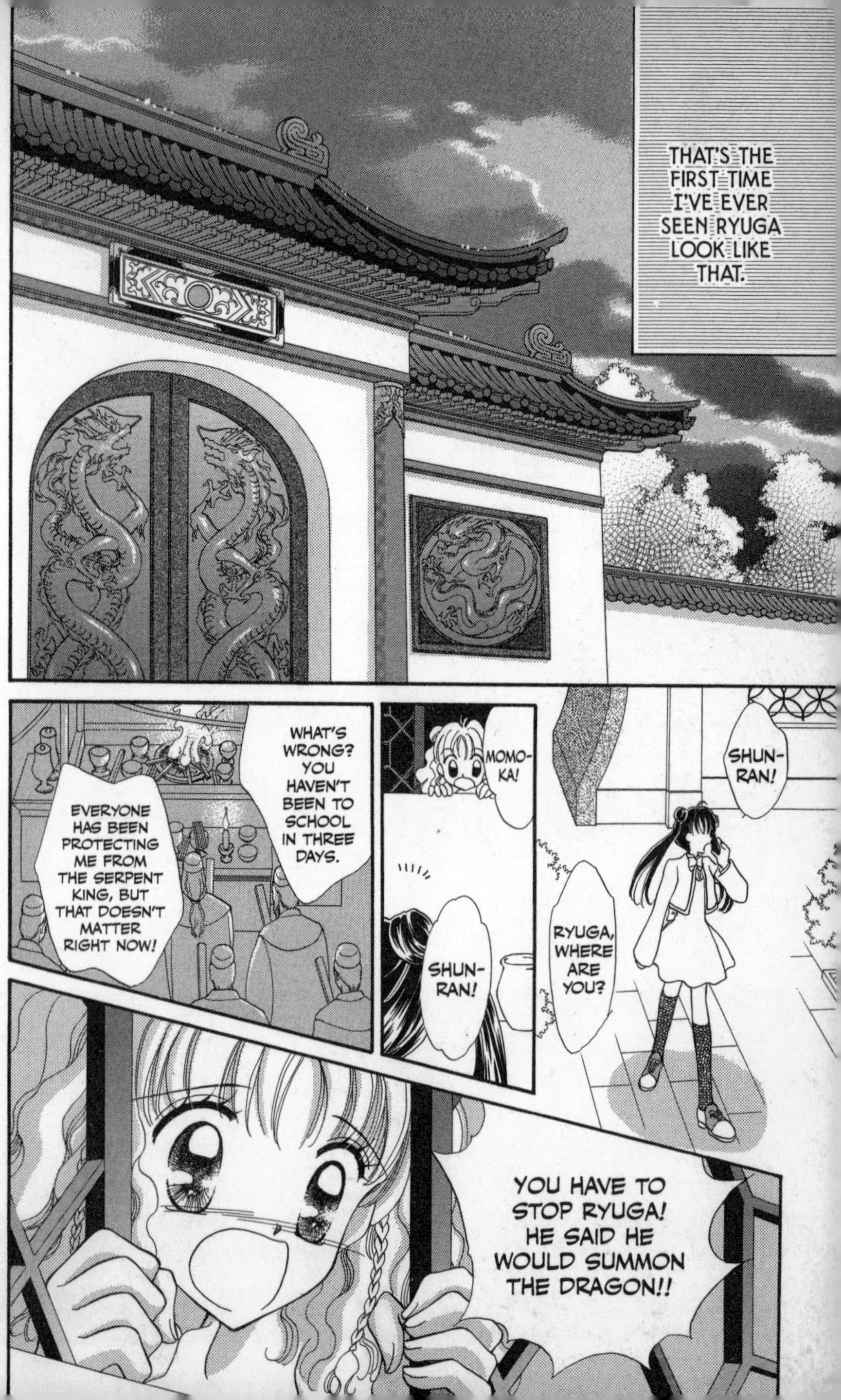
THAT'S THE FIRST TIME I'VE EVER SEEN RYUGA LOOK LIKE THAT.
SHUN-RAN!
RYUGA, WHERE ARE YOU?
MOMO-KA!
SHUN-RAN!
WHAT'S WRONG? YOU HAVEN'T BEEN TO SCHOOL IN THREE DAYS.
EVERYONE HAS BEEN PROTECTING ME FROM THE SERPENT KING, BUT THAT DOESN'T MATTER RIGHT NOW!
YOU HAVE TO STOP RYUGA! HE SAID HE WOULD SUMMON THE DRAGON!!

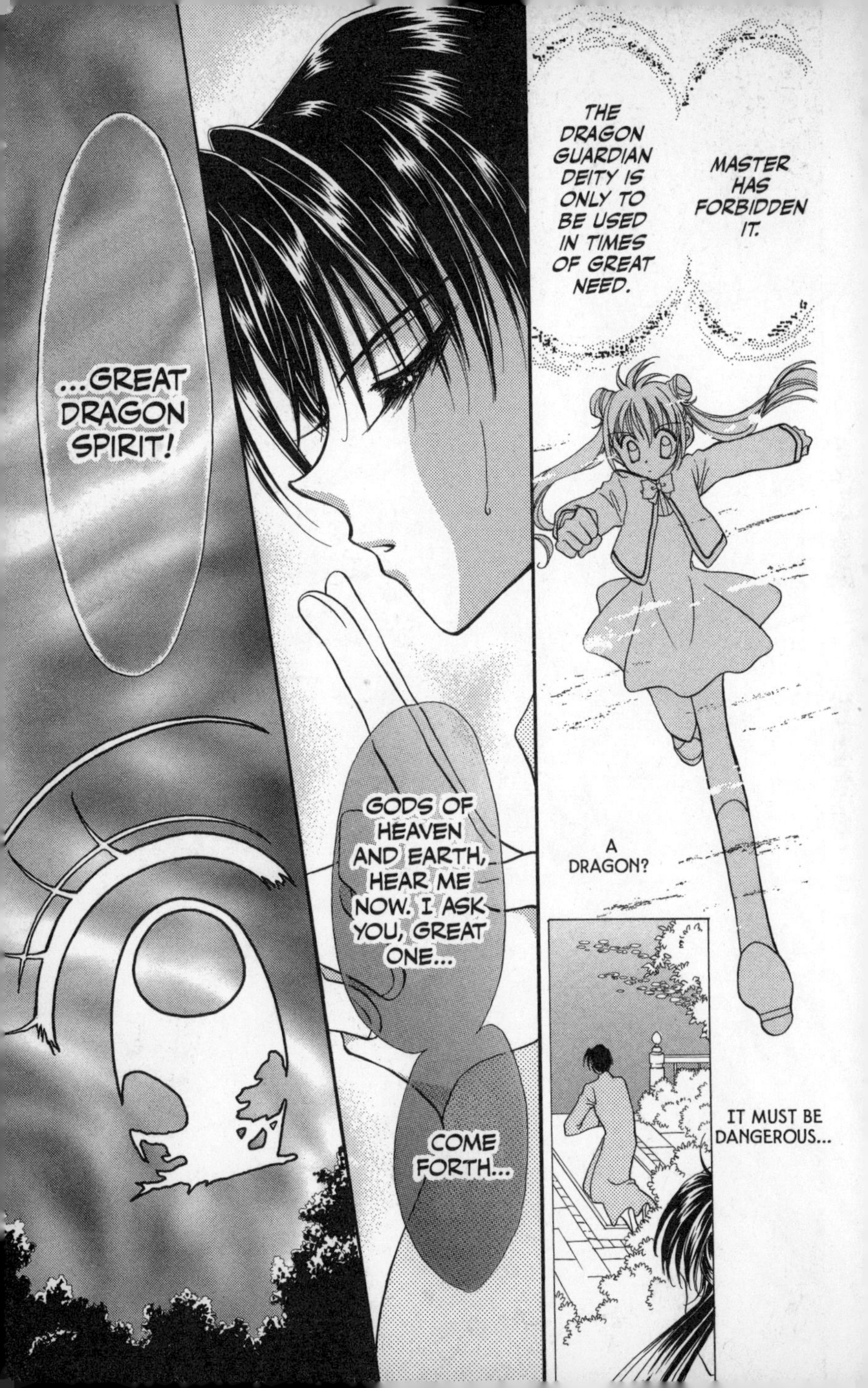
MASTER HAS FORBIDDEN IT.
THE DRAGON GUARDIAN DEITY IS ONLY TO BE USED IN TIMES OF GREAT NEED.
A DRAGON?
IT MUST BE DANGEROUS...
GODS OF HEAVEN AND EARTH, HEAR ME NOW. I ASK YOU, GREAT ONE...
COME FORTH...
...GREAT DRAGON SPIRIT!

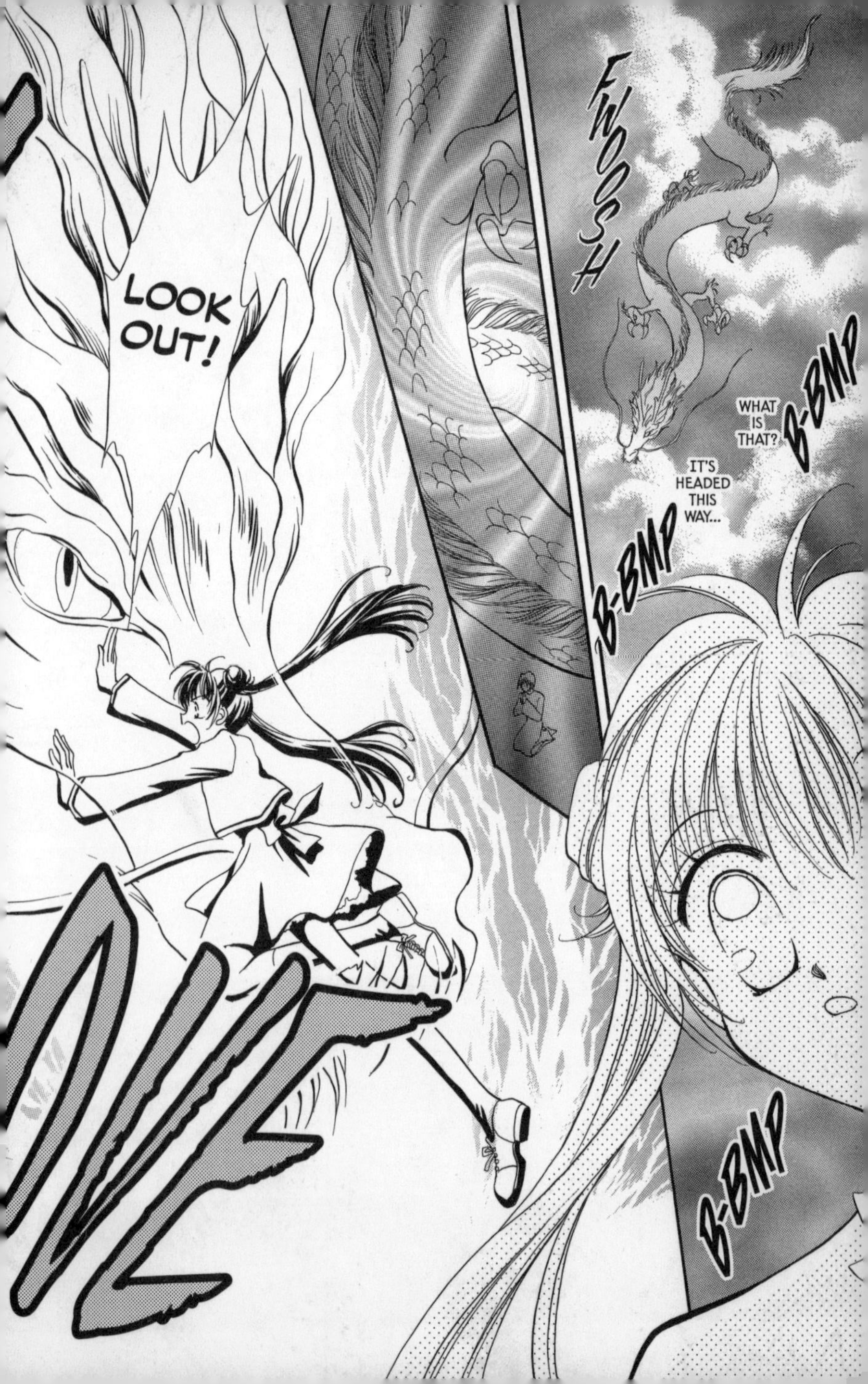
FWOOSH
B-BMP
WHAT IS THAT?
IT'S HEADED THIS WAY...
B-BMP
B-BMP
LOOK OUT!

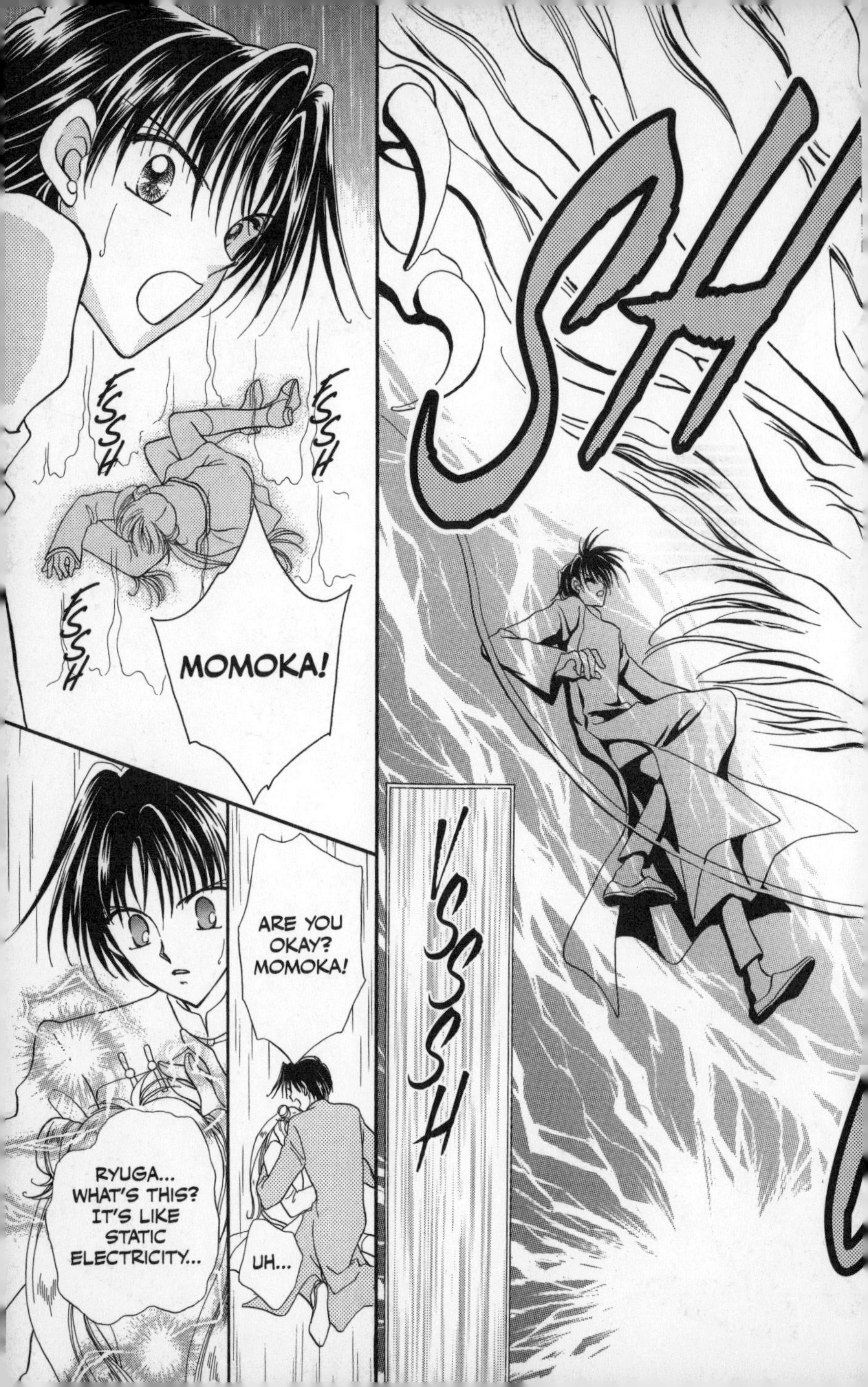

SH
VSSSH
FSSH
FSSH
FSSH
MOMOKA!
ARE YOU OKAY? MOMOKA!
UH...
RYUGA... WHAT'S THIS? IT'S LIKE STATIC ELECTRICITY...

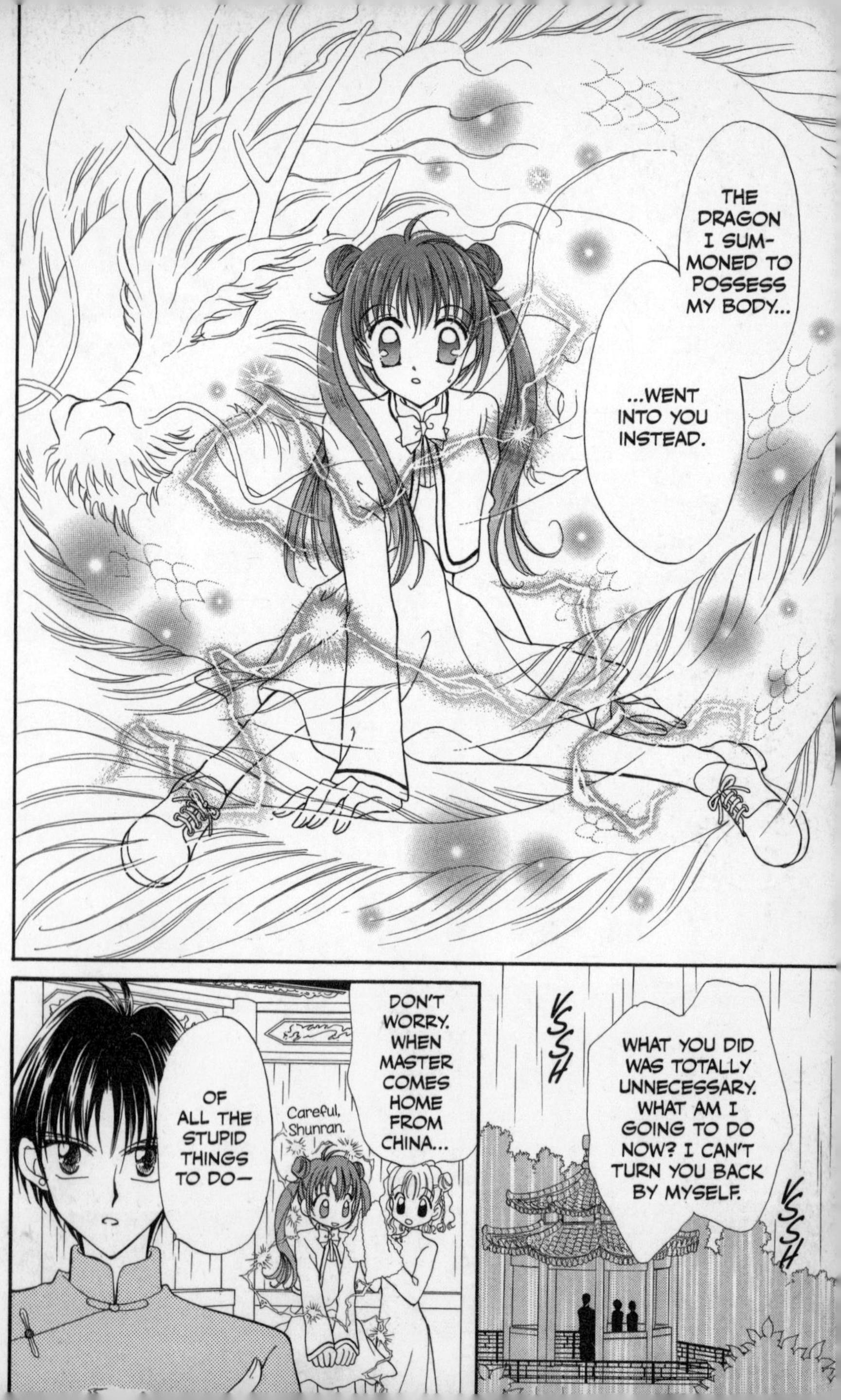
THE DRAGON I SUM-MONED TO POSSESS MY BODY...
...WENT INTO YOU INSTEAD.
VSSH
WHAT YOU DID WAS TOTALLY UNNECESSARY. WHAT AM I GOING TO DO NOW? I CAN'T TURN YOU BACK BY MYSELF.
VSSH
DON'T WORRY. WHEN MASTER COMES HOME FROM CHINA...
Careful, Shunran.
OF ALL THE STUPID THINGS TO DO—

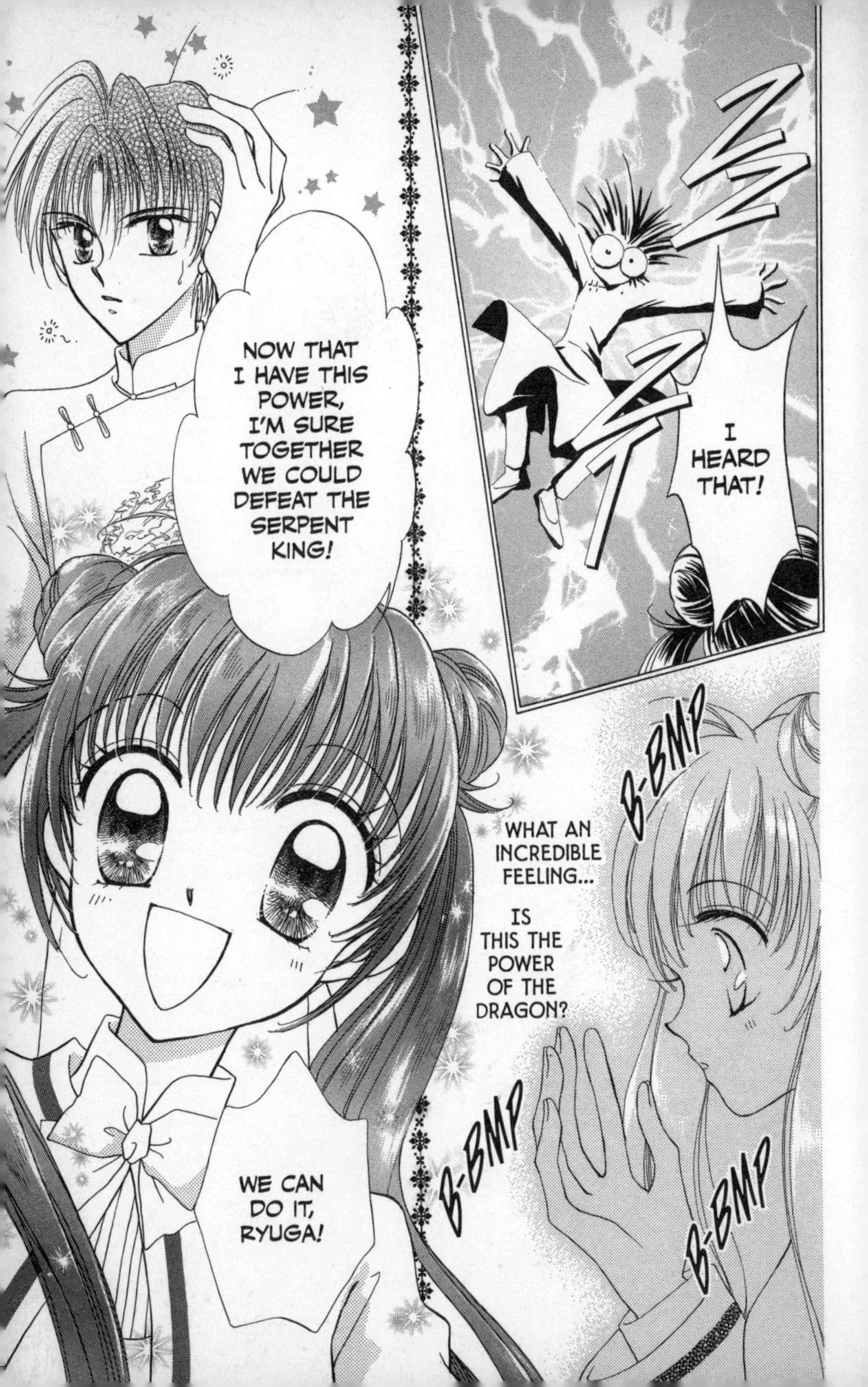
I HEARD THAT!
B-BMP
WHAT AN INCREDIBLE FEELING...
IS THIS THE POWER OF THE DRAGON?
B-BMP
B-BMP
NOW THAT I HAVE THIS POWER, I'M SURE TOGETHER WE COULD DEFEAT THE SERPENT KING!
WE CAN DO IT, RYUGA!

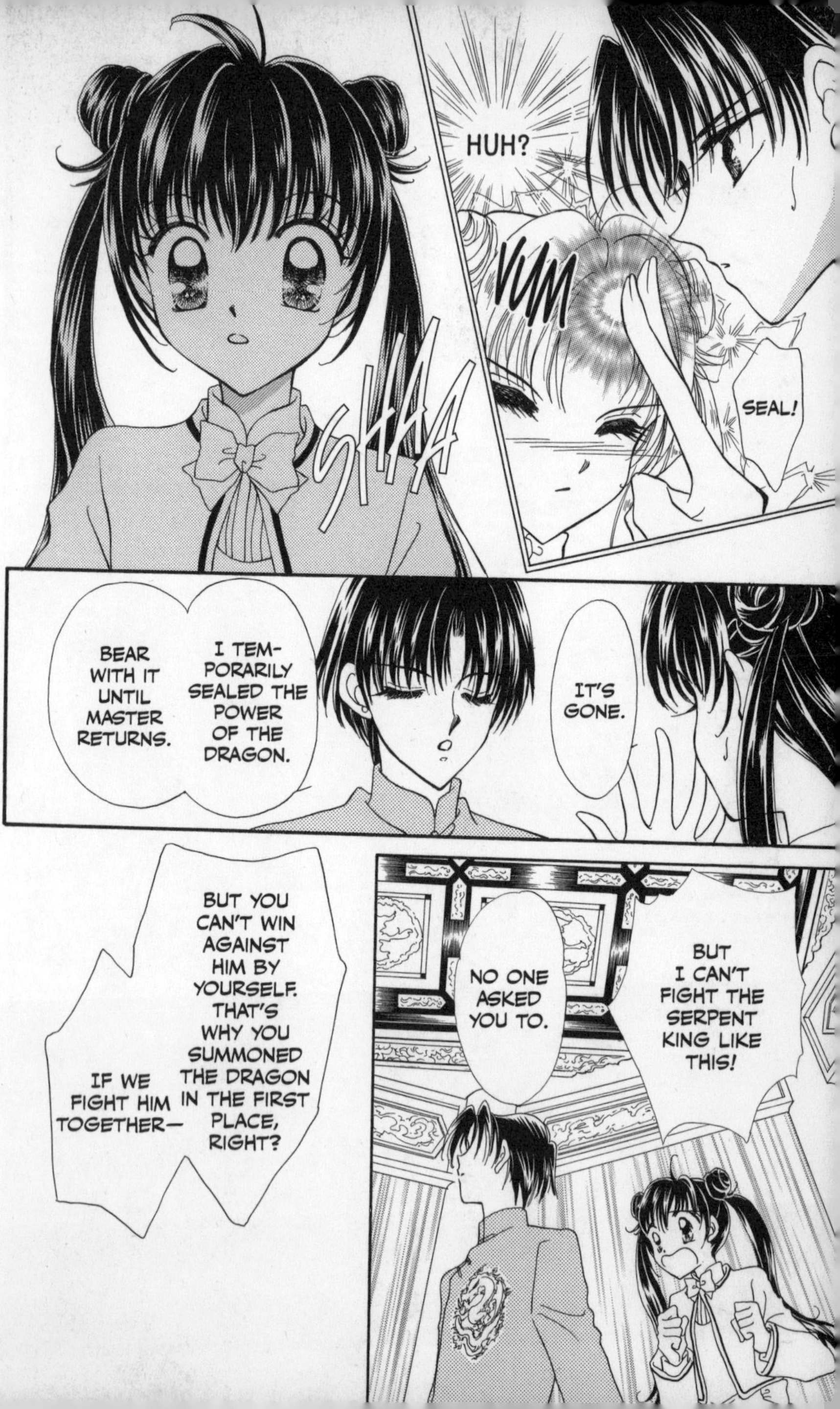
HUH?
VUM
SEAL!
SHAA
IT'S GONE.
I TEMPORARILY SEALED THE POWER OF THE DRAGON.
BEAR WITH IT UNTIL MASTER RETURNS.
BUT I CAN'T FIGHT THE SERPENT KING LIKE THIS!
NO ONE ASKED YOU TO.
BUT YOU CAN'T WIN AGAINST HIM BY YOURSELF. THAT'S WHY YOU SUMMONED THE DRAGON IN THE FIRST PLACE, RIGHT?
IF WE FIGHT HIM TOGETHER—

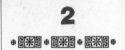

2

This time I wanted to draw both the hero and the heroine with black hair. (Basically I like characters with black hair.) It's hard (especially with Momoka), but it makes a strong impact in the action scenes, so I like it.

Momoka is the cheerful type of character who usually shows up in my manga. She's different, however, in that she has a small chest. (laugh)

When I was drawing the front cover, I had forgotten that I established she was an A-cup in chapter 1. My readers and beloved assistants all insisted that no matter how you look at it, Momoka is a D-cup. ...But the person who drew it has large breasts. It's amusing.

Please pretend the cover is of a future Momoka who has grown. Anyway, Chinese dresses look cool on girls with large chests...

It's fun to design various Chinese clothes.

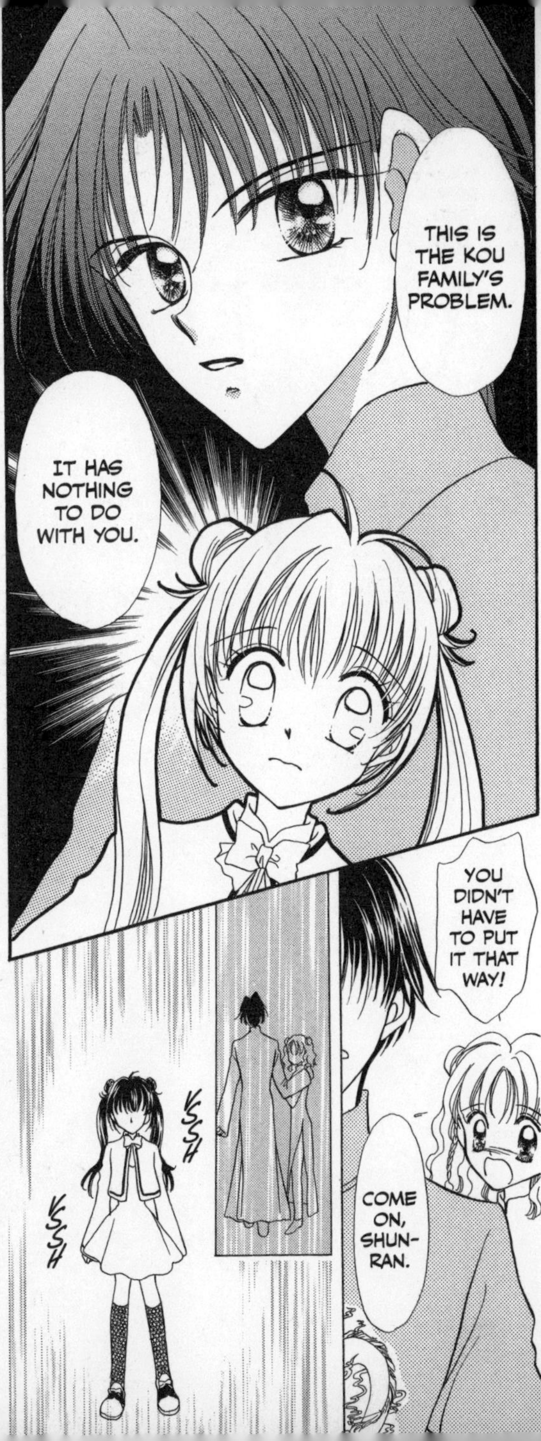
THIS IS THE KOU FAMILY'S PROBLEM.
IT HAS NOTHING TO DO WITH YOU.
YOU DIDN'T HAVE TO PUT IT THAT WAY!
COME ON, SHUN-RAN.
VSSH
VSSH

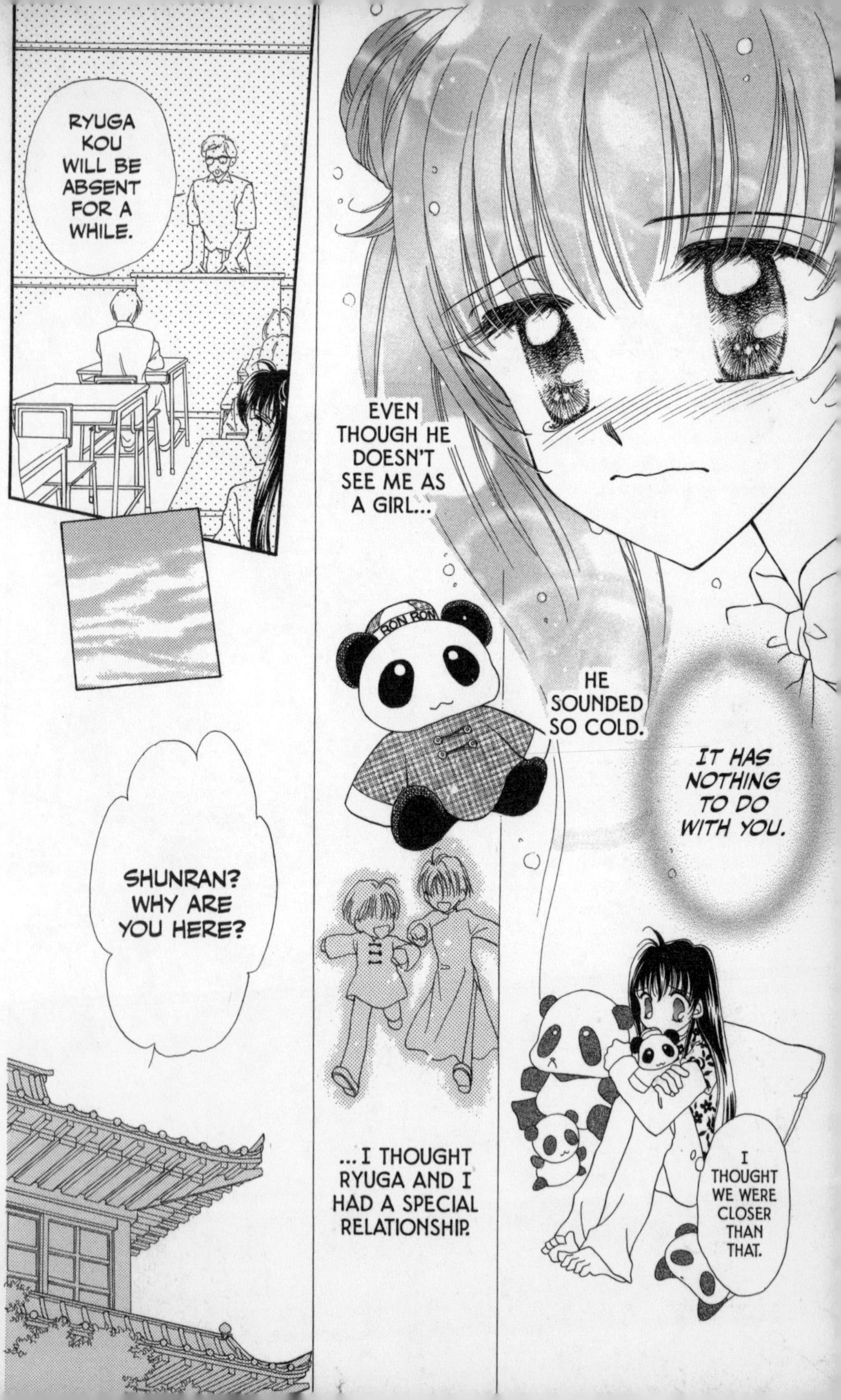
EVEN THOUGH HE DOESN'T SEE ME AS A GIRL...
HE SOUNDED SO COLD.
IT HAS NOTHING TO DO WITH YOU.
I THOUGHT WE WERE CLOSER THAN THAT.
RON RON
...I THOUGHT RYUGA AND I HAD A SPECIAL RELATIONSHIP.
RYUGA KOU WILL BE ABSENT FOR A WHILE.
SHUNRAN? WHY ARE YOU HERE?

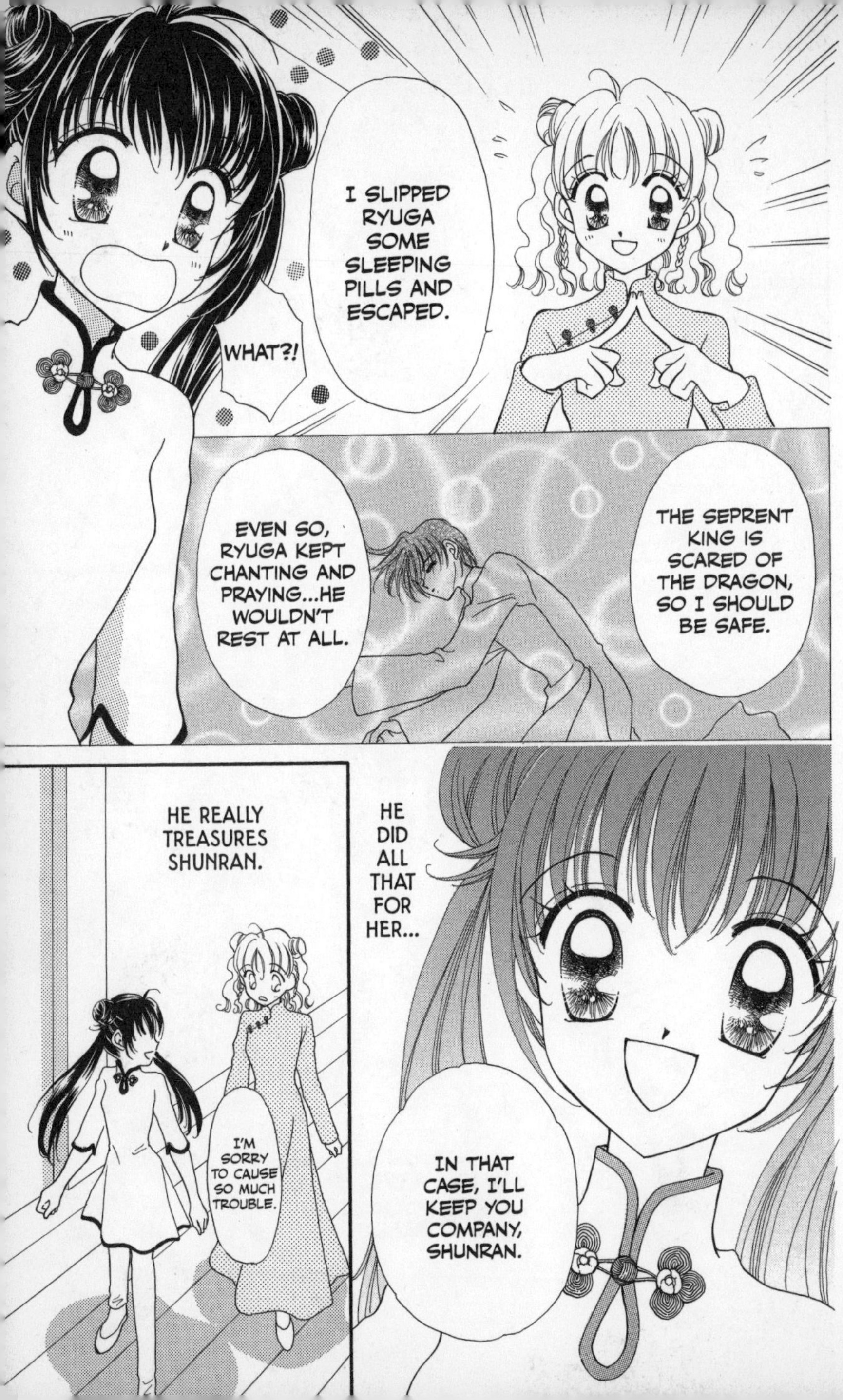
I SLIPPED RYUGA SOME SLEEPING PILLS AND ESCAPED.
WHAT?!
THE SEPRENT KING IS SCARED OF THE DRAGON, SO I SHOULD BE SAFE.
EVEN SO, RYUGA KEPT CHANTING AND PRAYING...HE WOULDN'T REST AT ALL.
HE DID ALL THAT FOR HER...
IN THAT CASE, I'LL KEEP YOU COMPANY, SHUNRAN.
HE REALLY TREASURES SHUNRAN.
I'M SORRY TO CAUSE SO MUCH TROUBLE.

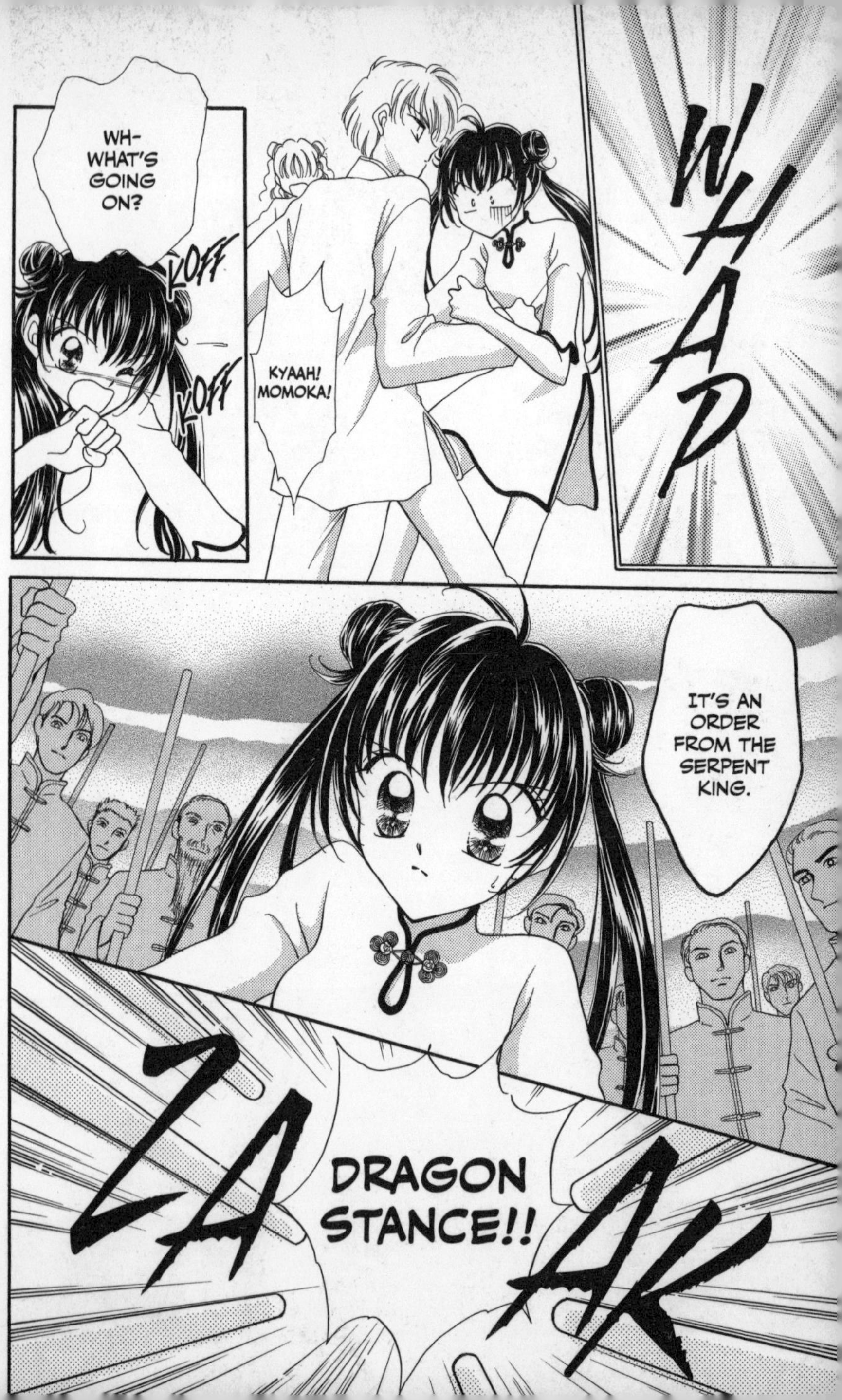
WHAP
KYAAH! MOMOKA!
WH- WHAT'S GOING ON?
KOFF
KOFF
IT'S AN ORDER FROM THE SERPENT KING.
ZAAK
DRAGON STANCE!!

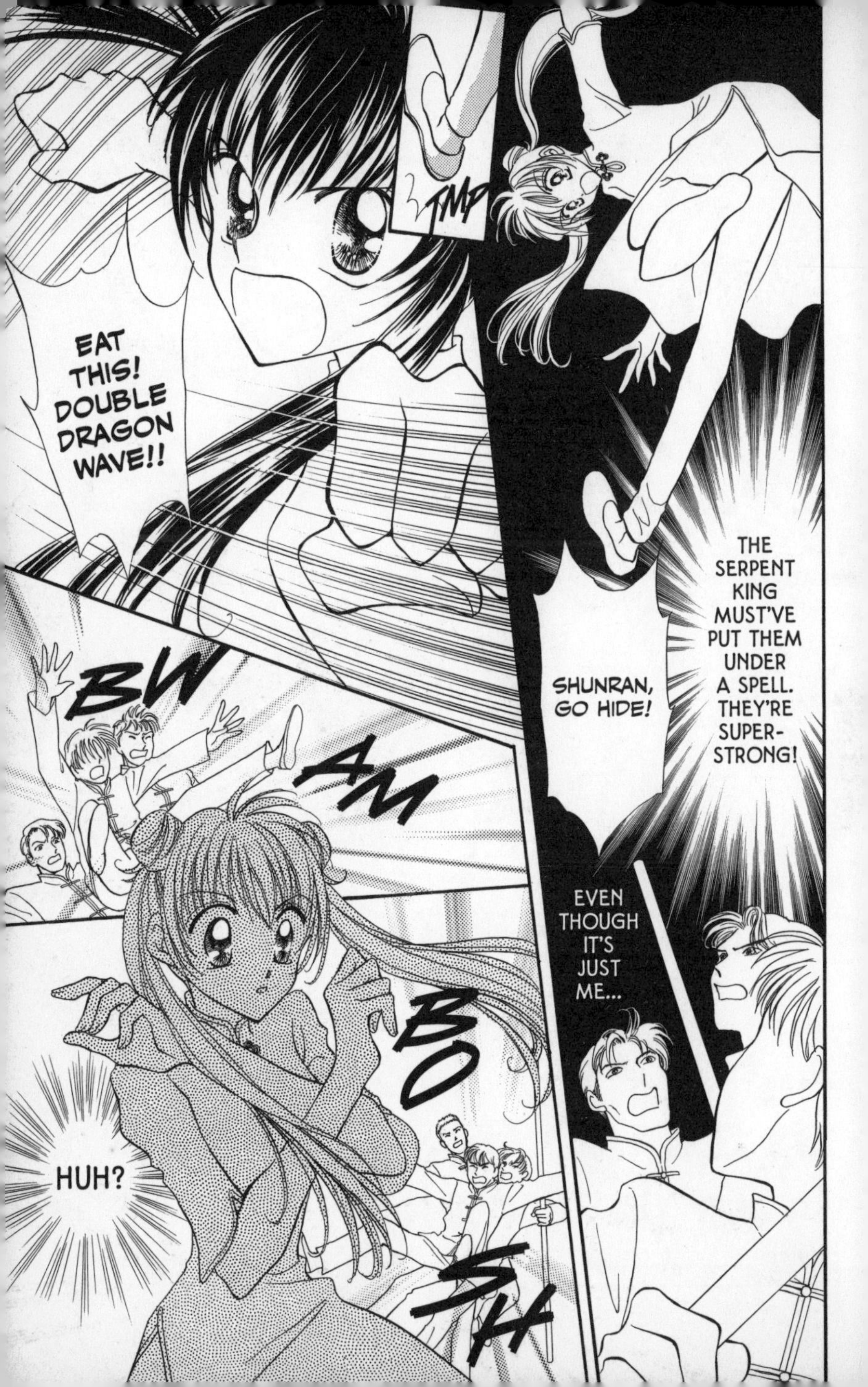
THE SERPENT KING MUST'VE PUT THEM UNDER A SPELL. THEY'RE SUPER-STRONG!
SHUNRAN, GO HIDE!
TMP
EAT THIS! DOUBLE DRAGON WAVE!!
BWAM
EVEN THOUGH IT'S JUST ME...
BOSH
HUH?

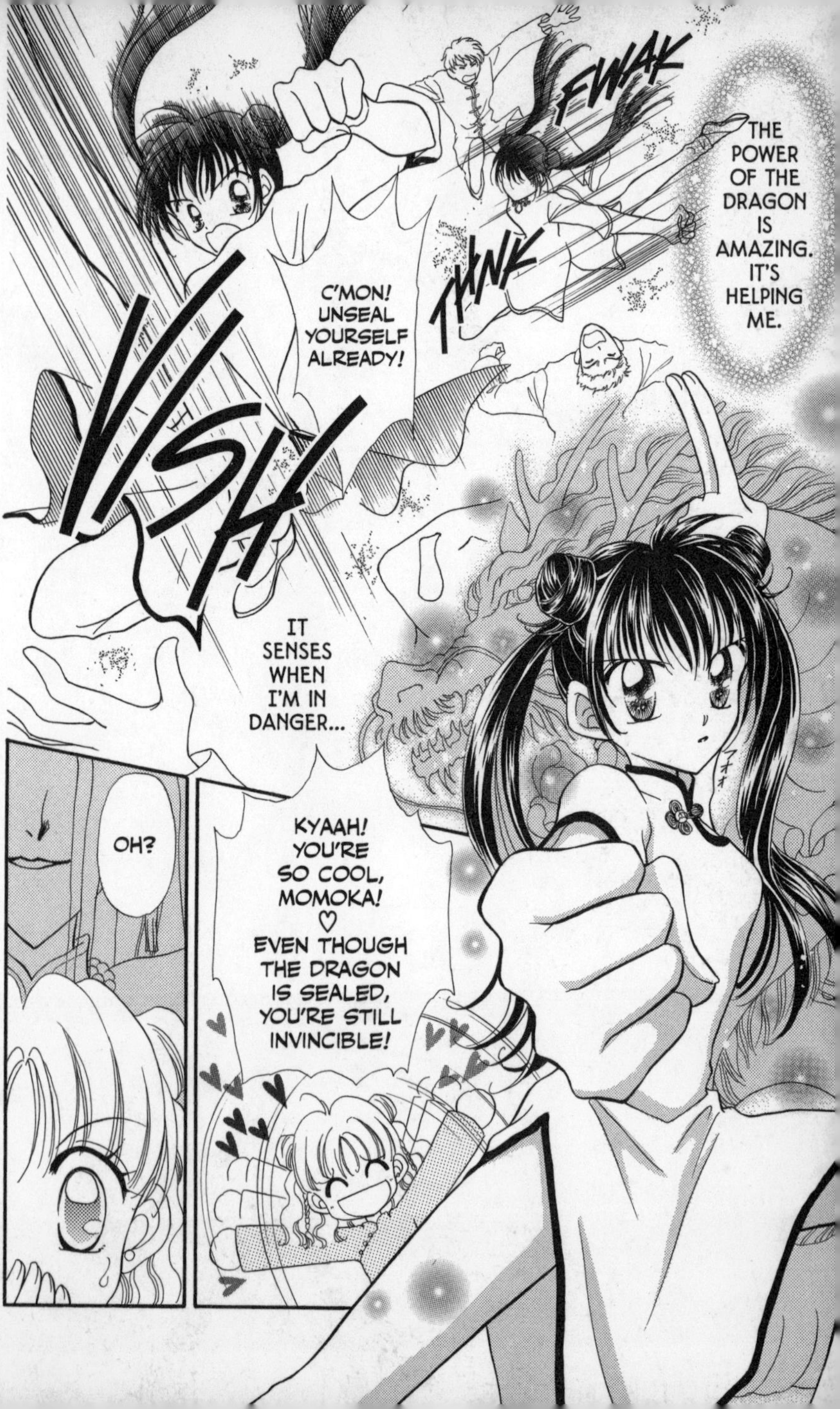

THE POWER OF THE DRAGON IS AMAZING. IT'S HELPING ME.
FWAK
THNK
C'MON! UNSEAL YOURSELF ALREADY!
VISH
IT SENSES WHEN I'M IN DANGER...
KYAAH! YOU'RE SO COOL, MOMOKA! ♡ EVEN THOUGH THE DRAGON IS SEALED, YOU'RE STILL INVINCIBLE!
OH?

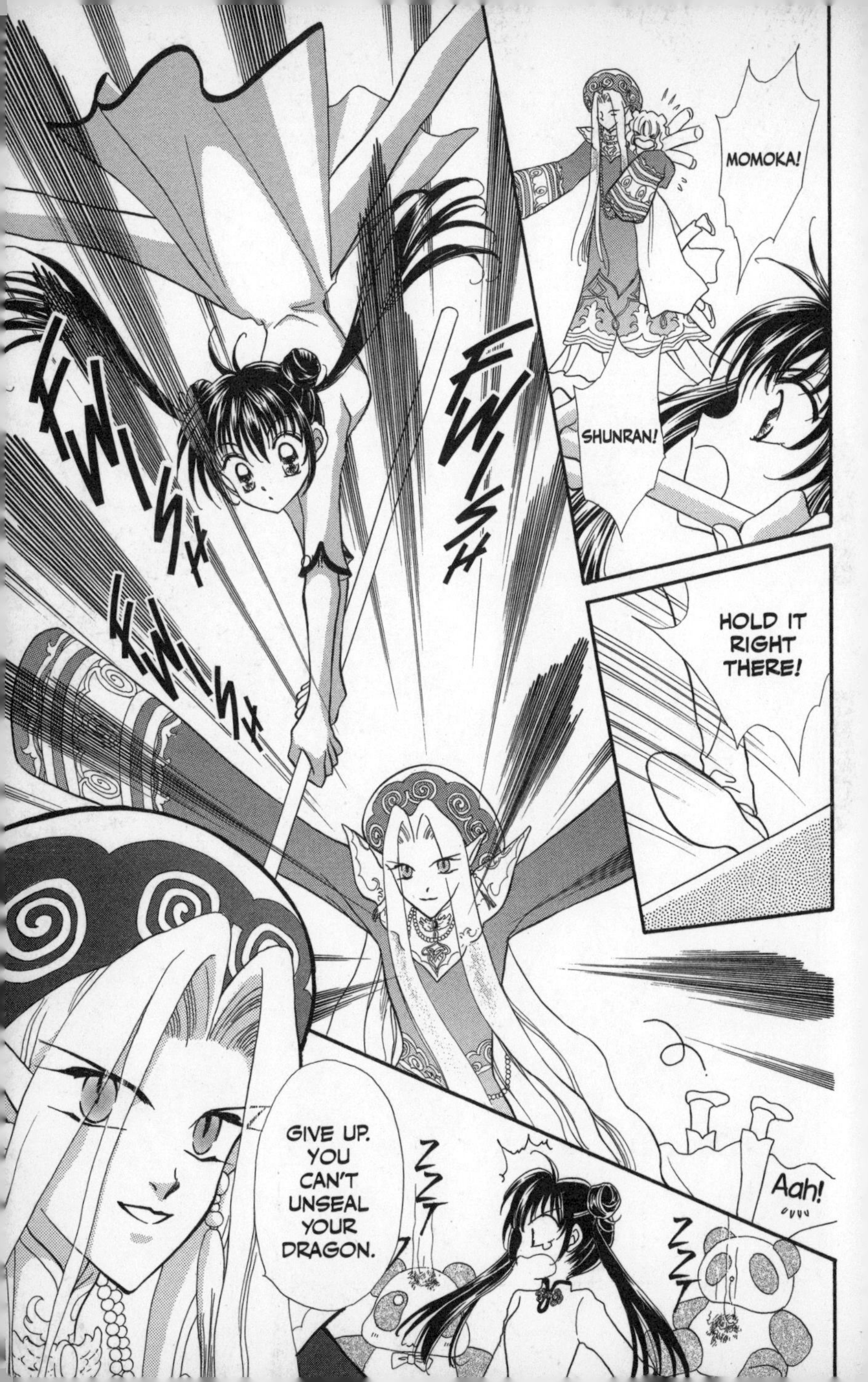
MOMOKA!
SHUNRAN!
HOLD IT RIGHT THERE!
FWISH
WHISH
WHISH
Aah!
ZZZ
ZZZ
GIVE UP. YOU CAN'T UNSEAL YOUR DRAGON.

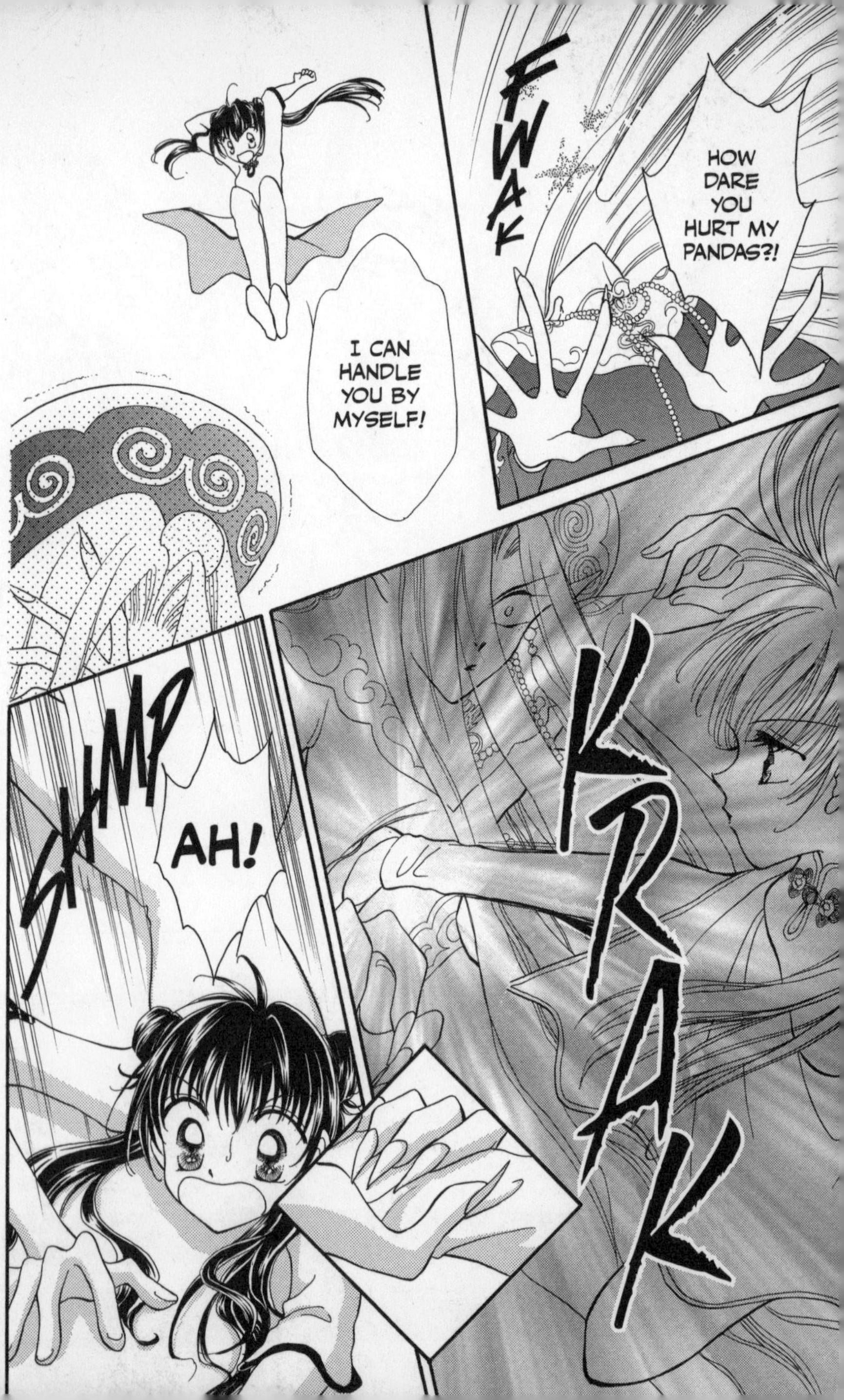
FWAK
HOW DARE YOU HURT MY PANDAS?!
I CAN HANDLE YOU BY MYSELF!
KRAK
SHMP
AH!

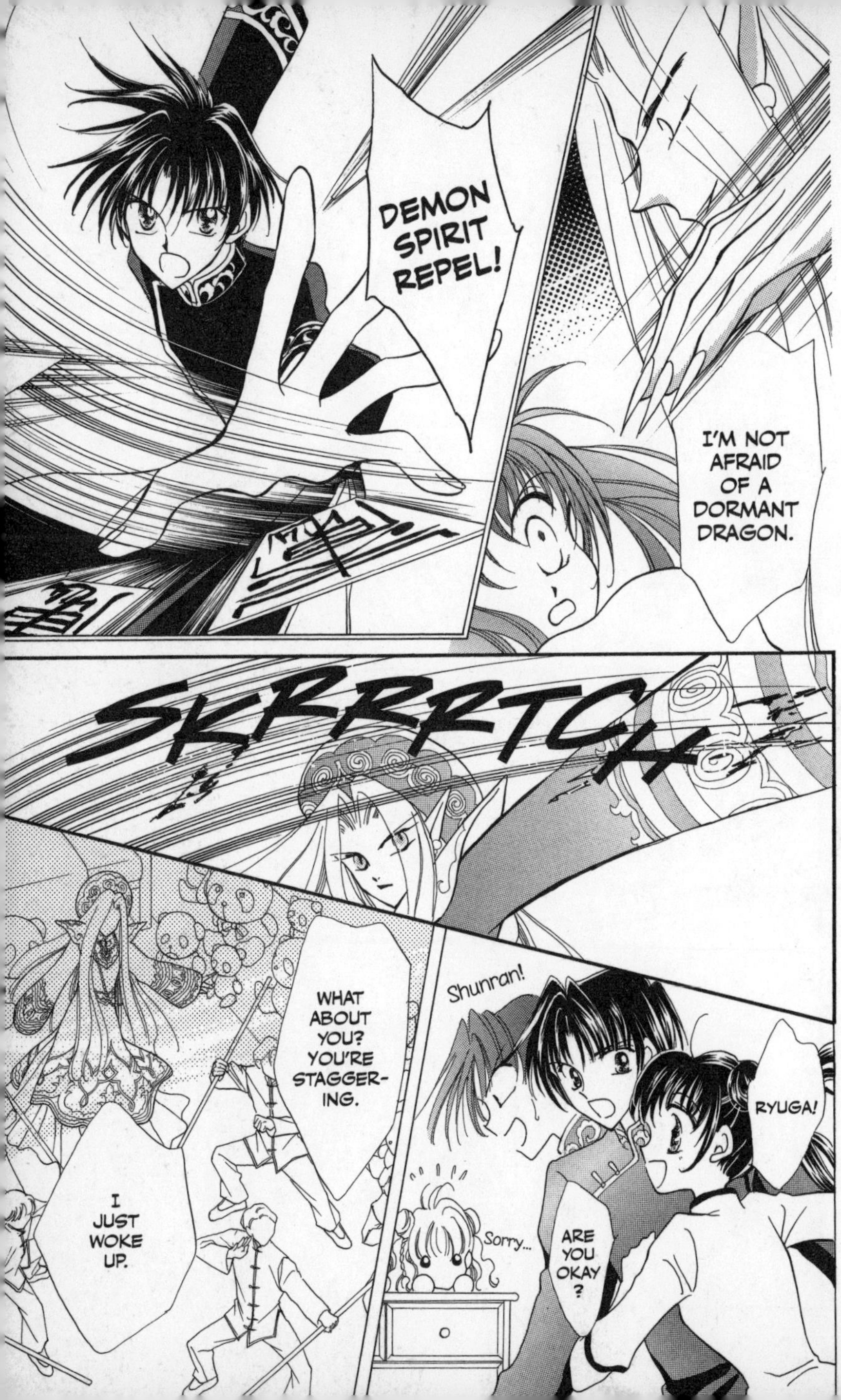
I'M NOT AFRAID OF A DORMANT DRAGON.
DEMON SPIRIT REPEL!
SKRRRTCH
Shunran!
RYUGA!
ARE YOU OKAY?
Sorry...
WHAT ABOUT YOU? YOU'RE STAGGER-ING.
I JUST WOKE UP.

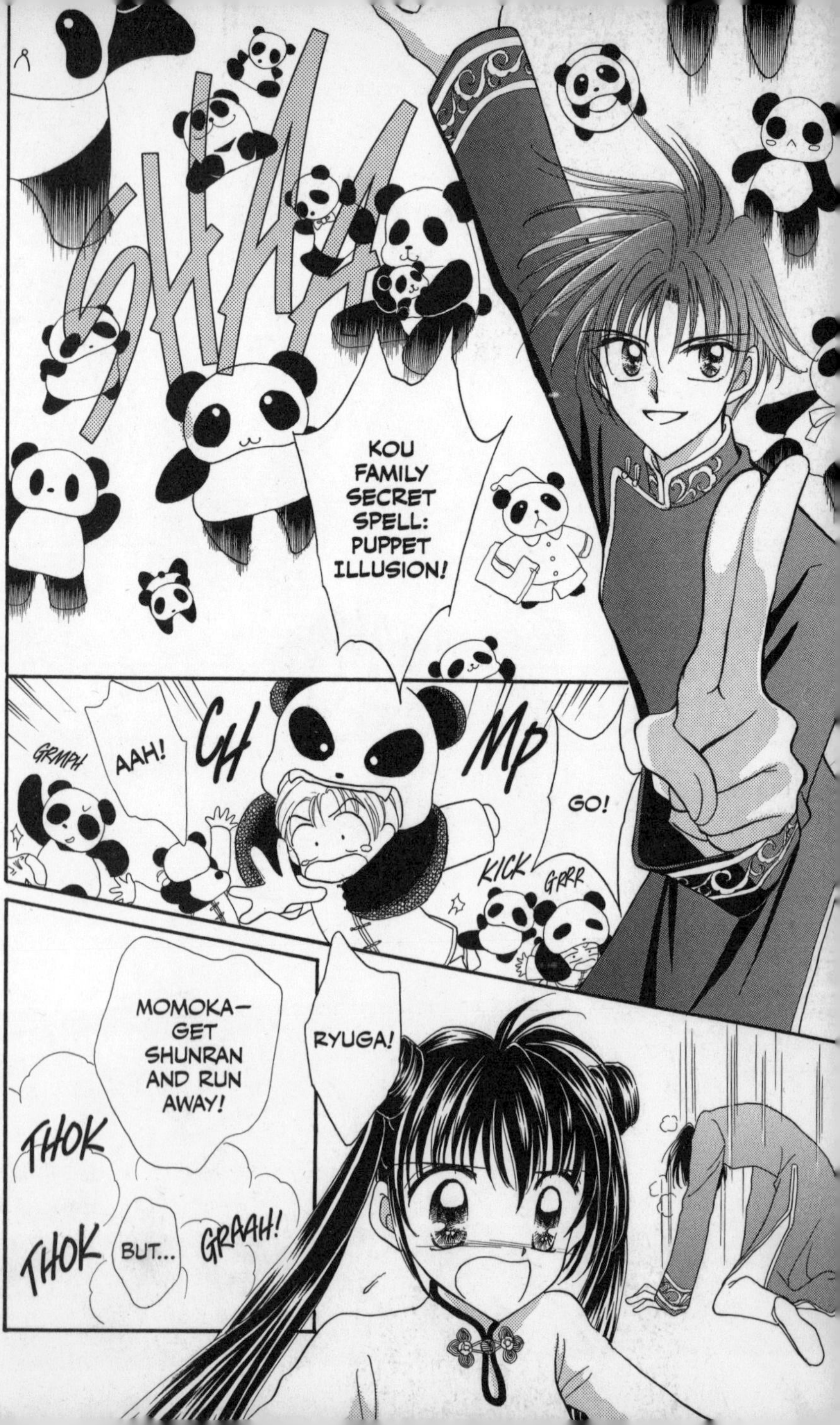
KOU FAMILY SECRET SPELL: PUPPET ILLUSION!
GO!
KICK
GRRR
CHOMP
AAH!
GRMPH
RYUGA!
MOMOKA— GET SHUNRAN AND RUN AWAY!
GRAAH!
BUT...
THOK
THOK

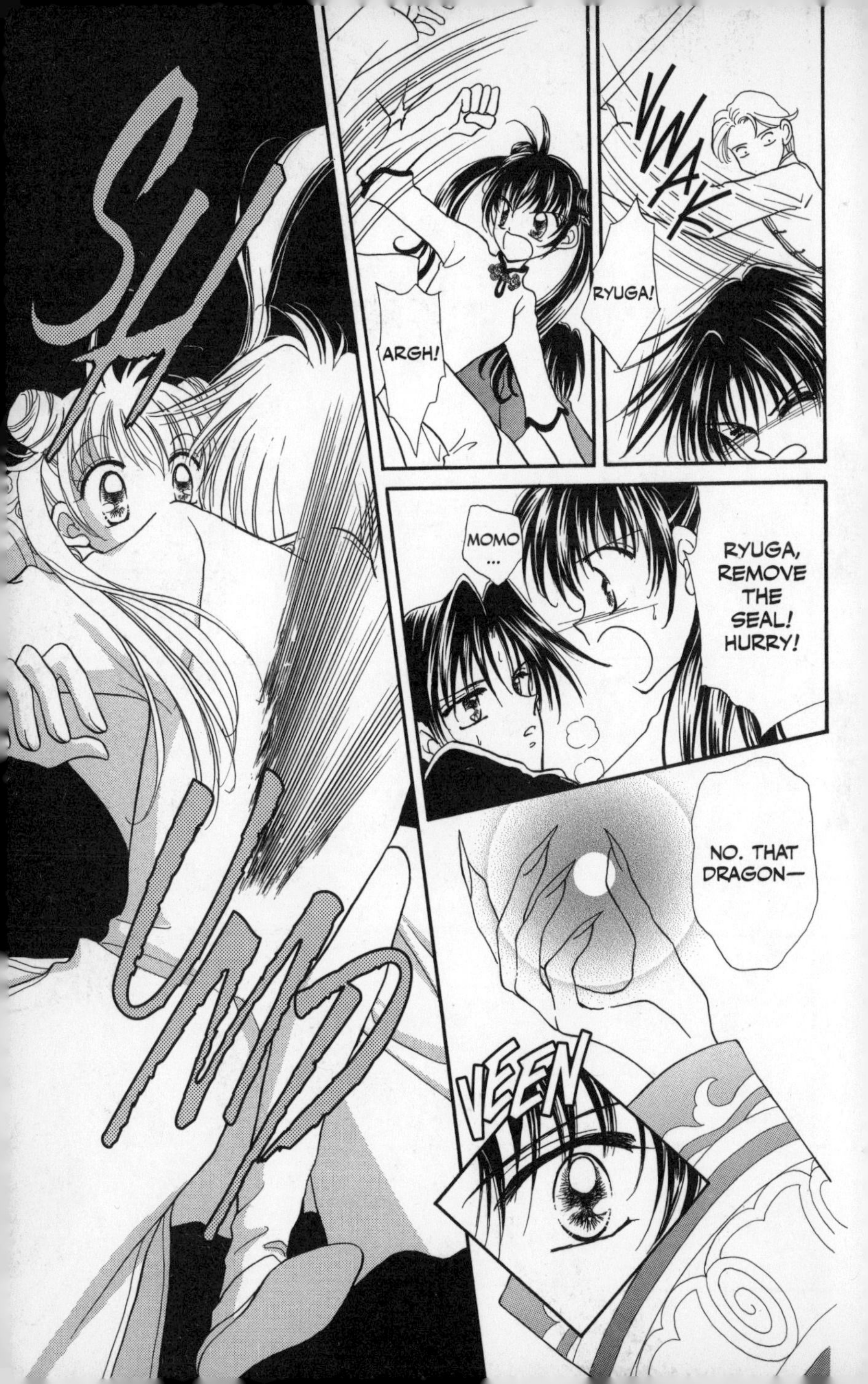
VWAK
RYUGA!
ARGH!
MOMO ...
RYUGA, REMOVE THE SEAL! HURRY!
NO. THAT DRAGON—
VEEN

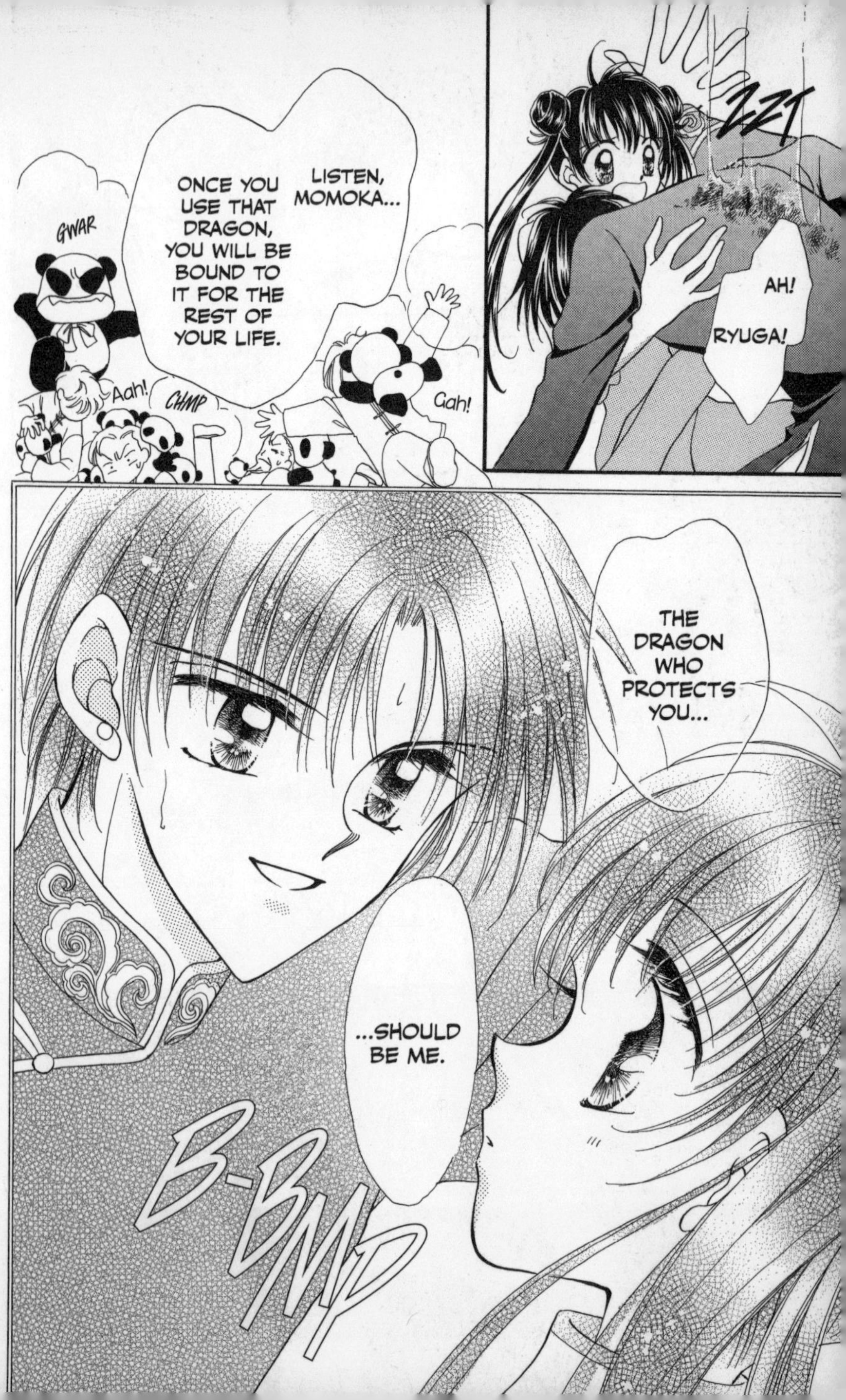
AH!
RYUGA!
LISTEN, MOMOKA...
ONCE YOU USE THAT DRAGON, YOU WILL BE BOUND TO IT FOR THE REST OF YOUR LIFE.
GWAR
Aah!
CHMP
Gah!
THE DRAGON WHO PROTECTS YOU...
...SHOULD BE ME.
B-BMP

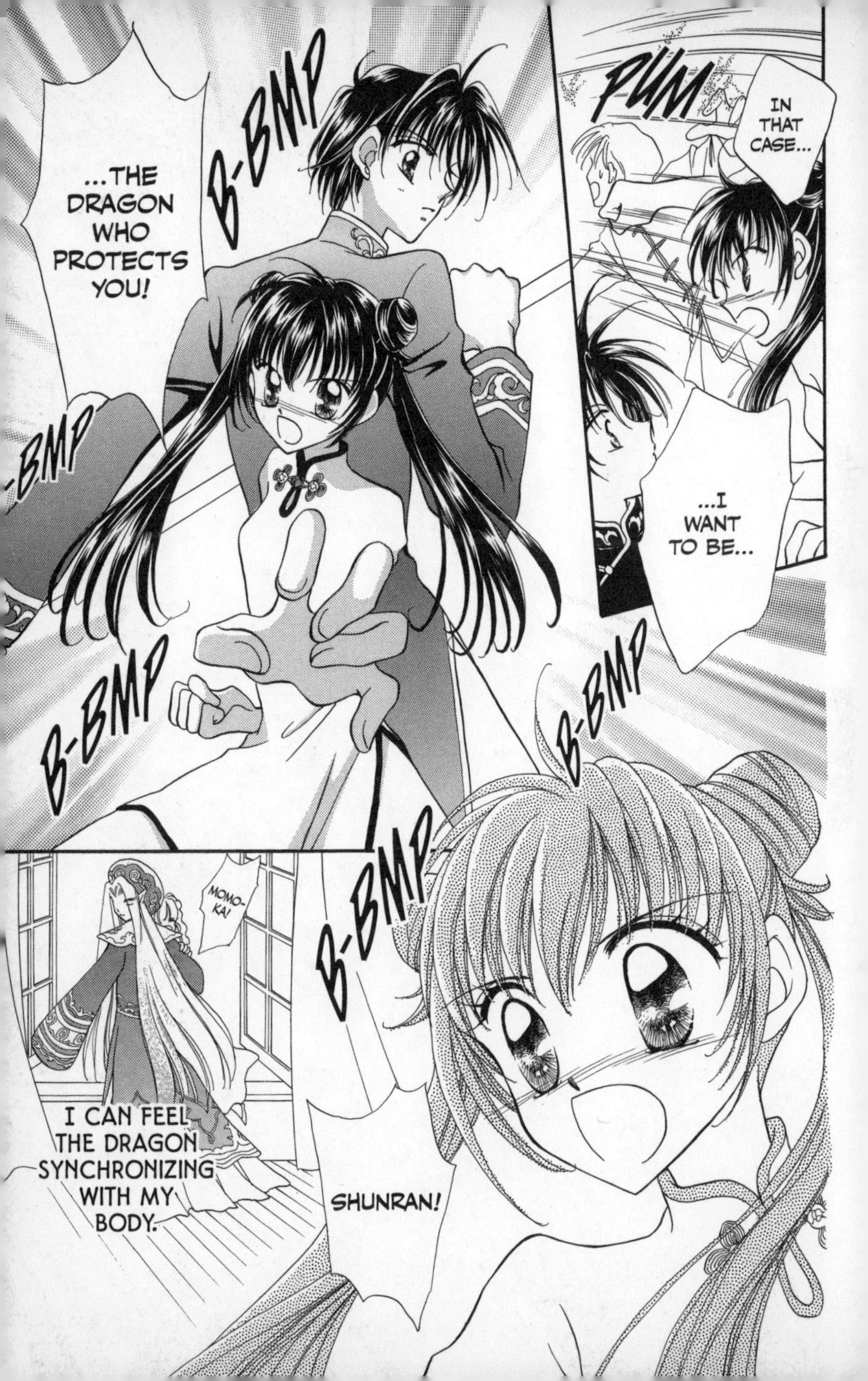
PUM
IN THAT CASE...
...I WANT TO BE...
...THE DRAGON WHO PROTECTS YOU!
B-BMP
-BMP
B-BMP
B-BMP
B-BMP
SHUNRAN!
MOMO-KA!
I CAN FEEL THE DRAGON SYNCHRONIZING WITH MY BODY.

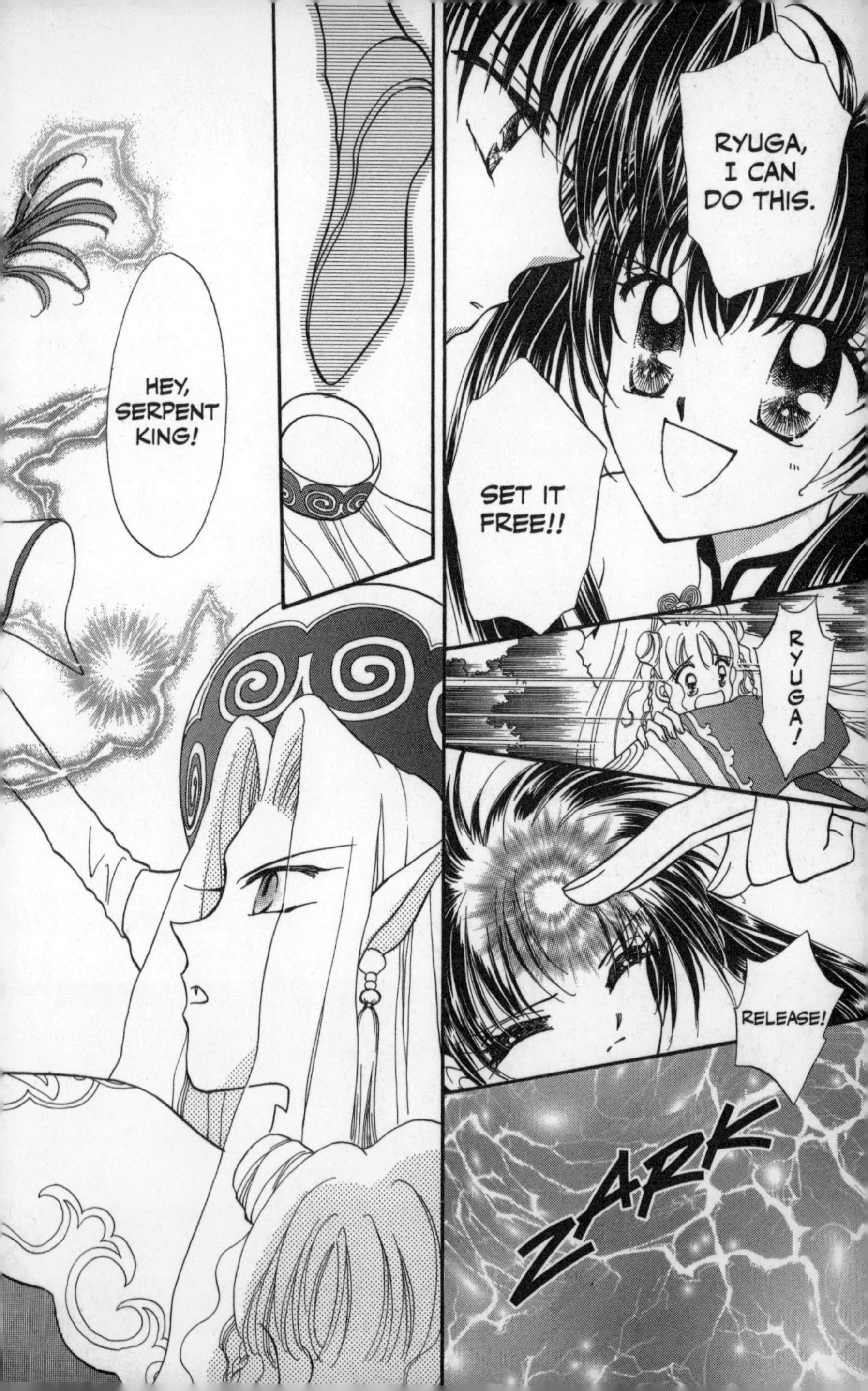
RYUGA, I CAN DO THIS.
SET IT FREE!!
RYUGA!
RELEASE!
ZARK
HEY, SERPENT KING!

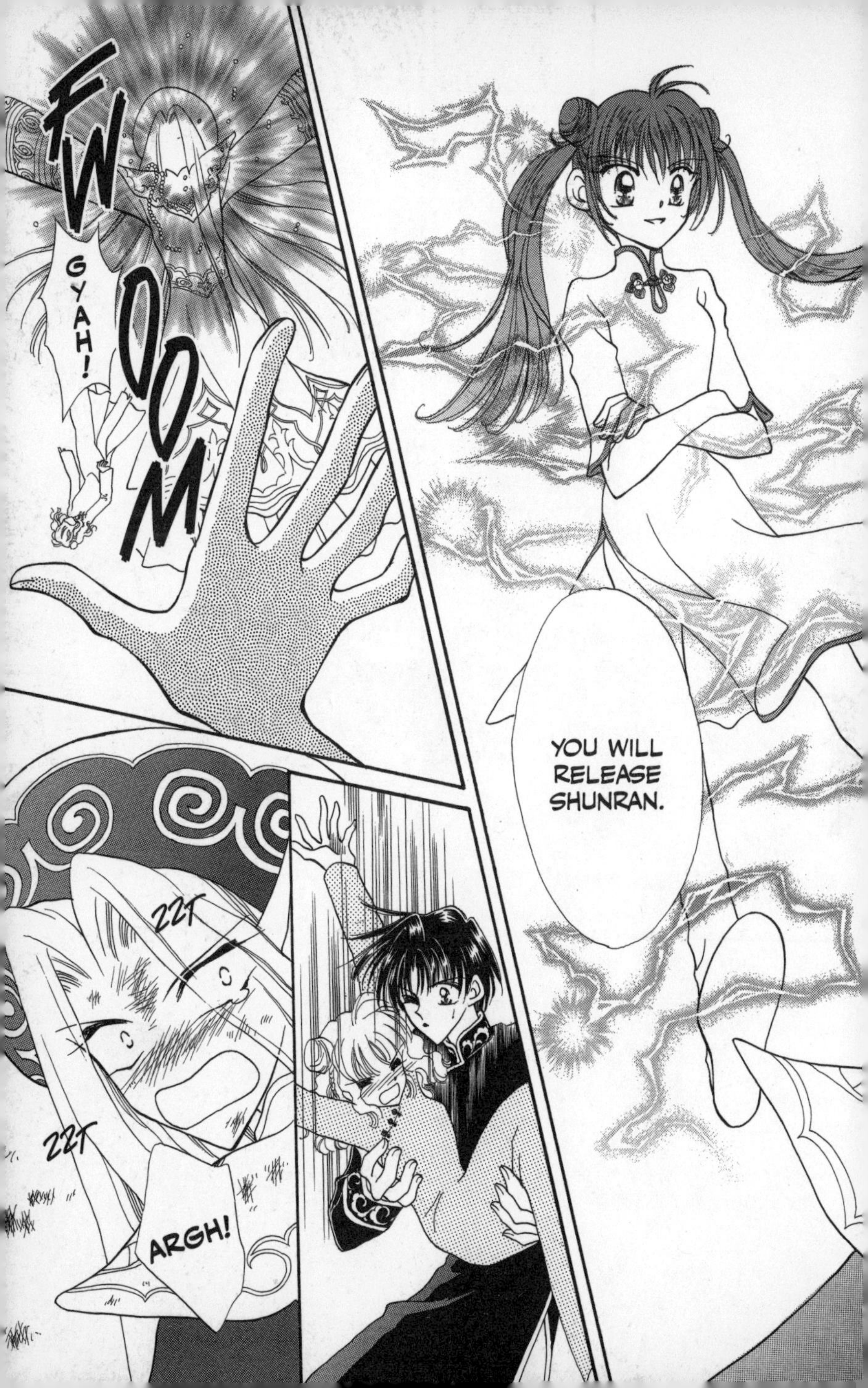

YOU WILL RELEASE SHUNRAN.
FWOOOM
GYAH!
ZZT
ZZT
ARGH!

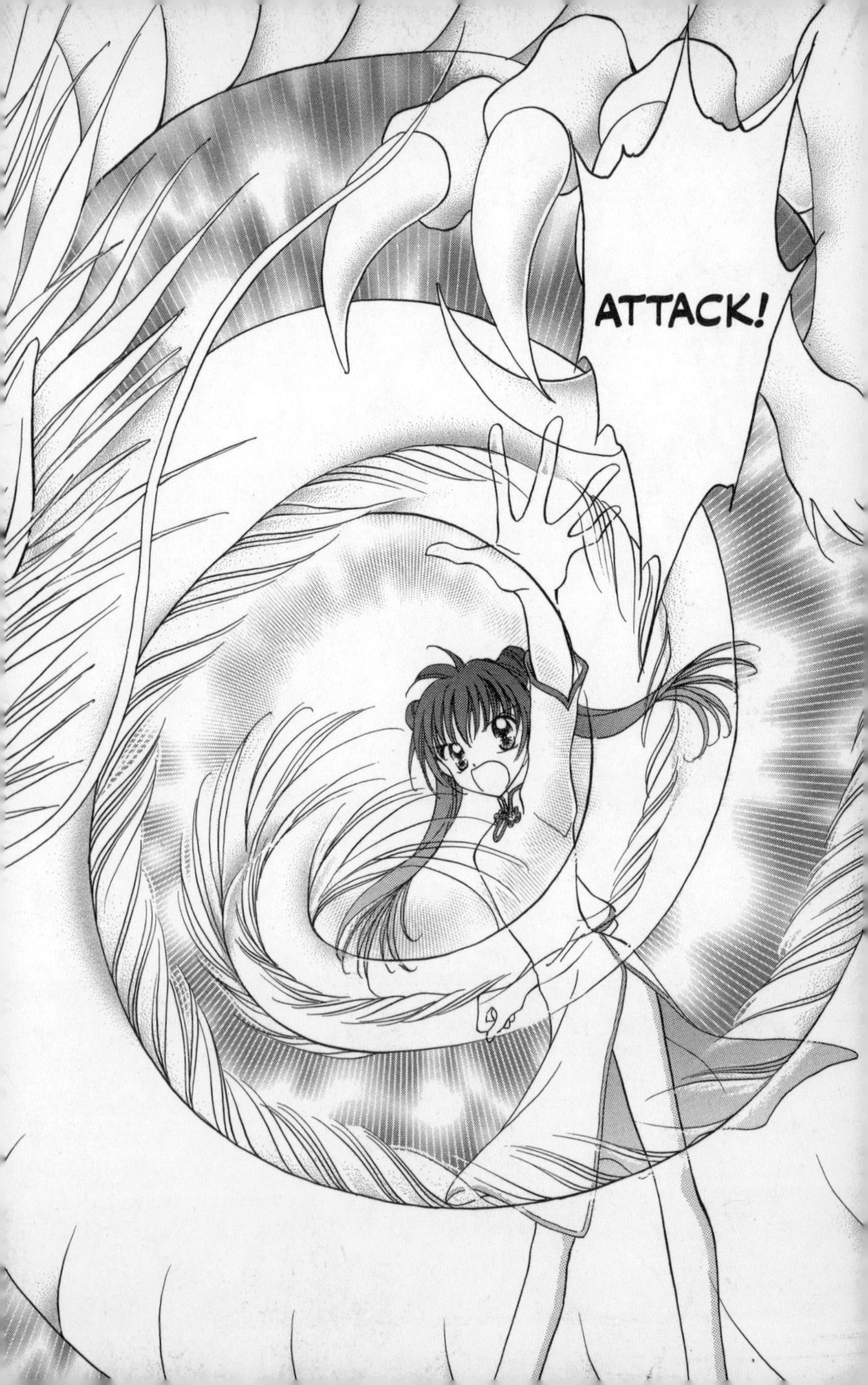
ATTACK!

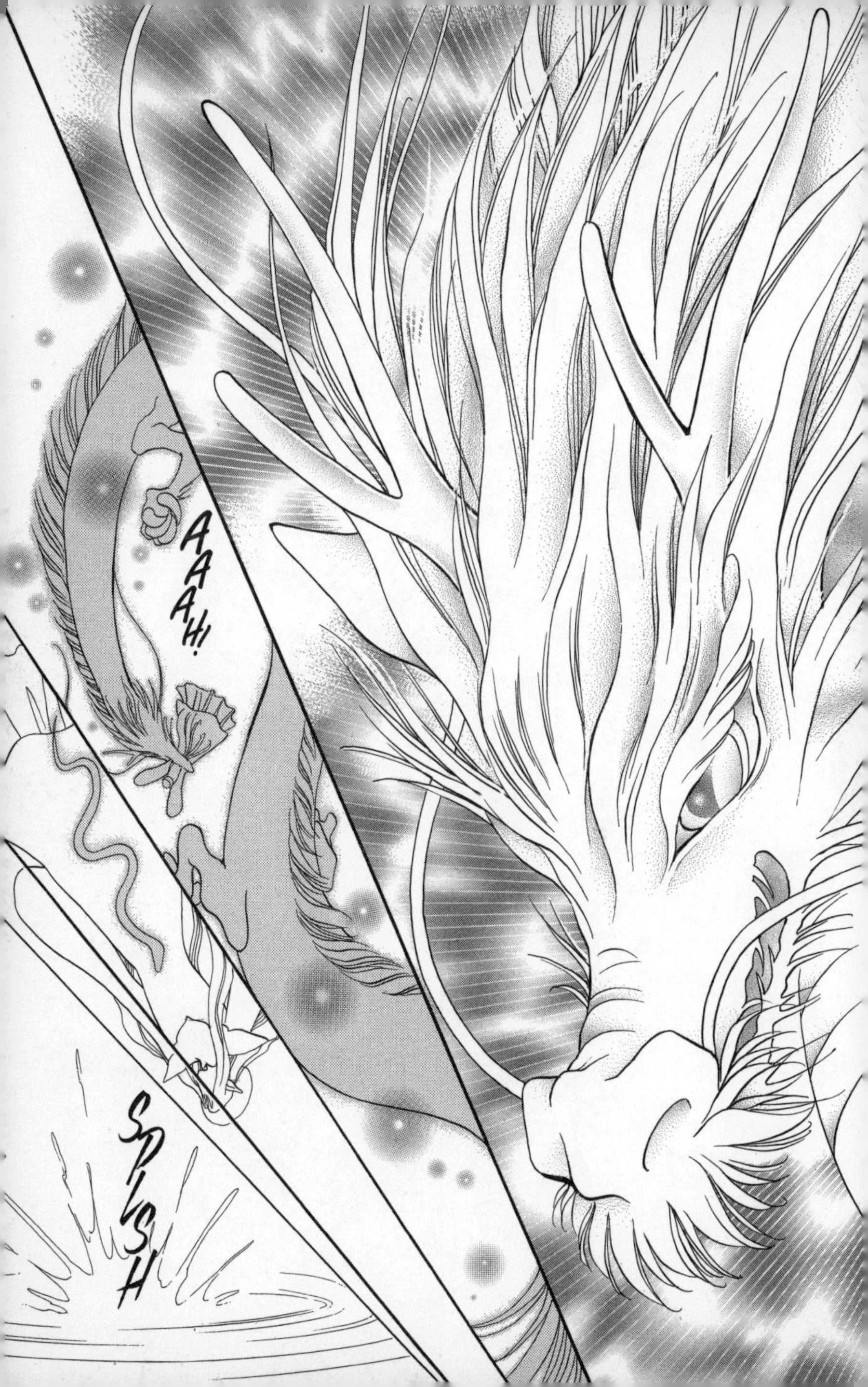
AAAAH!
SPLISH

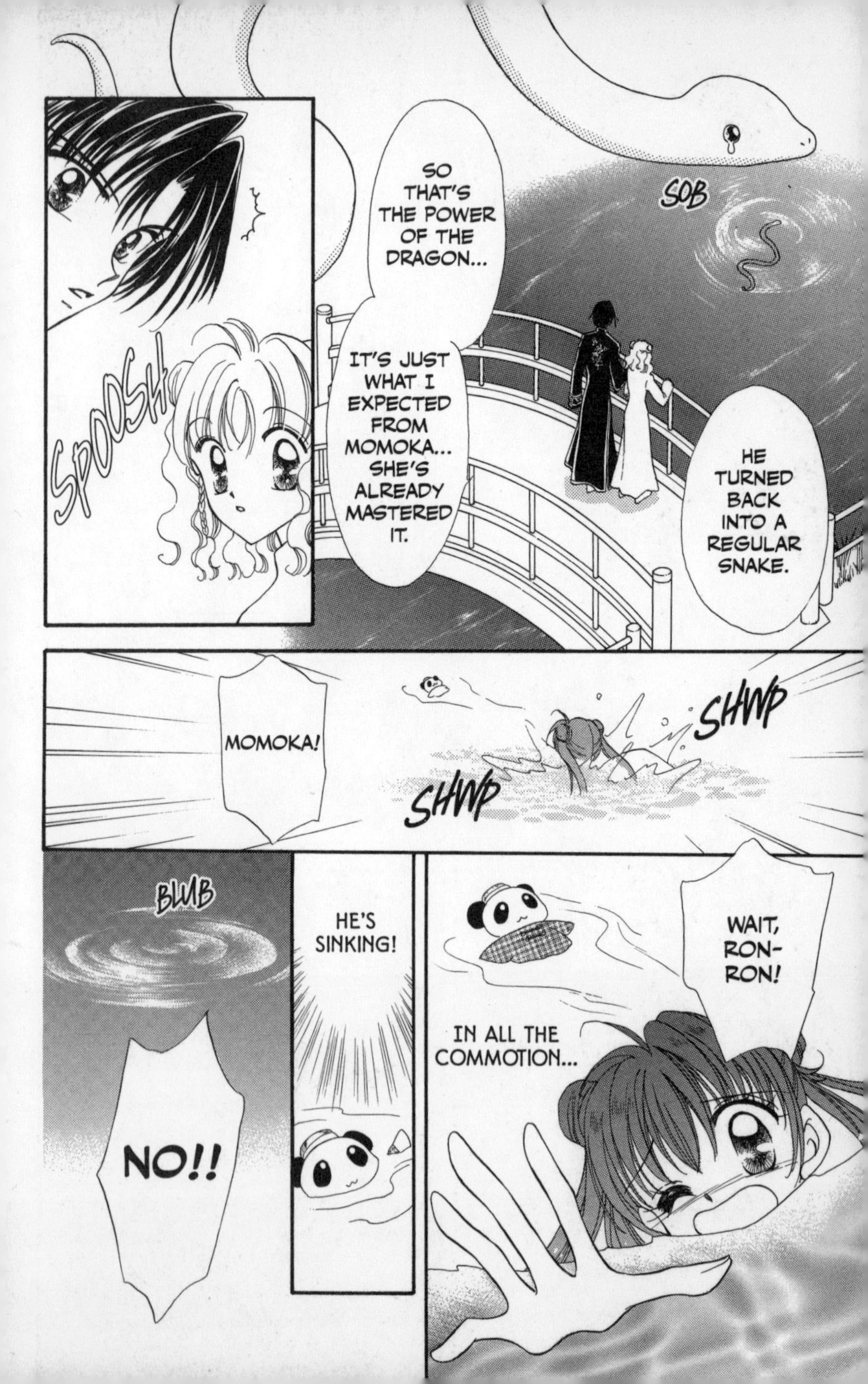

SOB
HE TURNED BACK INTO A REGULAR SNAKE.
SO THAT'S THE POWER OF THE DRAGON...
IT'S JUST WHAT I EXPECTED FROM MOMOKA... SHE'S ALREADY MASTERED IT.
SPOOSH
SHWP
SHWP
MOMOKA!
WAIT, RON-RON!
IN ALL THE COMMOTION...
HE'S SINKING!
BLUB
NO!!

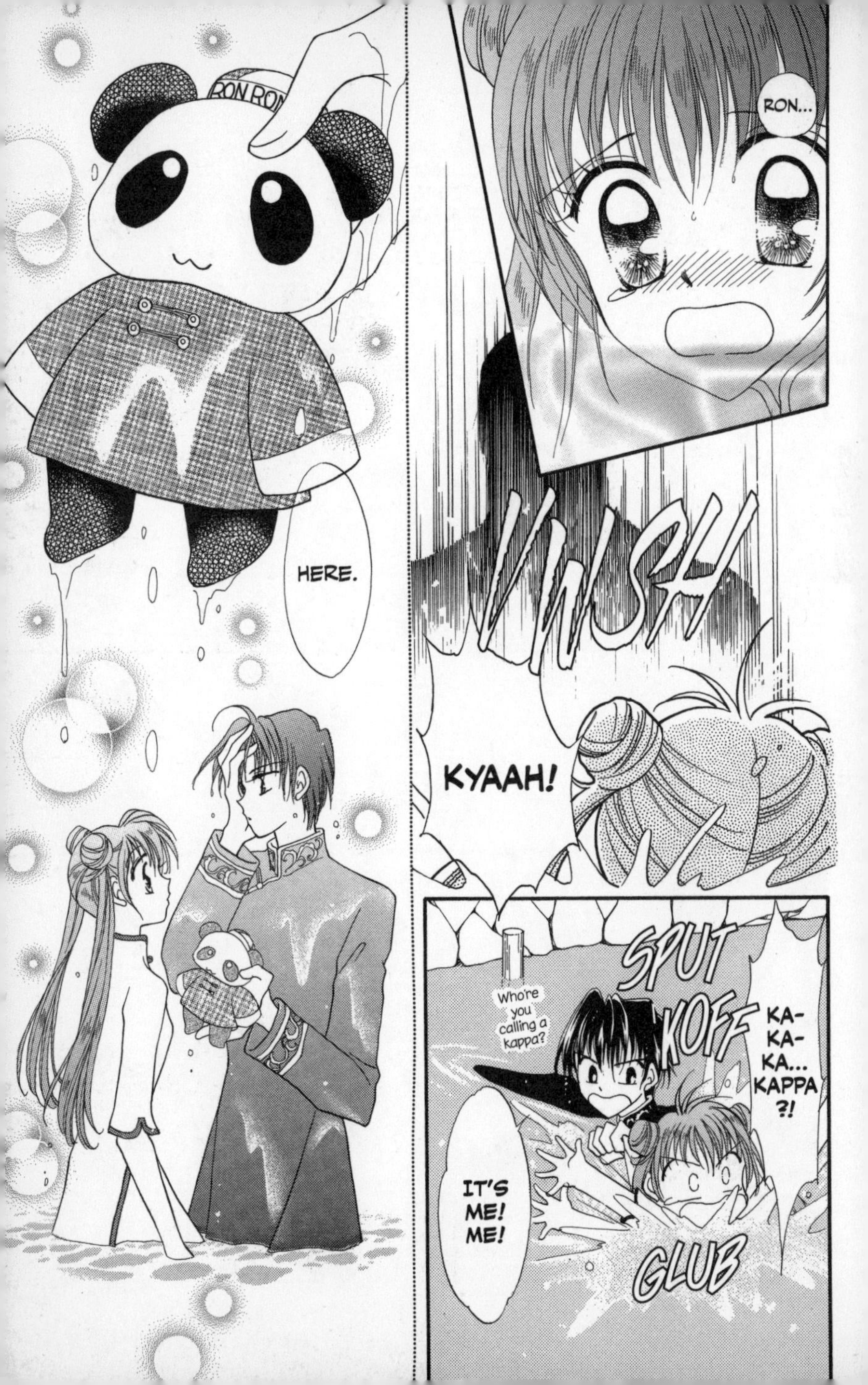
RON...
VWSH
KYAAH!
SPUT
KOFF
KA-
KA-
KA...
KAPPA
?!
Who're you calling a kappa?
IT'S ME! ME!
GLUB
RON RON
HERE.

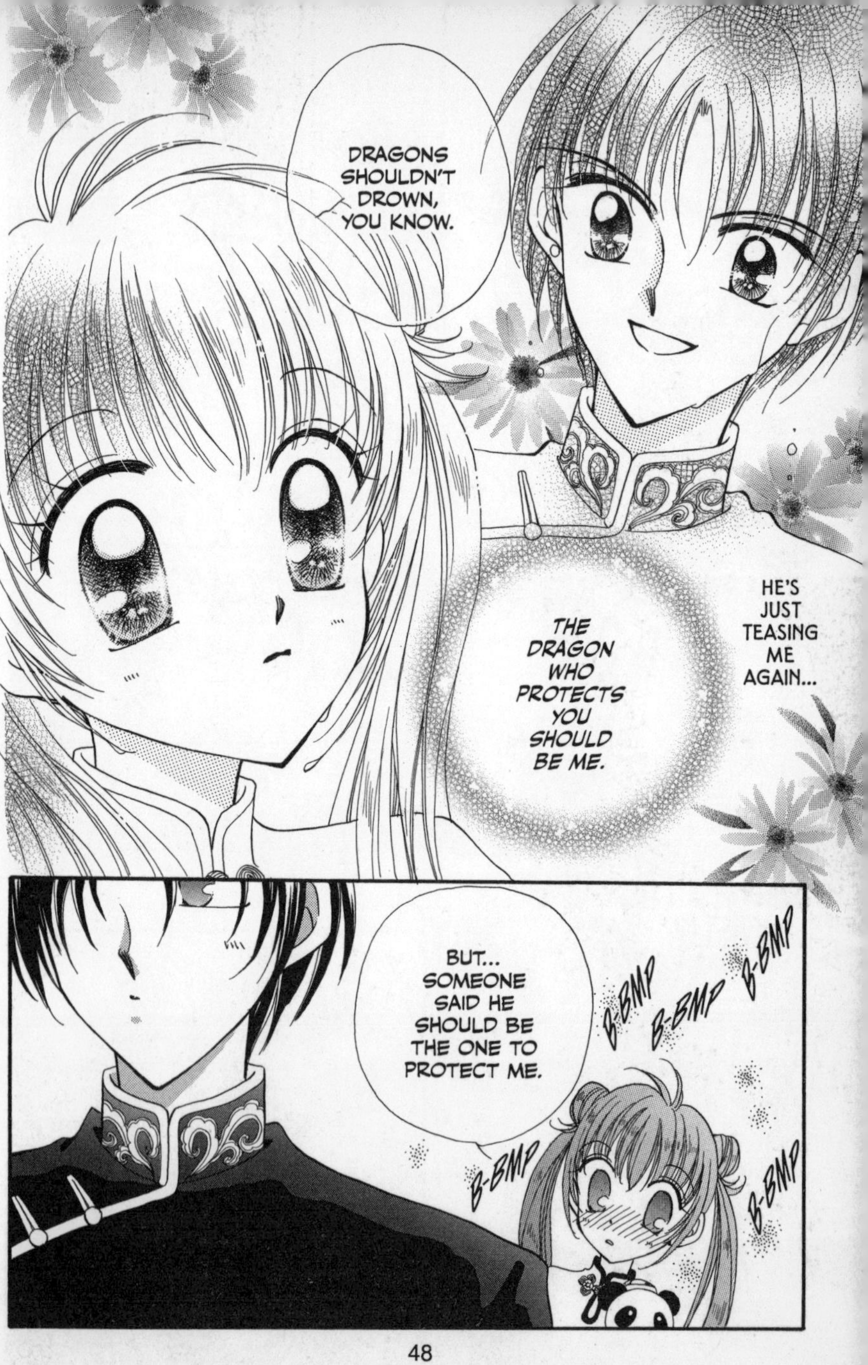
DRAGONS SHOULDN'T DROWN, YOU KNOW.
HE'S JUST TEASING ME AGAIN...
THE DRAGON WHO PROTECTS YOU SHOULD BE ME.
B-BMP B-BMP B-BMP B-BMP
BUT... SOMEONE SAID HE SHOULD BE THE ONE TO PROTECT ME.
B-BMP
B-BMP

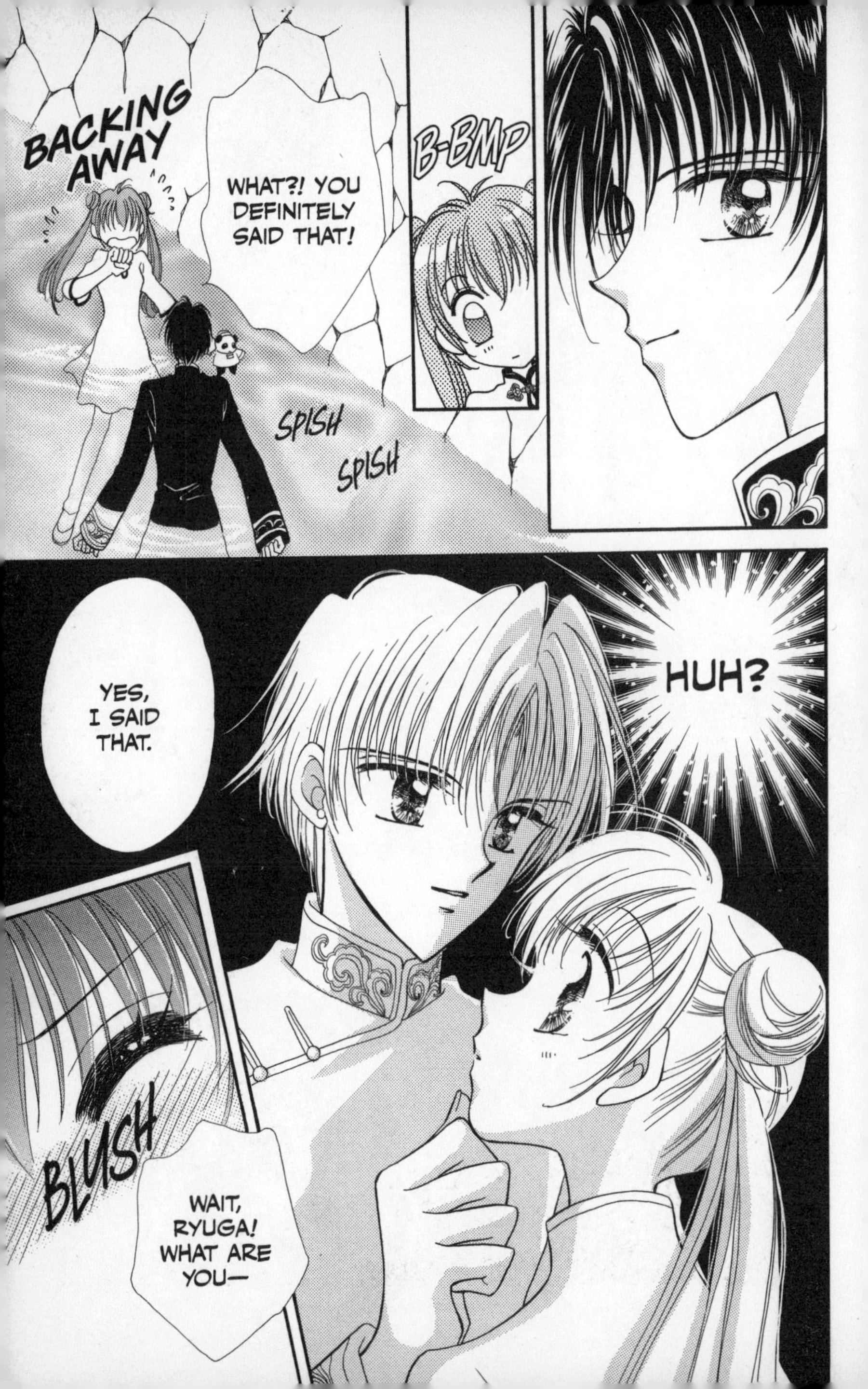
B-BMP
WHAT?! YOU DEFINITELY SAID THAT!
BACKING AWAY
SPISH
SPISH
HUH?
YES, I SAID THAT.
BLUSH
WAIT, RYUGA! WHAT ARE YOU—

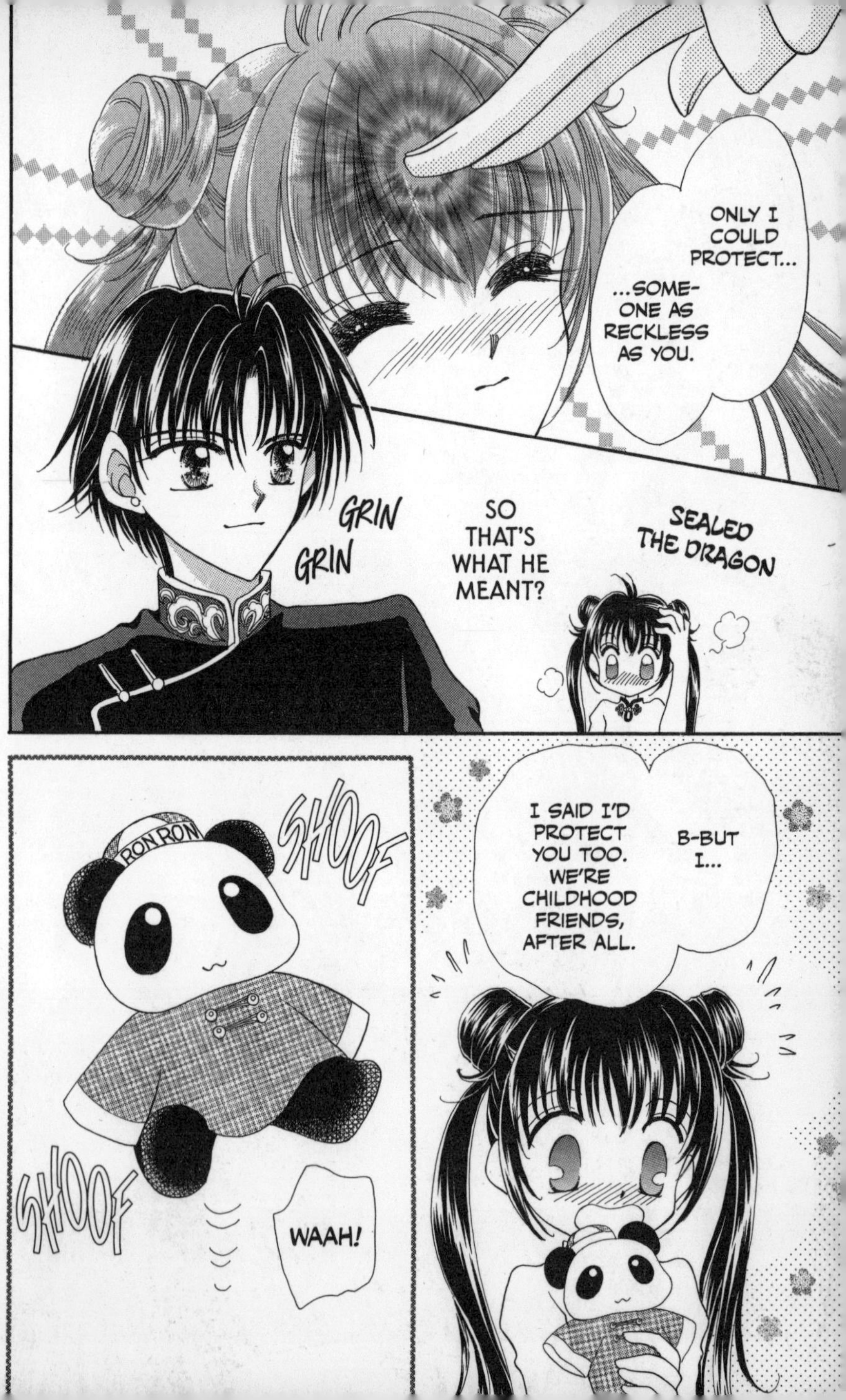
ONLY I COULD PROTECT...
...SOME-ONE AS RECKLESS AS YOU.
SEALED THE DRAGON
SO THAT'S WHAT HE MEANT?
GRIN GRIN
B-BUT I...
I SAID I'D PROTECT YOU TOO. WE'RE CHILDHOOD FRIENDS, AFTER ALL.
SHOOF
RON RON
WAAH!
SHOOF

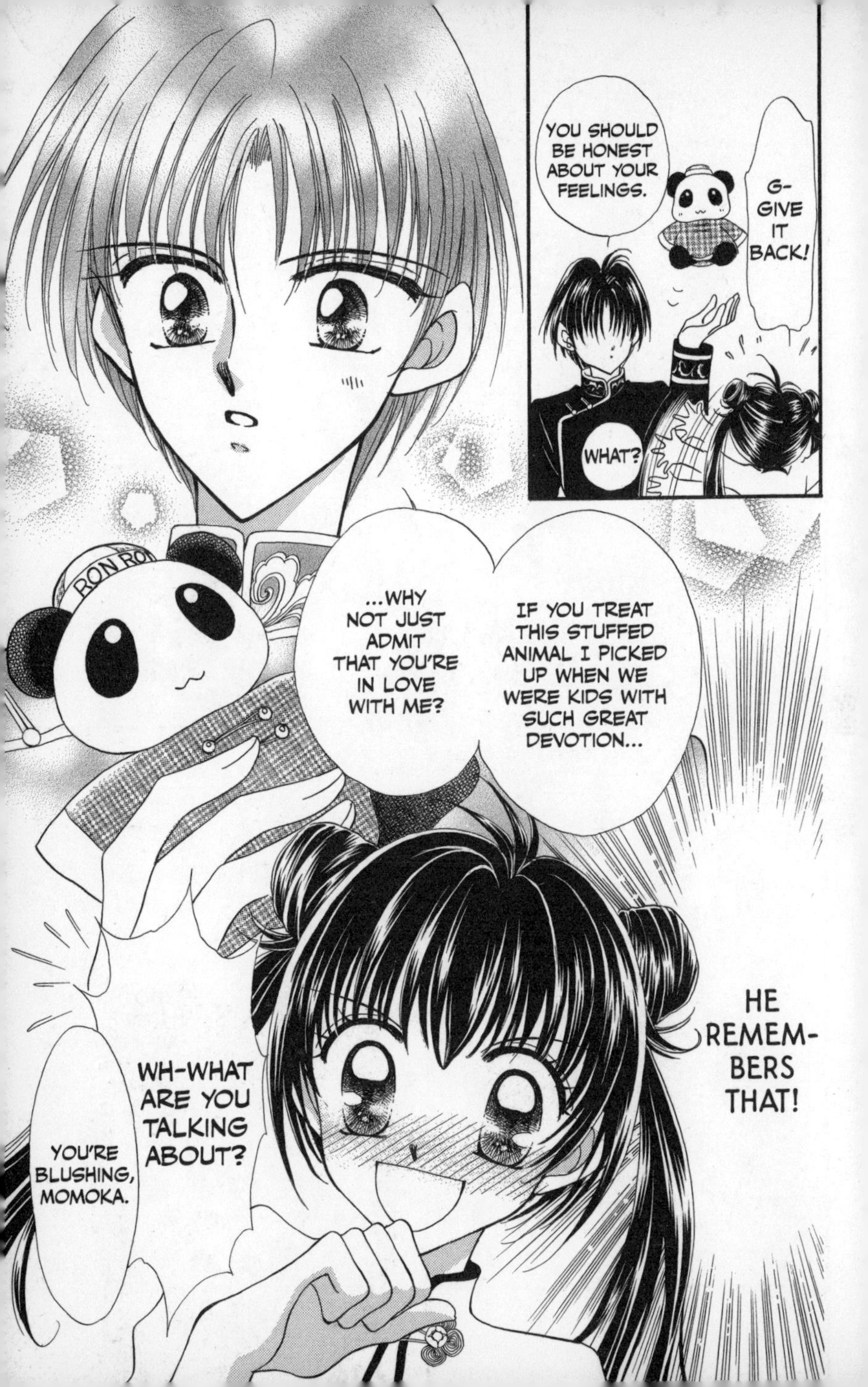
G-GIVE IT BACK!
YOU SHOULD BE HONEST ABOUT YOUR FEELINGS.
WHAT?
IF YOU TREAT THIS STUFFED ANIMAL I PICKED UP WHEN WE WERE KIDS WITH SUCH GREAT DEVOTION...
...WHY NOT JUST ADMIT THAT YOU'RE IN LOVE WITH ME?
RON RO
HE REMEM-BERS THAT!
WH-WHAT ARE YOU TALKING ABOUT?
YOU'RE BLUSHING, MOMOKA.

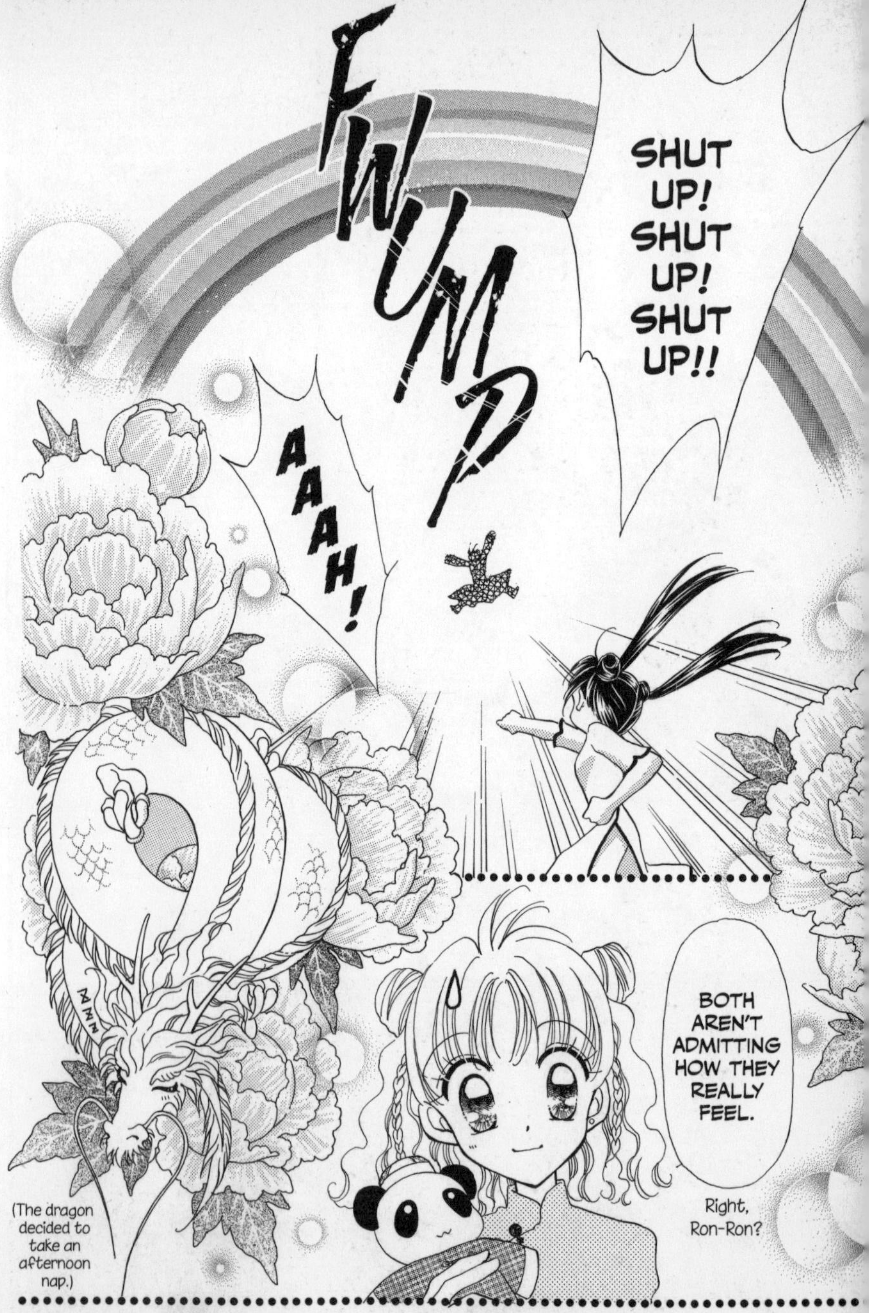
SHUT UP! SHUT UP! SHUT UP!!
FWUMP
AAAH!
BOTH AREN'T ADMITTING HOW THEY REALLY FEEL.
Right, Ron-Ron?
(The dragon decided to take an afternoon nap.)

CHAPTER 1/END

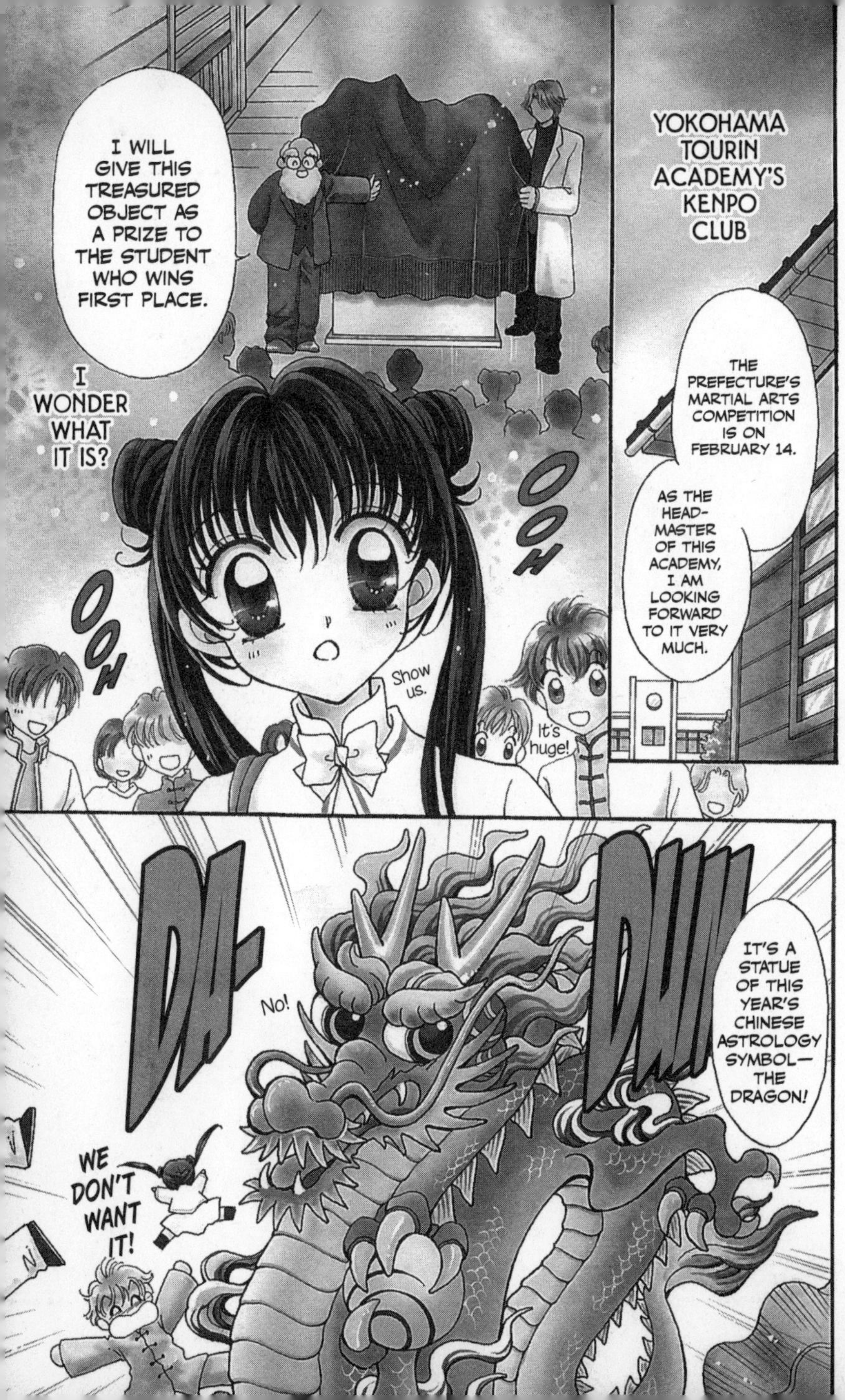
YOKOHAMA TOURIN ACADEMY'S KENPO CLUB
THE PREFECTURE'S MARTIAL ARTS COMPETITION IS ON FEBRUARY 14.
AS THE HEAD-MASTER OF THIS ACADEMY, I AM LOOKING FORWARD TO IT VERY MUCH.
I WILL GIVE THIS TREASURED OBJECT AS A PRIZE TO THE STUDENT WHO WINS FIRST PLACE.
I WONDER WHAT IT IS?
OOOH
OOOH
It's huge!
Show us.
IT'S A STATUE OF THIS YEAR'S CHINESE ASTROLOGY SYMBOL—THE DRAGON!
DA-
DUN
No!
WE DON'T WANT IT!

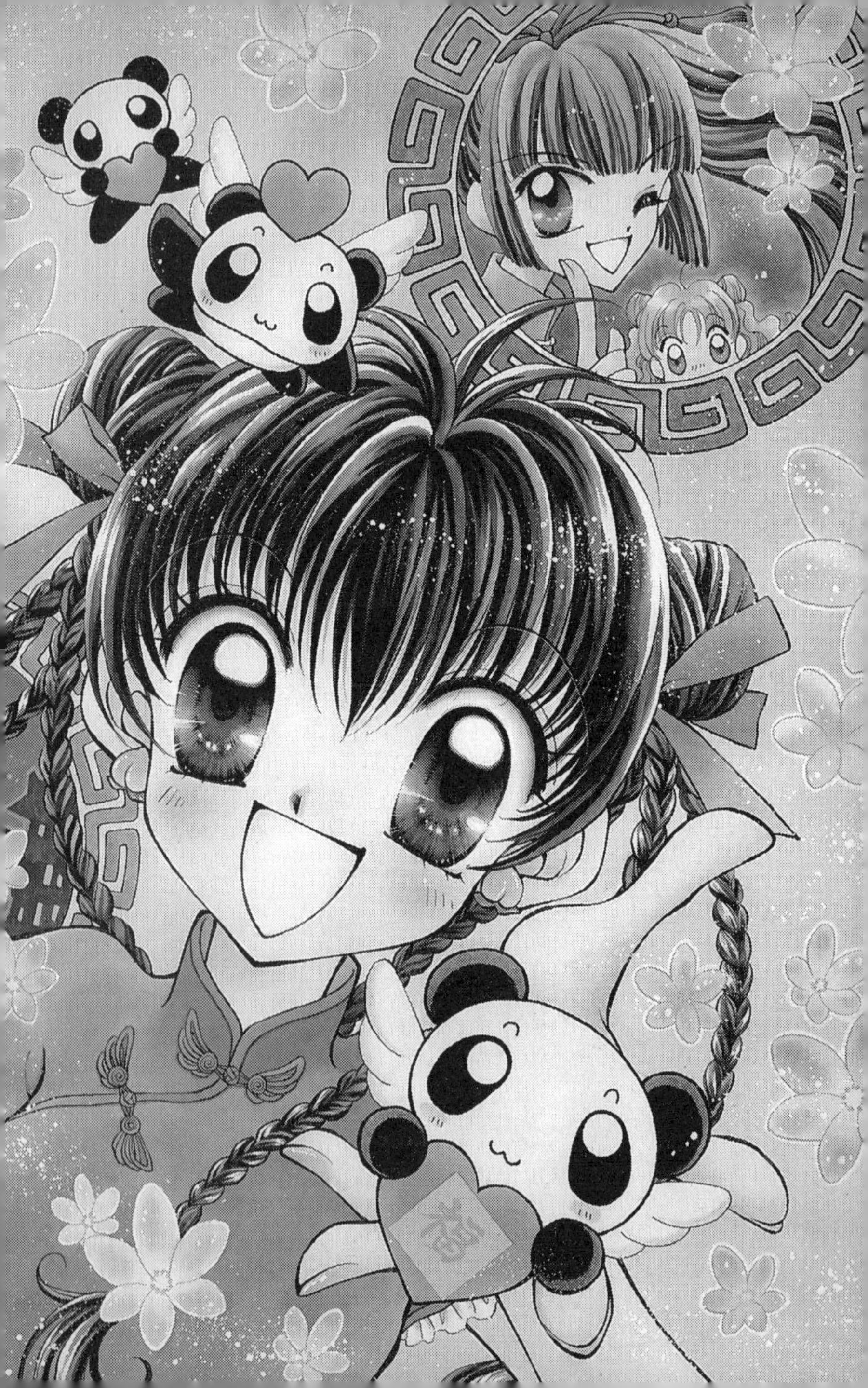

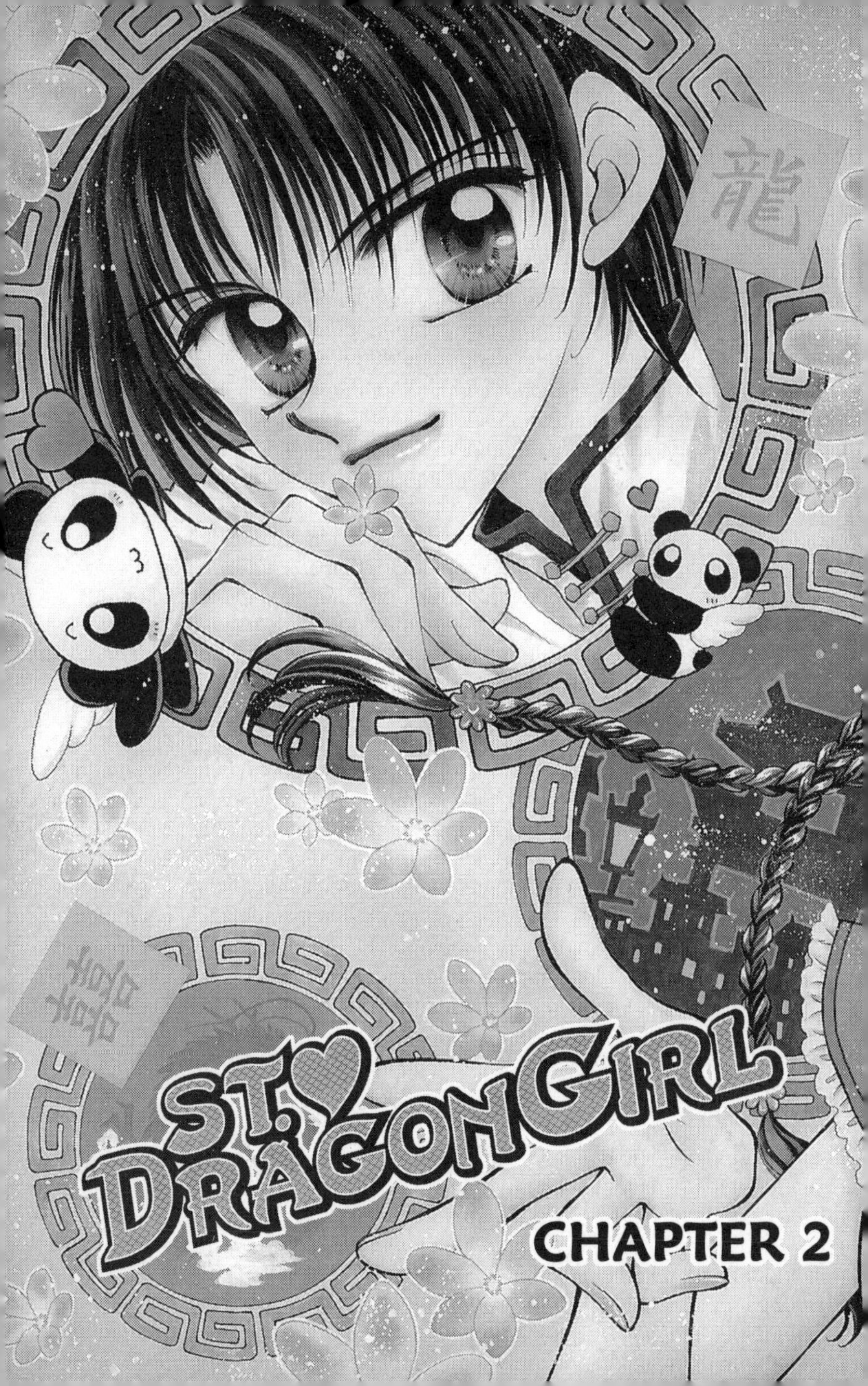

龍
ST.♥DRAGON GIRL
CHAPTER 2

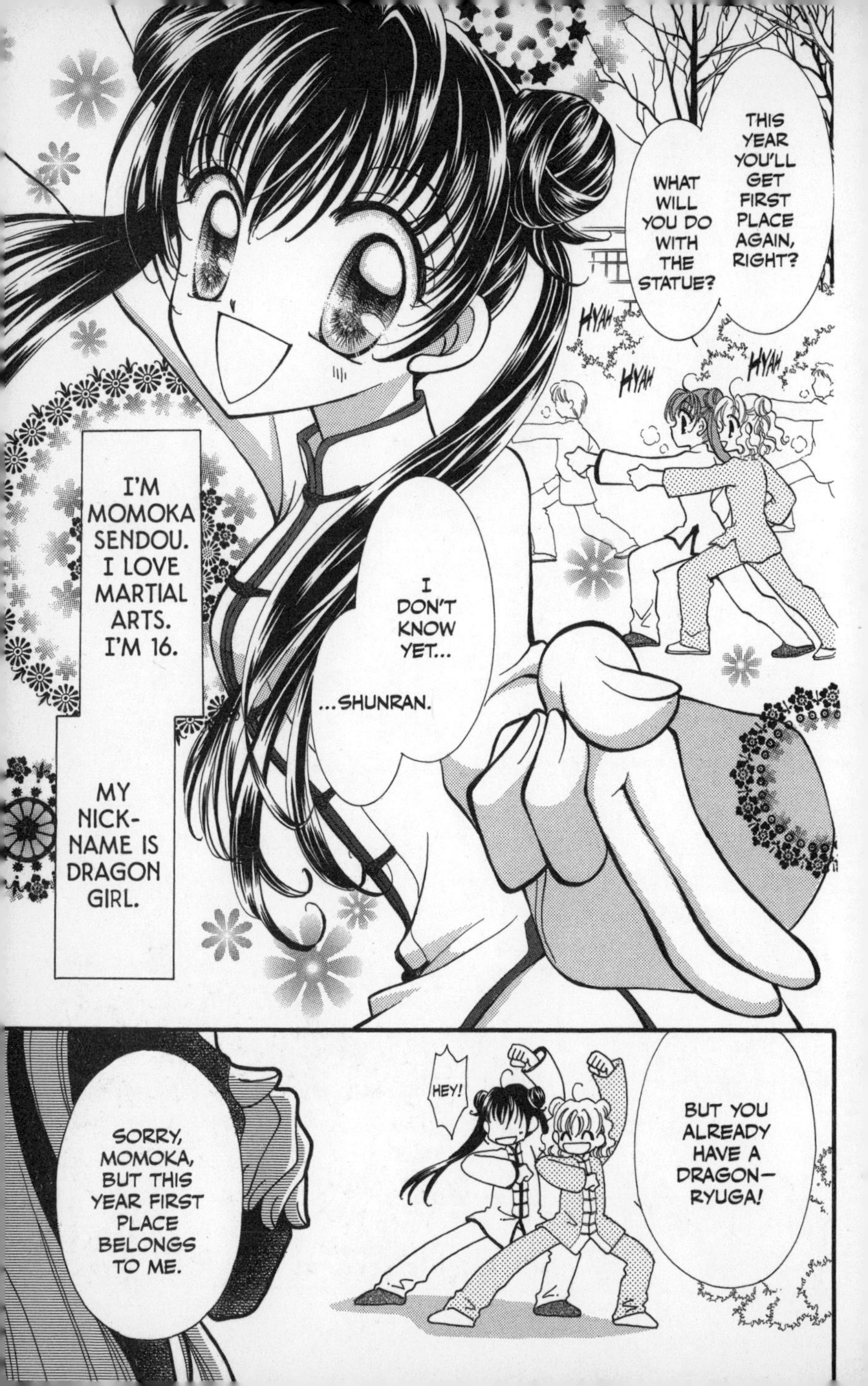
THIS YEAR YOU'LL GET FIRST PLACE AGAIN, RIGHT?
WHAT WILL YOU DO WITH THE STATUE?
HYAH
HYAH
HYAH
I DON'T KNOW YET...
...SHUNRAN.
I'M MOMOKA SENDOU. I LOVE MARTIAL ARTS. I'M 16.
MY NICK-NAME IS DRAGON GIRL.
BUT YOU ALREADY HAVE A DRAGON—RYUGA!
HEY!
SORRY, MOMOKA, BUT THIS YEAR FIRST PLACE BELONGS TO ME.

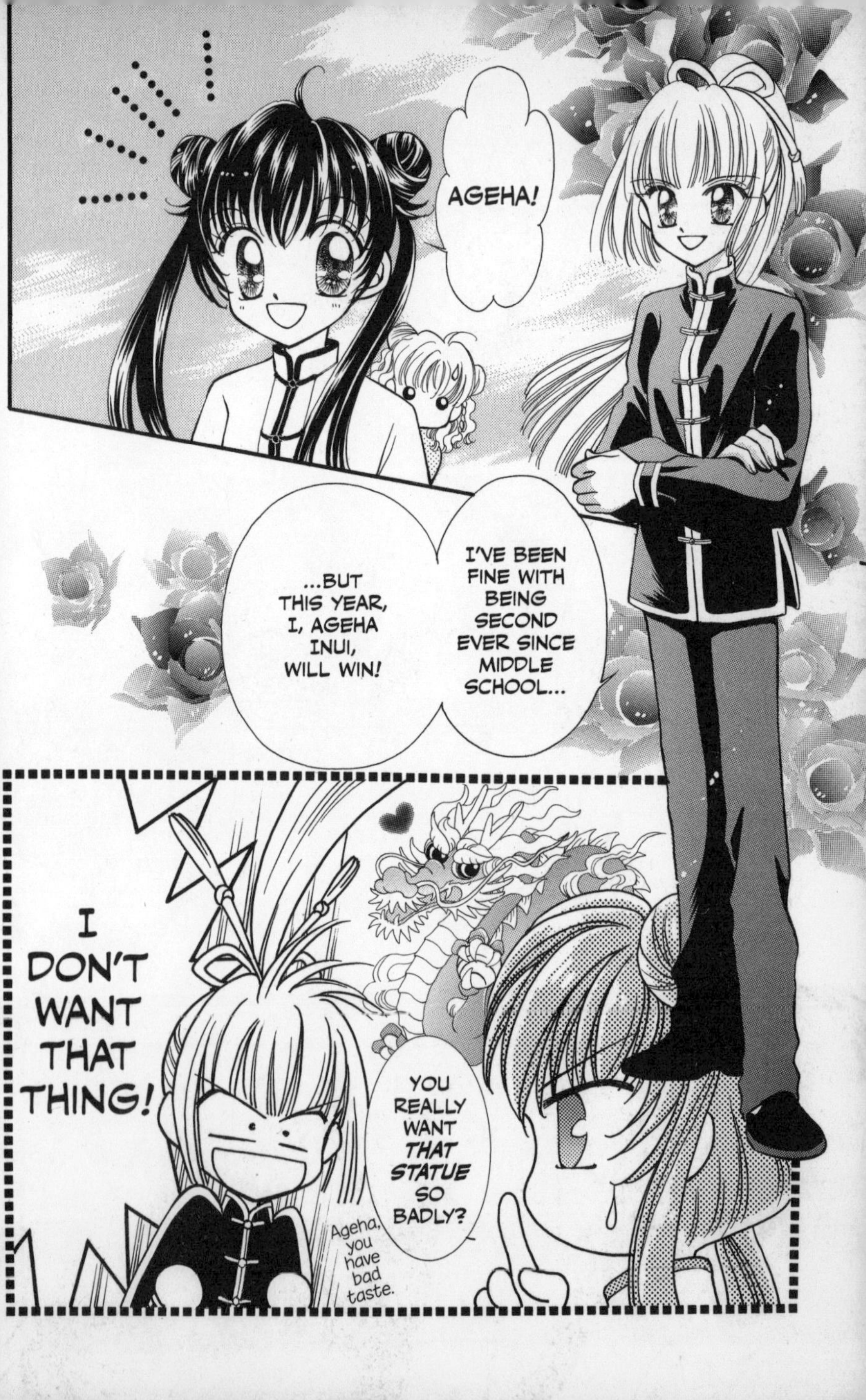

AGEHA!
I'VE BEEN FINE WITH BEING SECOND EVER SINCE MIDDLE SCHOOL...
...BUT THIS YEAR, I, AGEHA INUI, WILL WIN!
YOU REALLY WANT *THAT STATUE* SO BADLY?
I DON'T WANT THAT THING!
Ageha, you have bad taste.

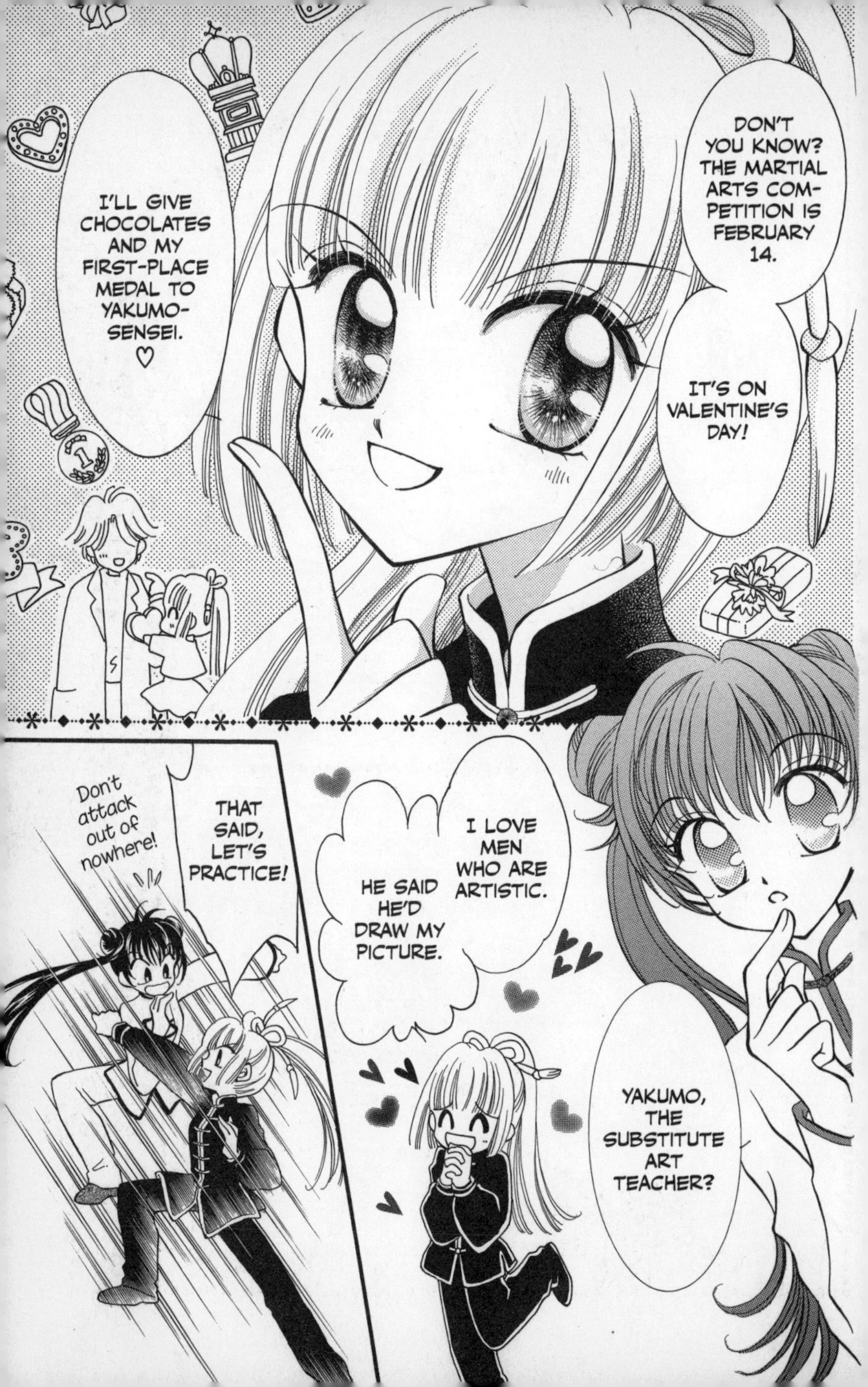
DON'T YOU KNOW? THE MARTIAL ARTS COMPETITION IS FEBRUARY 14.
IT'S ON VALENTINE'S DAY!
I'LL GIVE CHOCOLATES AND MY FIRST-PLACE MEDAL TO YAKUMO-SENSEI. ♡
YAKUMO, THE SUBSTITUTE ART TEACHER?
I LOVE MEN WHO ARE ARTISTIC.
HE SAID HE'D DRAW MY PICTURE.
THAT SAID, LET'S PRACTICE!
Don't attack out of nowhere!

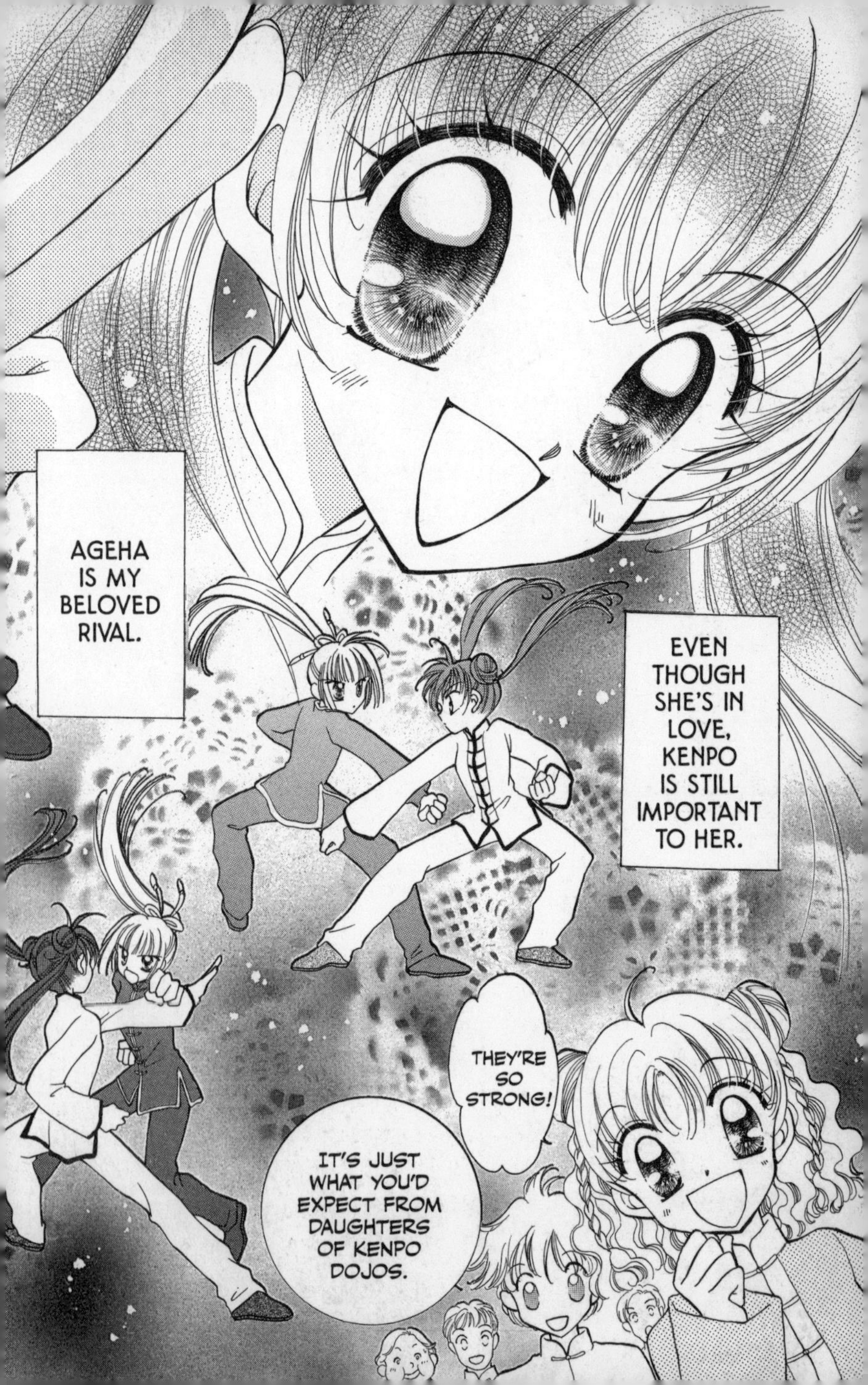
AGEHA IS MY BELOVED RIVAL.
EVEN THOUGH SHE'S IN LOVE, KENPO IS STILL IMPORTANT TO HER.
THEY'RE SO STRONG!
IT'S JUST WHAT YOU'D EXPECT FROM DAUGHTERS OF KENPO DOJOS.

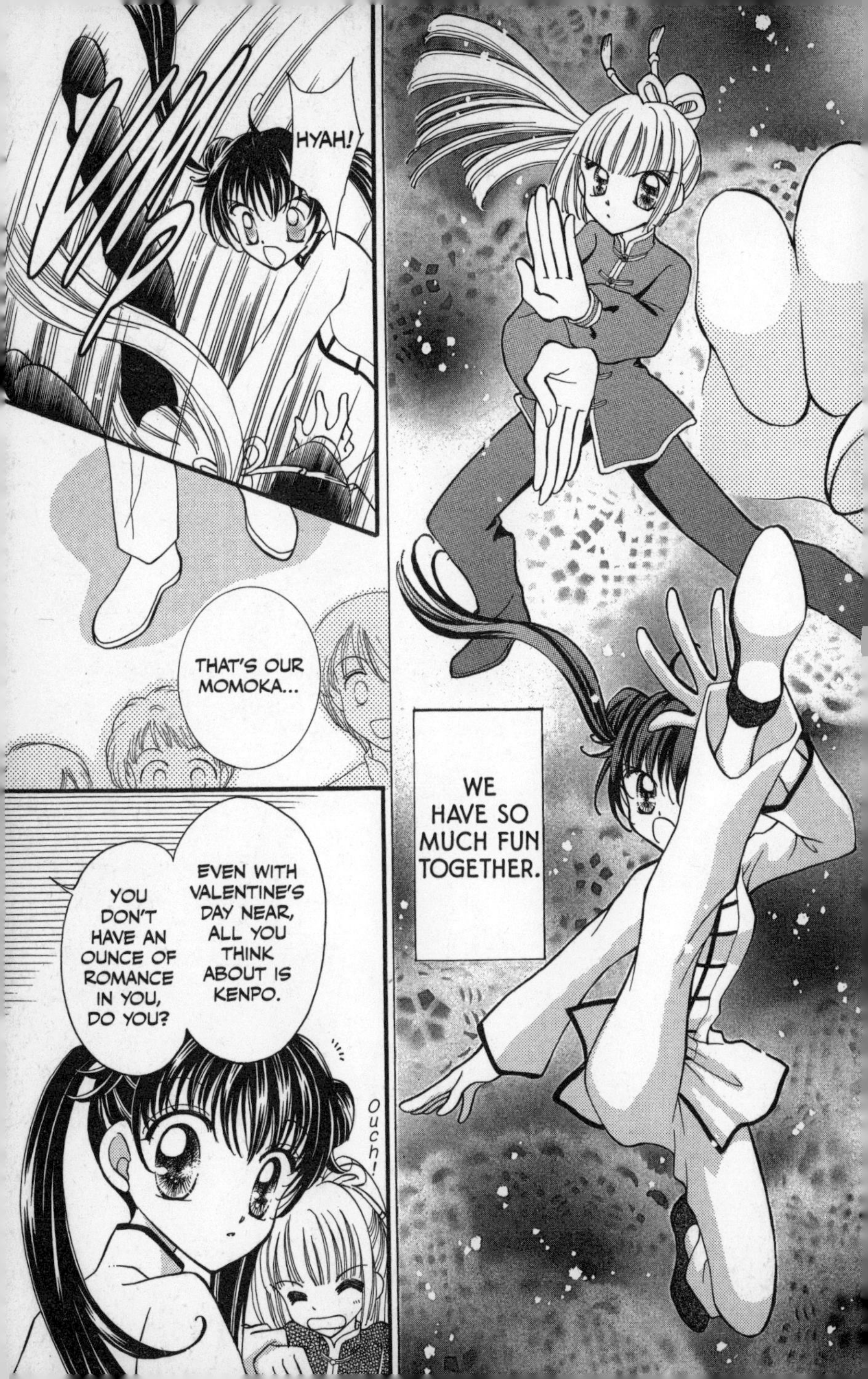

WE HAVE SO MUCH FUN TOGETHER.
HYAH!
THAT'S OUR MOMOKA...
EVEN WITH VALENTINE'S DAY NEAR, ALL YOU THINK ABOUT IS KENPO.
YOU DON'T HAVE AN OUNCE OF ROMANCE IN YOU, DO YOU?
Ouch!

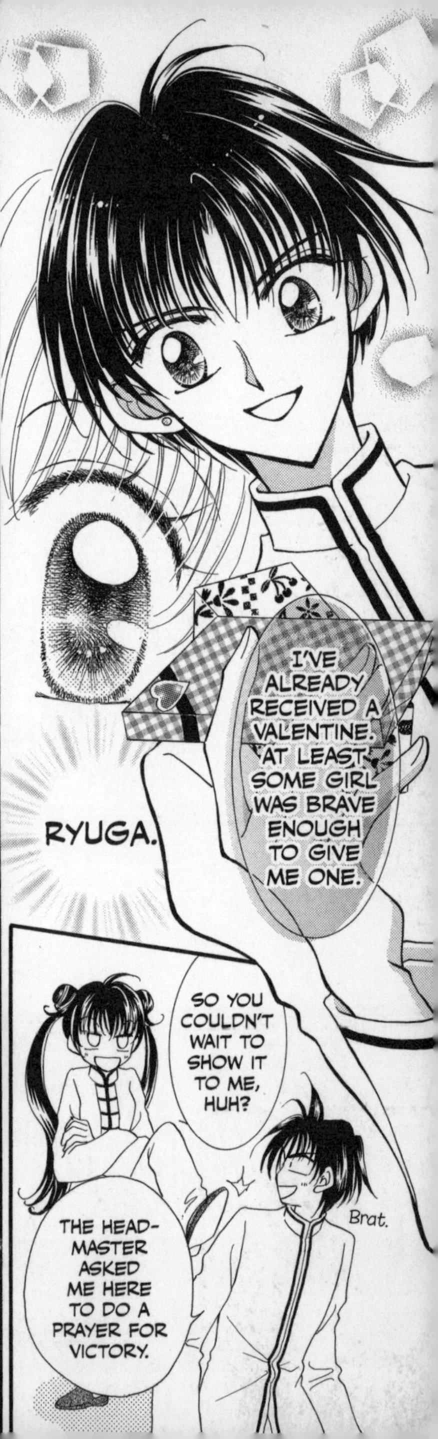
I'VE ALREADY RECEIVED A VALENTINE. AT LEAST SOME GIRL WAS BRAVE ENOUGH TO GIVE ME ONE.
RYUGA.
SO YOU COULDN'T WAIT TO SHOW IT TO ME, HUH?
Brat.
THE HEAD-MASTER ASKED ME HERE TO DO A PRAYER FOR VICTORY.

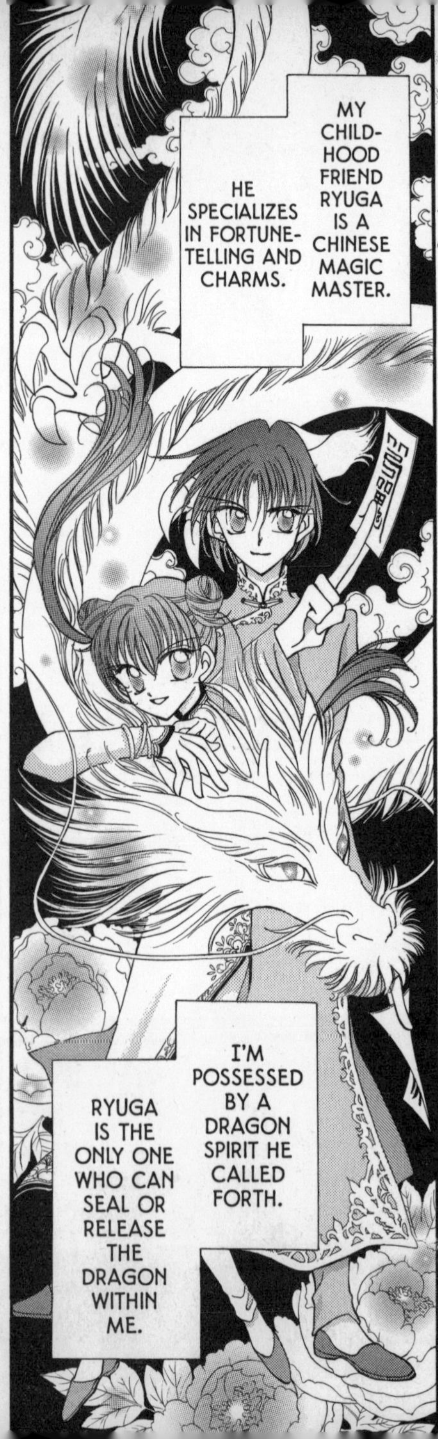
MY CHILD-HOOD FRIEND RYUGA IS A CHINESE MAGIC MASTER.
HE SPECIALIZES IN FORTUNE-TELLING AND CHARMS.
I'M POSSESSED BY A DRAGON SPIRIT HE CALLED FORTH.
RYUGA IS THE ONLY ONE WHO CAN SEAL OR RELEASE THE DRAGON WITHIN ME.

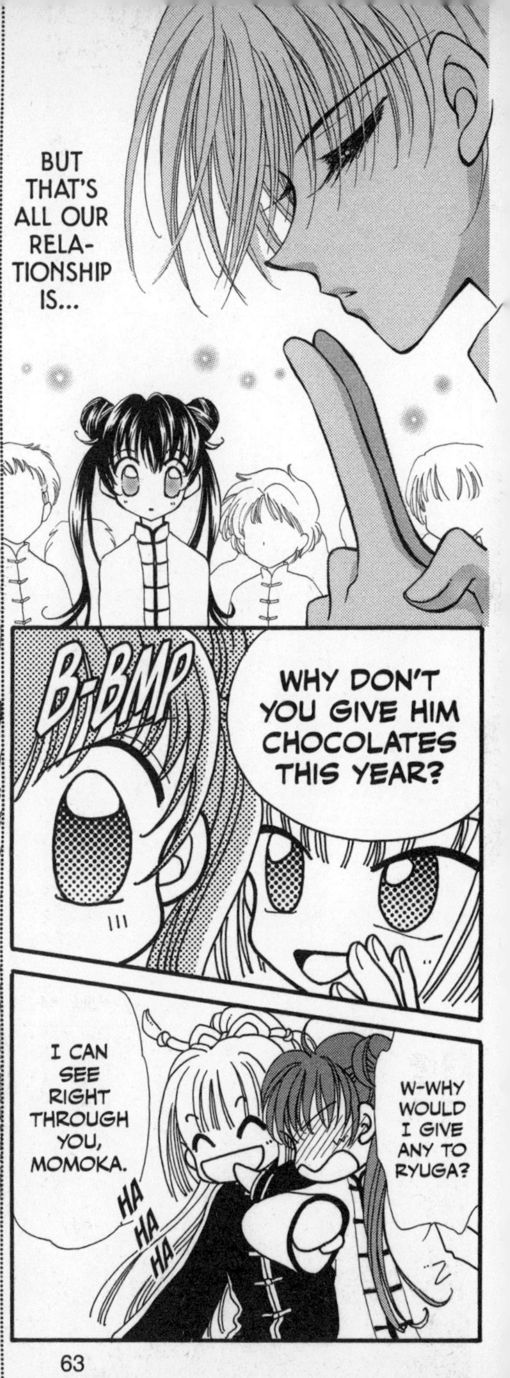
BUT THAT'S ALL OUR RELATIONSHIP IS...
B-BMP
WHY DON'T YOU GIVE HIM CHOCOLATES THIS YEAR?
W-WHY WOULD I GIVE ANY TO RYUGA?
I CAN SEE RIGHT THROUGH YOU, MOMOKA.
HA HA HA

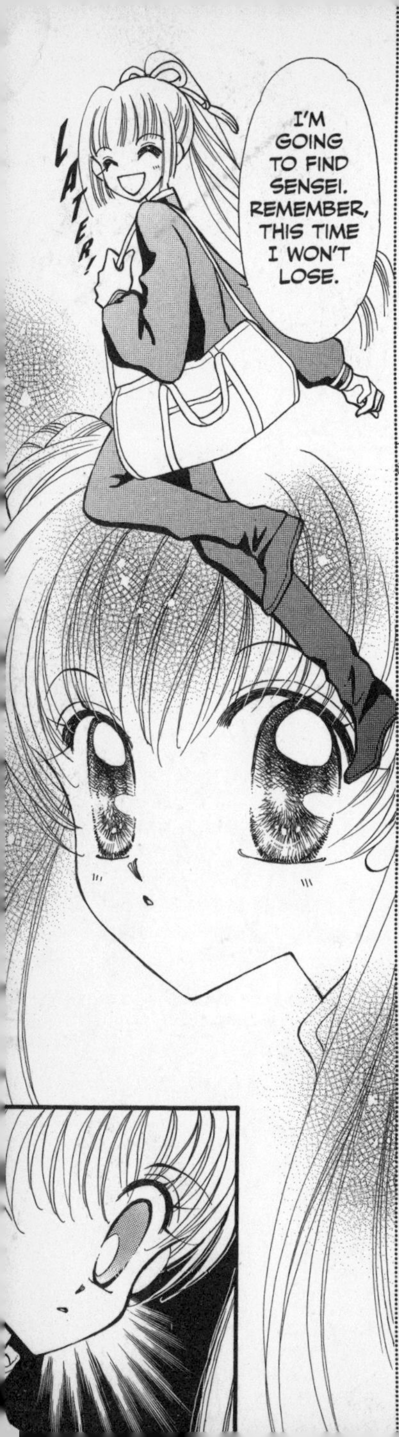
I'M GOING TO FIND SENSEI. REMEMBER, THIS TIME I WON'T LOSE.
LATER!

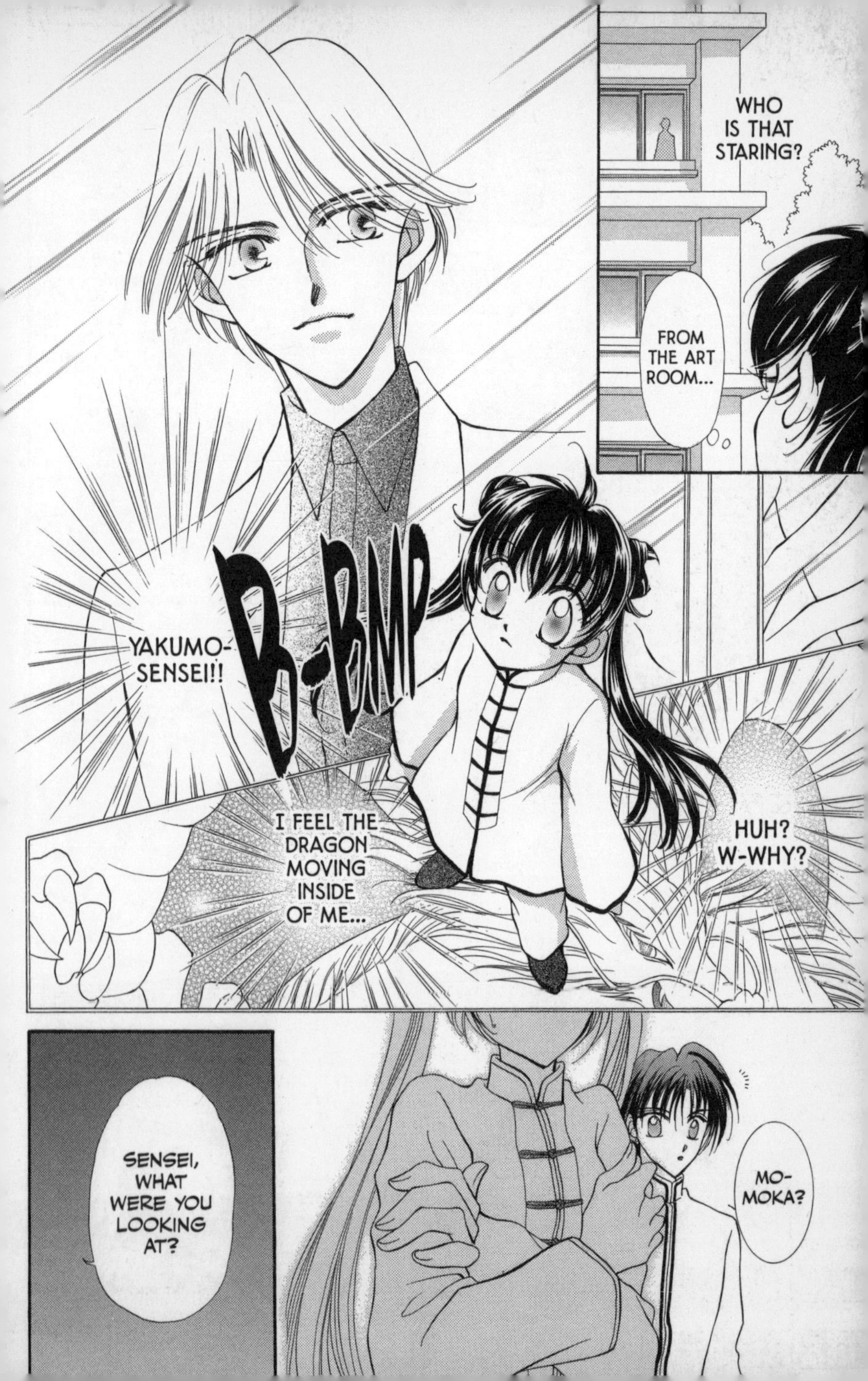
WHO IS THAT STARING?
FROM THE ART ROOM...
B-BMP
YAKUMO-SENSEI!!
HUH? W-WHY?
I FEEL THE DRAGON MOVING INSIDE OF ME...
MO-MOKA?
SENSEI, WHAT WERE YOU LOOKING AT?

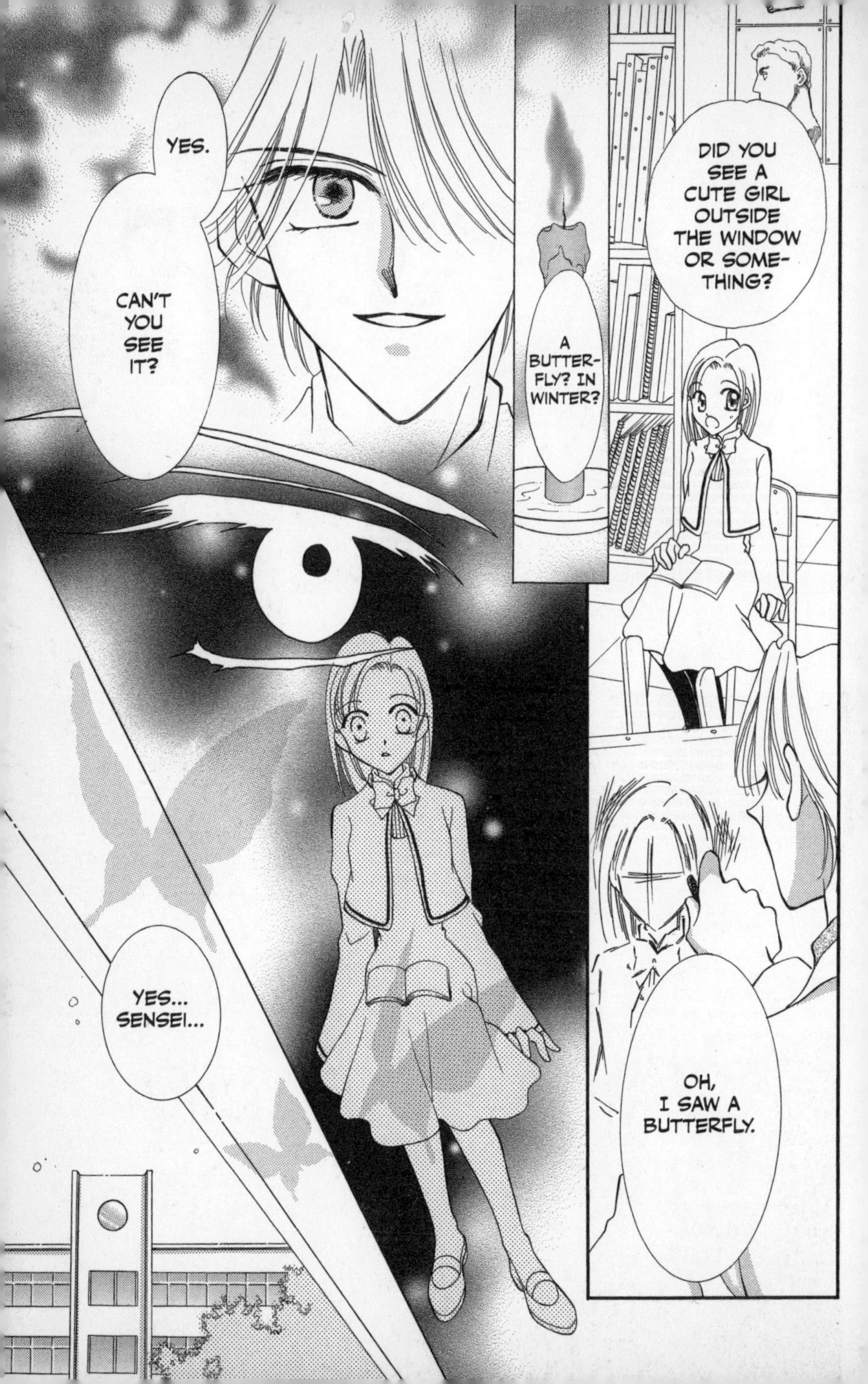

DID YOU SEE A CUTE GIRL OUTSIDE THE WINDOW OR SOME-THING?
OH, I SAW A BUTTERFLY.
A BUTTER-FLY? IN WINTER?
YES.
CAN'T YOU SEE IT?
YES... SENSEI...

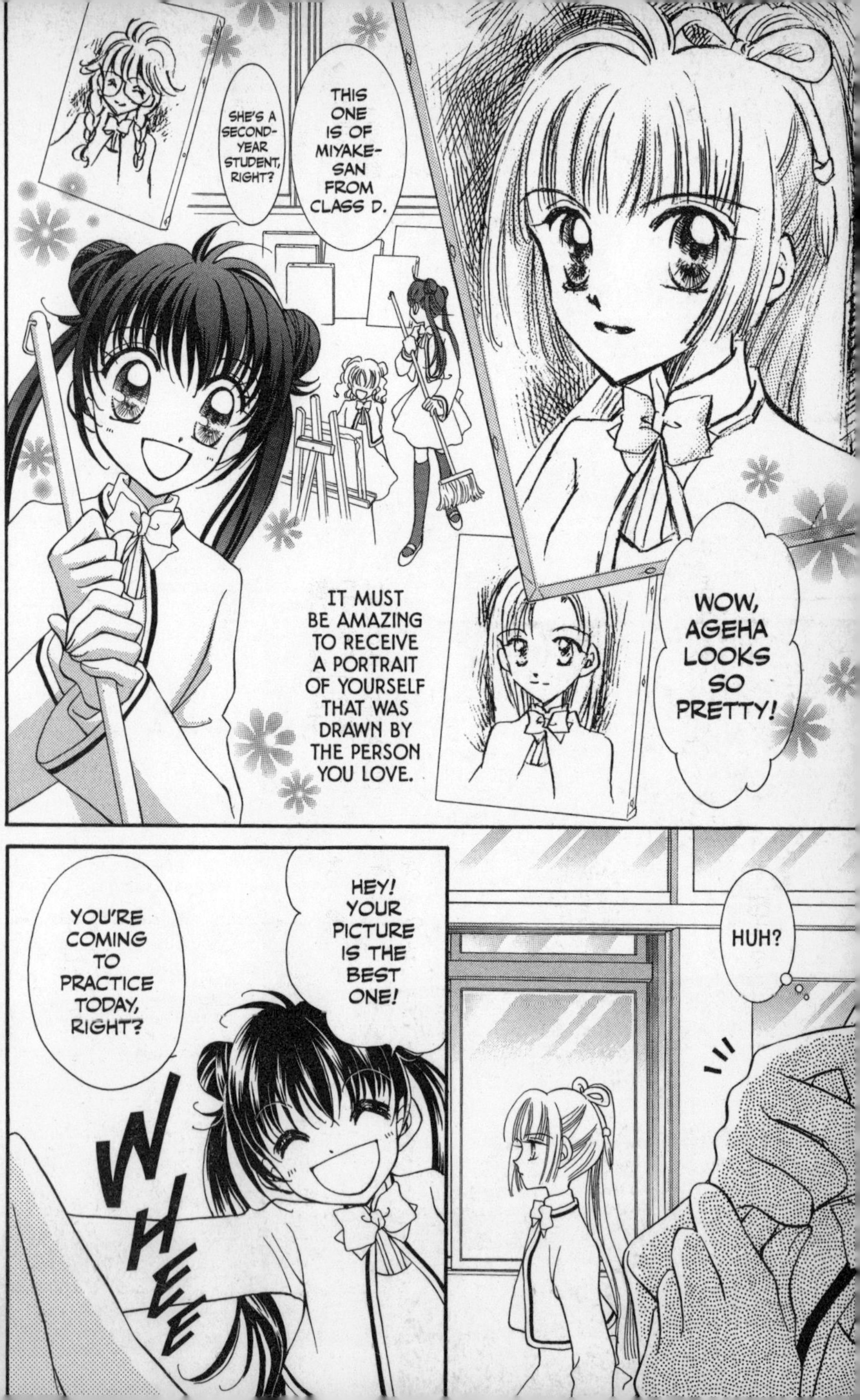
WOW, AGEHA LOOKS SO PRETTY!
THIS ONE IS OF MIYAKE-SAN FROM CLASS D.
SHE'S A SECOND-YEAR STUDENT, RIGHT?
IT MUST BE AMAZING TO RECEIVE A PORTRAIT OF YOURSELF THAT WAS DRAWN BY THE PERSON YOU LOVE.
HUH?
HEY! YOUR PICTURE IS THE BEST ONE!
YOU'RE COMING TO PRACTICE TODAY, RIGHT?
WHEE

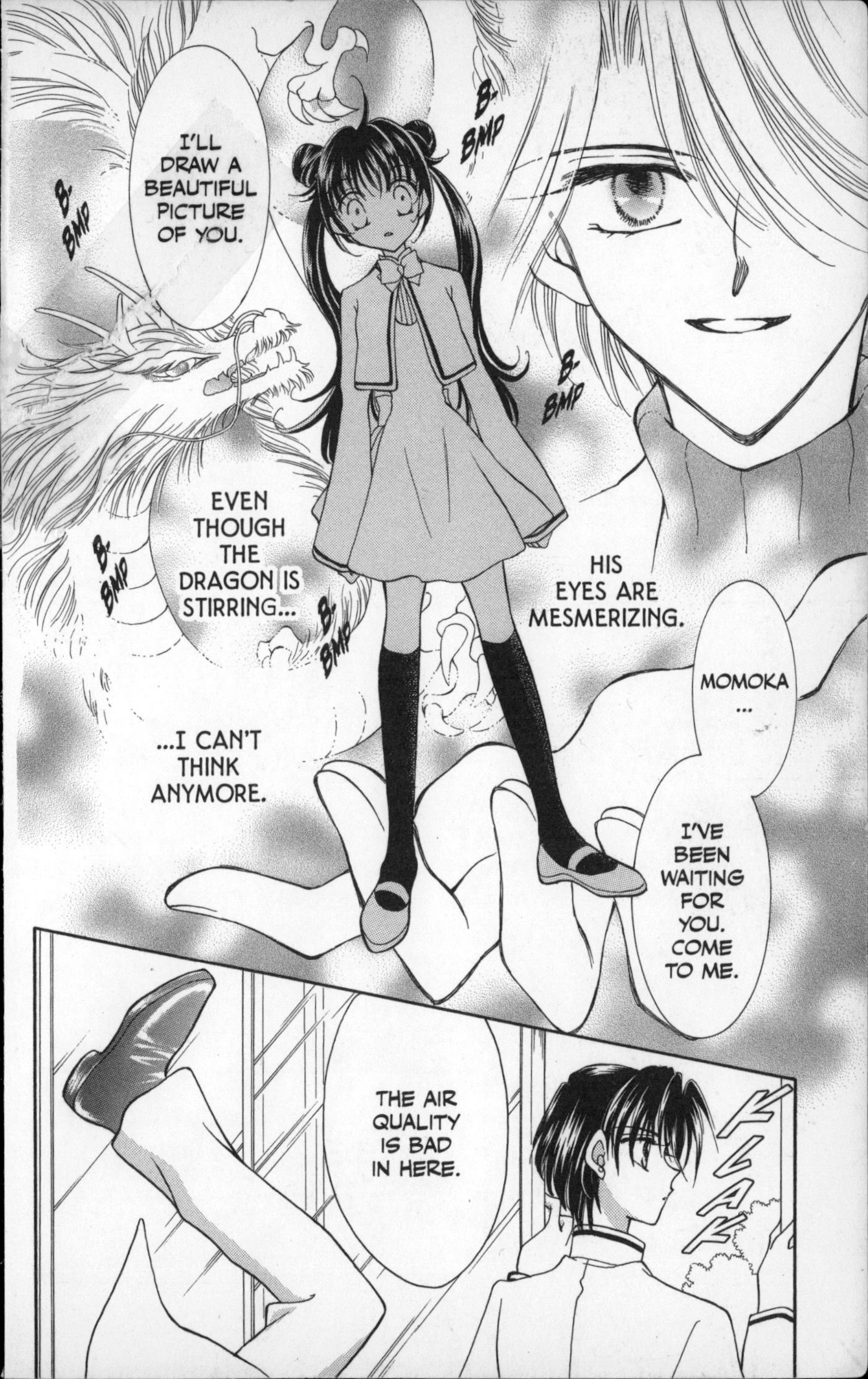
B-BMP
I'LL DRAW A BEAUTIFUL PICTURE OF YOU.
B-BMP
B-BMP
HIS EYES ARE MESMERIZING.
MOMOKA ...
EVEN THOUGH THE DRAGON IS STIRRING...
B-BMP
B-BMP
I'VE BEEN WAITING FOR YOU. COME TO ME.
...I CAN'T THINK ANYMORE.
FLAP
THE AIR QUALITY IS BAD IN HERE.

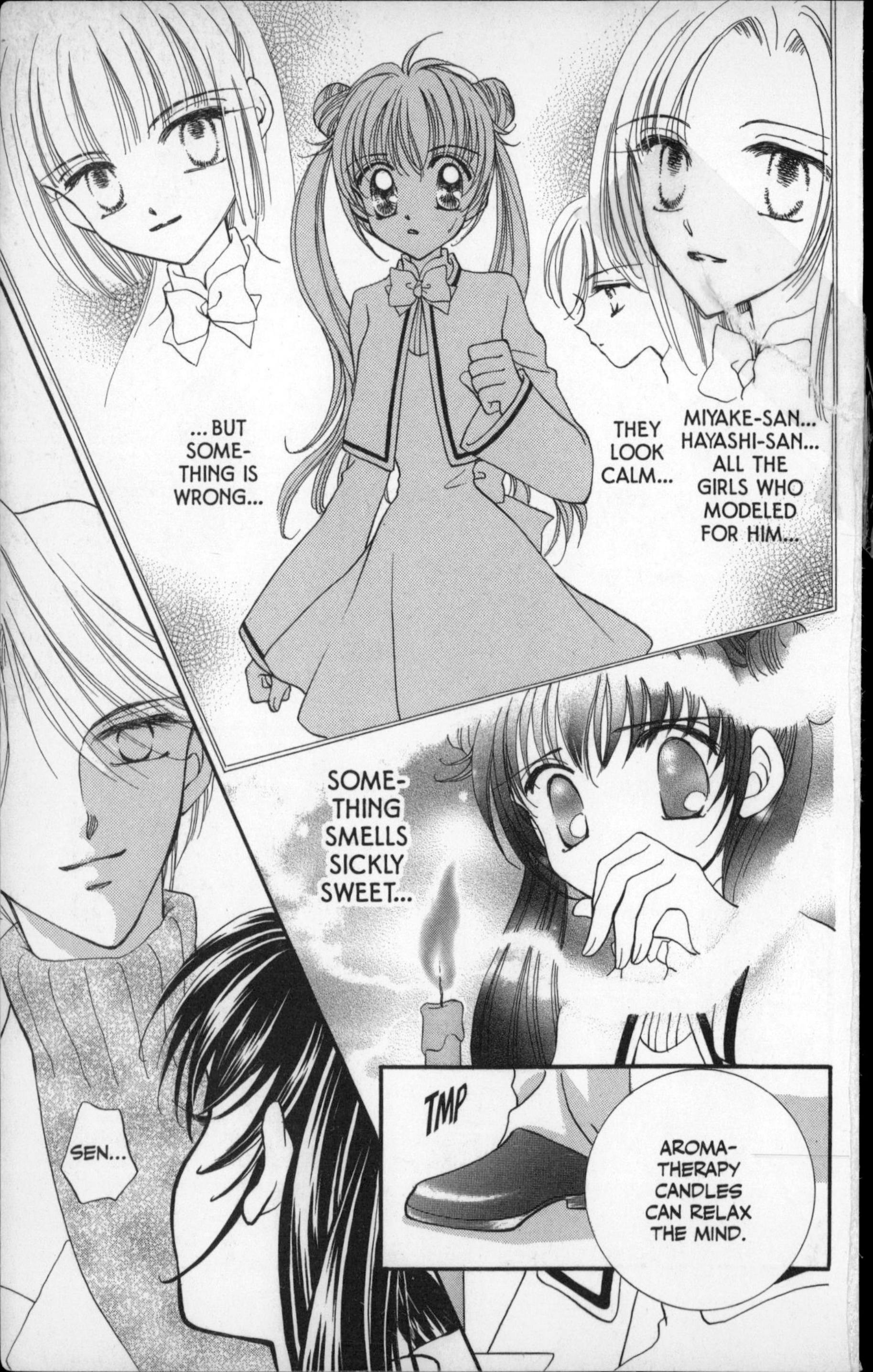
MIYAKE-SAN... HAYASHI-SAN... ALL THE GIRLS WHO MODELED FOR HIM...
THEY LOOK CALM...
... BUT SOME-THING IS WRONG...
SOME-THING SMELLS SICKLY SWEET...
TMP
AROMA-THERAPY CANDLES CAN RELAX THE MIND.
SEN...

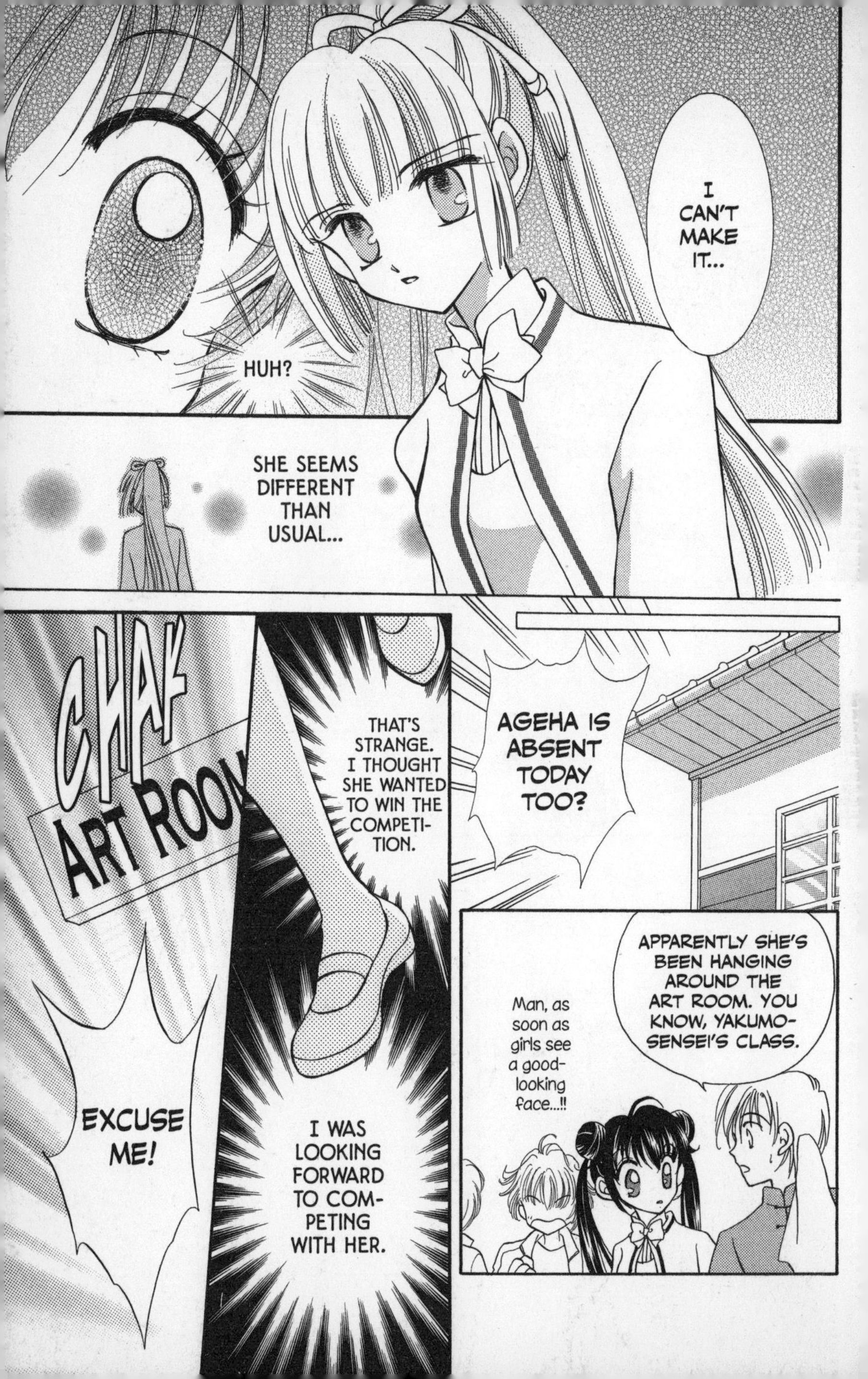
I CAN'T MAKE IT...
HUH?
SHE SEEMS DIFFERENT THAN USUAL...
AGEHA IS ABSENT TODAY TOO?
APPARENTLY SHE'S BEEN HANGING AROUND THE ART ROOM. YOU KNOW, YAKUMO-SENSEI'S CLASS.
Man, as soon as girls see a good-looking face...!!
THAT'S STRANGE. I THOUGHT SHE WANTED TO WIN THE COMPETITION.
I WAS LOOKING FORWARD TO COMPETING WITH HER.
CHAK
ART ROOM
EXCUSE ME!

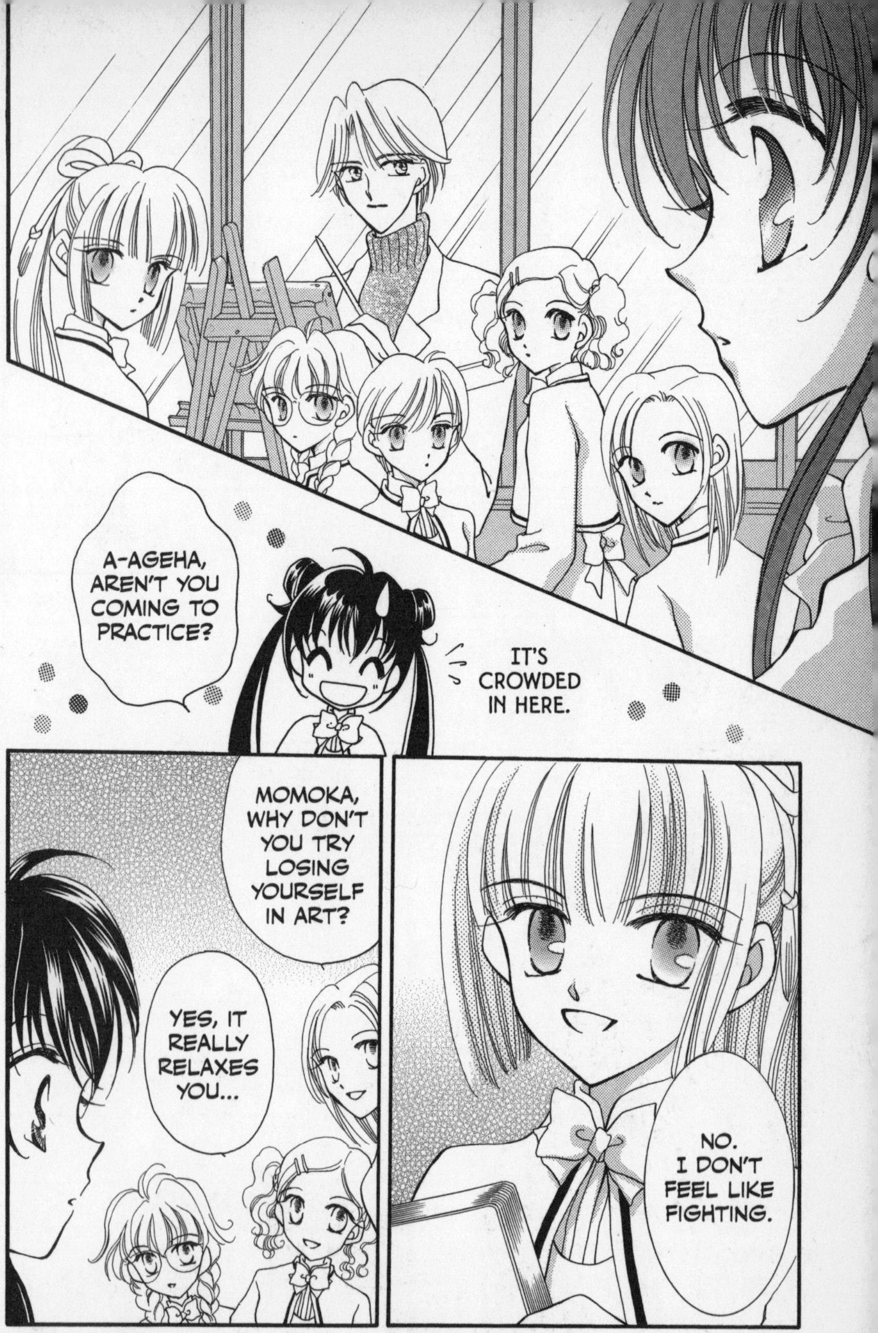
IT'S CROWDED IN HERE.
A-AGEHA, AREN'T YOU COMING TO PRACTICE?
NO. I DON'T FEEL LIKE FIGHTING.
MOMOKA, WHY DON'T YOU TRY LOSING YOURSELF IN ART?
YES, IT REALLY RELAXES YOU...

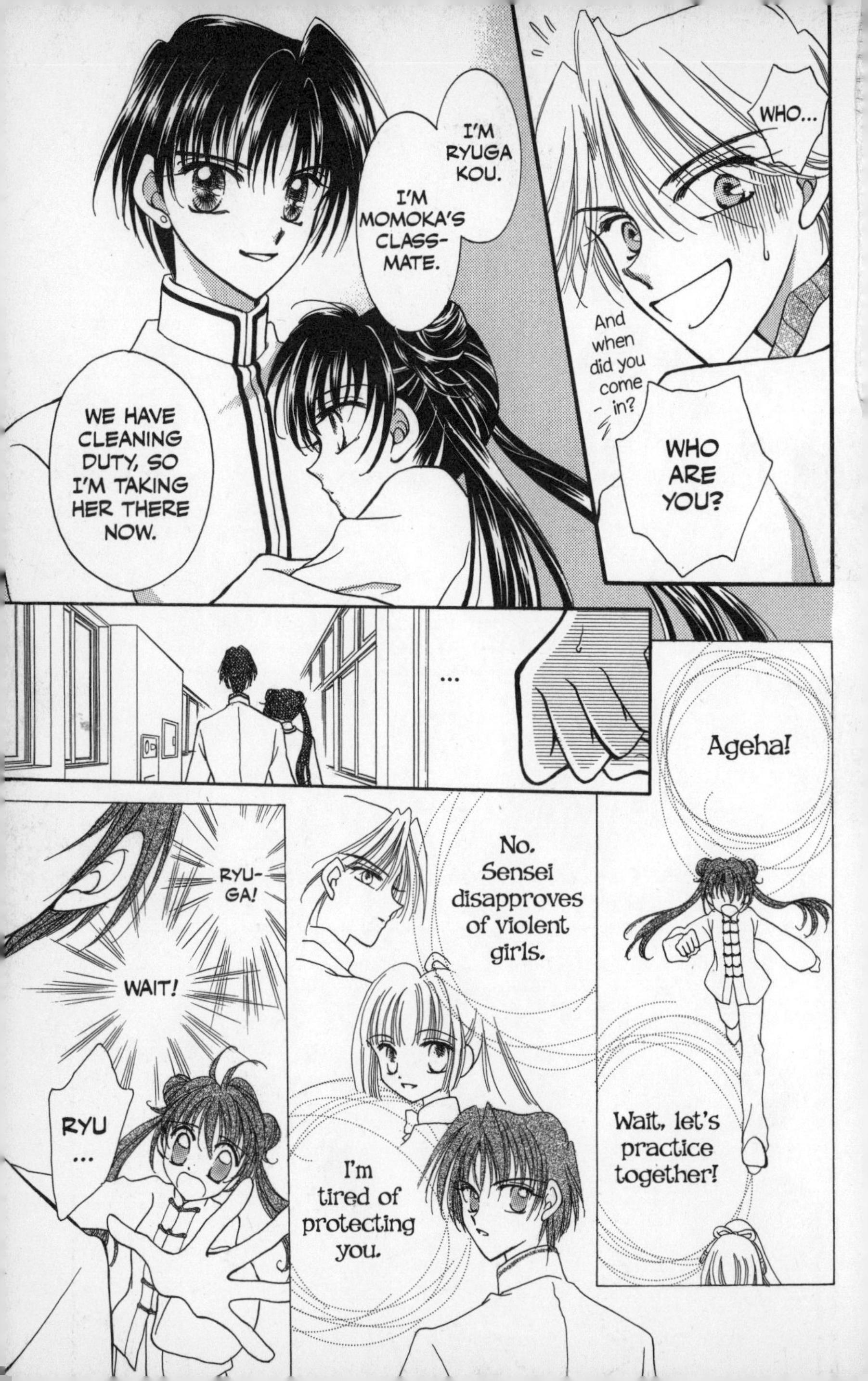
WHO...
And when did you come in?
WHO ARE YOU?
I'M RYUGA KOU.
I'M MOMOKA'S CLASSMATE.
WE HAVE CLEANING DUTY, SO I'M TAKING HER THERE NOW.
...
Ageha!
Wait, let's practice together!
No. Sensei disapproves of violent girls.
I'm tired of protecting you.
RYUGA!
WAIT!
RYU ...

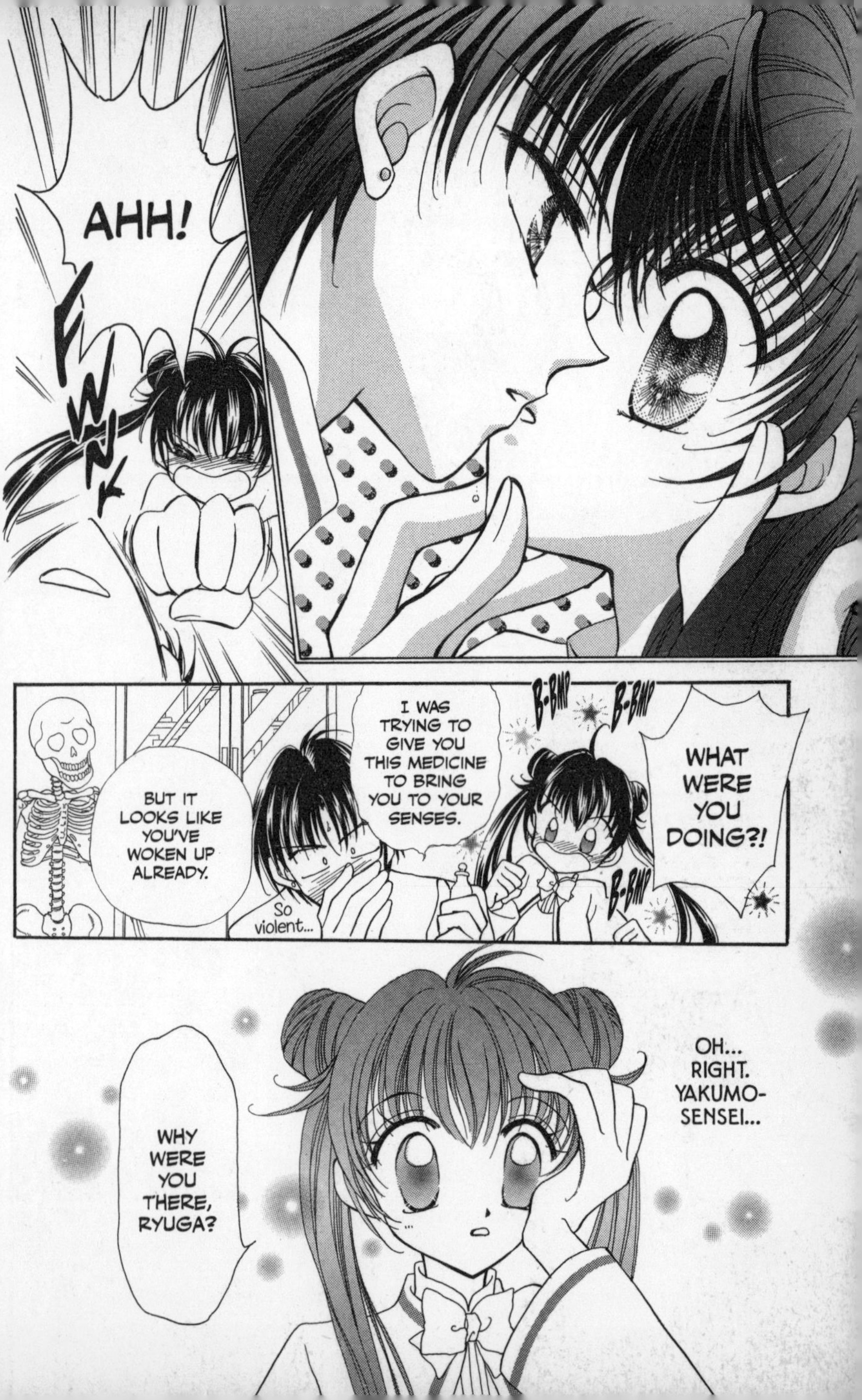
AHH!
FWUNK
WHAT WERE YOU DOING?!
B-BMP
B-BMP
B-BMP
I WAS TRYING TO GIVE YOU THIS MEDICINE TO BRING YOU TO YOUR SENSES.
So violent...
BUT IT LOOKS LIKE YOU'VE WOKEN UP ALREADY.
OH... RIGHT. YAKUMO-SENSEI...
WHY WERE YOU THERE, RYUGA?

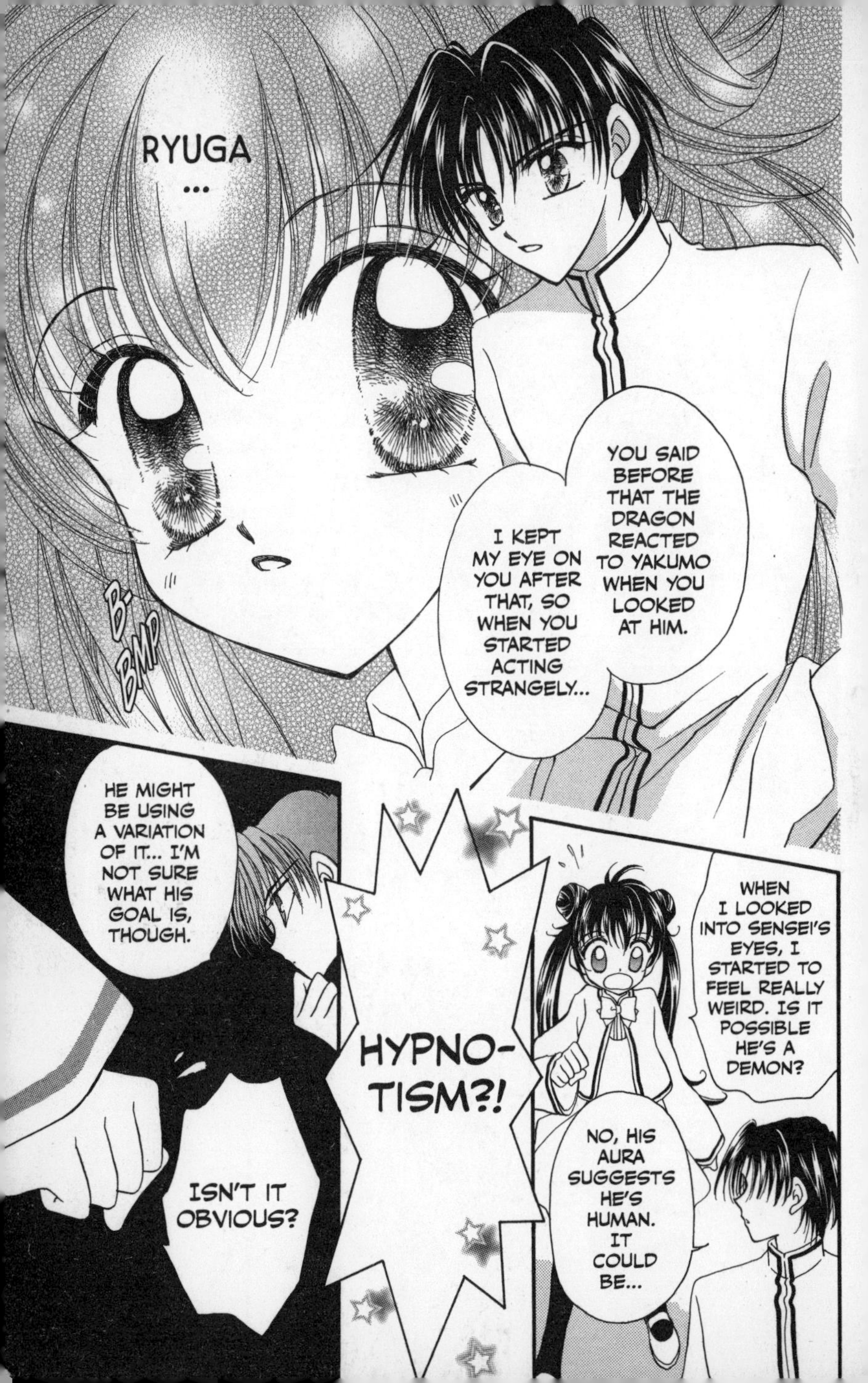
YOU SAID BEFORE THAT THE DRAGON REACTED TO YAKUMO WHEN YOU LOOKED AT HIM.
I KEPT MY EYE ON YOU AFTER THAT, SO WHEN YOU STARTED ACTING STRANGELY...
RYUGA ...
B-BMP
WHEN I LOOKED INTO SENSEI'S EYES, I STARTED TO FEEL REALLY WEIRD. IS IT POSSIBLE HE'S A DEMON?
NO, HIS AURA SUGGESTS HE'S HUMAN. IT COULD BE...
ISN'T IT OBVIOUS?
HYPNO-TISM?!
HE MIGHT BE USING A VARIATION OF IT... I'M NOT SURE WHAT HIS GOAL IS, THOUGH.

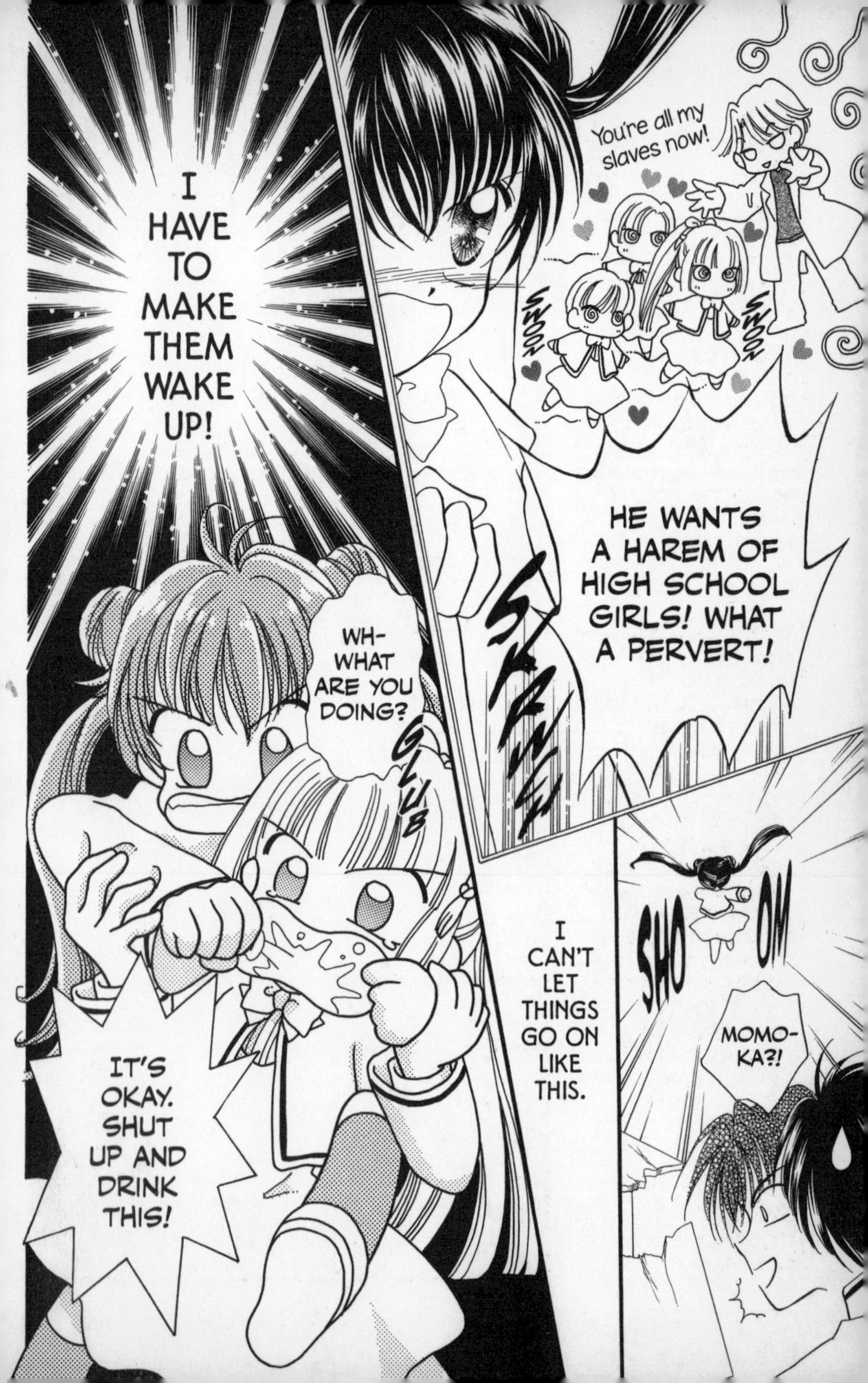
You're all my slaves now!
SWOON
SWOON
HE WANTS A HAREM OF HIGH SCHOOL GIRLS! WHAT A PERVERT!
I CAN'T LET THINGS GO ON LIKE THIS.
SHOOM
MOMOKA?!
I HAVE TO MAKE THEM WAKE UP!
WH-WHAT ARE YOU DOING?
GLUB
IT'S OKAY. SHUT UP AND DRINK THIS!

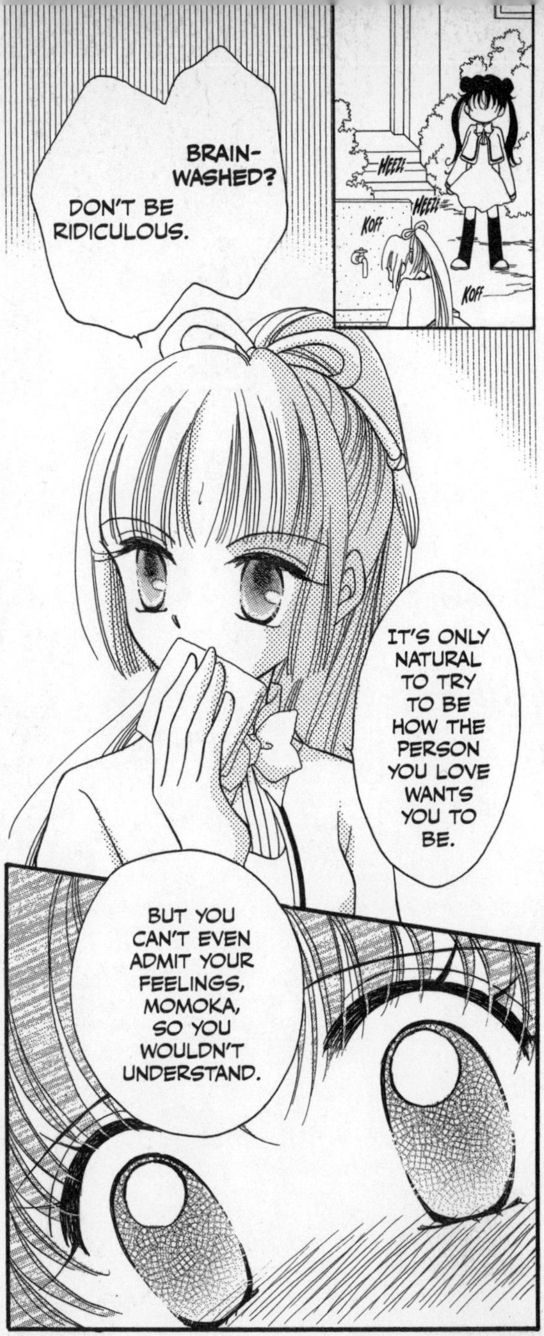
HEEZE
HEEZE
KOFF
KOFF
BRAIN-WASHED?
DON'T BE RIDICULOUS.
IT'S ONLY NATURAL TO TRY TO BE HOW THE PERSON YOU LOVE WANTS YOU TO BE.
BUT YOU CAN'T EVEN ADMIT YOUR FEELINGS, MOMOKA, SO YOU WOULDN'T UNDERSTAND.

3

Up until now, I've done a lot of stories in which the protagonists were mermaids or vampires. This time, however, I decided to make the protagonists normal humans, although Momoka is possessed by a dragon and Ryuga has one trick after another. I have a feeling that these two are the farthest removed from humans yet. But I guess that's okay, as long as I'm having fun. (laugh)

This manga became serialized from chapter 2 on. I was surprised that, of all the side characters, Ageha turned out to be very popular for some reason. I guess it's because she is strong-willed and her feelings of love are sincere. There were many voices saying, "Bring out Ageha again!" I understand. I'll bring her back again. Personally, action scenes between two girls make me very happy. Speaking of which, I received a letter from a girl who joined her school's kenpo club. I thought, wow, there really is such a thing as kenpo. (Hey!) I wanted to ask her all kinds of things about it. ♡ Maybe I should go do some research.

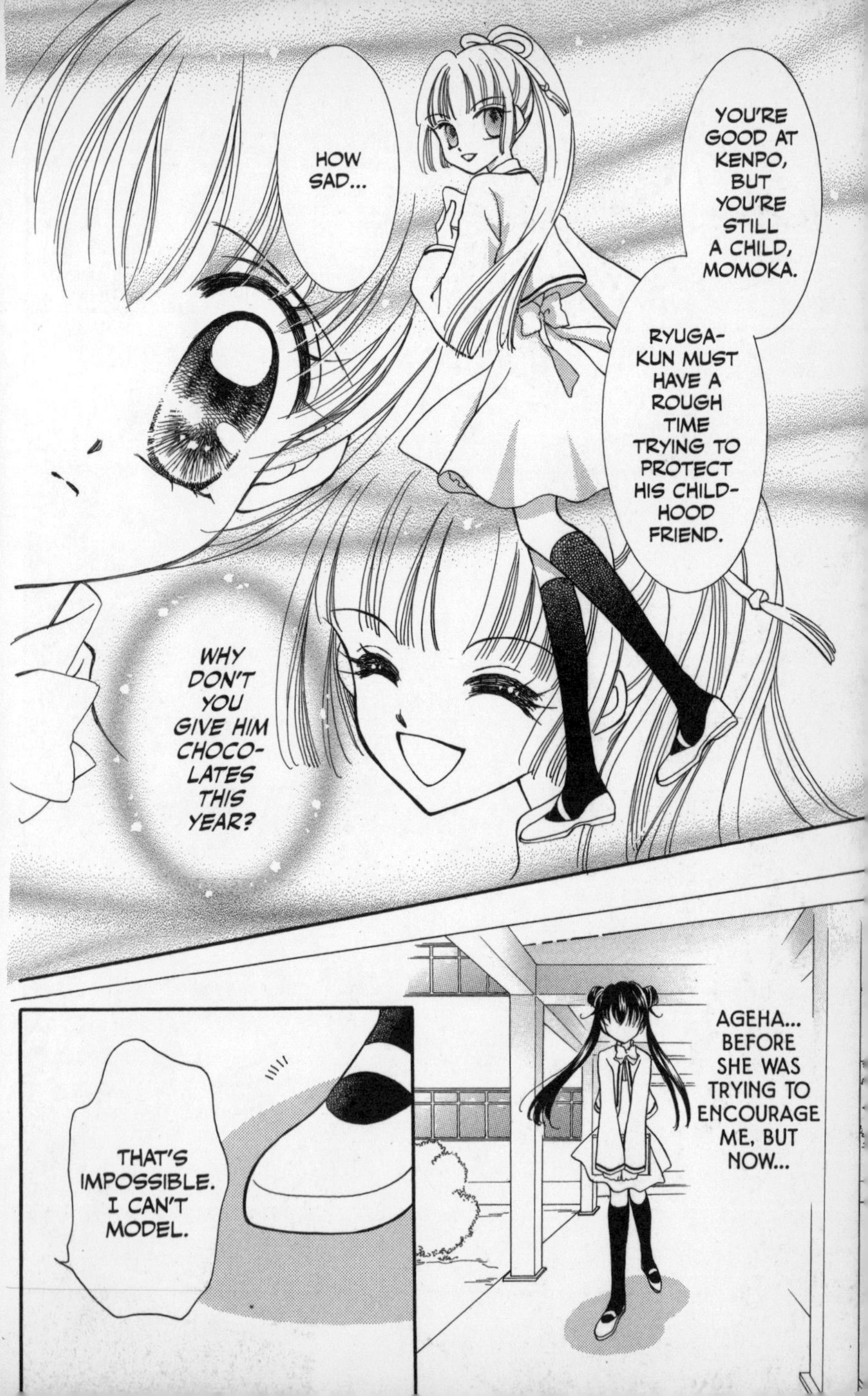
YOU'RE GOOD AT KENPO, BUT YOU'RE STILL A CHILD, MOMOKA.
HOW SAD...
RYUGA-KUN MUST HAVE A ROUGH TIME TRYING TO PROTECT HIS CHILD-HOOD FRIEND.
WHY DON'T YOU GIVE HIM CHOCO-LATES THIS YEAR?
AGEHA... BEFORE SHE WAS TRYING TO ENCOURAGE ME, BUT NOW...
THAT'S IMPOSSIBLE. I CAN'T MODEL.

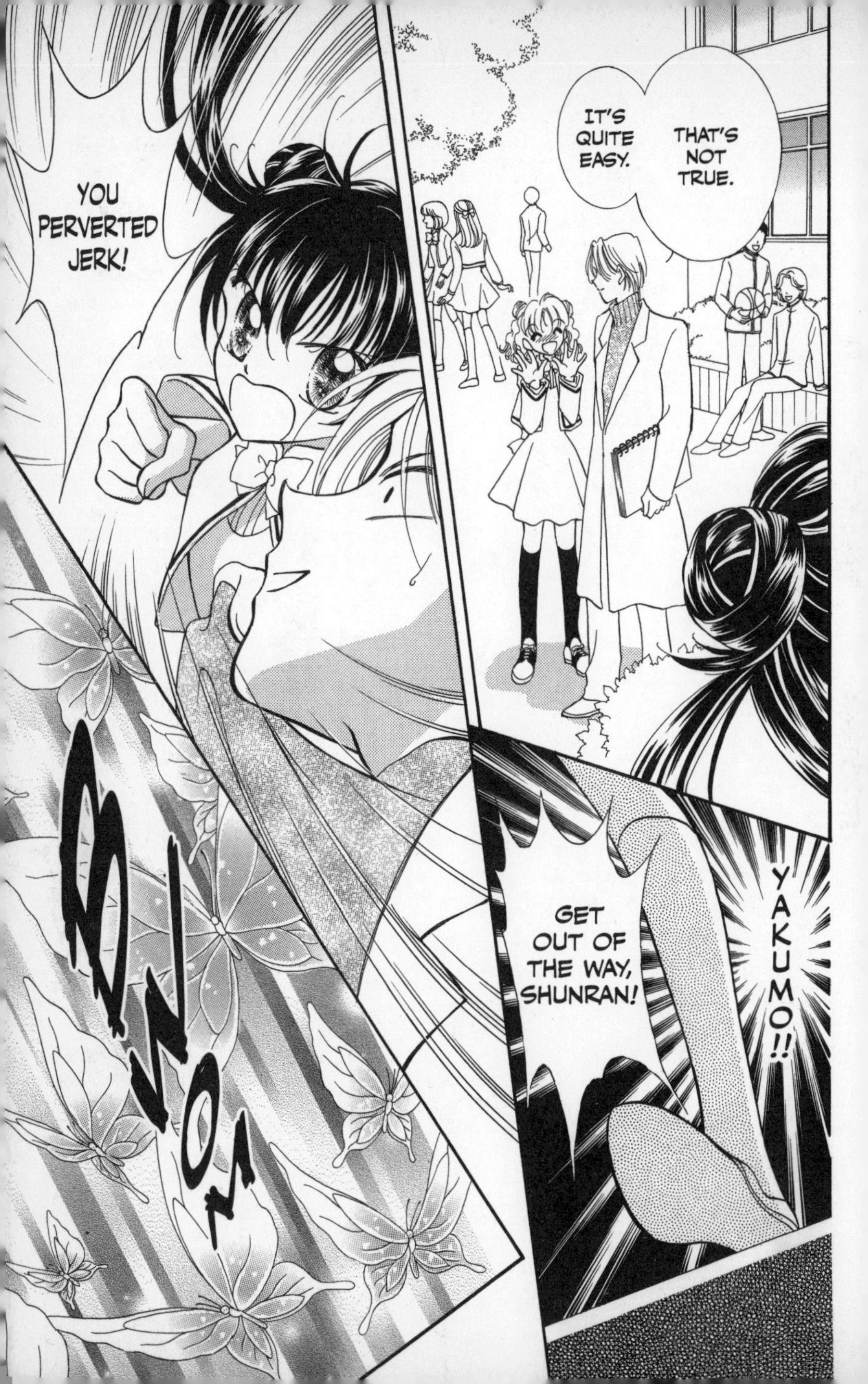
THAT'S NOT TRUE.
IT'S QUITE EASY.
YOU PERVERTED JERK!
YAKUMO!!
GET OUT OF THE WAY, SHUNRAN!

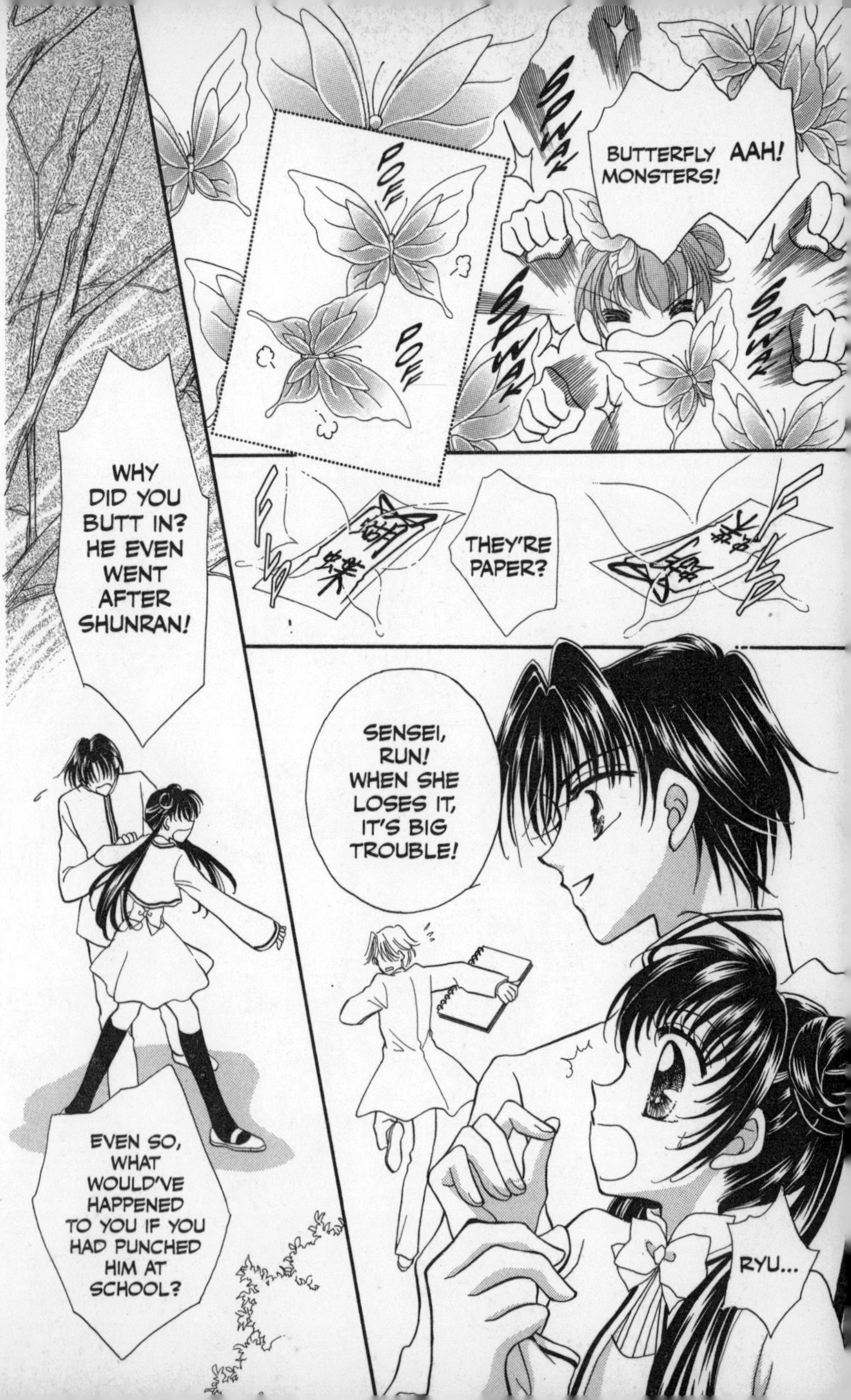
SWAP
AAH! BUTTERFLY MONSTERS!
SWAP
SWAP
POFF
POFF
THEY'RE PAPER?
SENSEI, RUN! WHEN SHE LOSES IT, IT'S BIG TROUBLE!
RYU...
WHY DID YOU BUTT IN? HE EVEN WENT AFTER SHUNRAN!
EVEN SO, WHAT WOULD'VE HAPPENED TO YOU IF YOU HAD PUNCHED HIM AT SCHOOL?

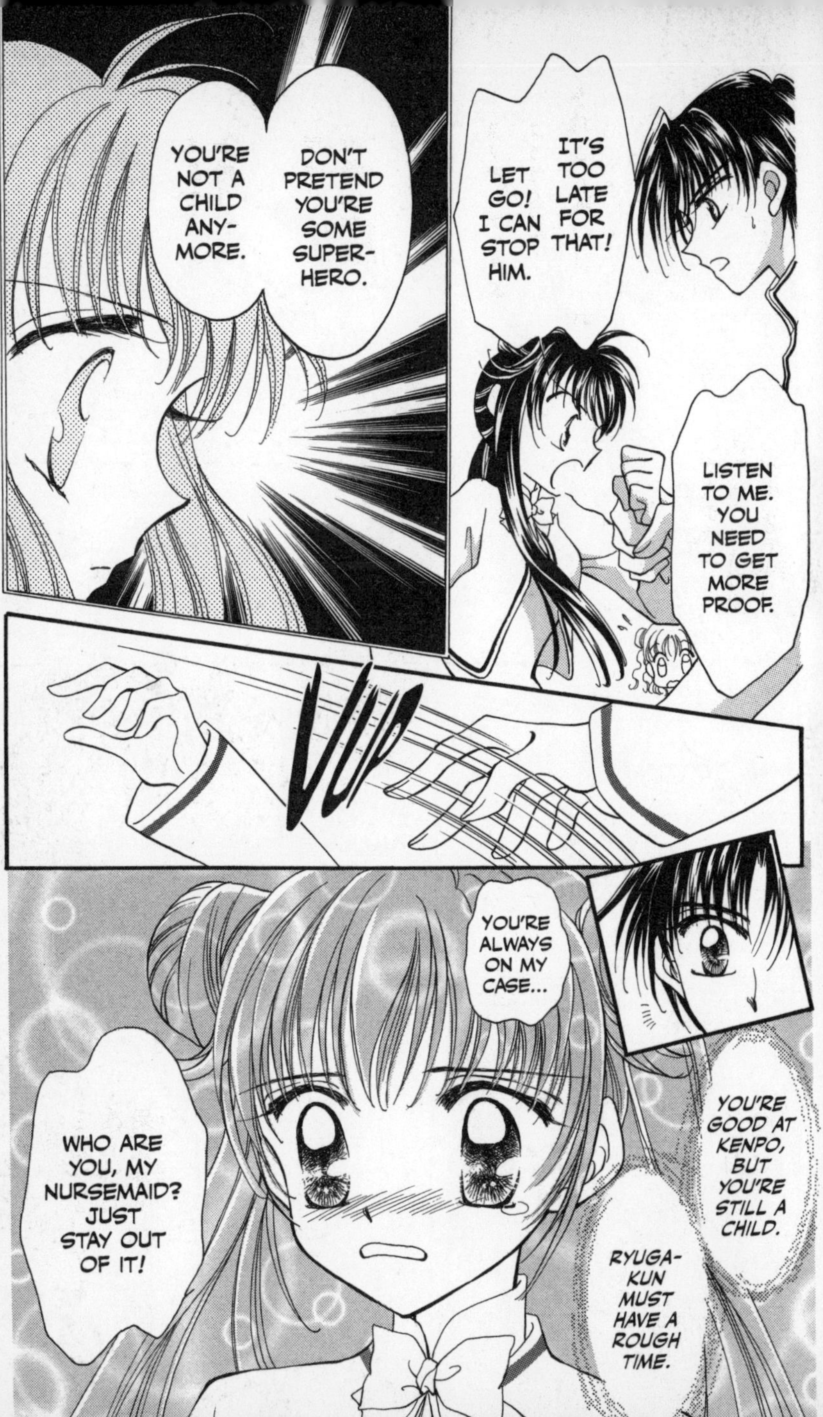
IT'S TOO LATE FOR THAT!
LET GO! I CAN STOP HIM.
LISTEN TO ME. YOU NEED TO GET MORE PROOF.
DON'T PRETEND YOU'RE SOME SUPER-HERO.
YOU'RE NOT A CHILD ANY-MORE.
VUP
YOU'RE ALWAYS ON MY CASE...
WHO ARE YOU, MY NURSEMAID? JUST STAY OUT OF IT!
YOU'RE GOOD AT KENPO, BUT YOU'RE STILL A CHILD.
RYUGA-KUN MUST HAVE A ROUGH TIME.

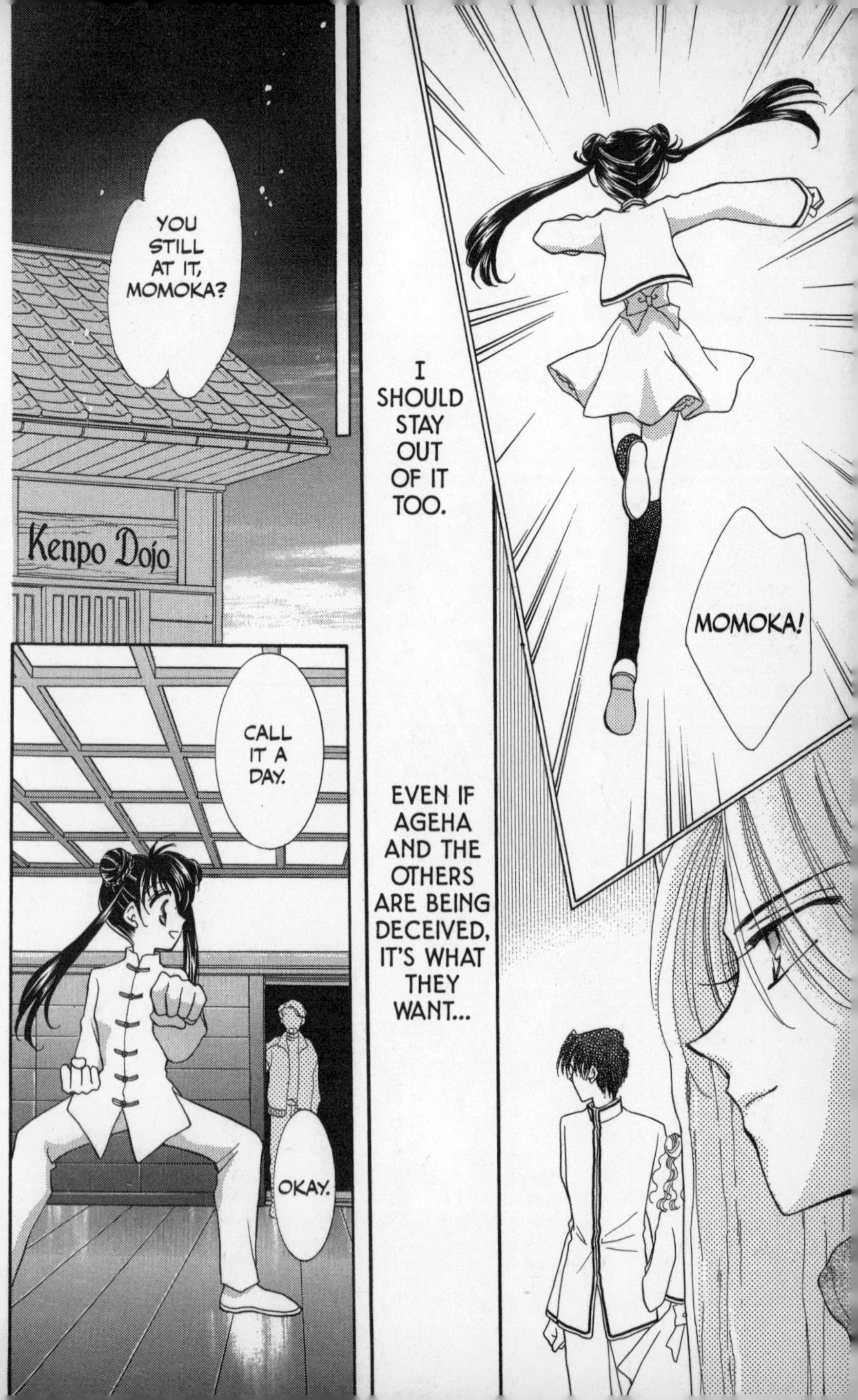
I SHOULD STAY OUT OF IT TOO.
MOMOKA!
EVEN IF AGEHA AND THE OTHERS ARE BEING DECEIVED, IT'S WHAT THEY WANT...
YOU STILL AT IT, MOMOKA?
Kenpo Dojo
CALL IT A DAY.
OKAY.

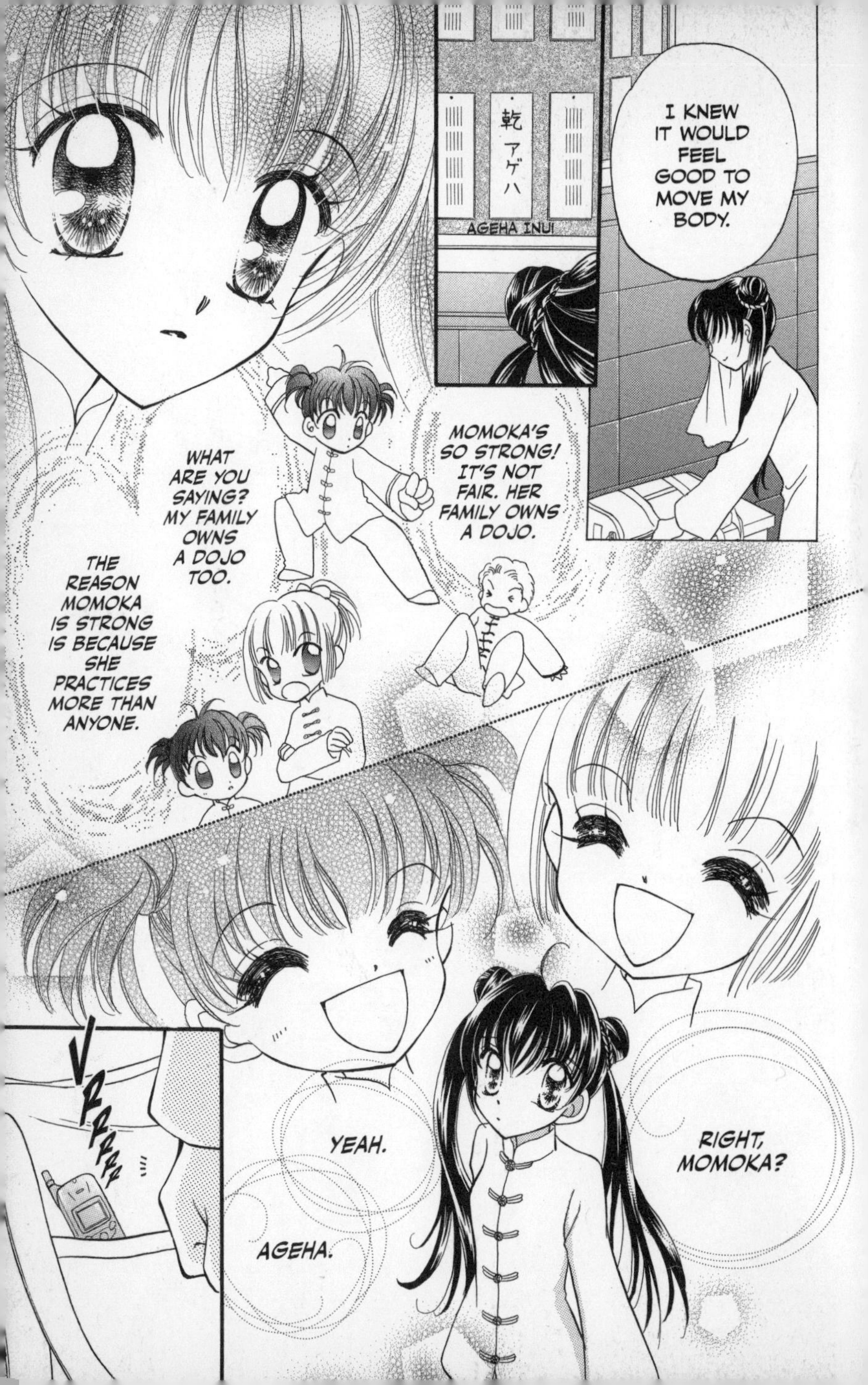
I KNEW IT WOULD FEEL GOOD TO MOVE MY BODY.
乾 アゲハ
AGEHA INUI
MOMOKA'S SO STRONG! IT'S NOT FAIR. HER FAMILY OWNS A DOJO.
WHAT ARE YOU SAYING? MY FAMILY OWNS A DOJO TOO.
THE REASON MOMOKA IS STRONG IS BECAUSE SHE PRACTICES MORE THAN ANYONE.
RIGHT, MOMOKA?
YEAH.
AGEHA.
VRRRR

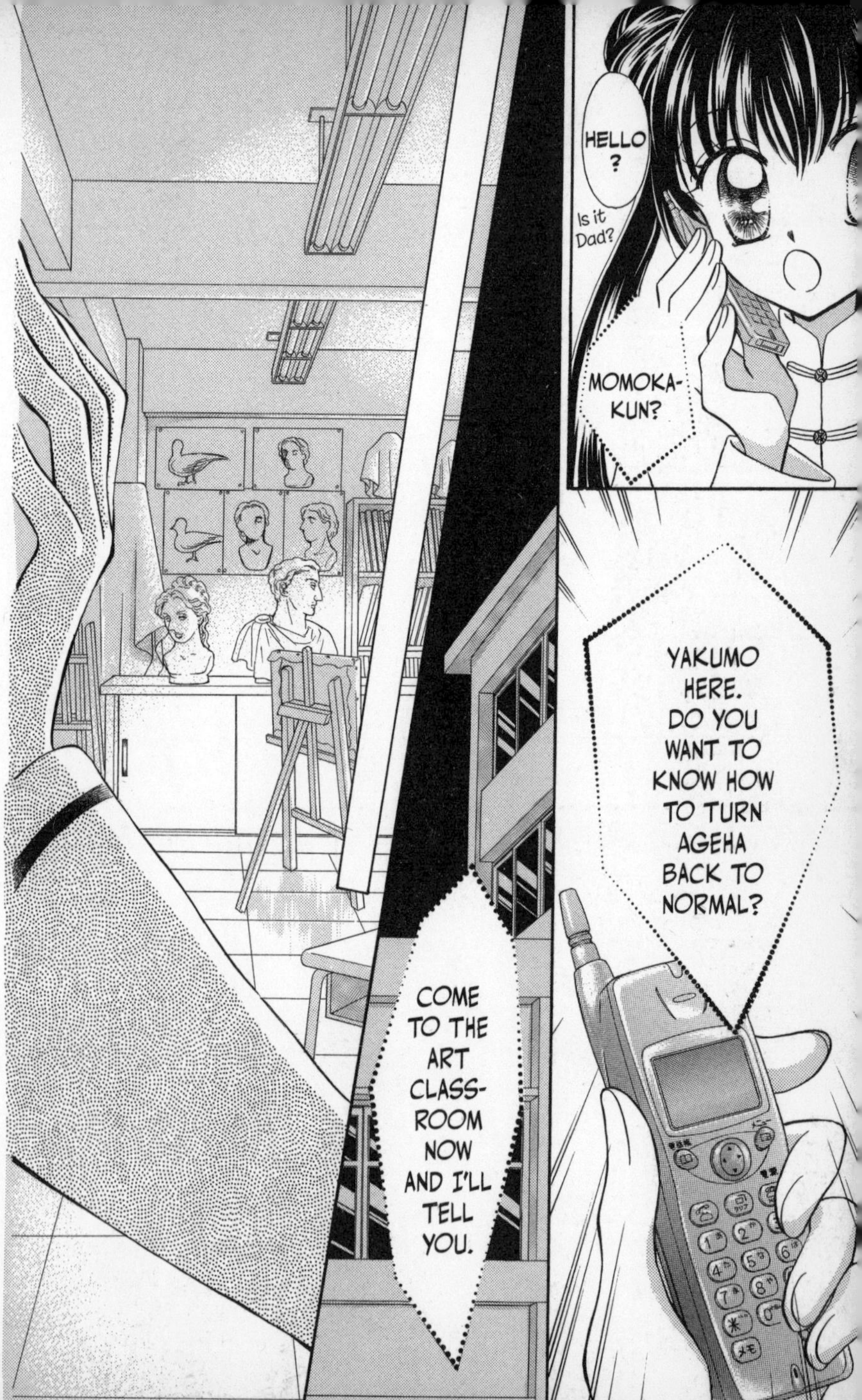
HELLO?
Is it Dad?
MOMOKA-KUN?
YAKUMO HERE. DO YOU WANT TO KNOW HOW TO TURN AGEHA BACK TO NORMAL?
COME TO THE ART CLASS-ROOM NOW AND I'LL TELL YOU.

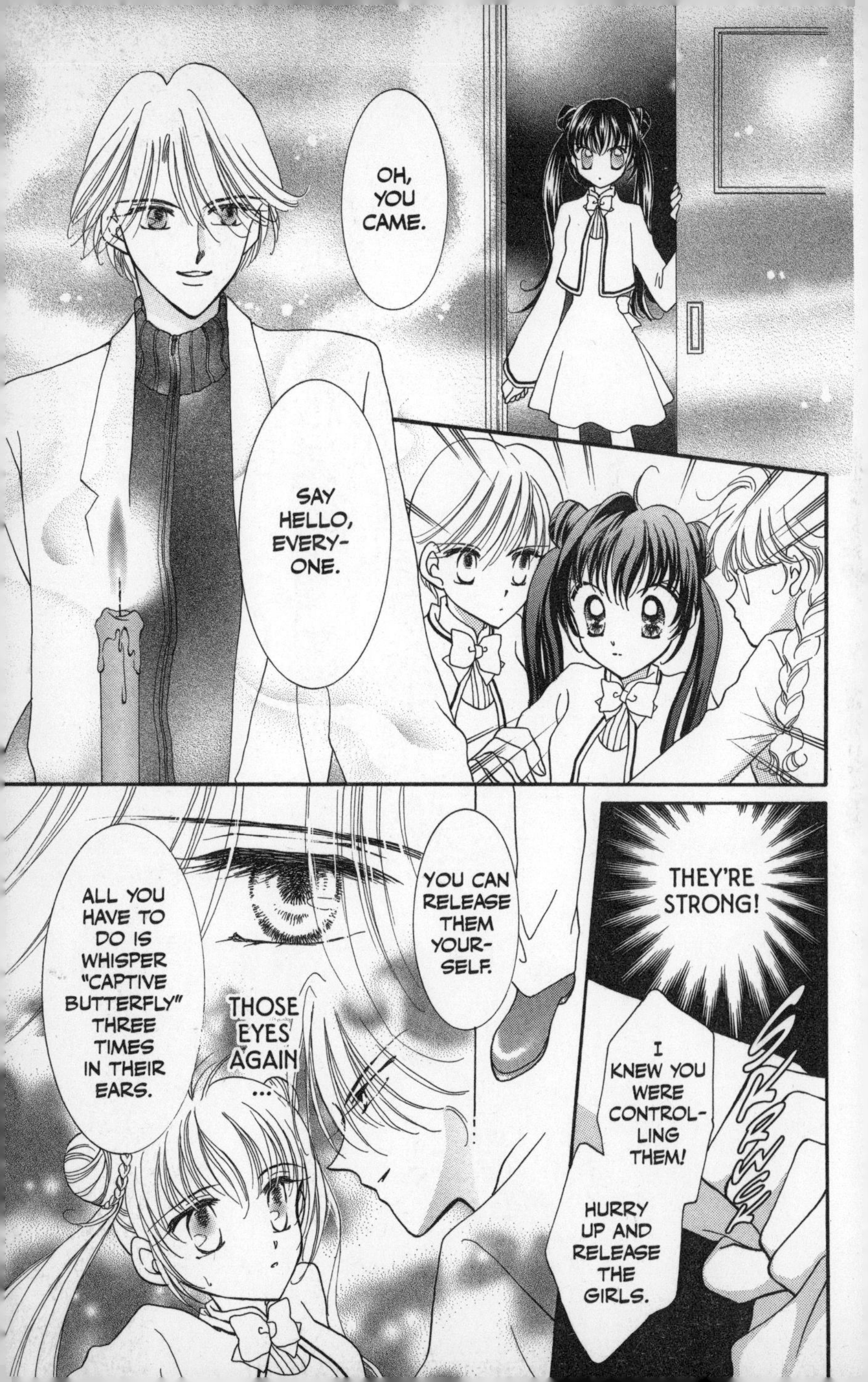
OH, YOU CAME.
SAY HELLO, EVERYONE.
THEY'RE STRONG!
I KNEW YOU WERE CONTROLLING THEM!
HURRY UP AND RELEASE THE GIRLS.
YOU CAN RELEASE THEM YOURSELF.
ALL YOU HAVE TO DO IS WHISPER "CAPTIVE BUTTERFLY" THREE TIMES IN THEIR EARS.
THOSE EYES AGAIN...

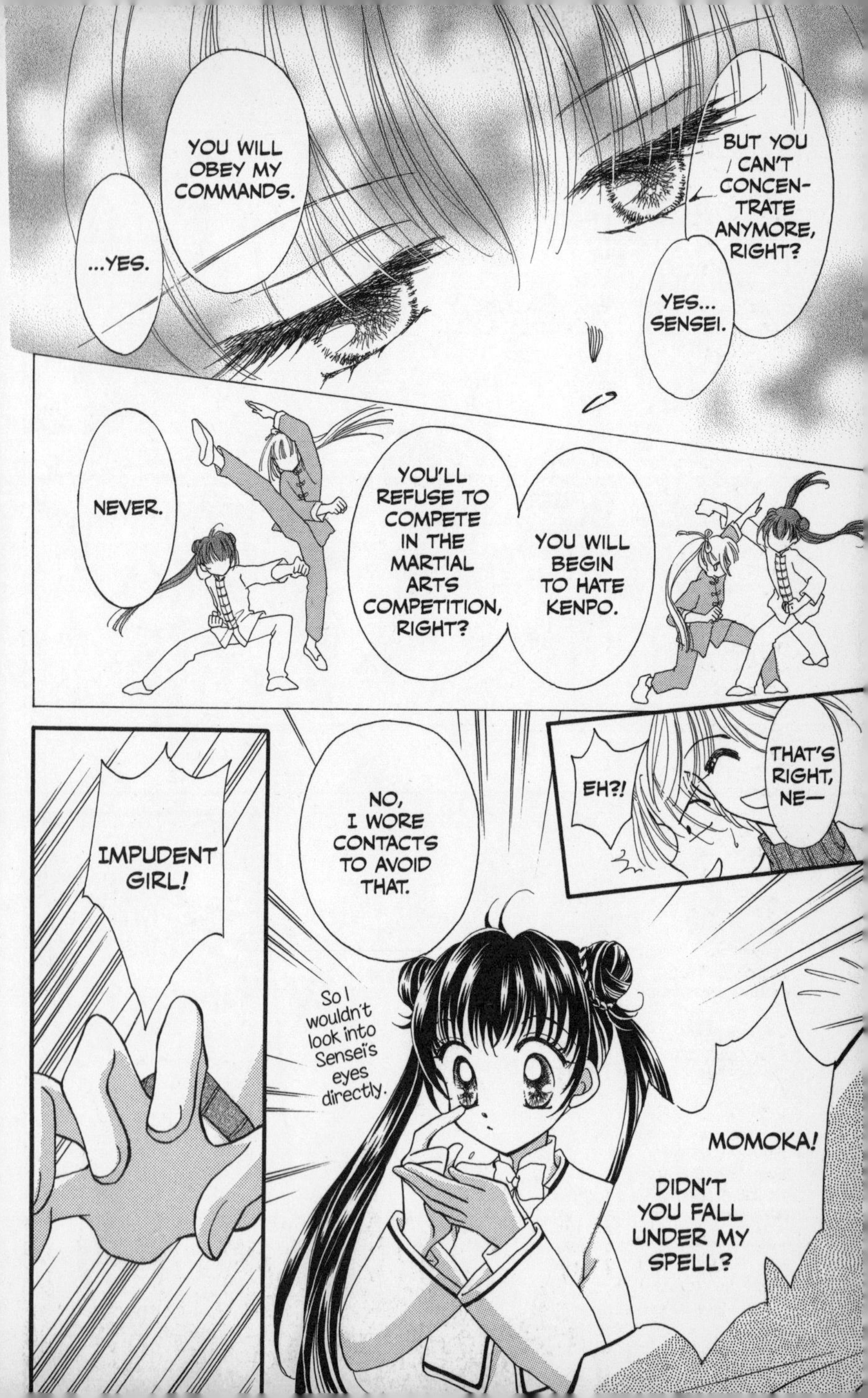
BUT YOU CAN'T CONCEN-TRATE ANYMORE, RIGHT?
YES... SENSEI.
YOU WILL OBEY MY COMMANDS.
...YES.
YOU WILL BEGIN TO HATE KENPO.
YOU'LL REFUSE TO COMPETE IN THE MARTIAL ARTS COMPETITION, RIGHT?
NEVER.
THAT'S RIGHT, NE—
EH?!
MOMOKA!
DIDN'T YOU FALL UNDER MY SPELL?
NO, I WORE CONTACTS TO AVOID THAT.
So I wouldn't look into Sensei's eyes directly.
IMPUDENT GIRL!

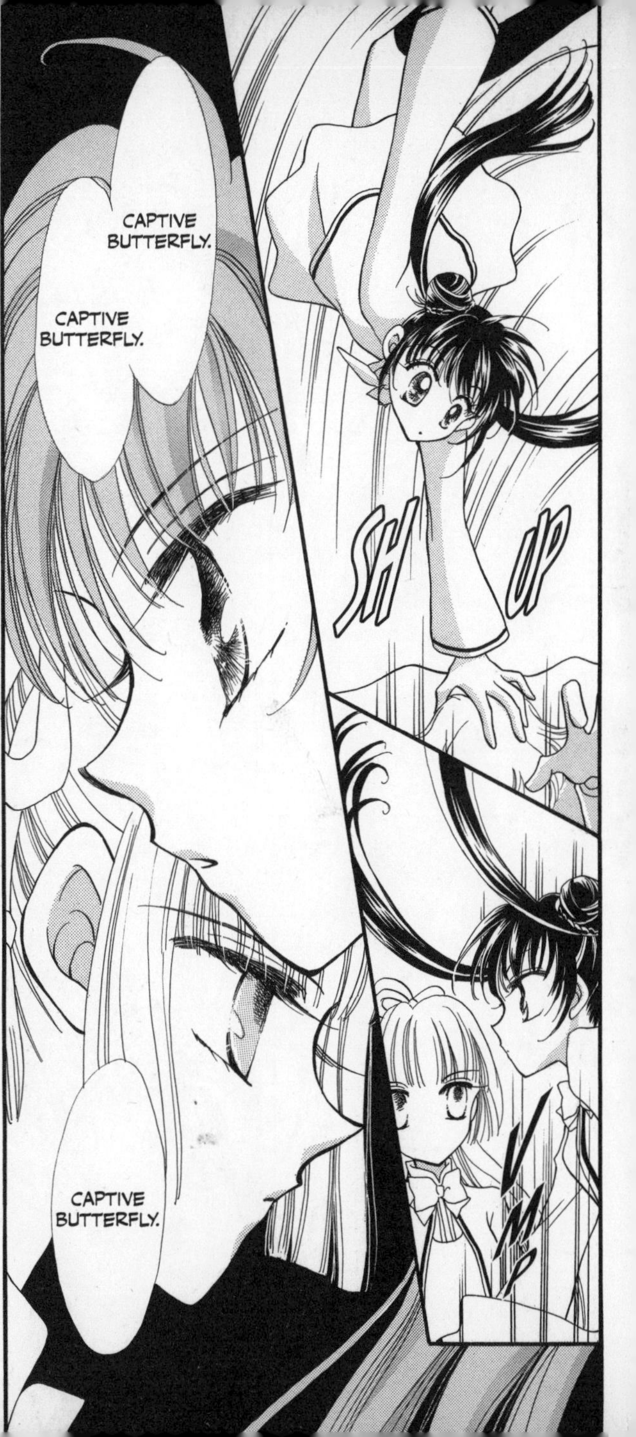
SH UP
CAPTIVE BUTTERFLY.
CAPTIVE BUTTERFLY.
CAPTIVE BUTTERFLY.

4

There seemed to be a lot of people who read chapter 1 and thought there were many Chinese things in it. Everyone wears Chinese clothes, but the setting is more or less Yokohama in Japan.

In the fall of 1999, I went with my assistant to Yokohama's Chinatown to do some research. There were dragons everywhere. We took tons of pictures.

Oh yeah. I had an old Chinese man tell me the fortune for my name. It seems my pen name is better than my real name. That's good... I'll have luck with work...

He said that 2000 is a lucky year for me. I guess so, since I got my own series running in a magazine.

I've had two series serialized. My luck continues.

Ahh. And there's this manga too. The old man was right!

After that, my assistant and I drank some tea, bought some Chinese souvenirs, then went home.

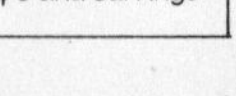

Peach clips and earrings

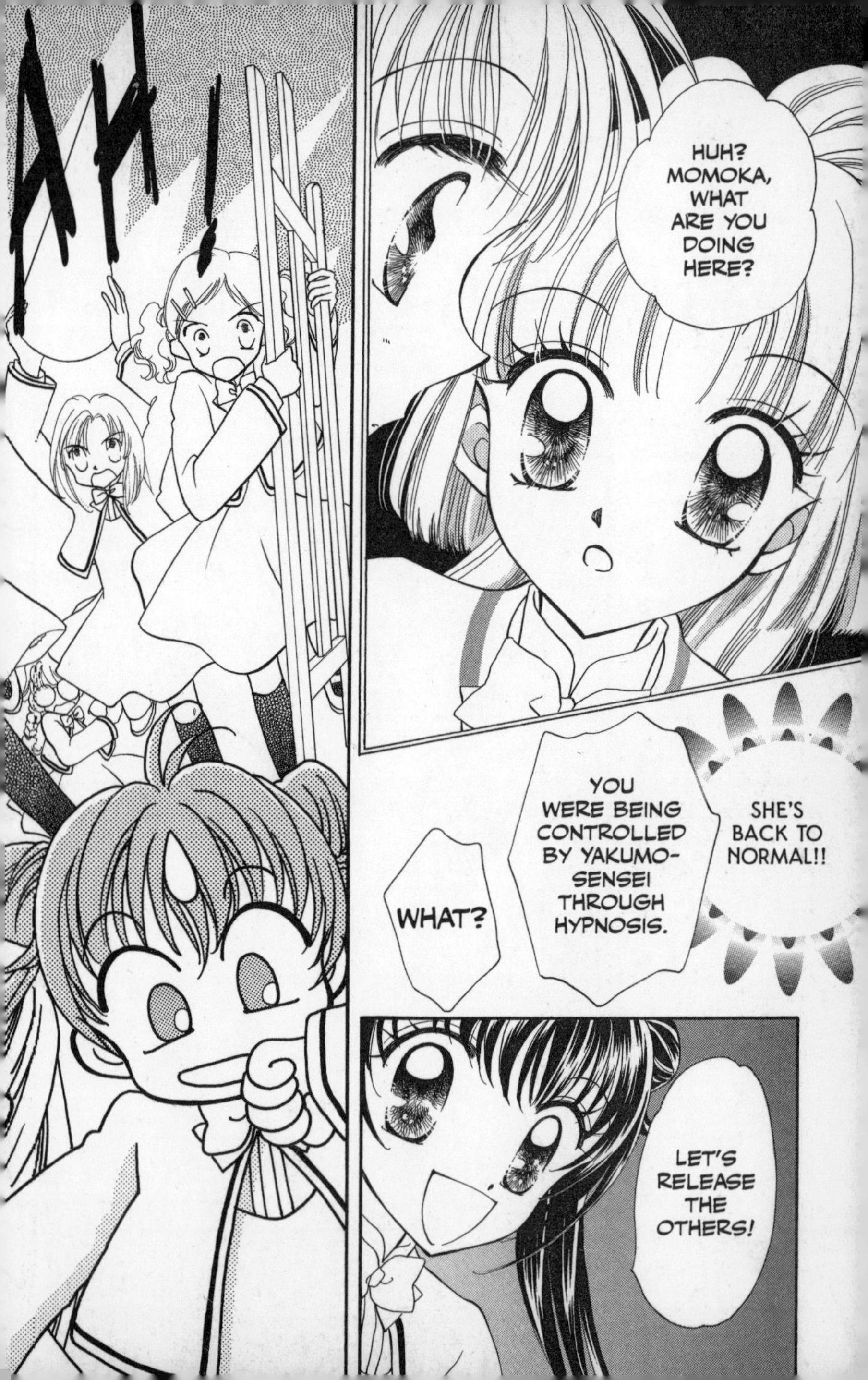
HUH? MOMOKA, WHAT ARE YOU DOING HERE?
SHE'S BACK TO NORMAL!!
YOU WERE BEING CONTROLLED BY YAKUMO-SENSEI THROUGH HYPNOSIS.
WHAT?
LET'S RELEASE THE OTHERS!
AH!

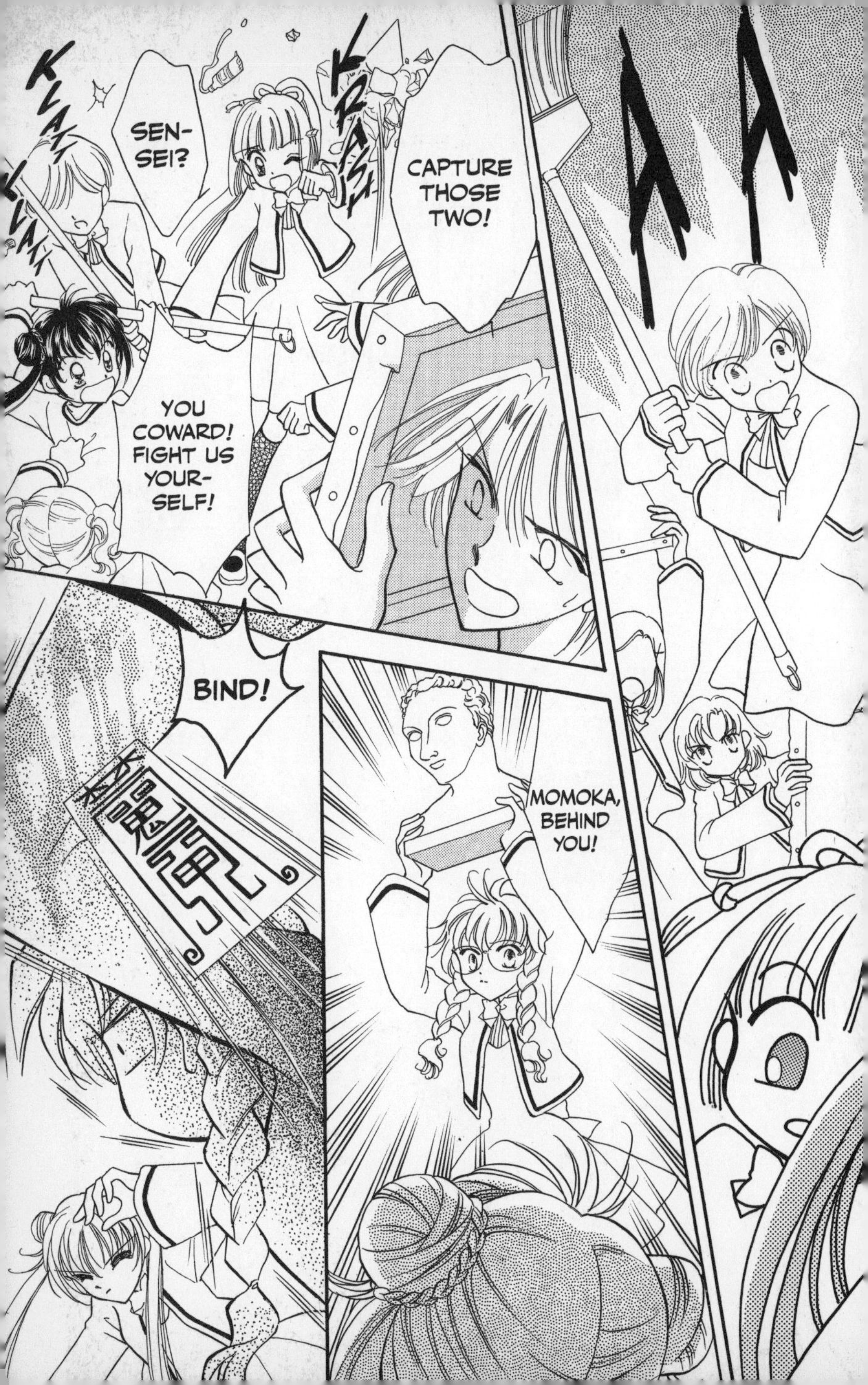
CAPTURE THOSE TWO!
KRASH
SEN-SEI?
KLAK
KLAK
YOU COWARD! FIGHT US YOUR-SELF!
MOMOKA, BEHIND YOU!
BIND!

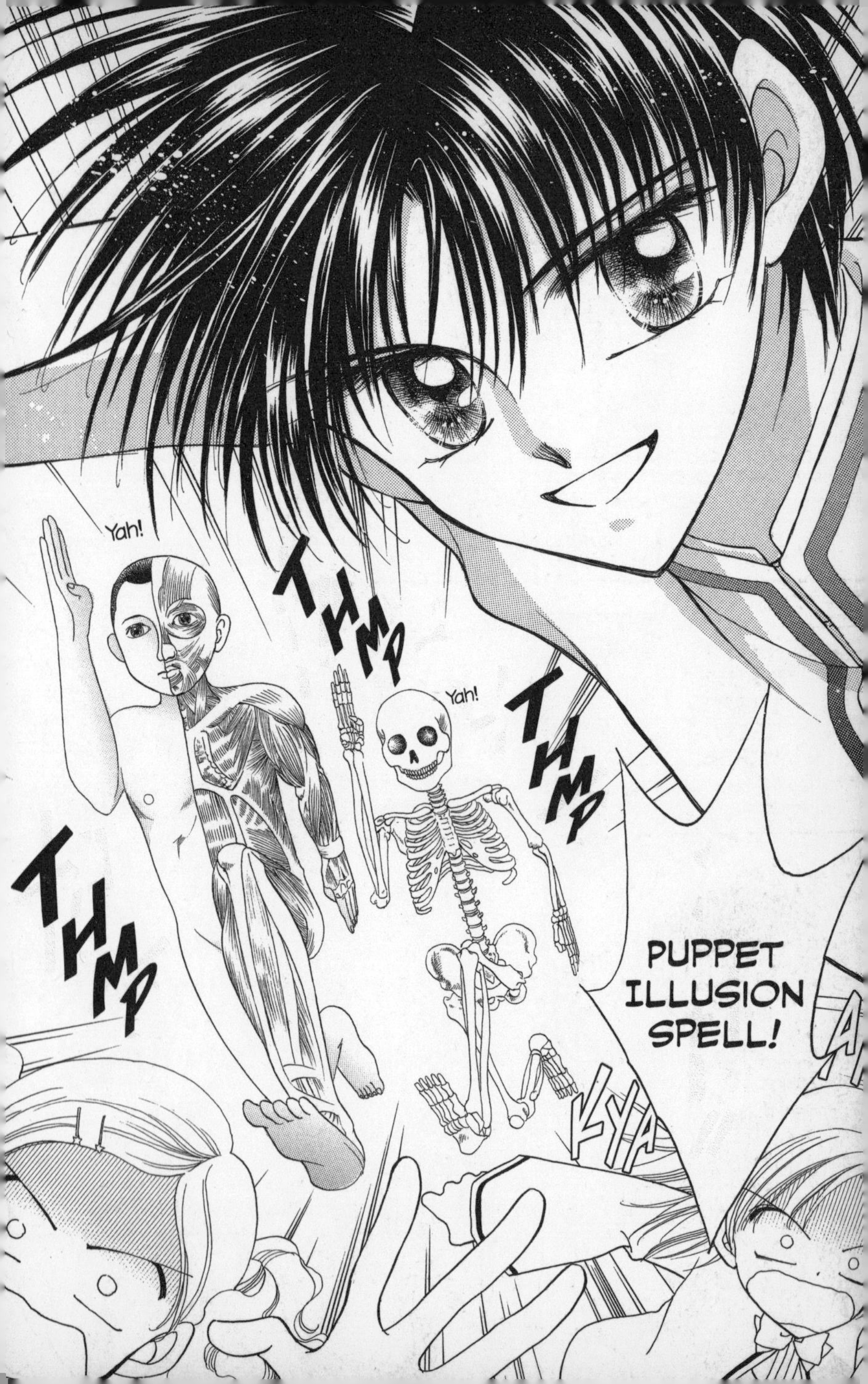
PUPPET ILLUSION SPELL!
A
KYA
THMP
THMP
Yah!
Yah!
THMP

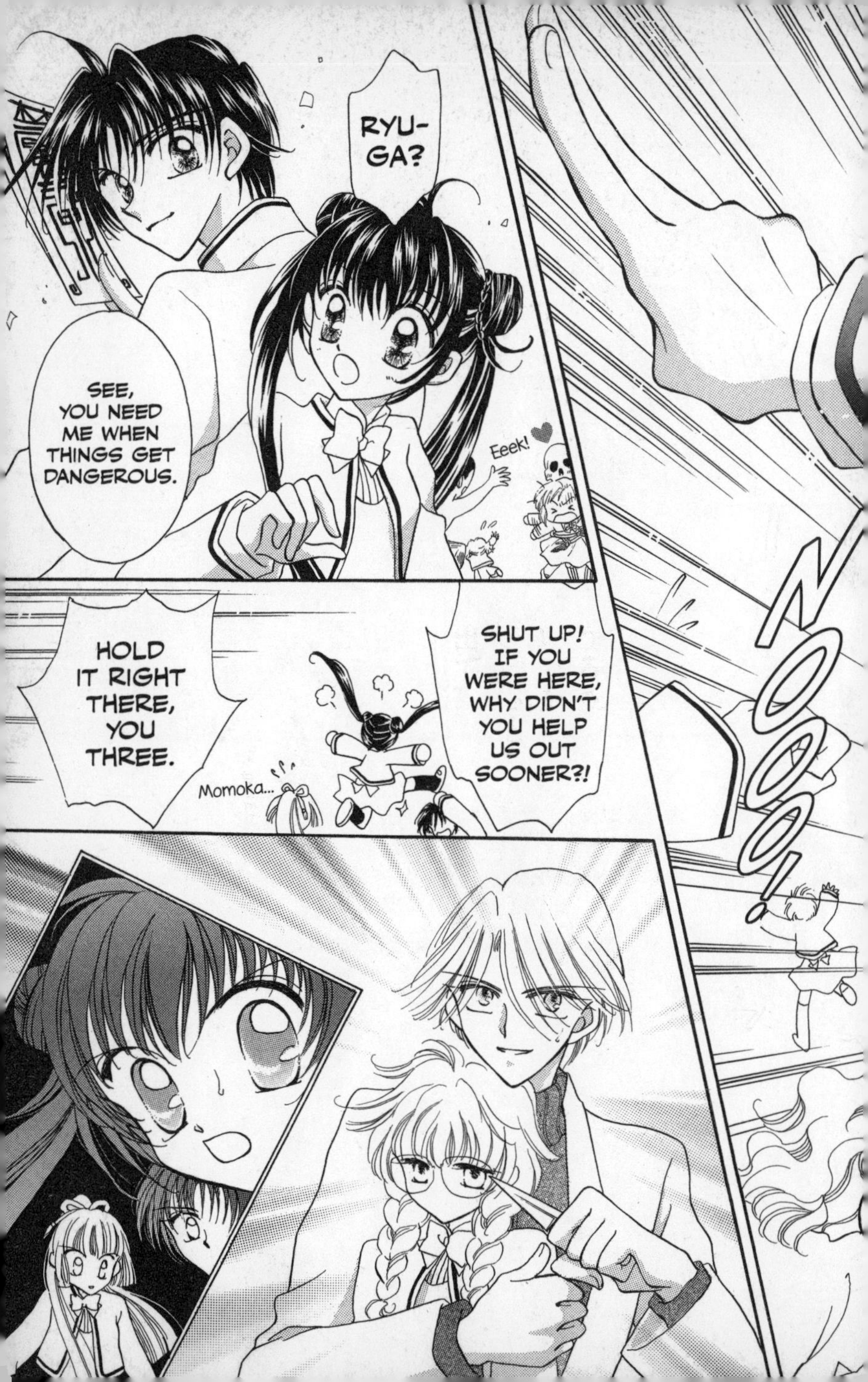
NOOOO!
RYU-GA?
SEE, YOU NEED ME WHEN THINGS GET DANGEROUS.
Eeek!
SHUT UP! IF YOU WERE HERE, WHY DIDN'T YOU HELP US OUT SOONER?!
Momoka...
HOLD IT RIGHT THERE, YOU THREE.

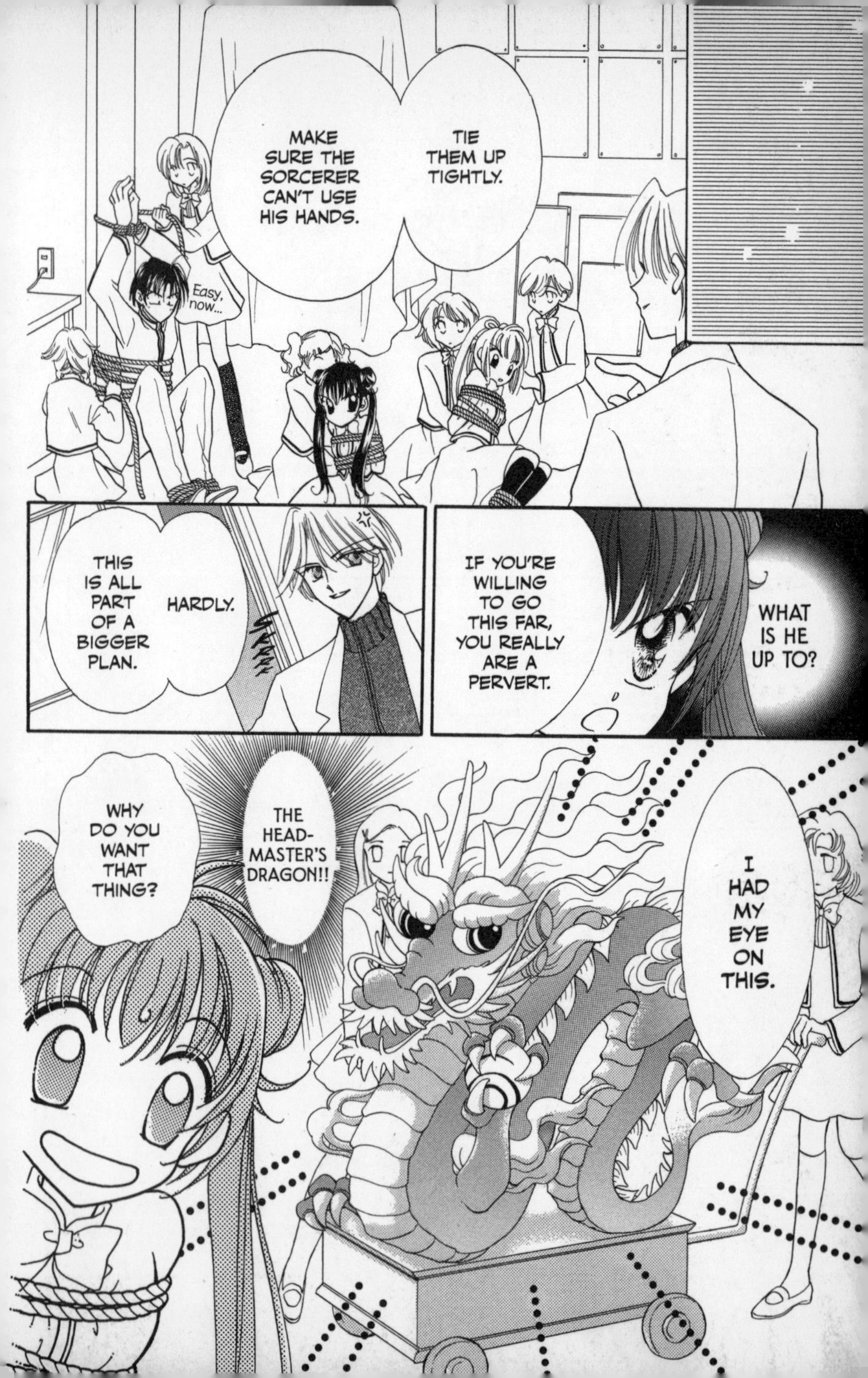
TIE THEM UP TIGHTLY.
MAKE SURE THE SORCERER CAN'T USE HIS HANDS.
Easy, now...
WHAT IS HE UP TO?
IF YOU'RE WILLING TO GO THIS FAR, YOU REALLY ARE A PERVERT.
HARDLY.
THIS IS ALL PART OF A BIGGER PLAN.
I HAD MY EYE ON THIS.
THE HEAD-MASTER'S DRAGON!!
WHY DO YOU WANT THAT THING?

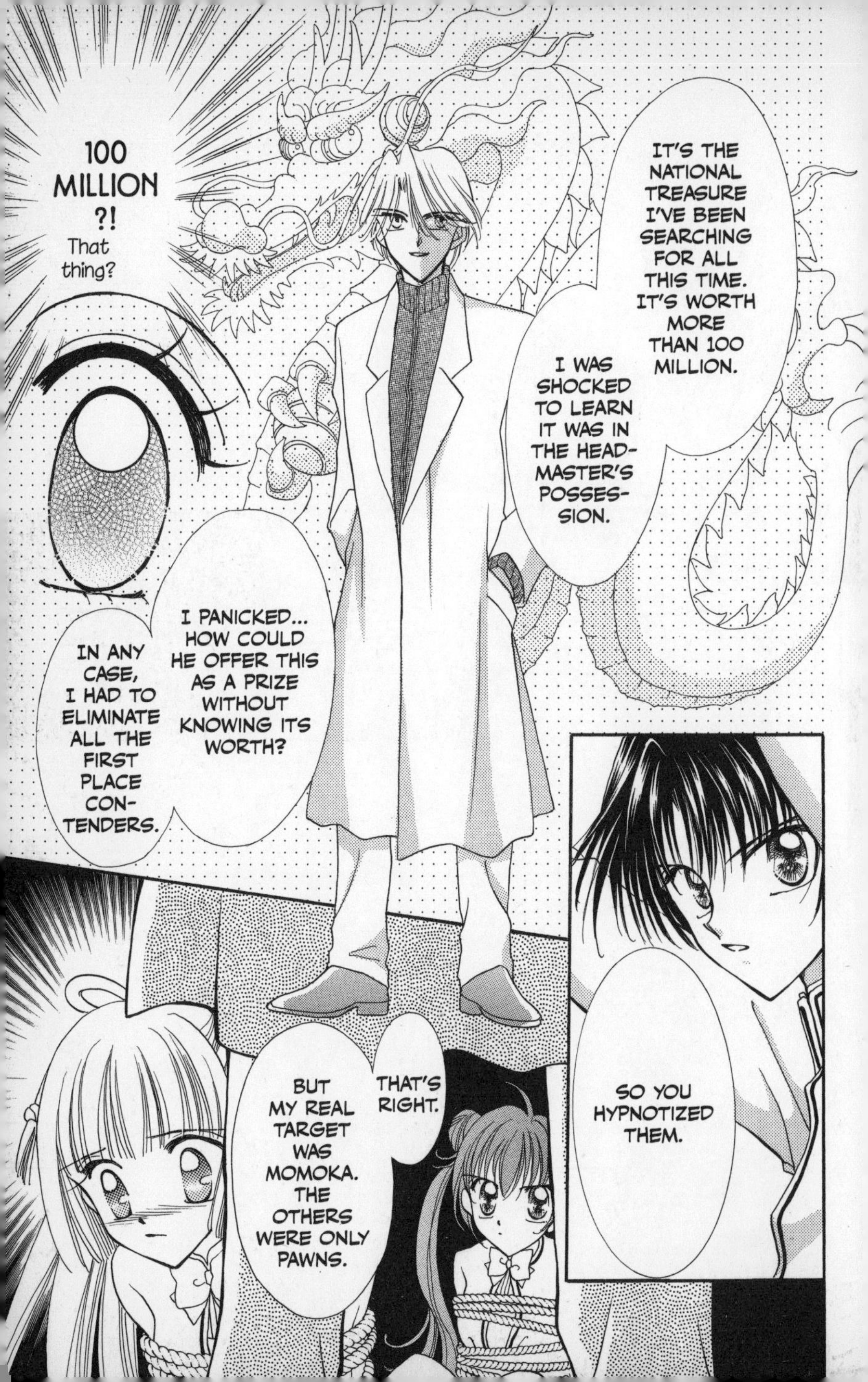
IT'S THE NATIONAL TREASURE I'VE BEEN SEARCHING FOR ALL THIS TIME. IT'S WORTH MORE THAN 100 MILLION.
I WAS SHOCKED TO LEARN IT WAS IN THE HEAD-MASTER'S POSSES-SION.
100 MILLION ?!
That thing?
I PANICKED... HOW COULD HE OFFER THIS AS A PRIZE WITHOUT KNOWING ITS WORTH?
IN ANY CASE, I HAD TO ELIMINATE ALL THE FIRST PLACE CON-TENDERS.
SO YOU HYPNOTIZED THEM.
THAT'S RIGHT.
BUT MY REAL TARGET WAS MOMOKA. THE OTHERS WERE ONLY PAWNS.

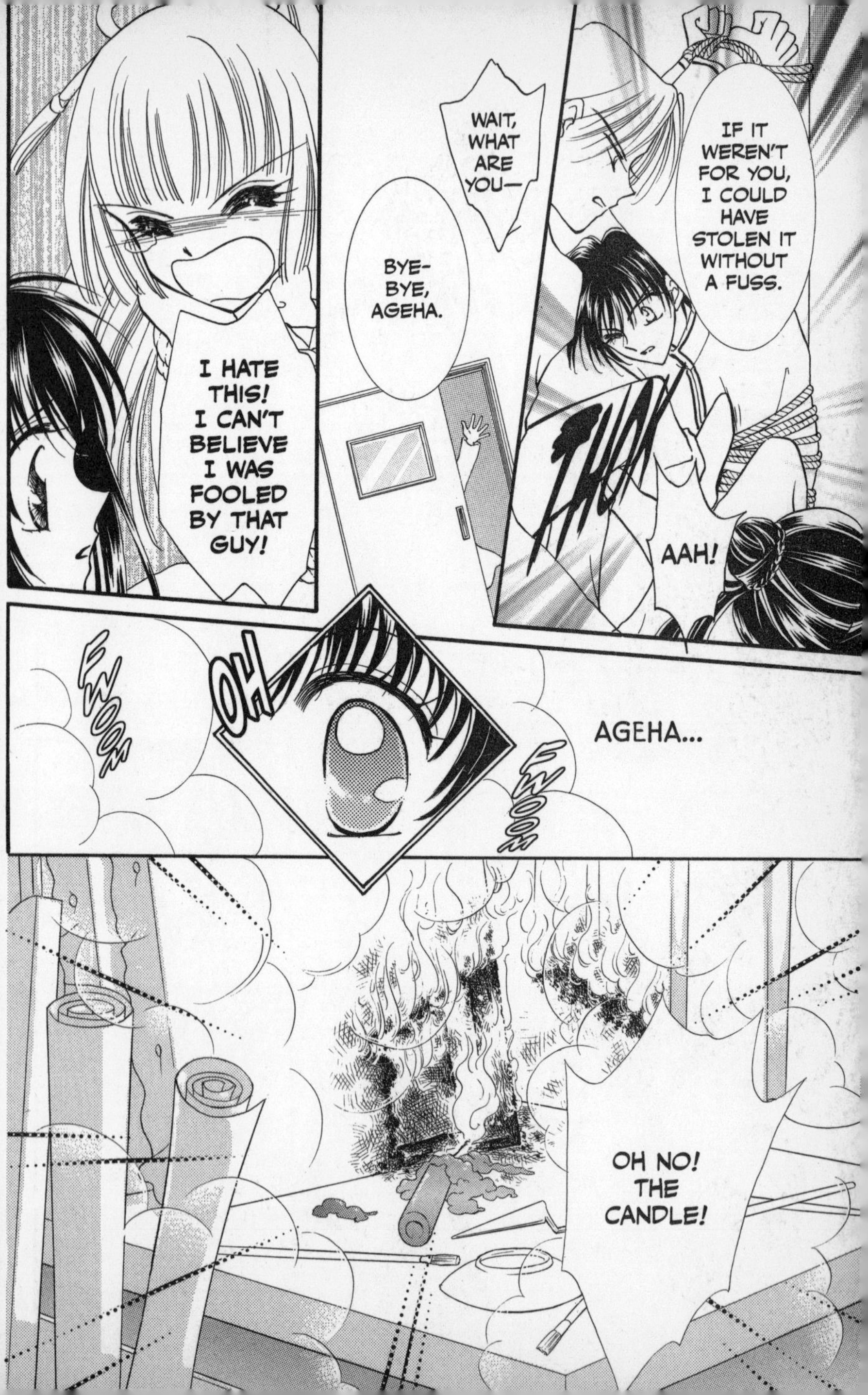
IF IT WEREN'T FOR YOU, I COULD HAVE STOLEN IT WITHOUT A FUSS.
AAH!
WAIT, WHAT ARE YOU—
BYE-BYE, AGEHA.
I HATE THIS! I CAN'T BELIEVE I WAS FOOLED BY THAT GUY!
AGEHA...
FWOOF
OH
FWOOF
OH NO! THE CANDLE!

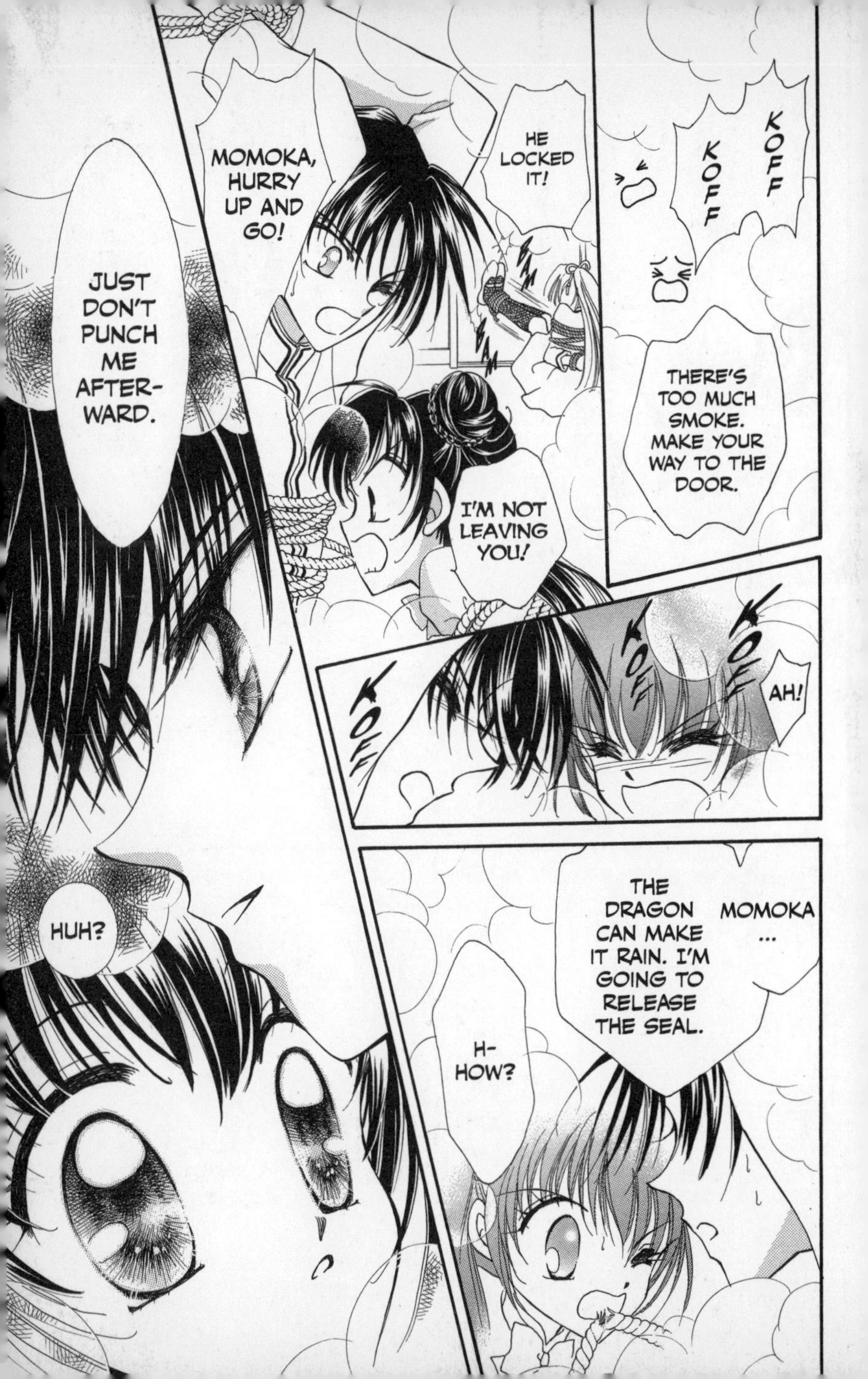
KOFF KOFF
THERE'S TOO MUCH SMOKE. MAKE YOUR WAY TO THE DOOR.
HE LOCKED IT!
BAM BAM
MOMOKA, HURRY UP AND GO!
I'M NOT LEAVING YOU!
KOFF KOFF
AH!
MOMOKA ...
THE DRAGON CAN MAKE IT RAIN. I'M GOING TO RELEASE THE SEAL.
H-HOW?
JUST DON'T PUNCH ME AFTER-WARD.
HUH?

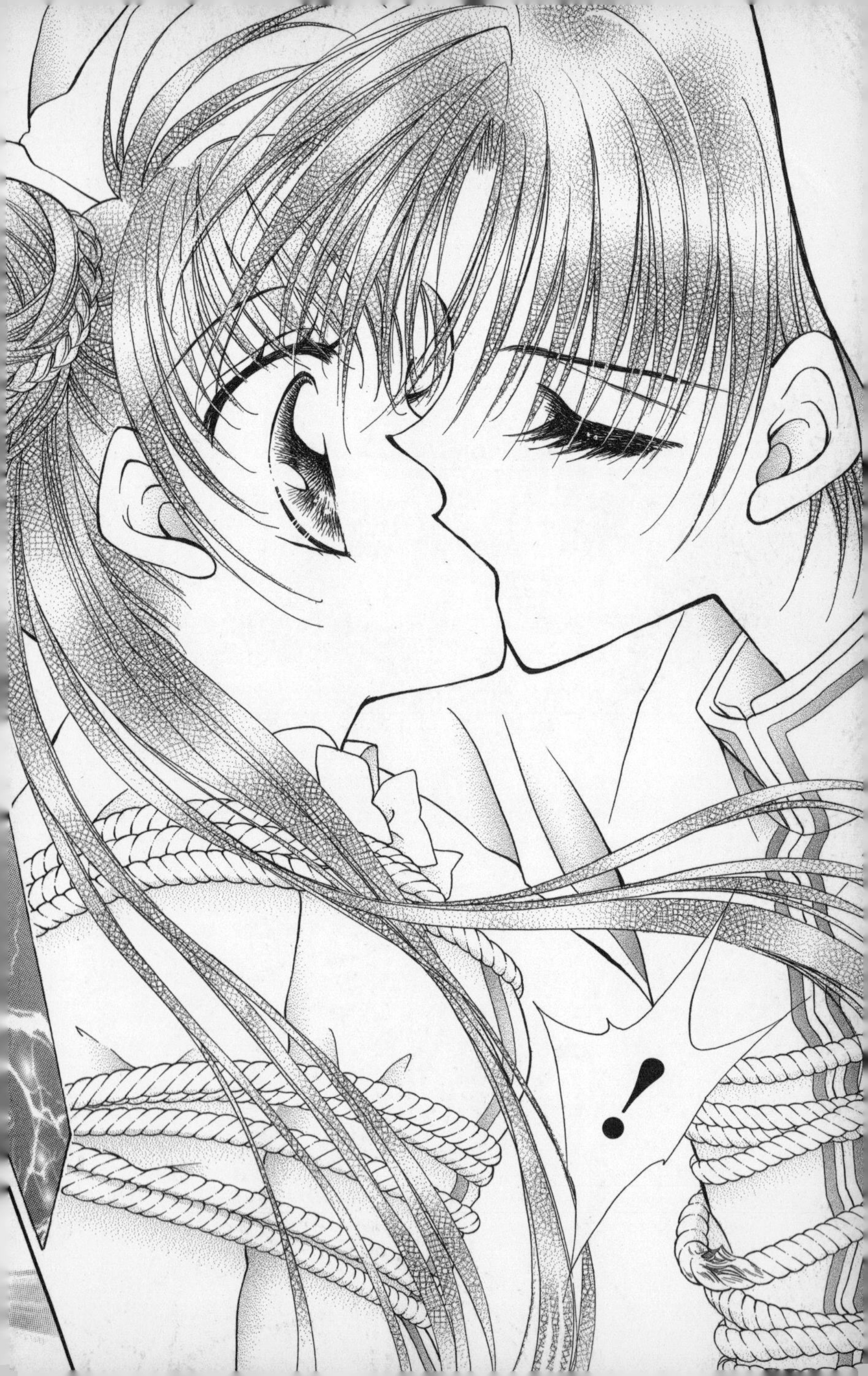
!

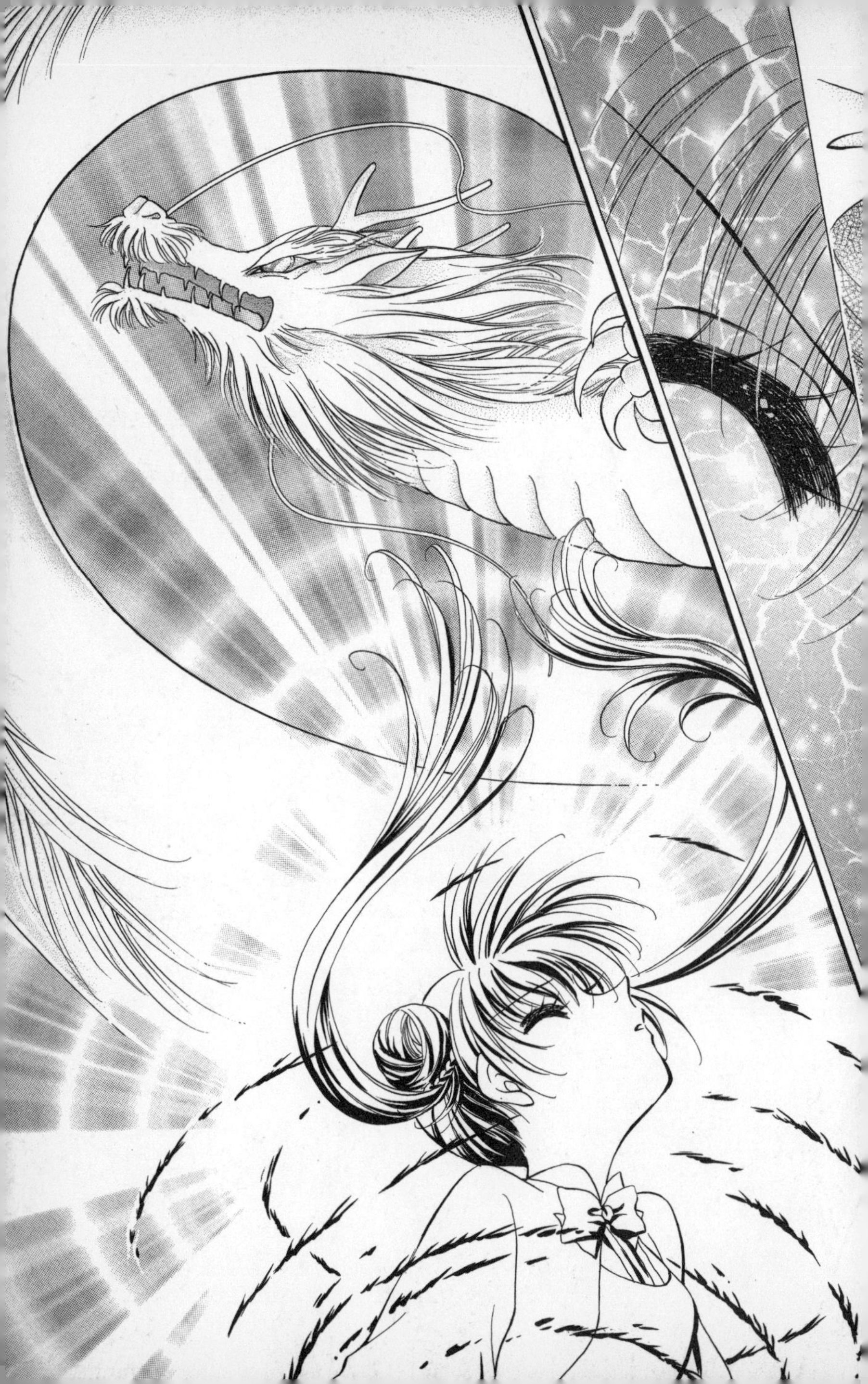

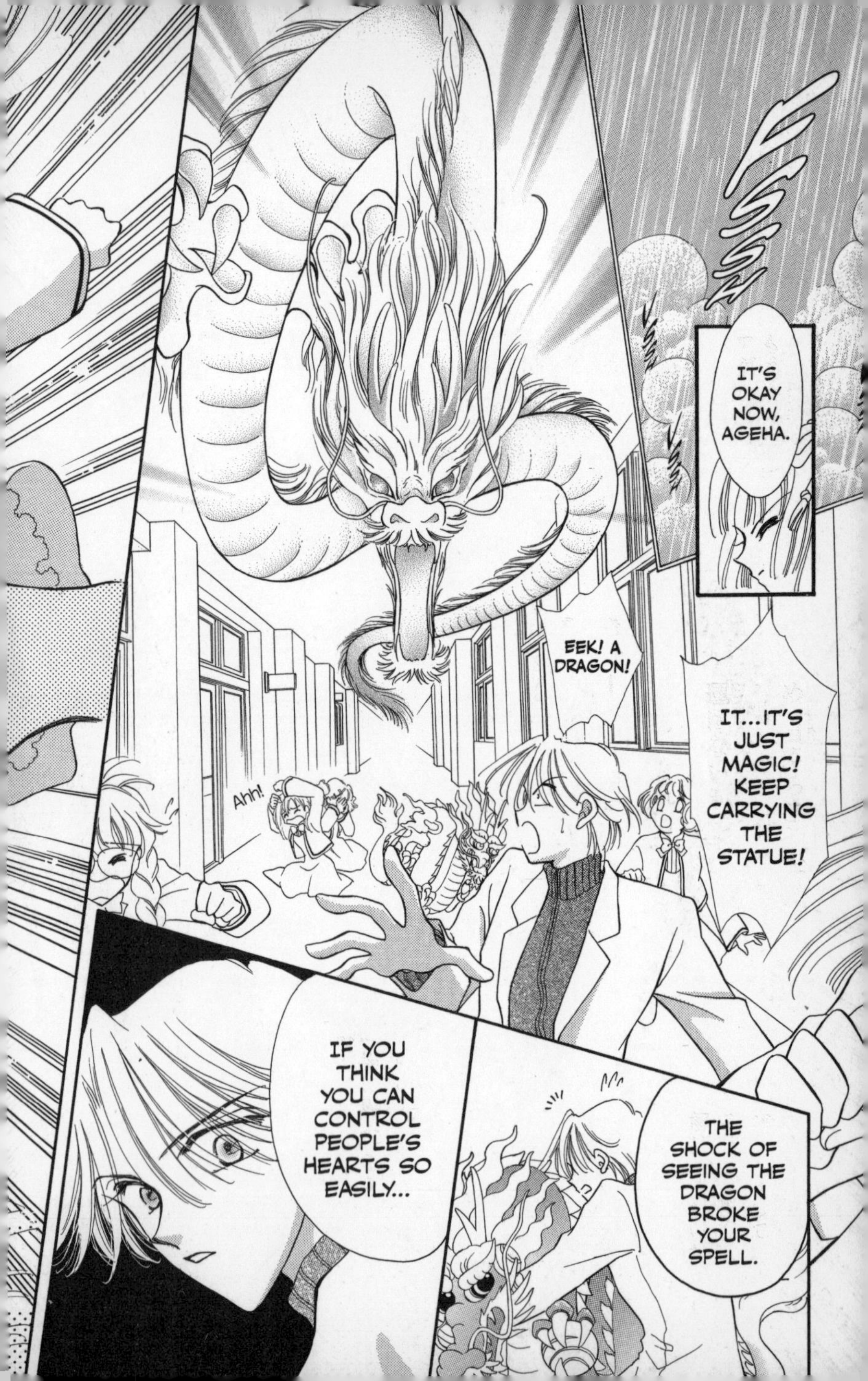
IT'S OKAY NOW, AGEHA.
EEK! A DRAGON!
IT...IT'S JUST MAGIC! KEEP CARRYING THE STATUE!
Ahh!
THE SHOCK OF SEEING THE DRAGON BROKE YOUR SPELL.
IF YOU THINK YOU CAN CONTROL PEOPLE'S HEARTS SO EASILY...

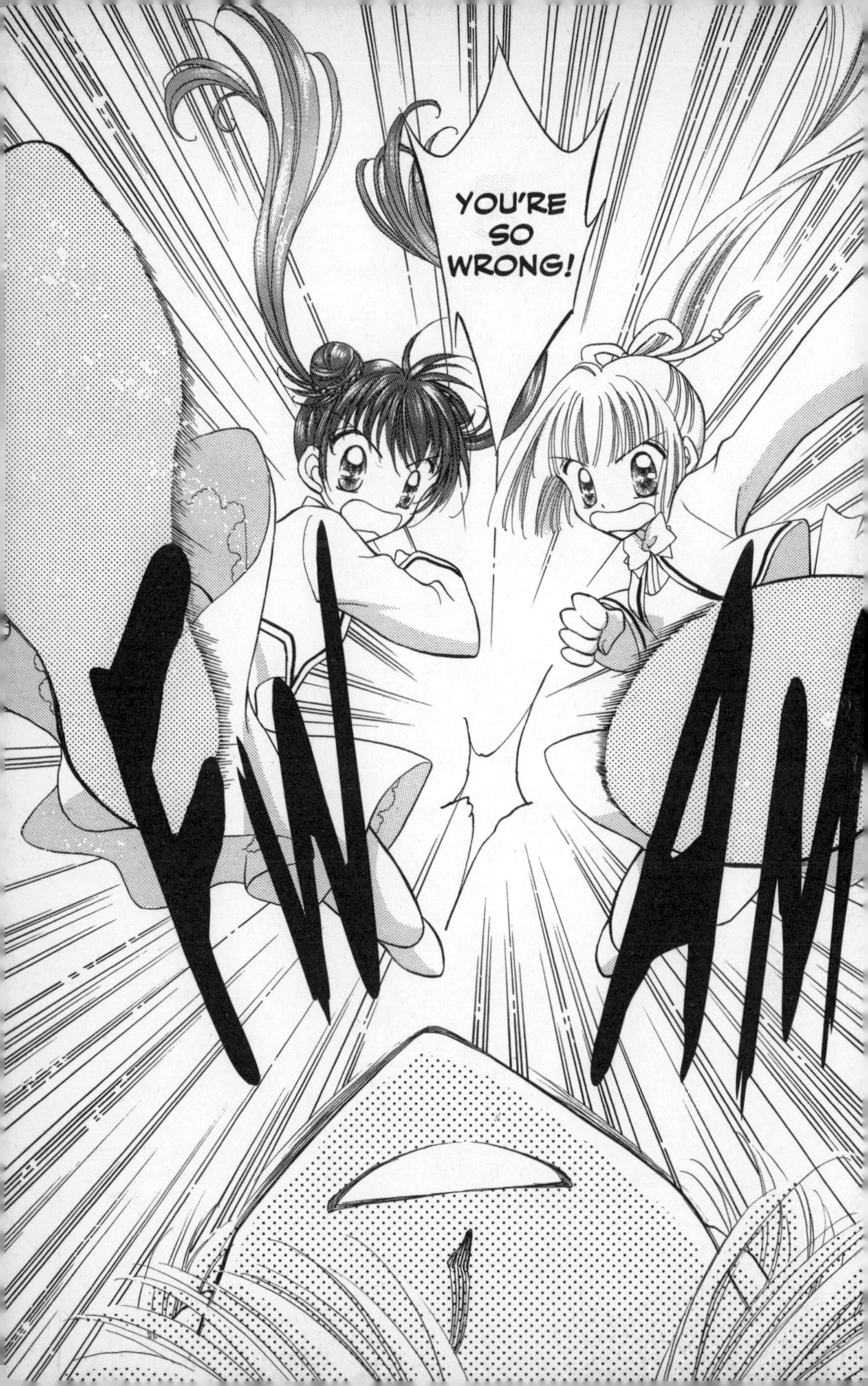
YOU'RE SO WRONG!

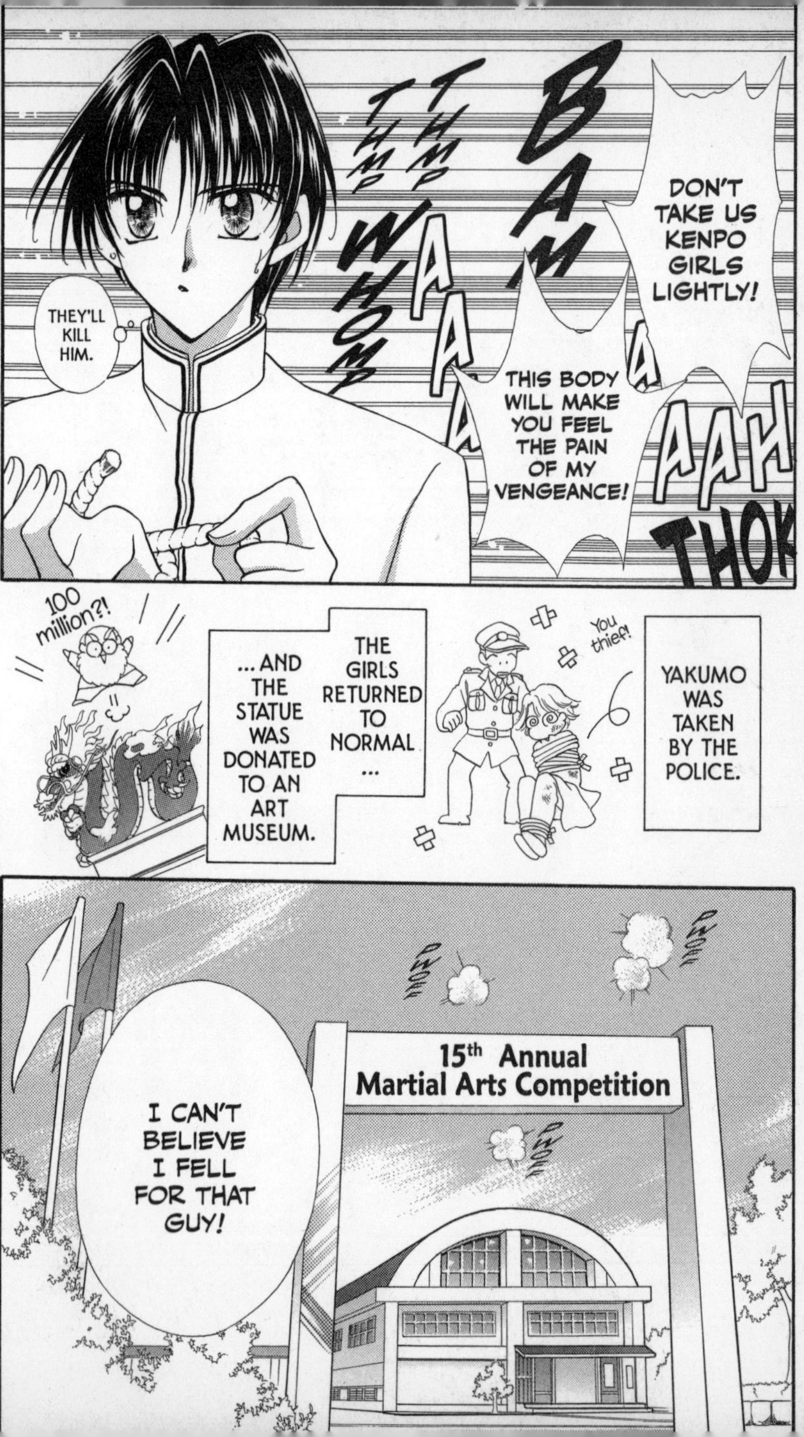
BAM
DON'T TAKE US KENPO GIRLS LIGHTLY!
THIS BODY WILL MAKE YOU FEEL THE PAIN OF MY VENGEANCE!
AAH
THOK
WHOMP
THUMP THUMP
THEY'LL KILL HIM.
YAKUMO WAS TAKEN BY THE POLICE.
You thief!
THE GIRLS RETURNED TO NORMAL ...
... AND THE STATUE WAS DONATED TO AN ART MUSEUM.
100 million?!
15th Annual Martial Arts Competition
I CAN'T BELIEVE I FELL FOR THAT GUY!

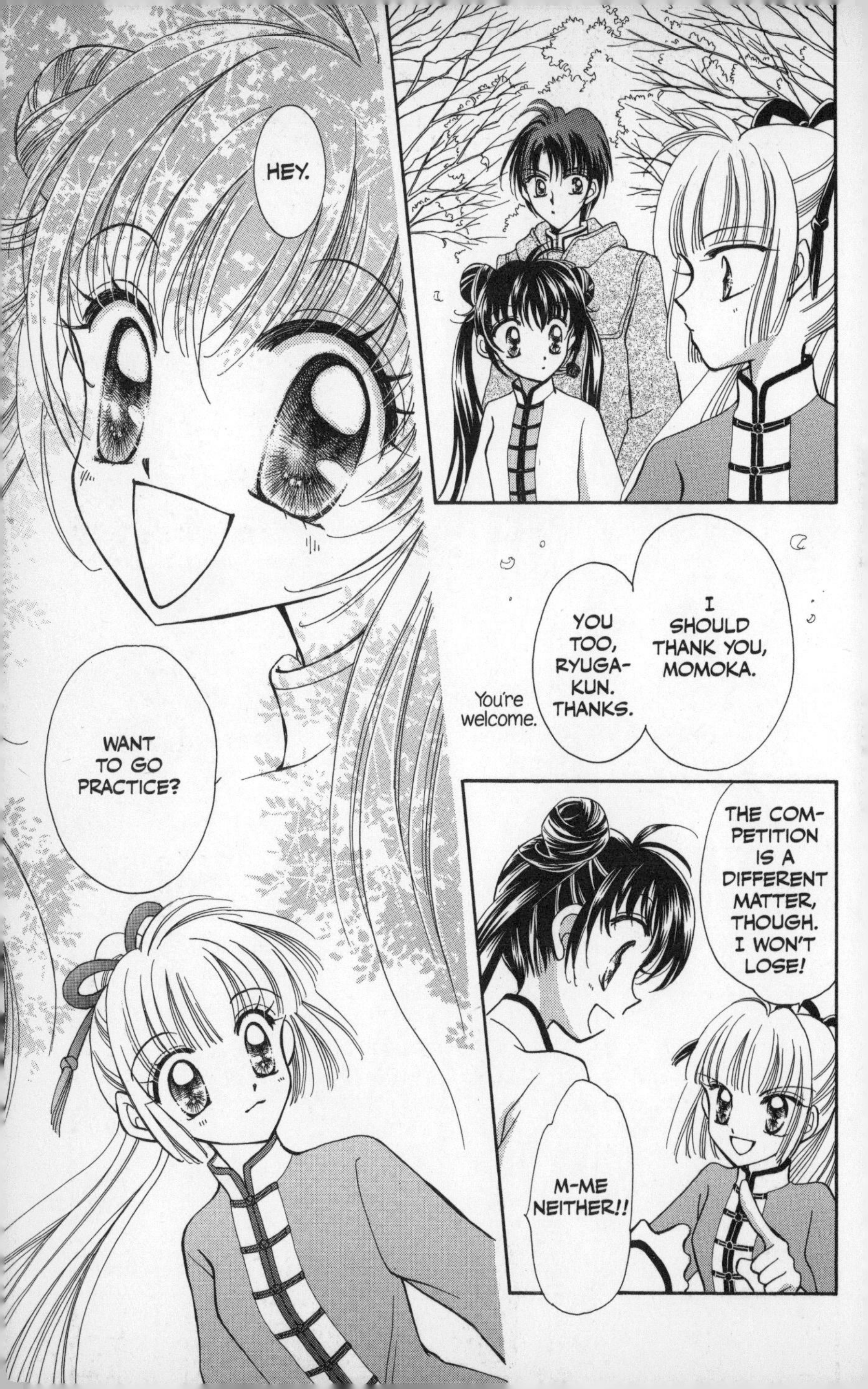
I SHOULD THANK YOU, MOMOKA.
YOU TOO, RYUGA-KUN. THANKS.
You're welcome.
THE COM-PETITION IS A DIFFERENT MATTER, THOUGH. I WON'T LOSE!
M-ME NEITHER!!
HEY.
WANT TO GO PRACTICE?

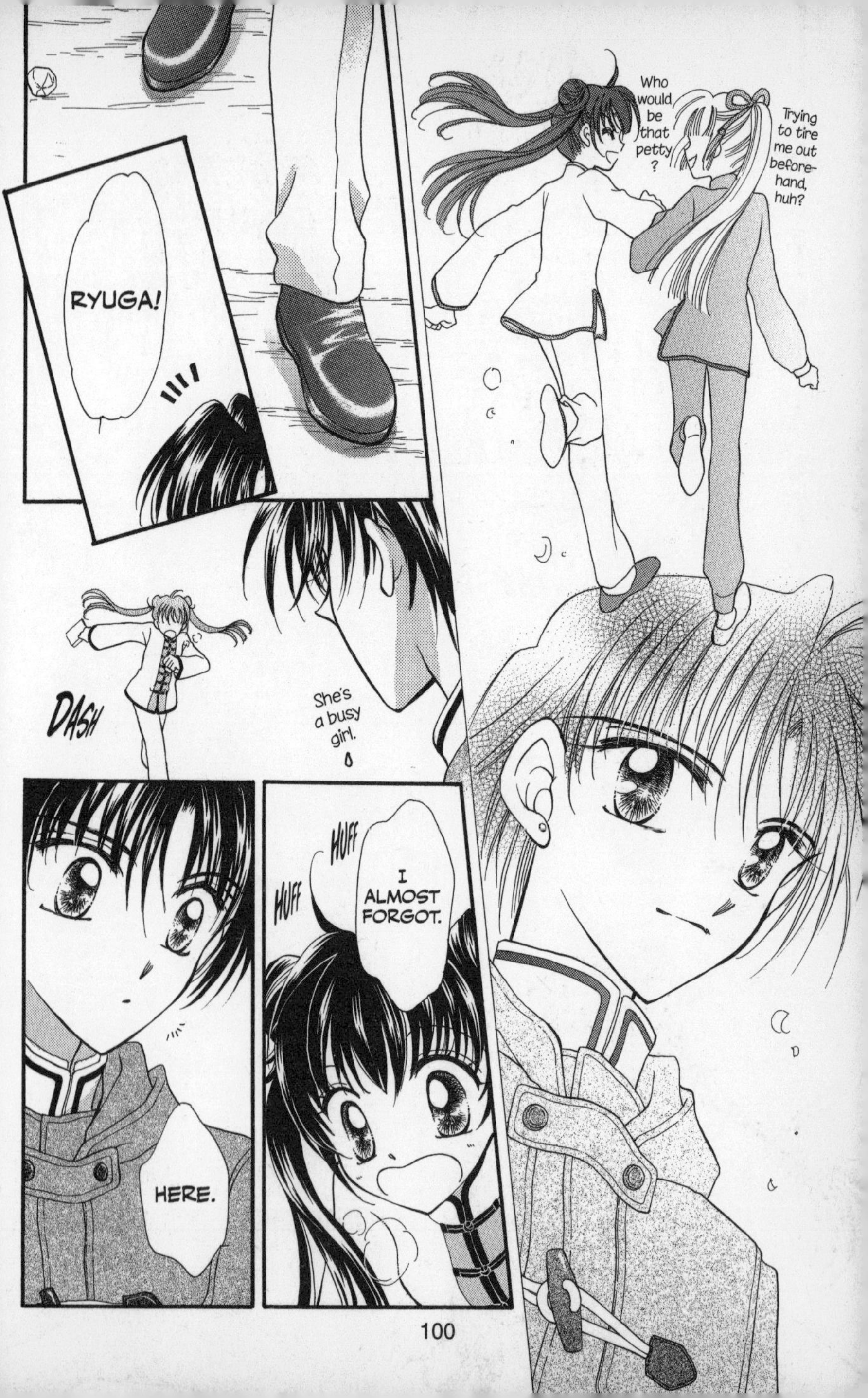
Trying to tire me out beforehand, huh?
Who would be that petty?
RYUGA!
She's a busy girl.
DASH
HUFF
HUFF
I ALMOST FORGOT.
HERE.

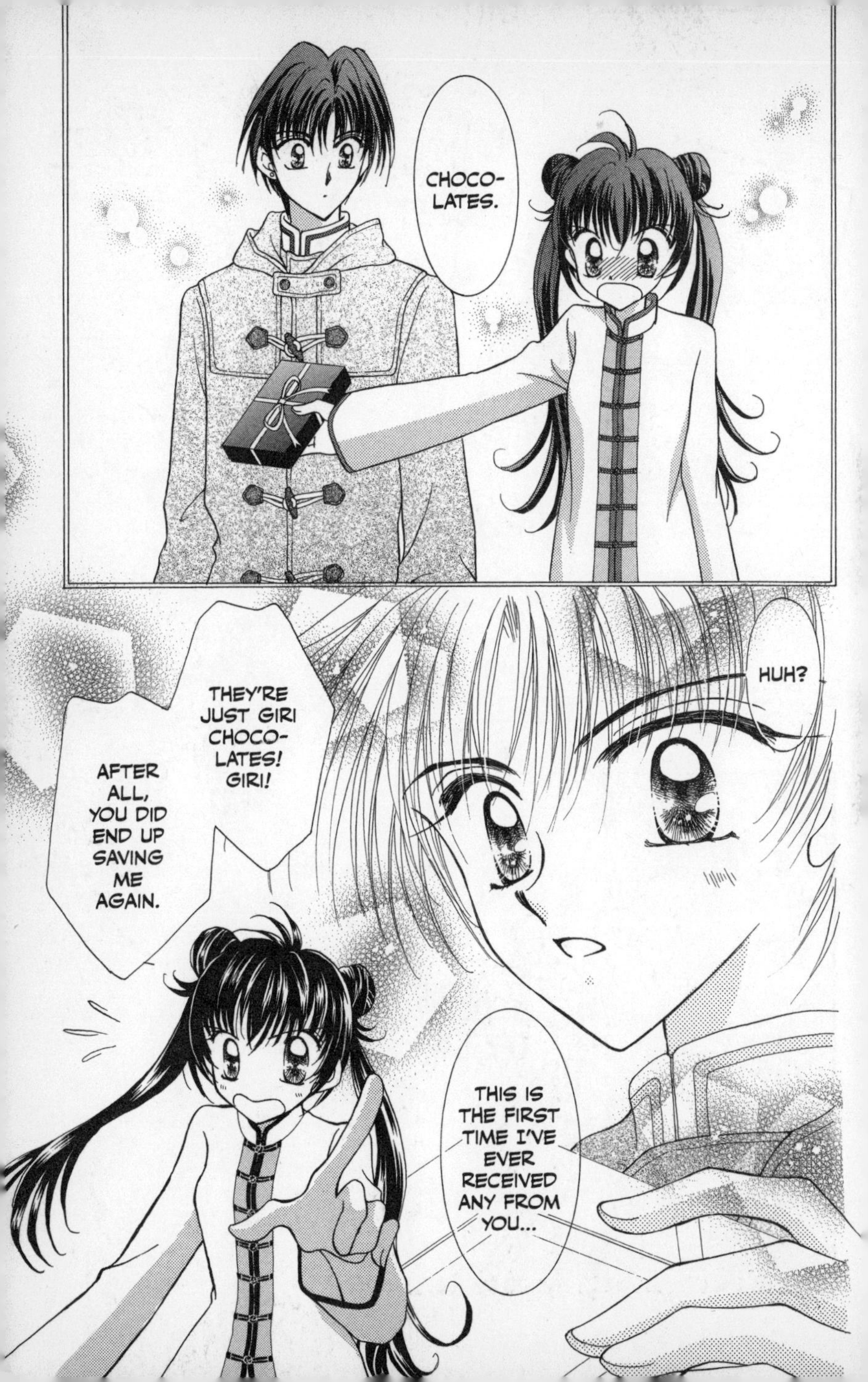
CHOCO-LATES.
HUH?
THEY'RE JUST GIRI CHOCO-LATES! GIRI!
AFTER ALL, YOU DID END UP SAVING ME AGAIN.
THIS IS THE FIRST TIME I'VE EVER RECEIVED ANY FROM YOU...

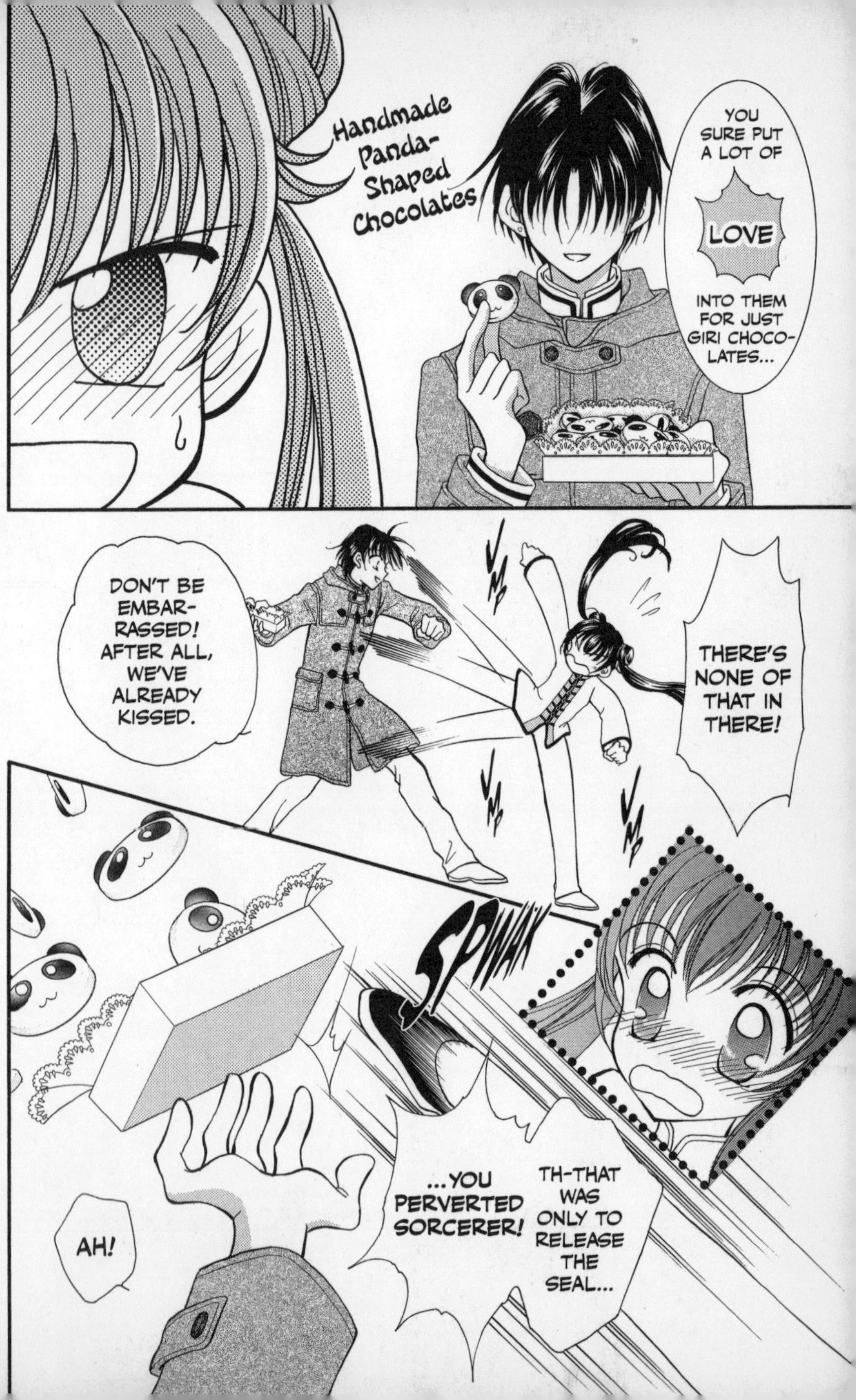
YOU SURE PUT A LOT OF LOVE INTO THEM FOR JUST GIRI CHOCOLATES...
Handmade Panda-Shaped Chocolates
THERE'S NONE OF THAT IN THERE!
DON'T BE EMBARRASSED! AFTER ALL, WE'VE ALREADY KISSED.
SPWAK
TH-THAT WAS ONLY TO RELEASE THE SEAL...
...YOU PERVERTED SORCERER!
AH!

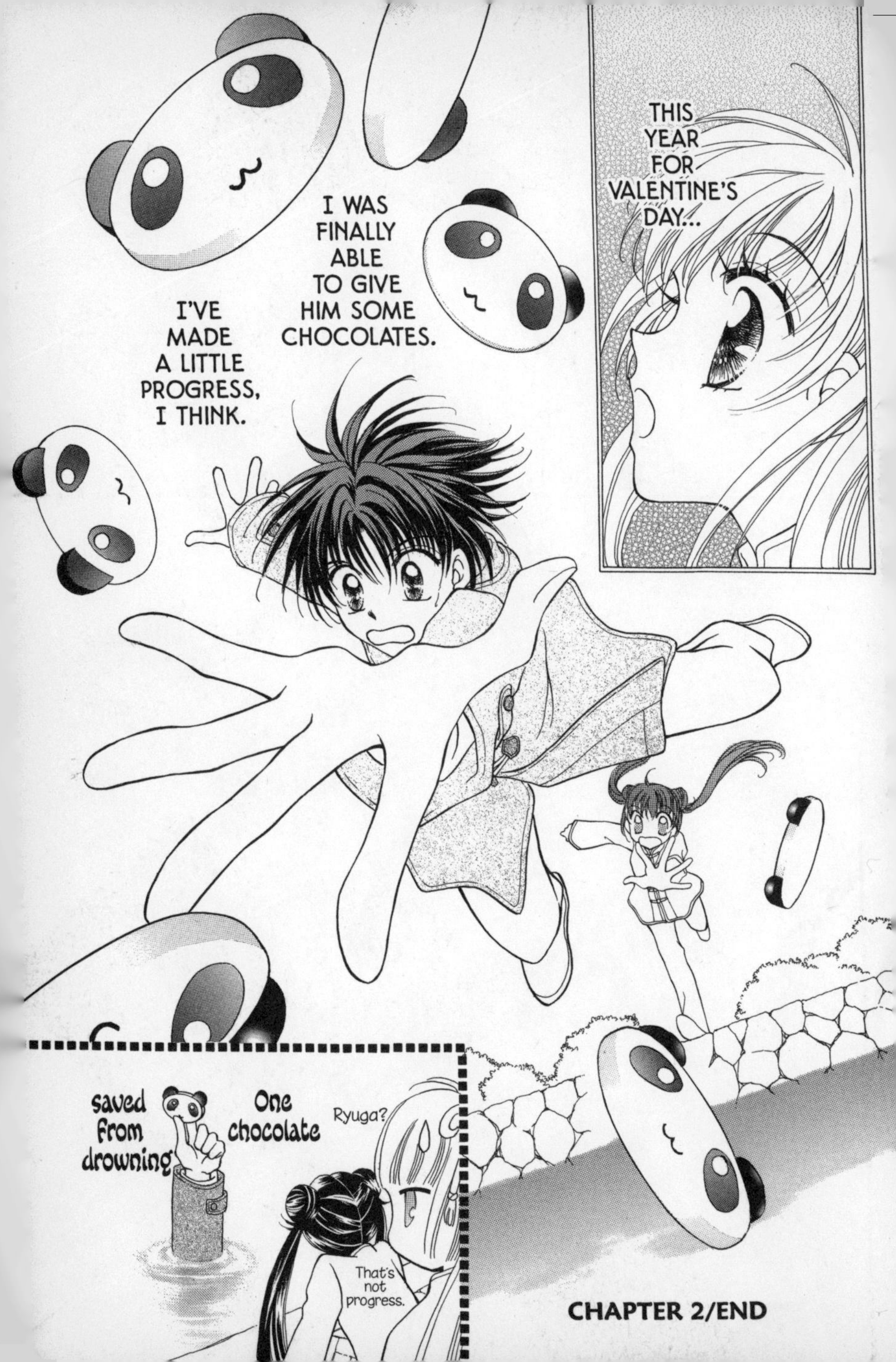
THIS YEAR FOR VALENTINE'S DAY...
I WAS FINALLY ABLE TO GIVE HIM SOME CHOCOLATES.
I'VE MADE A LITTLE PROGRESS, I THINK.
Ryuga?
One chocolate
saved from drowning
That's not progress.
CHAPTER 2/END

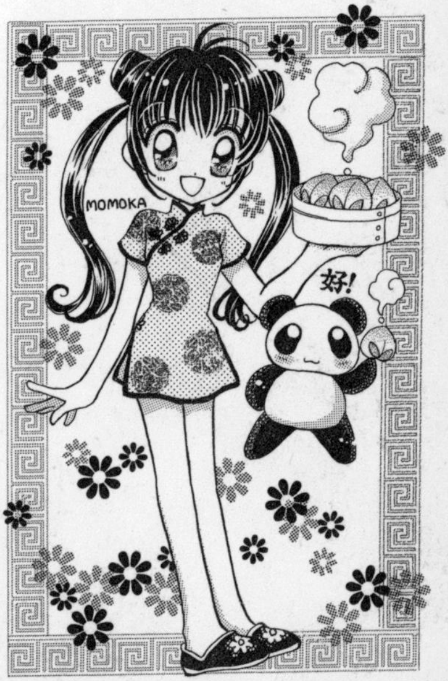
MOMOKA
好!

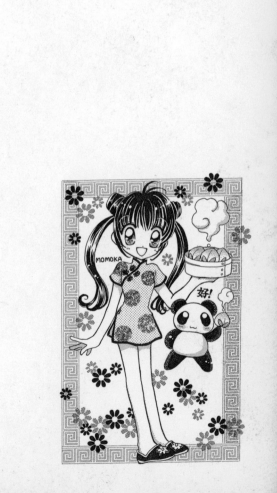

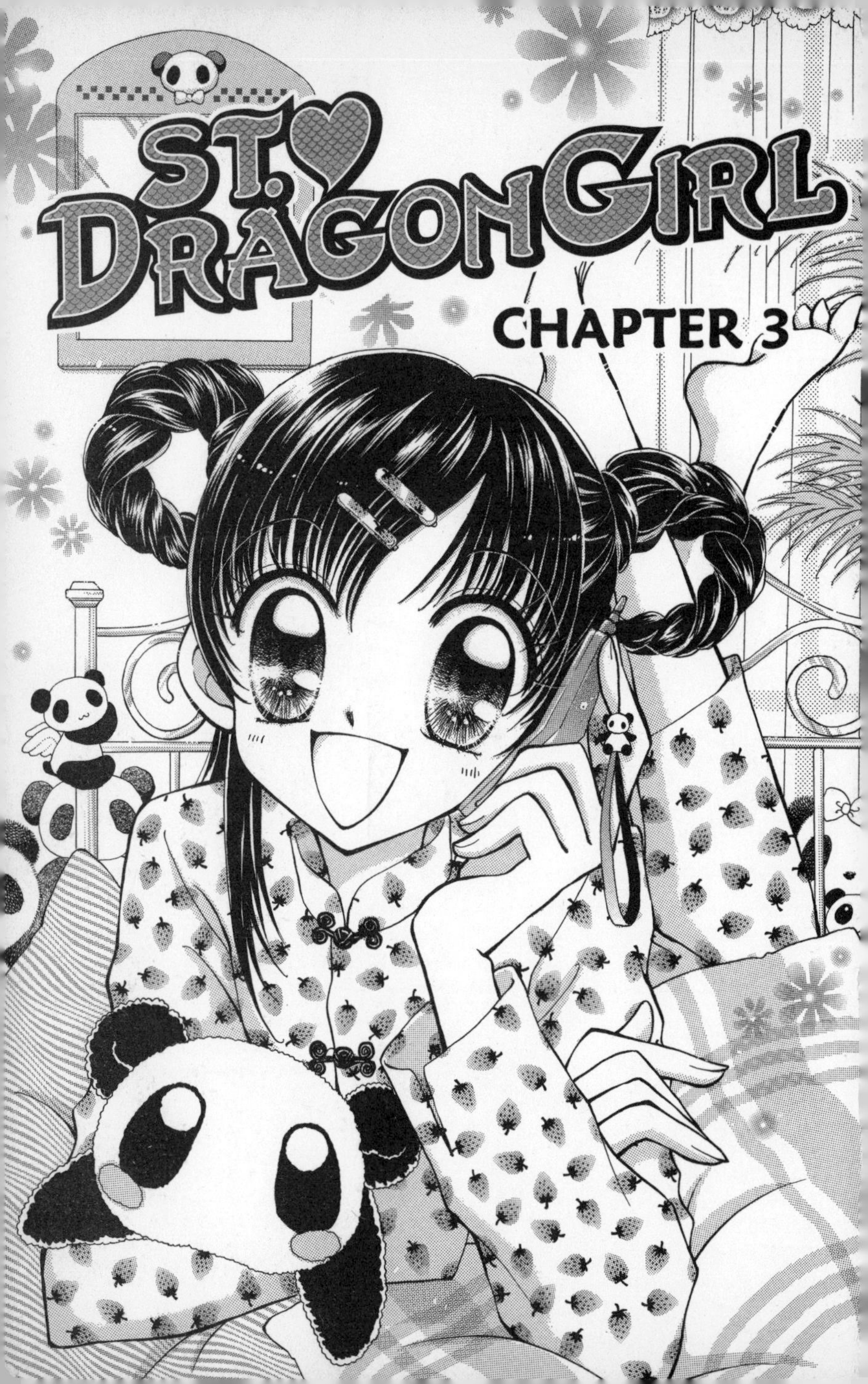

ST. ♥ DRAGON GIRL
CHAPTER 3

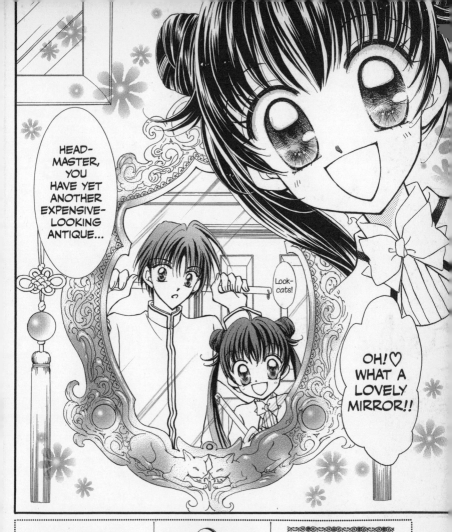

OH! ♡ WHAT A LOVELY MIRROR!!
Look-cats!
HEAD-MASTER, YOU HAVE YET ANOTHER EXPENSIVE-LOOKING ANTIQUE...

She is the type to talk with her hands. She can't ignore people in need. She has been possessed by the dragon that Ryuga summoned. When the seal is lifted, she becomes an invincible dragon girl. Will she and Ryuga become a couple in the future?

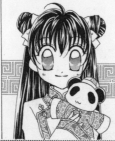

Momoka Sendou

Born May 1.
Taurus, Blood-Type: O.
Raised in Yokohama. Her family owns a kenpo dojo, and she is highly skilled in martial arts. She really loves pandas. Her hobby is collecting stuffed animals. She is secretly in love with Ryuga.

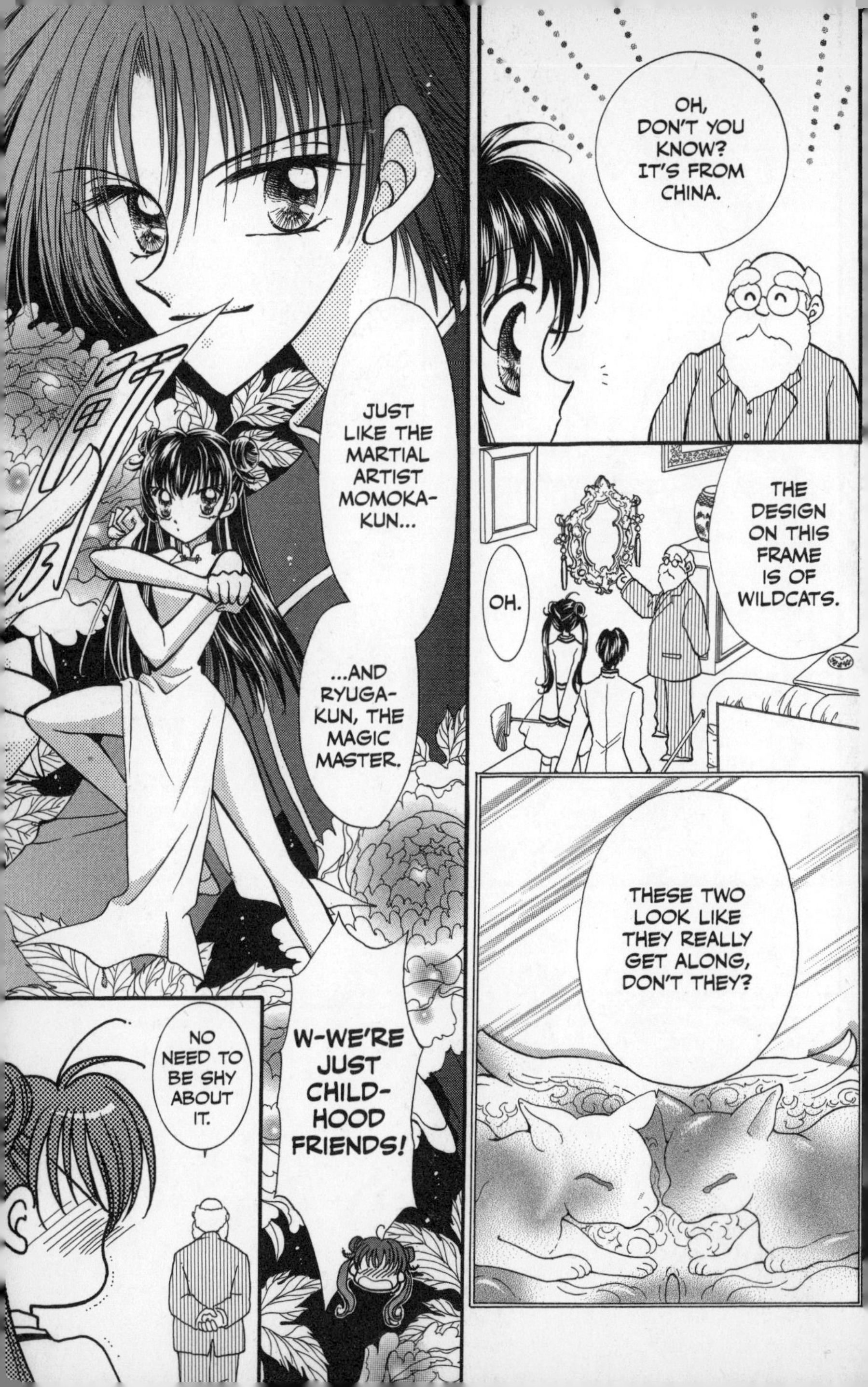
OH, DON'T YOU KNOW? IT'S FROM CHINA.
THE DESIGN ON THIS FRAME IS OF WILDCATS.
OH.
THESE TWO LOOK LIKE THEY REALLY GET ALONG, DON'T THEY?
JUST LIKE THE MARTIAL ARTIST MOMOKA-KUN...
...AND RYUGA-KUN, THE MAGIC MASTER.
W-WE'RE JUST CHILDHOOD FRIENDS!
NO NEED TO BE SHY ABOUT IT.

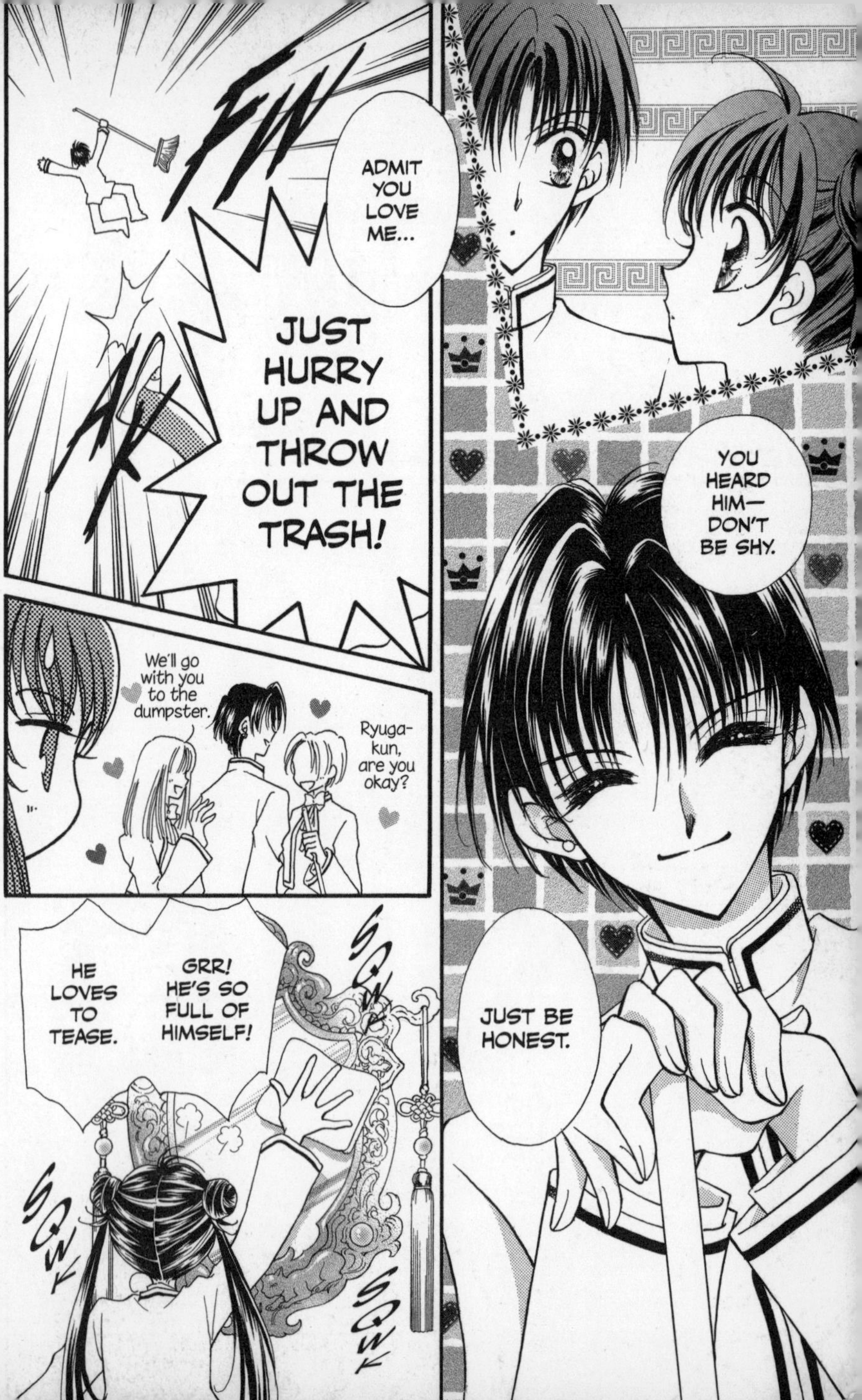
YOU HEARD HIM— DON'T BE SHY.
JUST BE HONEST.
ADMIT YOU LOVE ME...
JUST HURRY UP AND THROW OUT THE TRASH!
FWAK
Ryuga-kun, are you okay?
We'll go with you to the dumpster.
GRR! HE'S SO FULL OF HIMSELF!
HE LOVES TO TEASE.
SQWK
SQWK
SQWK

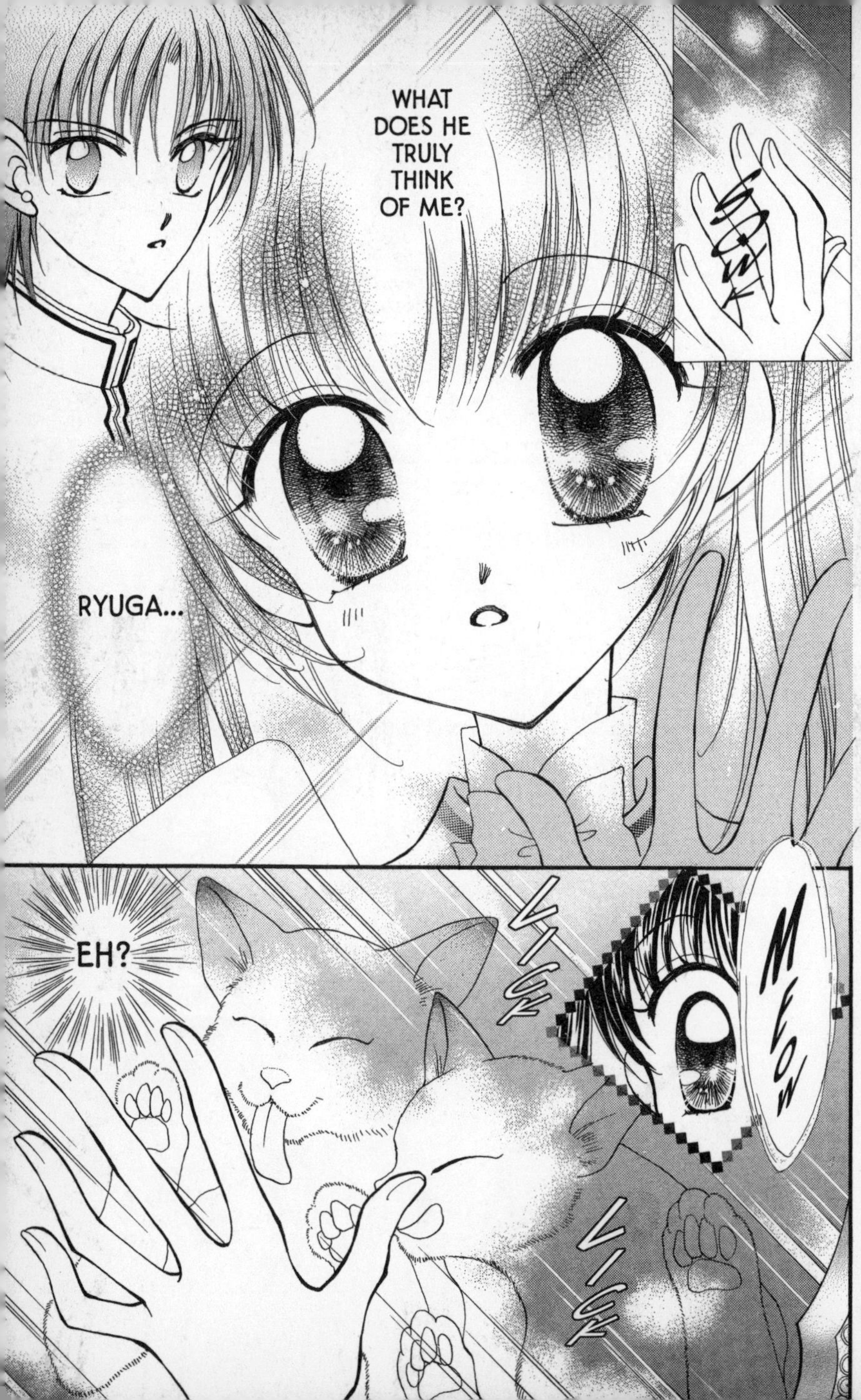
WHAT DOES HE TRULY THINK OF ME?
RYUGA...
MEOW
LICK
EH?
LICK

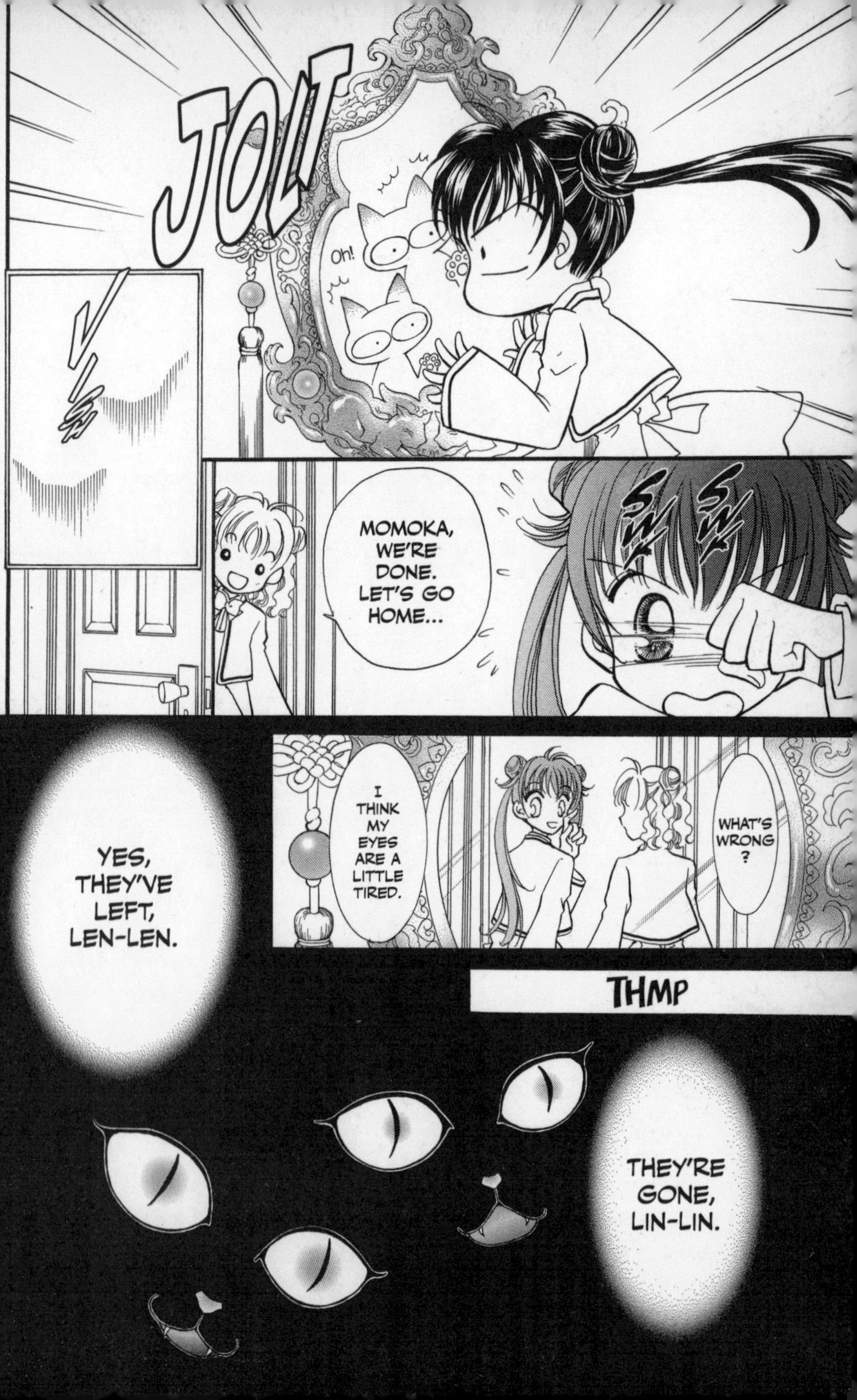
JOLT
Oh!
SW SW
MOMOKA, WE'RE DONE. LET'S GO HOME...
WHAT'S WRONG?
I THINK MY EYES ARE A LITTLE TIRED.
THMP
YES, THEY'VE LEFT, LEN-LEN.
THEY'RE GONE, LIN-LIN.

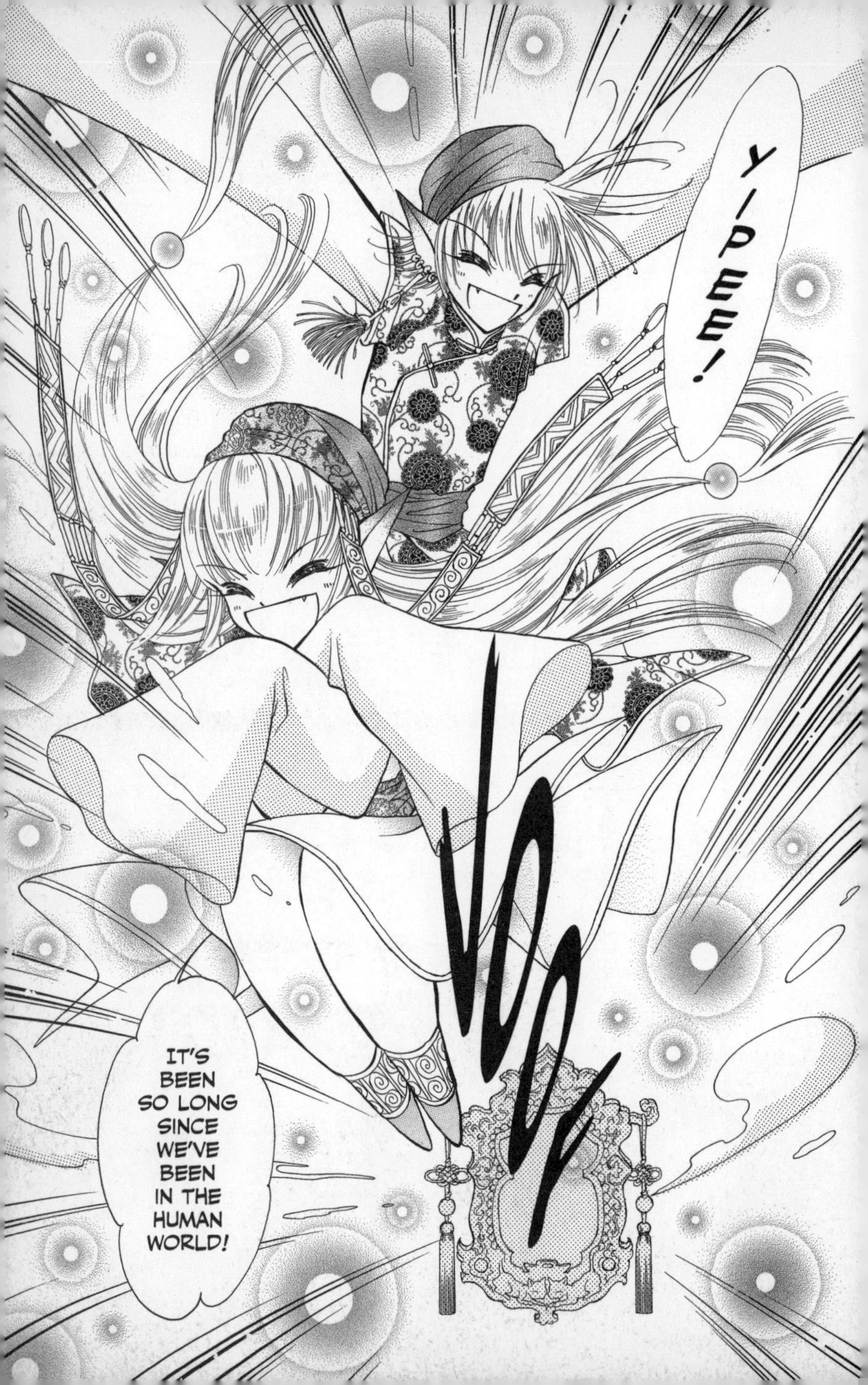
YIPEE!
IT'S BEEN SO LONG SINCE WE'VE BEEN IN THE HUMAN WORLD!

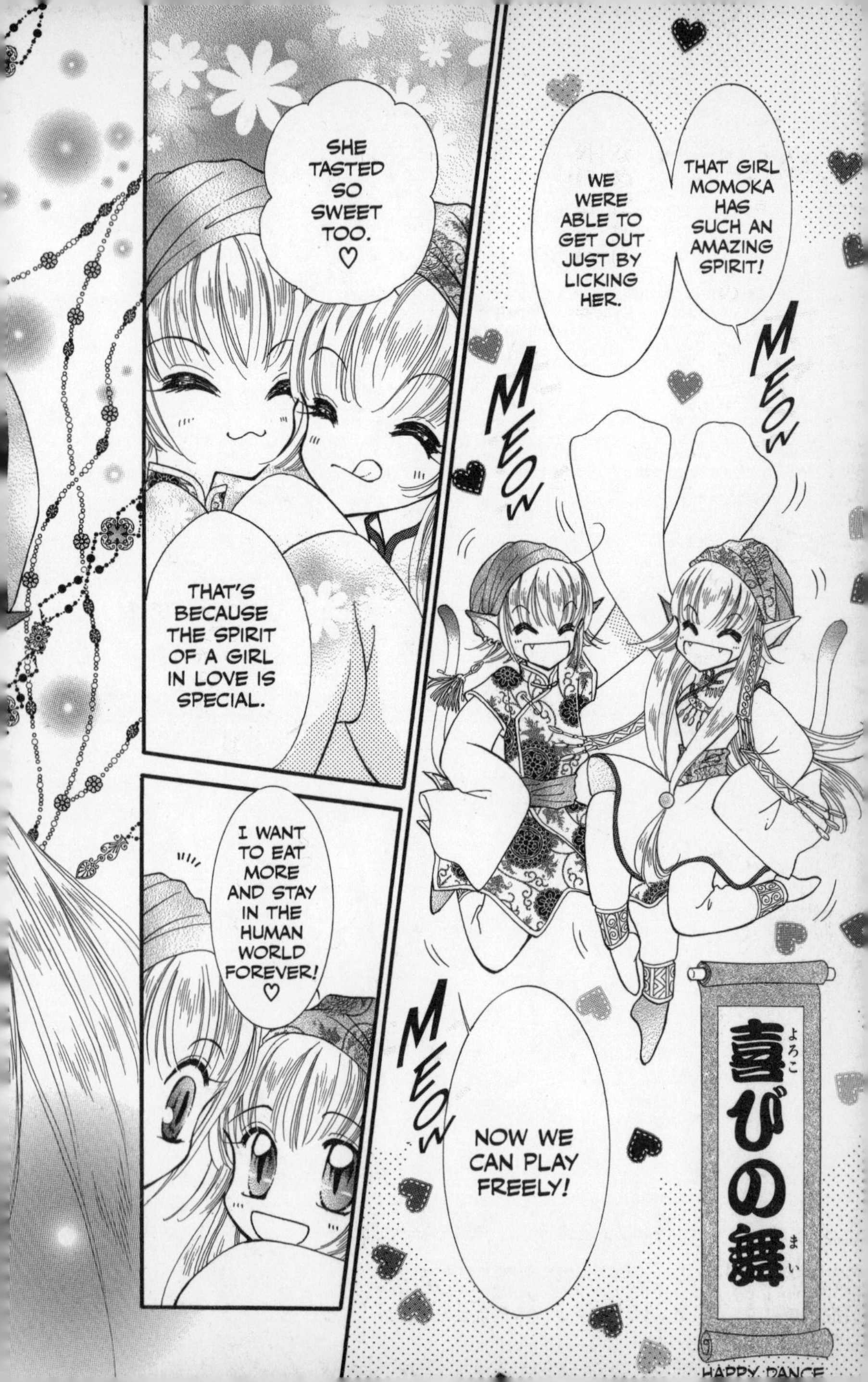
THAT GIRL MOMOKA HAS SUCH AN AMAZING SPIRIT!
WE WERE ABLE TO GET OUT JUST BY LICKING HER.
MEOW
MEOW
MEOW
NOW WE CAN PLAY FREELY!
喜(よろこ)びの舞(まい)
HAPPY DANCE
SHE TASTED SO SWEET TOO. ♡
THAT'S BECAUSE THE SPIRIT OF A GIRL IN LOVE IS SPECIAL.
I WANT TO EAT MORE AND STAY IN THE HUMAN WORLD FOREVER! ♡

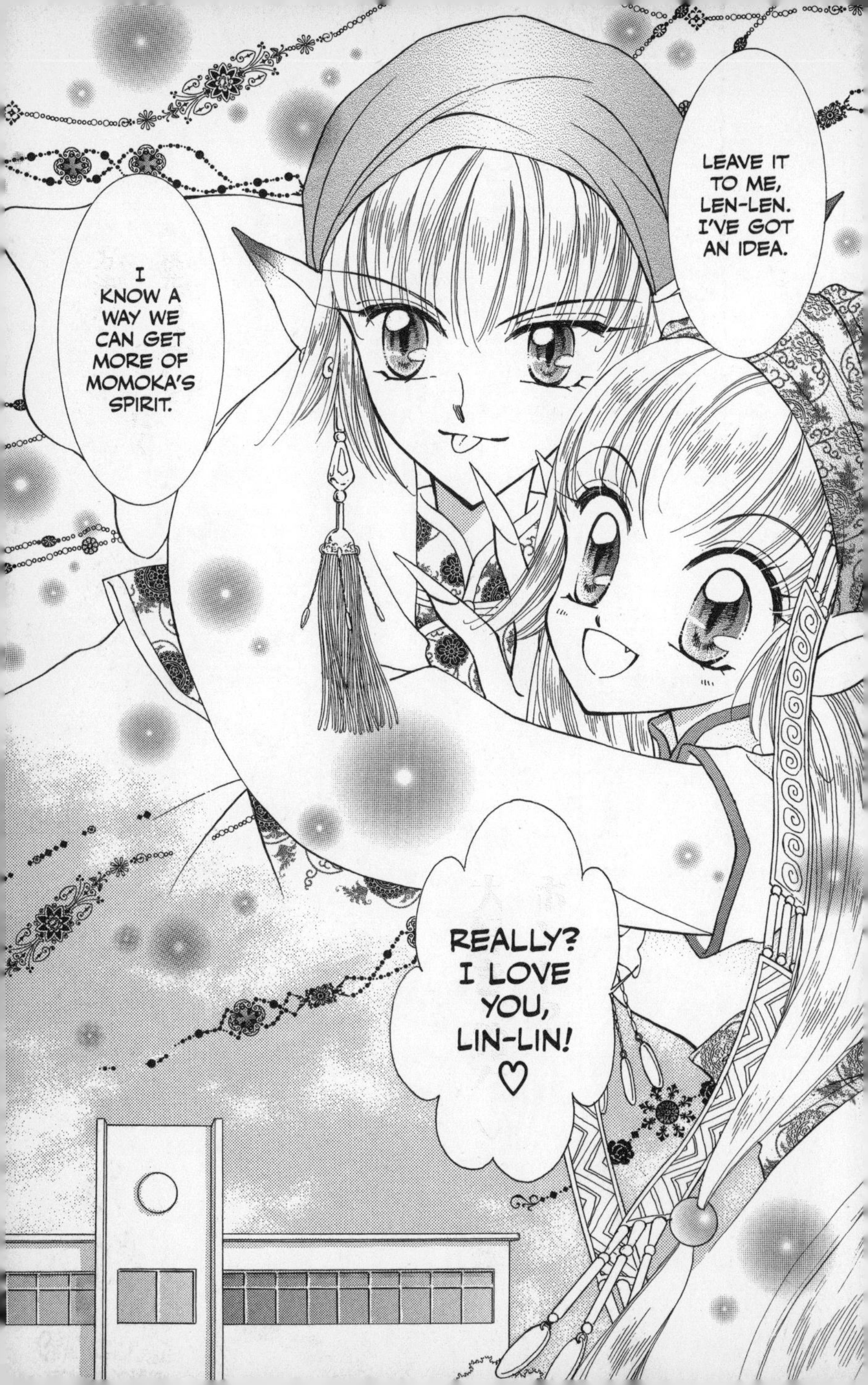
LEAVE IT TO ME, LEN-LEN. I'VE GOT AN IDEA.
I KNOW A WAY WE CAN GET MORE OF MOMOKA'S SPIRIT.
REALLY? I LOVE YOU, LIN-LIN! ♡

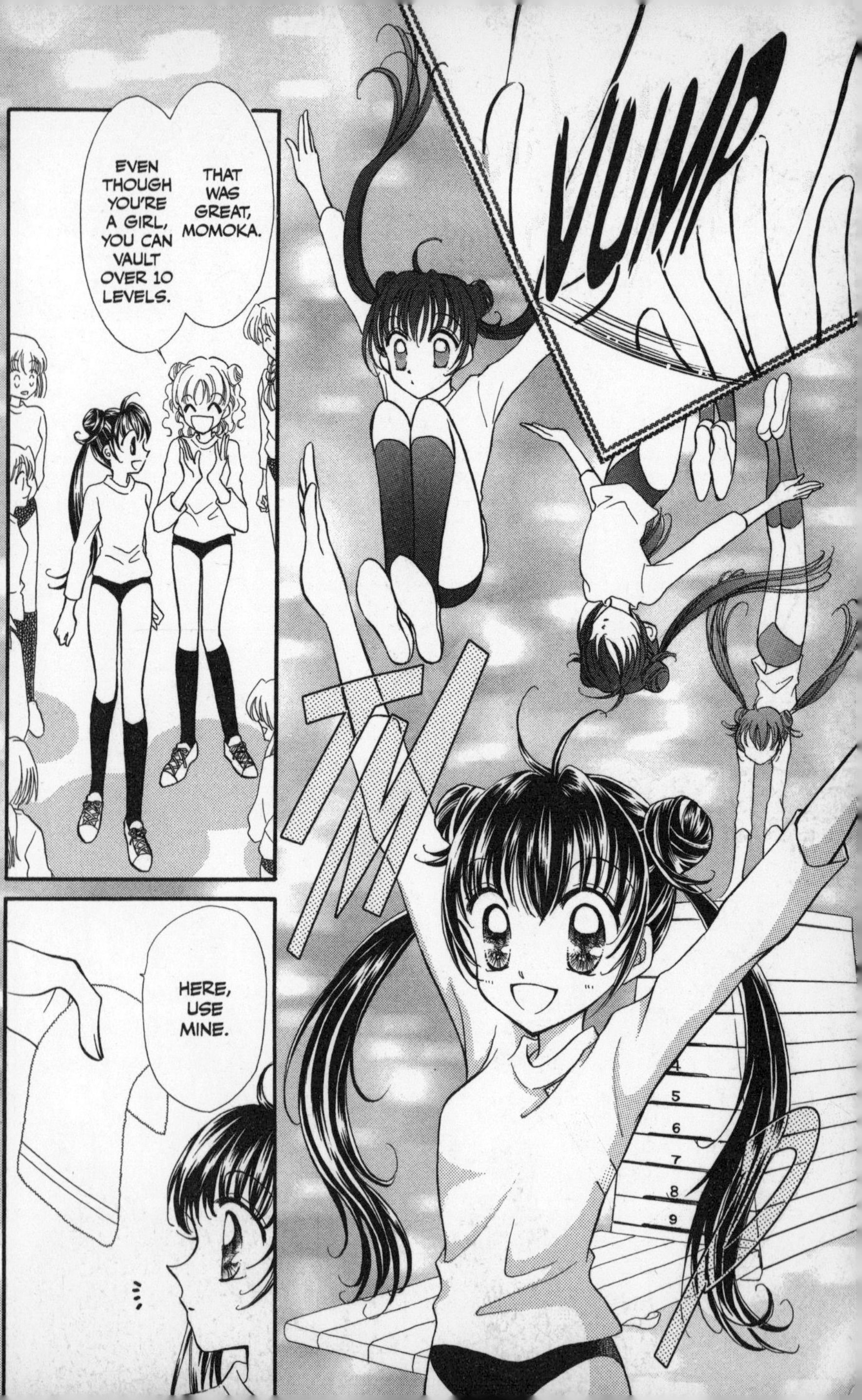
JUMP
THAT WAS GREAT, MOMOKA.
EVEN THOUGH YOU'RE A GIRL, YOU CAN VAULT OVER 10 LEVELS.
HERE, USE MINE.

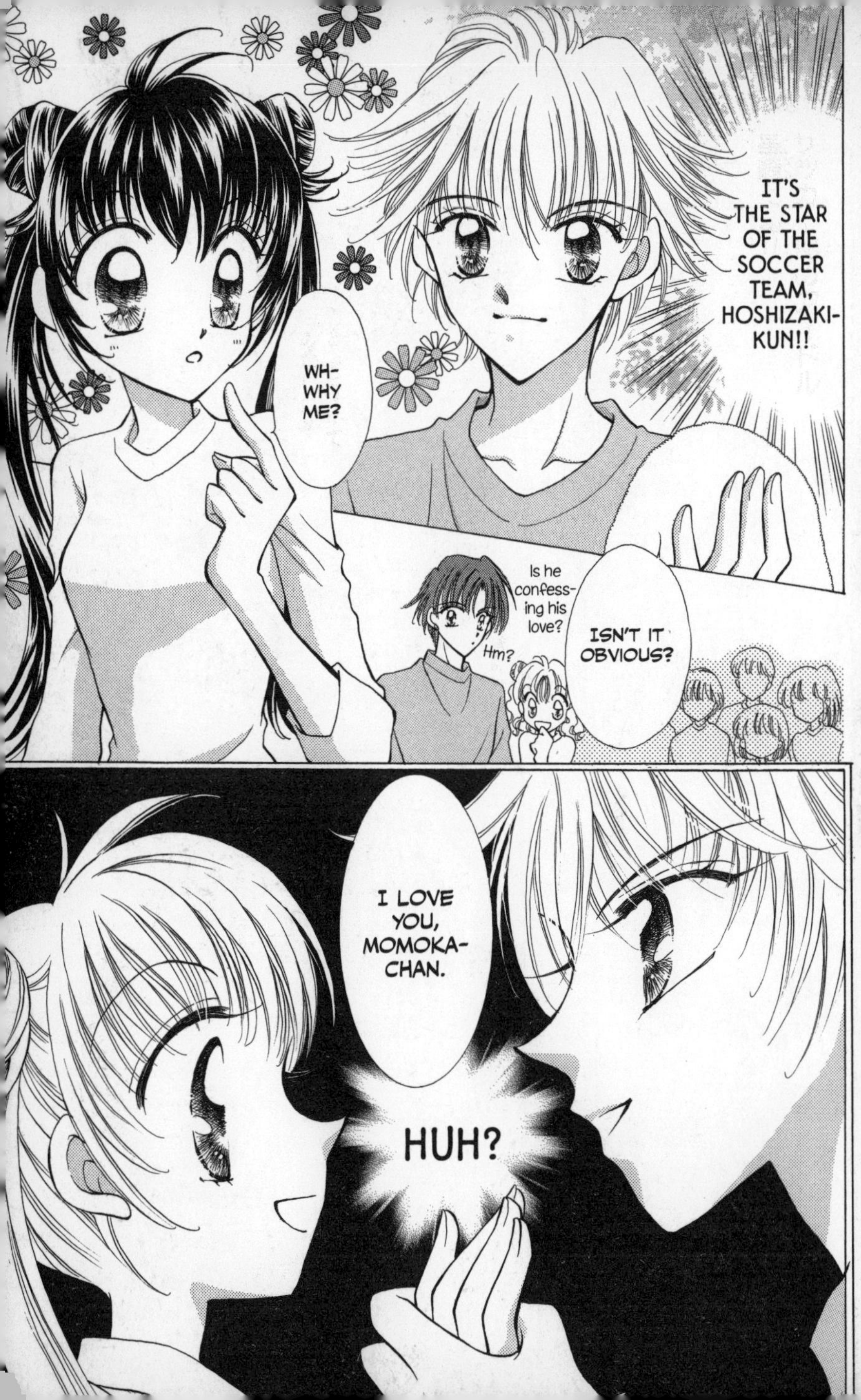
IT'S THE STAR OF THE SOCCER TEAM, HOSHIZAKI-KUN!!
WH-WHY ME?
ISN'T IT OBVIOUS?
Is he confess-ing his love?
Hm?
I LOVE YOU, MOMOKA-CHAN.
HUH?

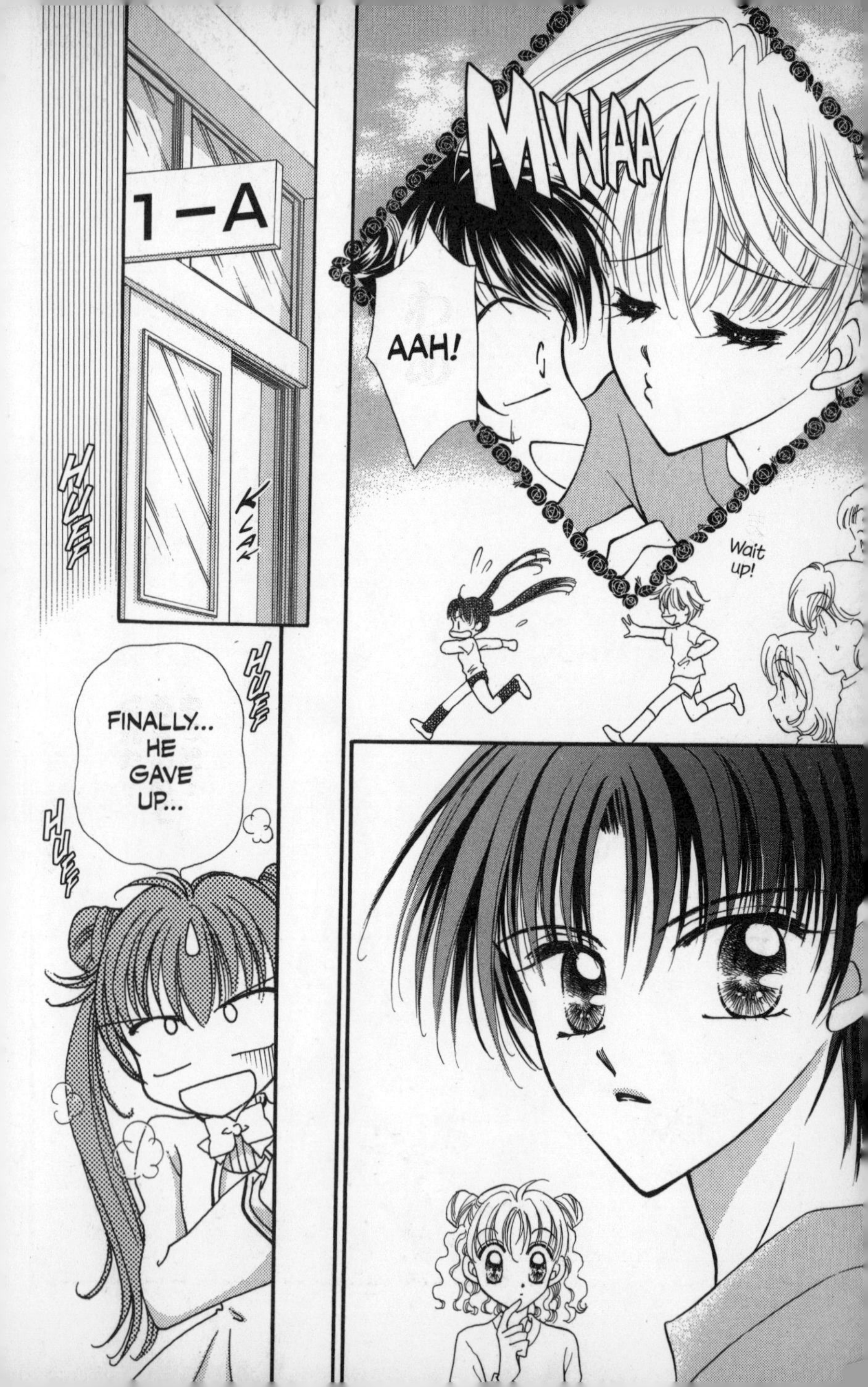
MINAA
AAH!
Wait up!
1-A
HUFF
KLAK
FINALLY... HE GAVE UP...
HUFF
HUFF

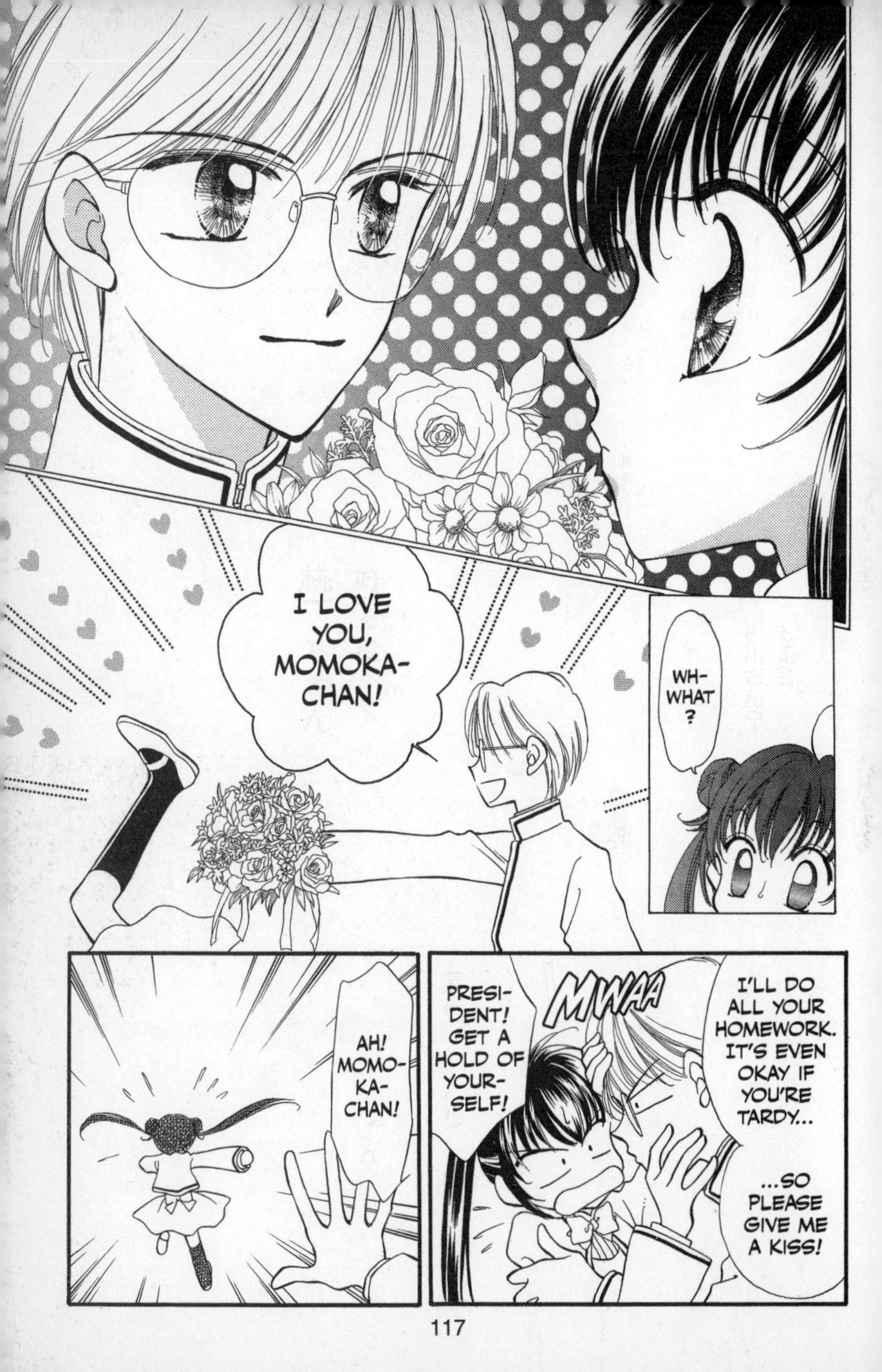
I LOVE YOU, MOMOKA-CHAN!
WH-WHAT?
I'LL DO ALL YOUR HOMEWORK. IT'S EVEN OKAY IF YOU'RE TARDY...
...SO PLEASE GIVE ME A KISS!
MWAA
PRESI-DENT! GET A HOLD OF YOUR-SELF!
AH! MOMO-KA-CHAN!

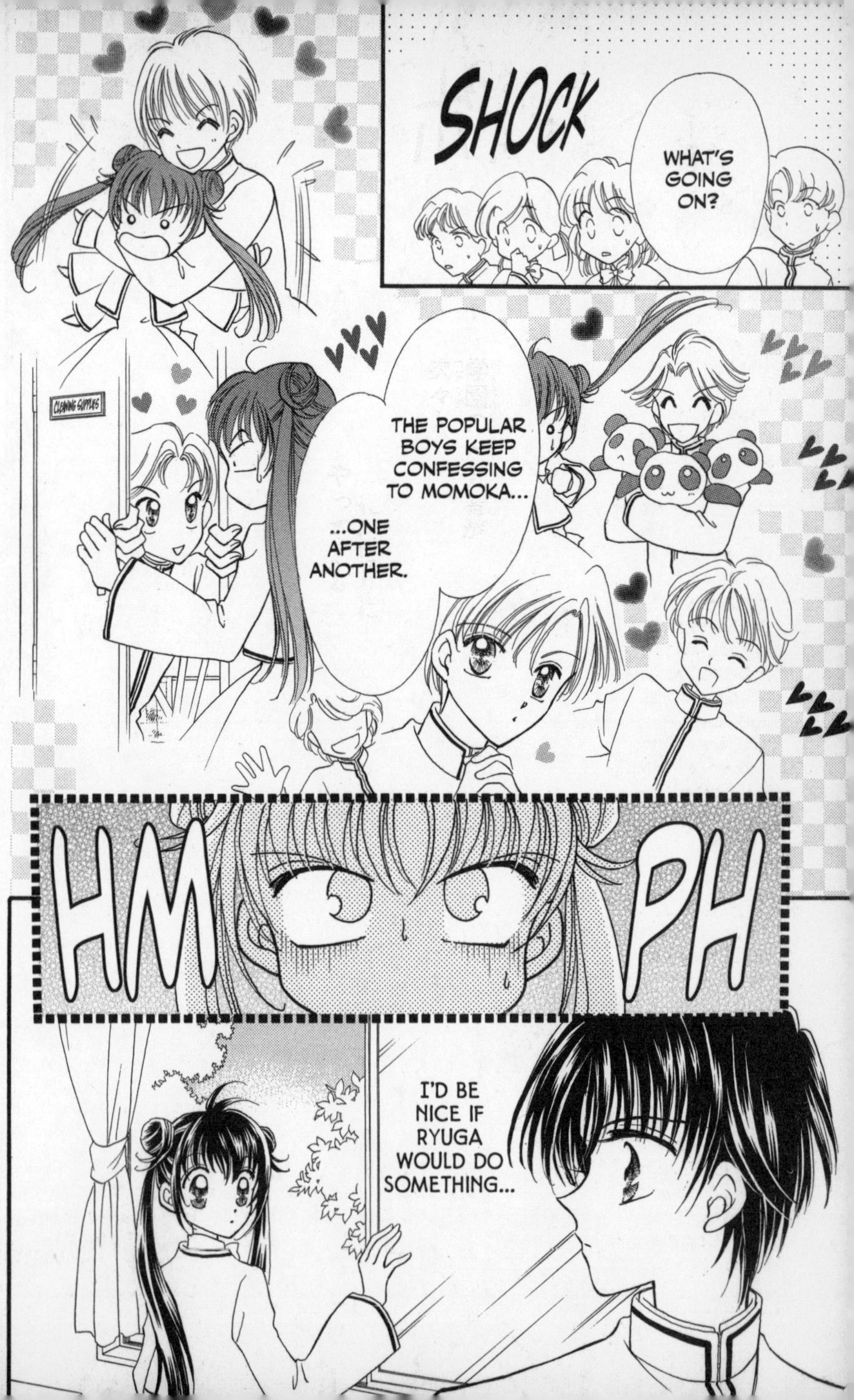
SHOCK
WHAT'S GOING ON?
THE POPULAR BOYS KEEP CONFESSING TO MOMOKA...
...ONE AFTER ANOTHER.
CLEANING SUPPLIES
HMPH
I'D BE NICE IF RYUGA WOULD DO SOMETHING...

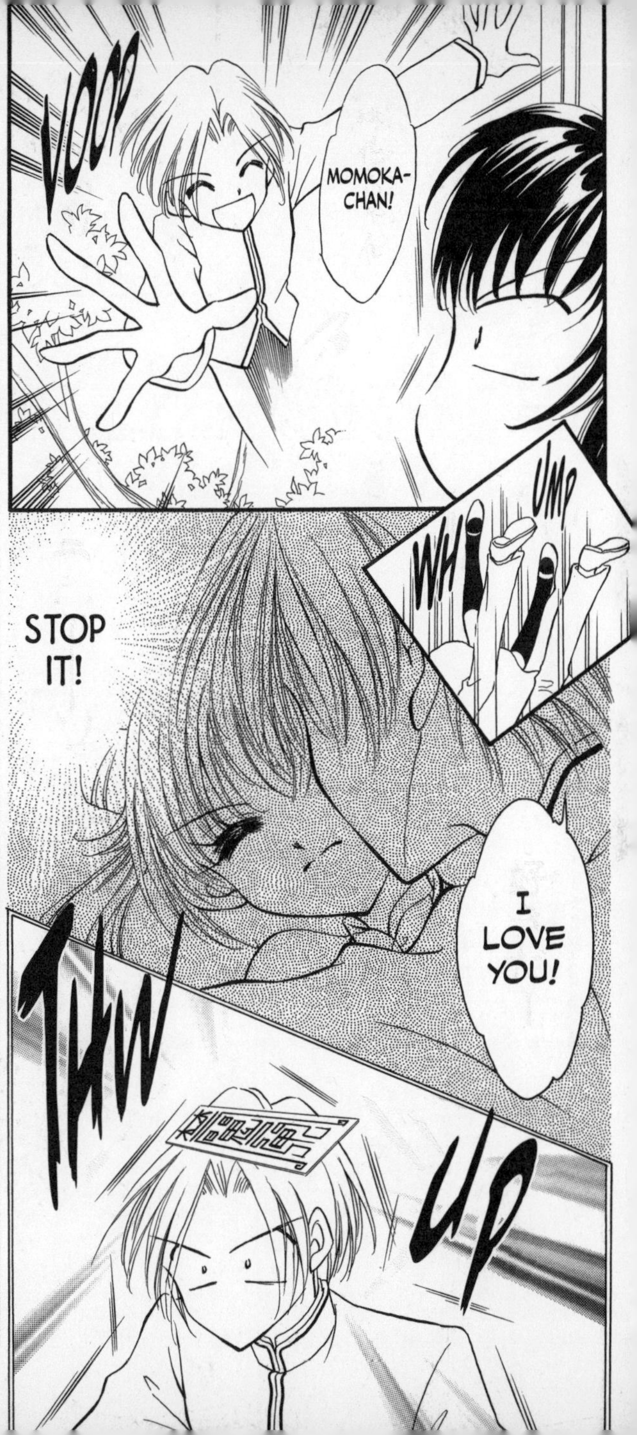
VOOP
MOMOKA-CHAN!
WHUMP
STOP IT!
I LOVE YOU!
THWUP

5

Both humans and demons can be baddies in *St.♥Dragon Girl*. The demons dress in Chinese clothes. However, it's funny that the serpent king and demon cats have more gorgeous costumes than the protagonists.

I've always liked traditional Asian clothing and I've collected pictures of many pieces. I get ideas for the characters' costumes from them (as well as from Hong Kong movies).

Anything is possible in this series, isn't it? Maybe I'll make them wear flashier clothing.

Sometimes I get letters with drawings of the characters wearing those kinds of outfits. Everyone draws me cute Chinese dresses. They really help give me ideas. ♥♥♥

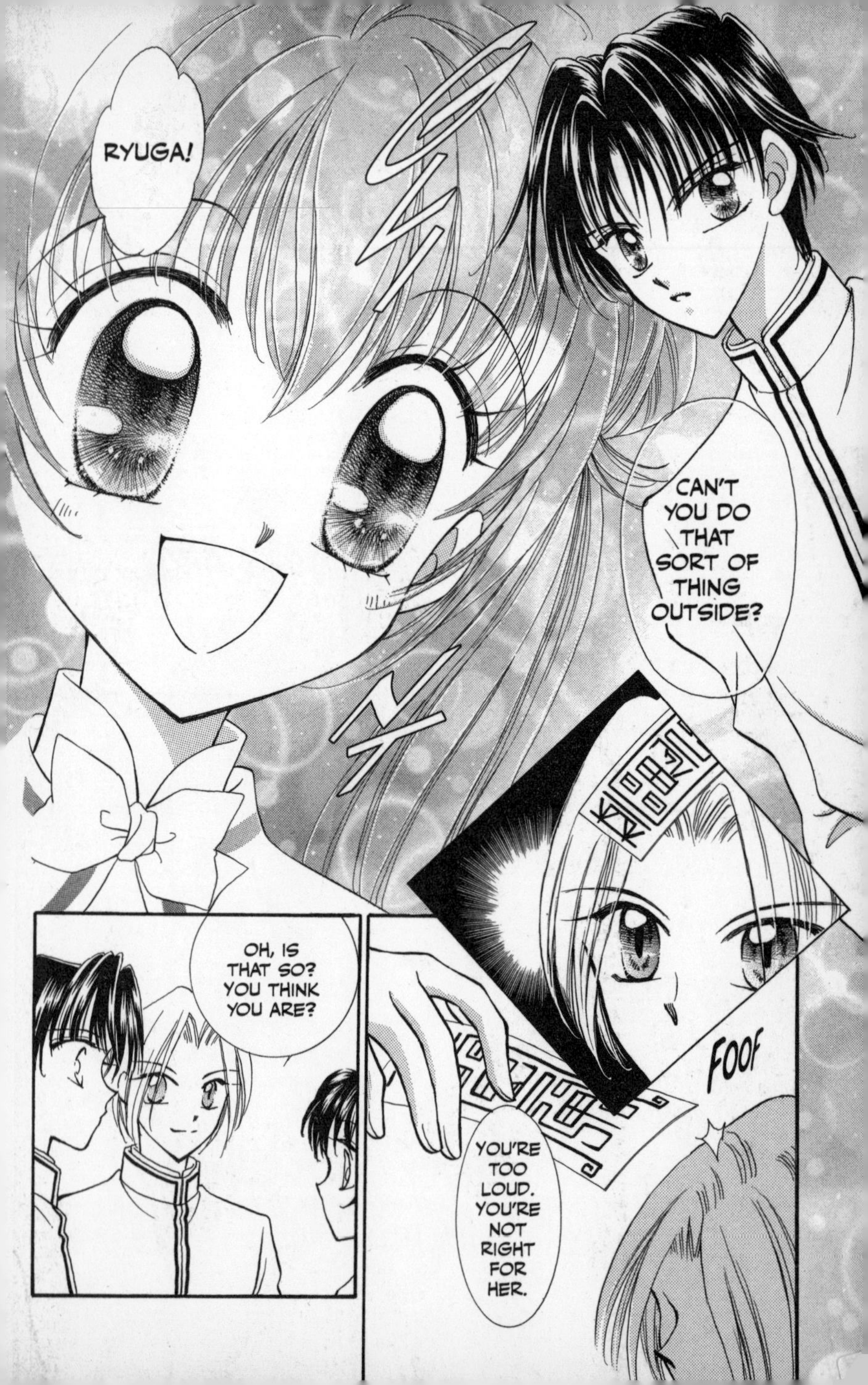
RYUGA!
CAN'T YOU DO THAT SORT OF THING OUTSIDE?
FOOF
YOU'RE TOO LOUD. YOU'RE NOT RIGHT FOR HER.
OH, IS THAT SO? YOU THINK YOU ARE?

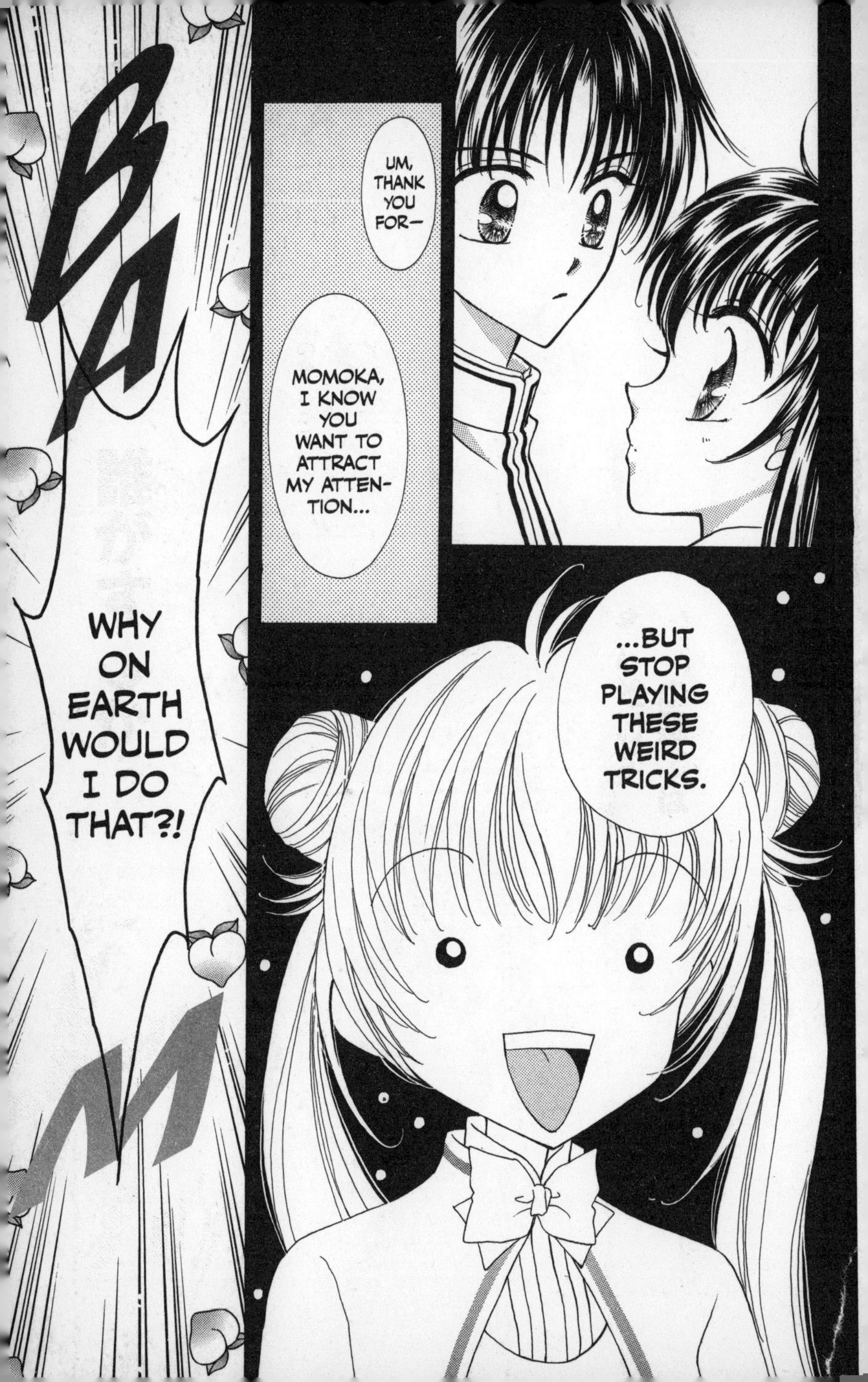
UM, THANK YOU FOR—
MOMOKA, I KNOW YOU WANT TO ATTRACT MY ATTENTION...
...BUT STOP PLAYING THESE WEIRD TRICKS.
BAM
WHY ON EARTH WOULD I DO THAT?!

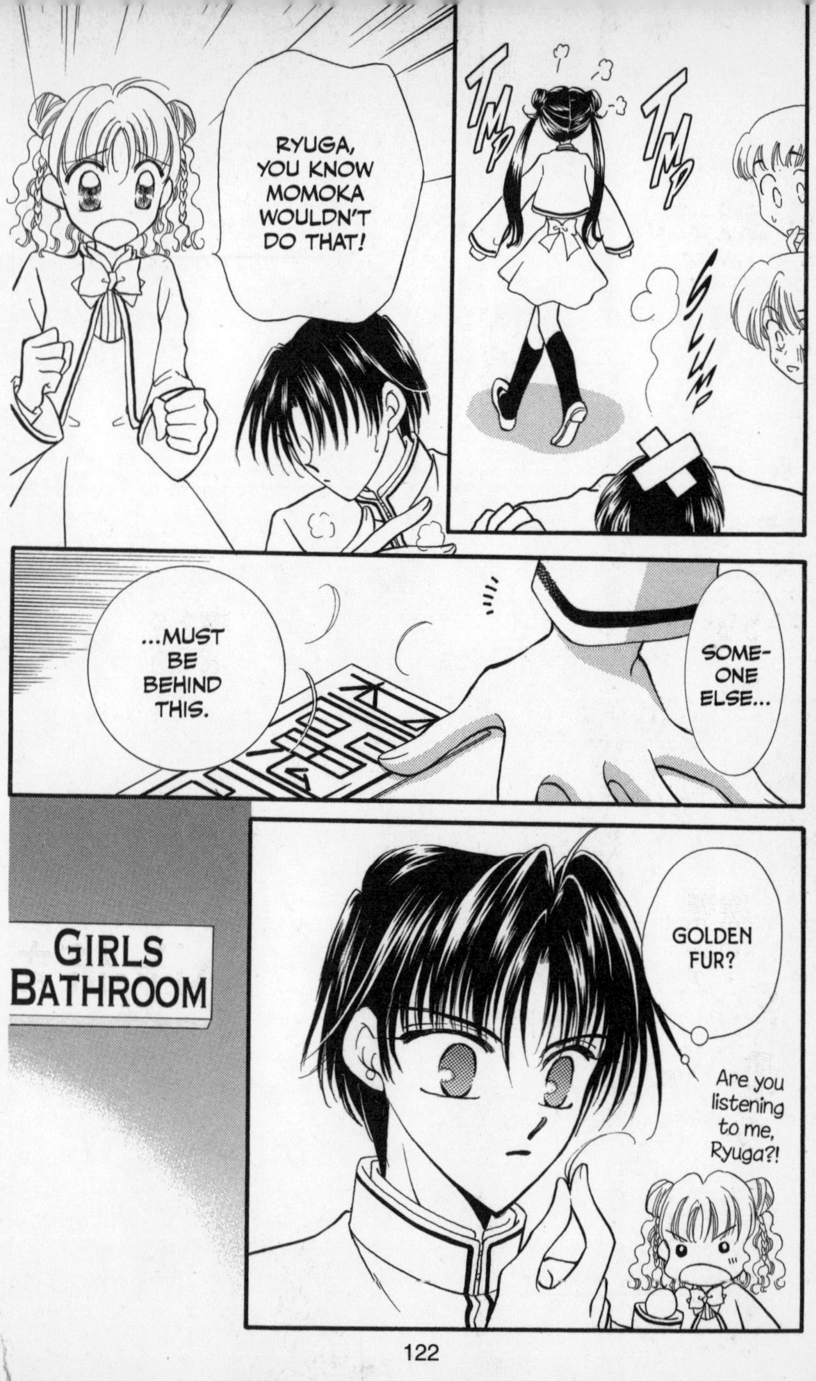
TMP
TMP
SLUMP
RYUGA, YOU KNOW MOMOKA WOULDN'T DO THAT!
SOME-ONE ELSE...
...MUST BE BEHIND THIS.
GOLDEN FUR?
Are you listening to me, Ryuga?!
GIRLS BATHROOM

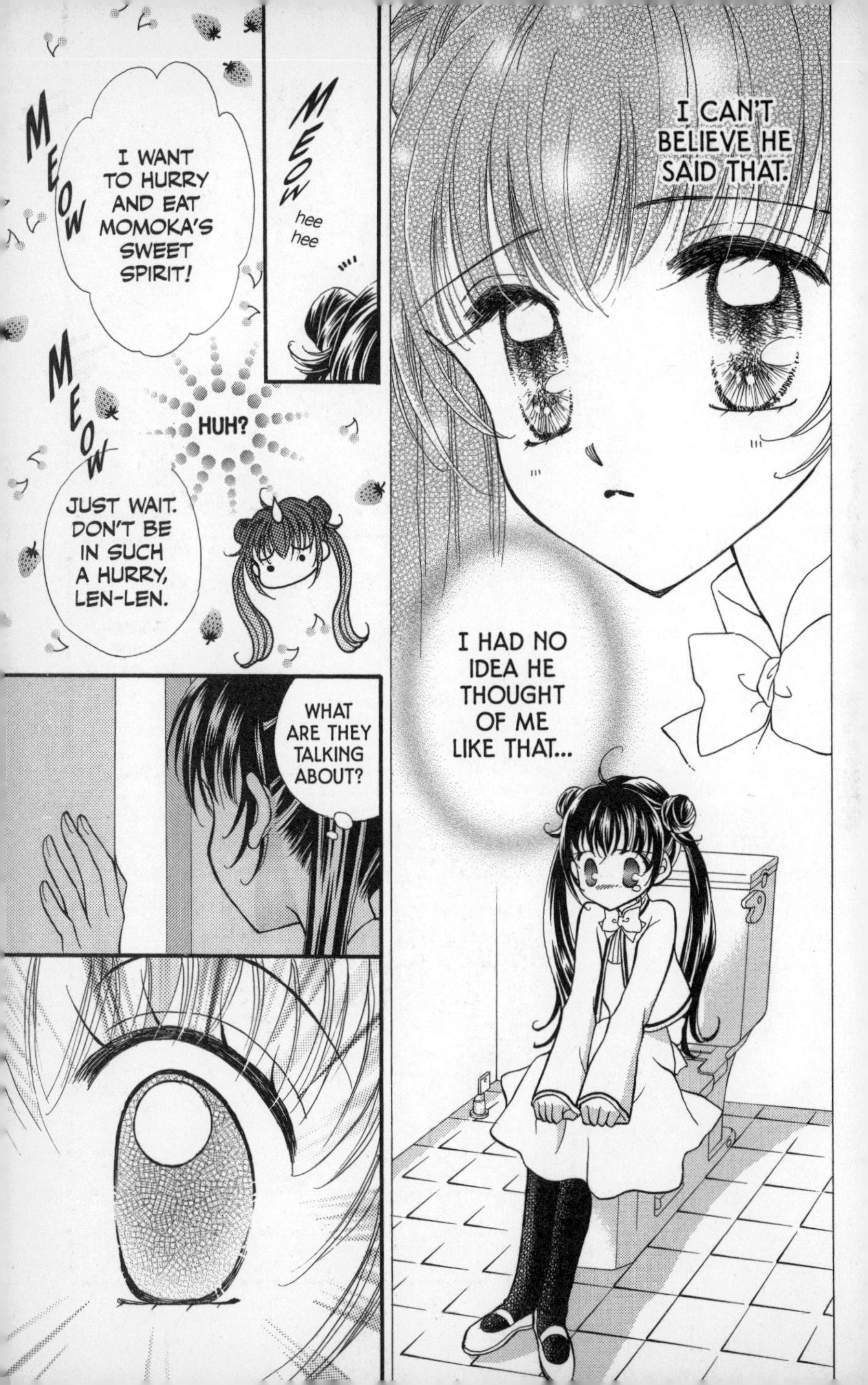
I CAN'T BELIEVE HE SAID THAT.
I HAD NO IDEA HE THOUGHT OF ME LIKE THAT...
MEOW
hee hee
MEOW
I WANT TO HURRY AND EAT MOMOKA'S SWEET SPIRIT!
HUH?
MEOW
JUST WAIT. DON'T BE IN SUCH A HURRY, LEN-LEN.
WHAT ARE THEY TALKING ABOUT?

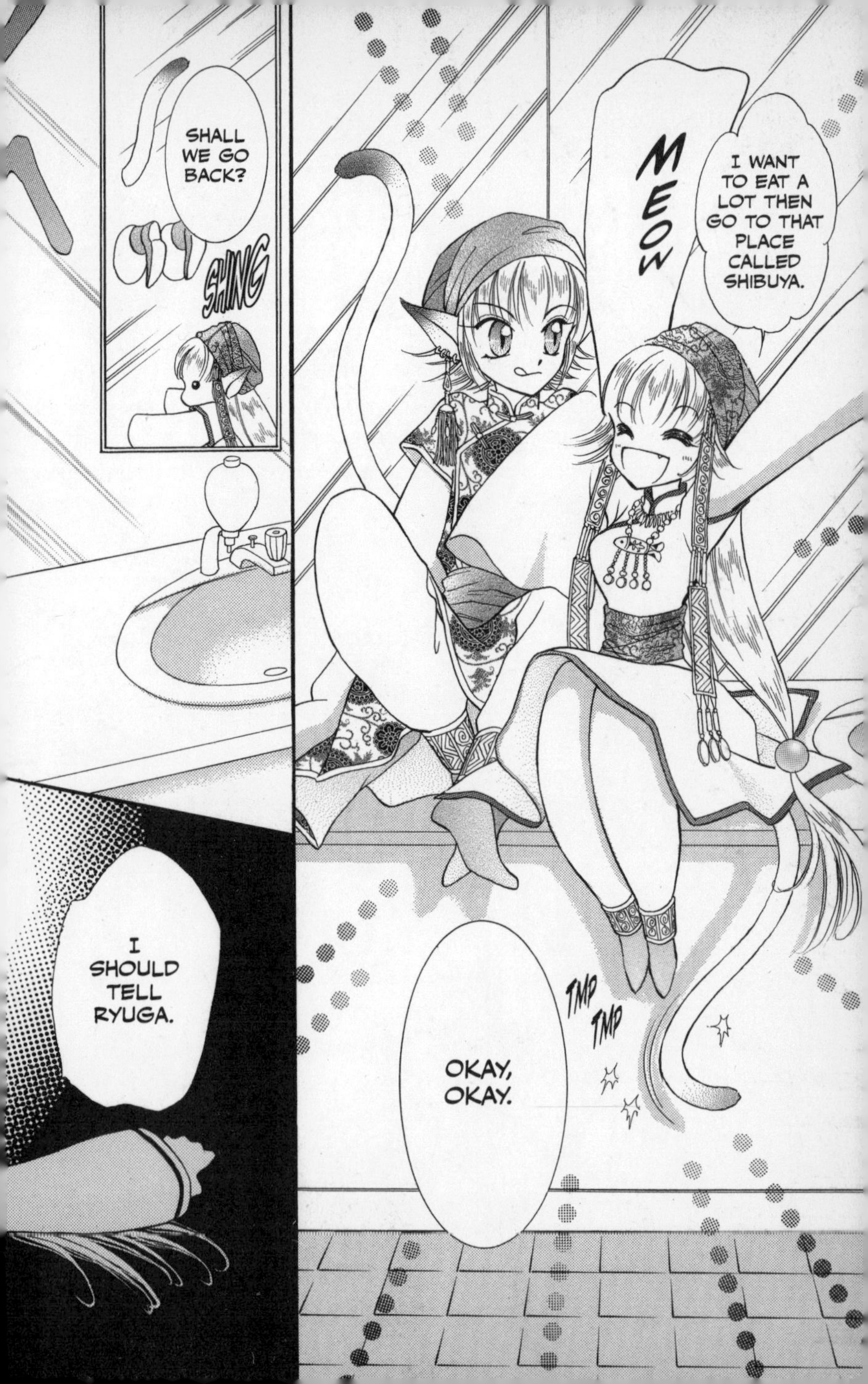
I WANT TO EAT A LOT THEN GO TO THAT PLACE CALLED SHIBUYA.
MEOW
TMP TMP
OKAY, OKAY.
SHALL WE GO BACK?
SHING
I SHOULD TELL RYUGA.

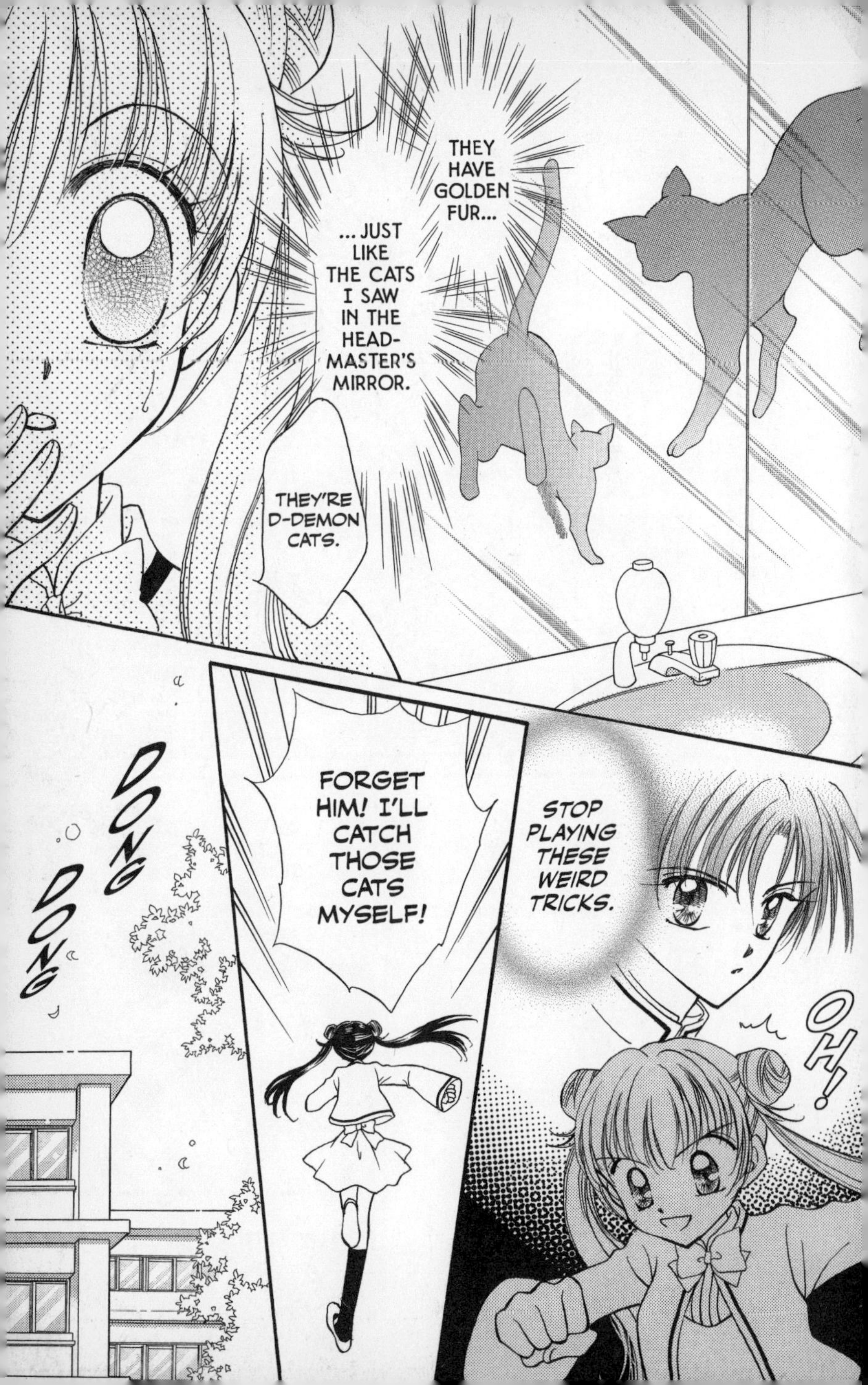
THEY HAVE GOLDEN FUR...
...JUST LIKE THE CATS I SAW IN THE HEAD-MASTER'S MIRROR.
THEY'RE D-DEMON CATS.
STOP PLAYING THESE WEIRD TRICKS.
OH!
FORGET HIM! I'LL CATCH THOSE CATS MYSELF!
DONG
DONG

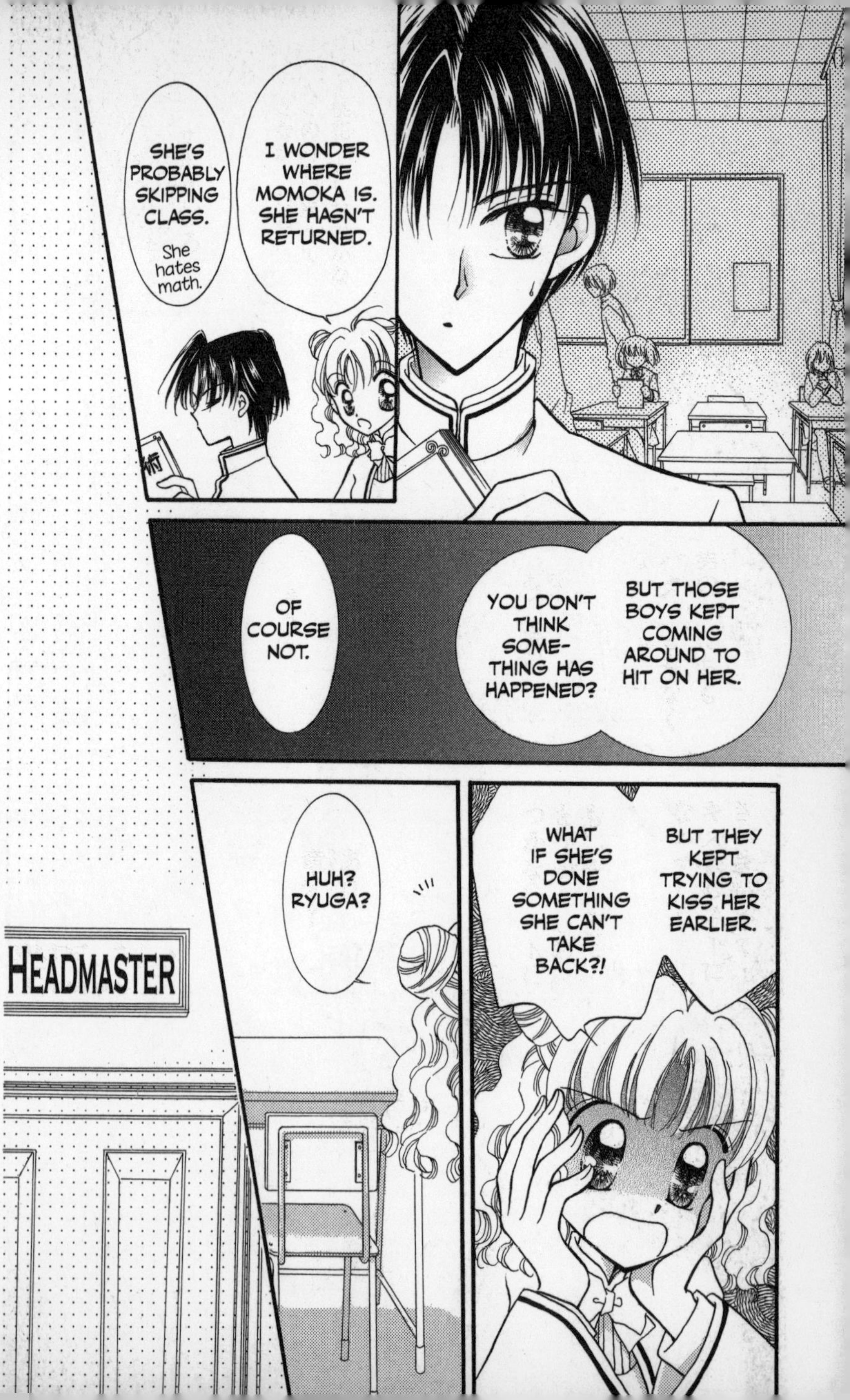
I WONDER WHERE MOMOKA IS. SHE HASN'T RETURNED.
SHE'S PROBABLY SKIPPING CLASS.
She hates math.
BUT THOSE BOYS KEPT COMING AROUND TO HIT ON HER.
YOU DON'T THINK SOME-THING HAS HAPPENED?
OF COURSE NOT.
BUT THEY KEPT TRYING TO KISS HER EARLIER.
WHAT IF SHE'S DONE SOMETHING SHE CAN'T TAKE BACK?!
HUH? RYUGA?
HEADMASTER

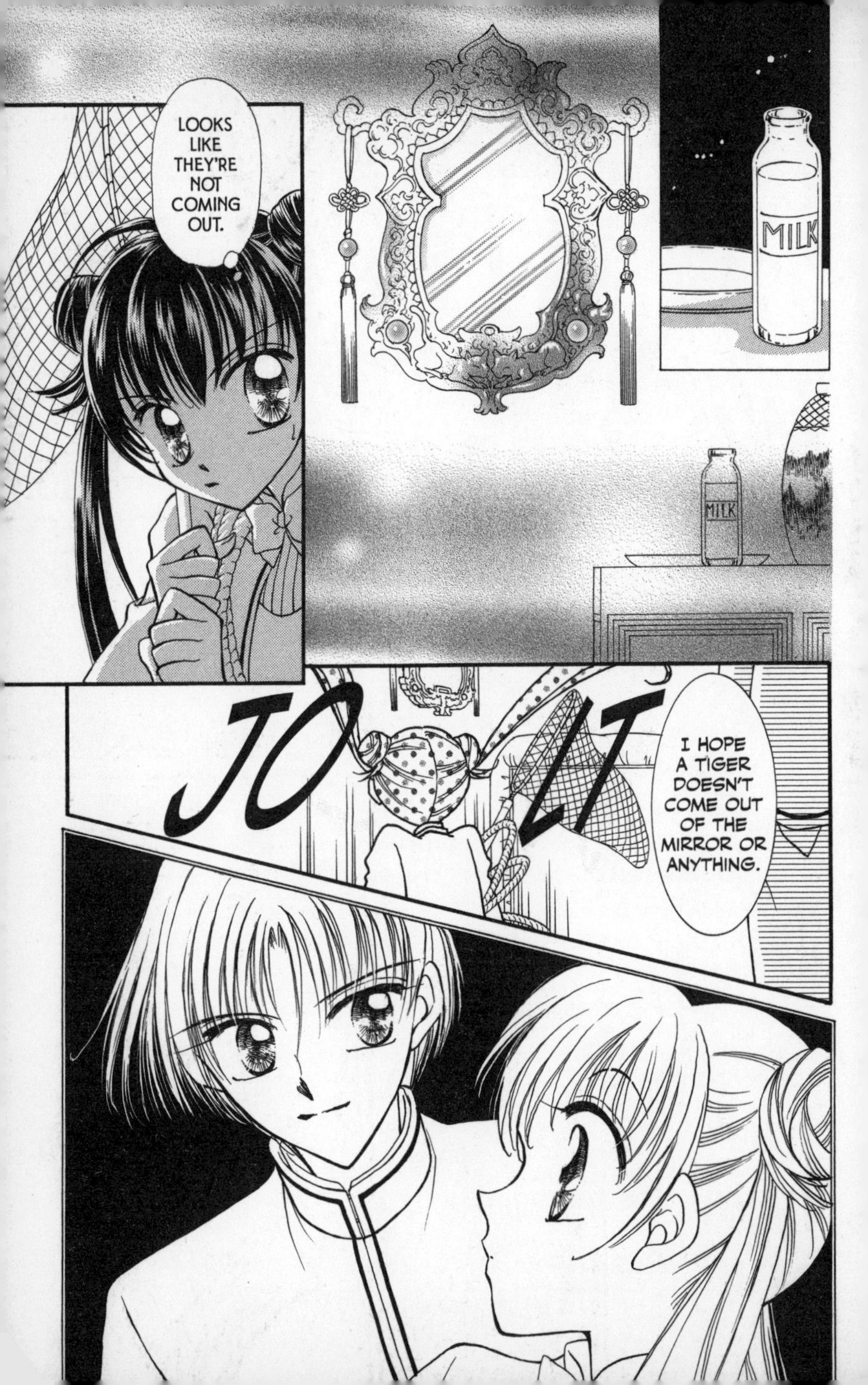
LOOKS LIKE THEY'RE NOT COMING OUT.
I HOPE A TIGER DOESN'T COME OUT OF THE MIRROR OR ANYTHING.
JOLT

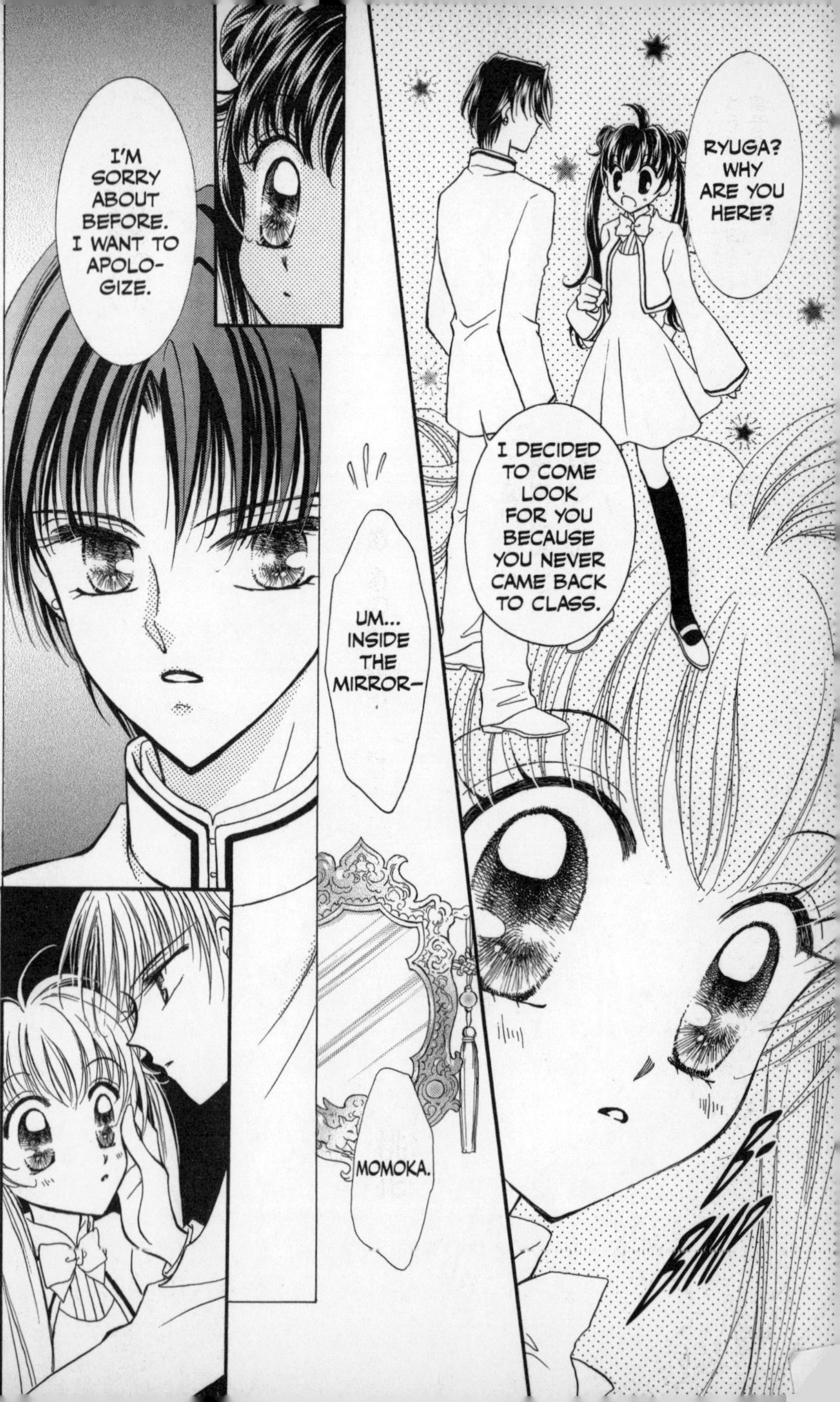
RYUGA? WHY ARE YOU HERE?
I DECIDED TO COME LOOK FOR YOU BECAUSE YOU NEVER CAME BACK TO CLASS.
UM... INSIDE THE MIRROR—
I'M SORRY ABOUT BEFORE. I WANT TO APOLOGIZE.
MOMOKA.

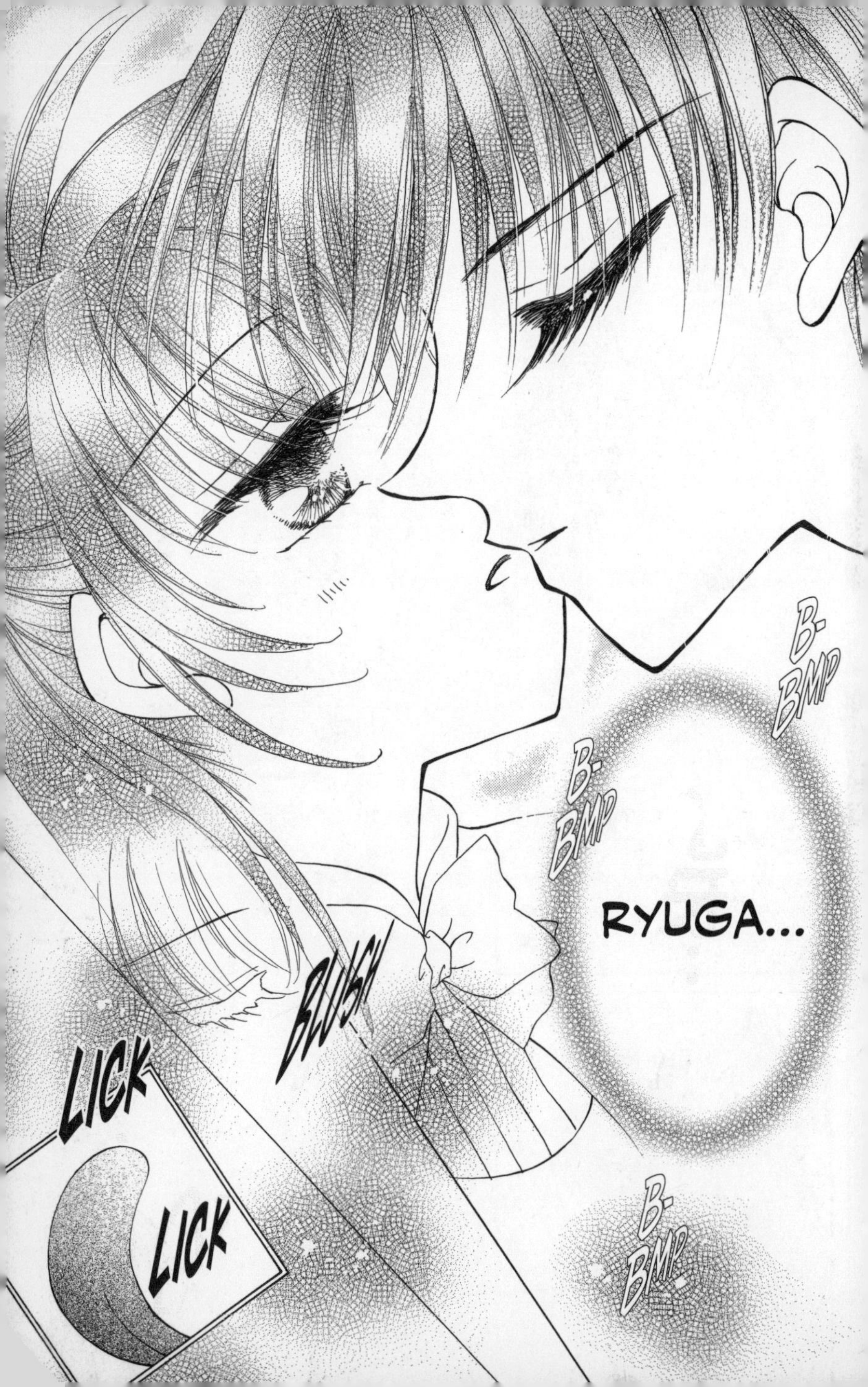
B-BMP
B-BMP
RYUGA...
BLUSH
B-BMP
LICK
LICK

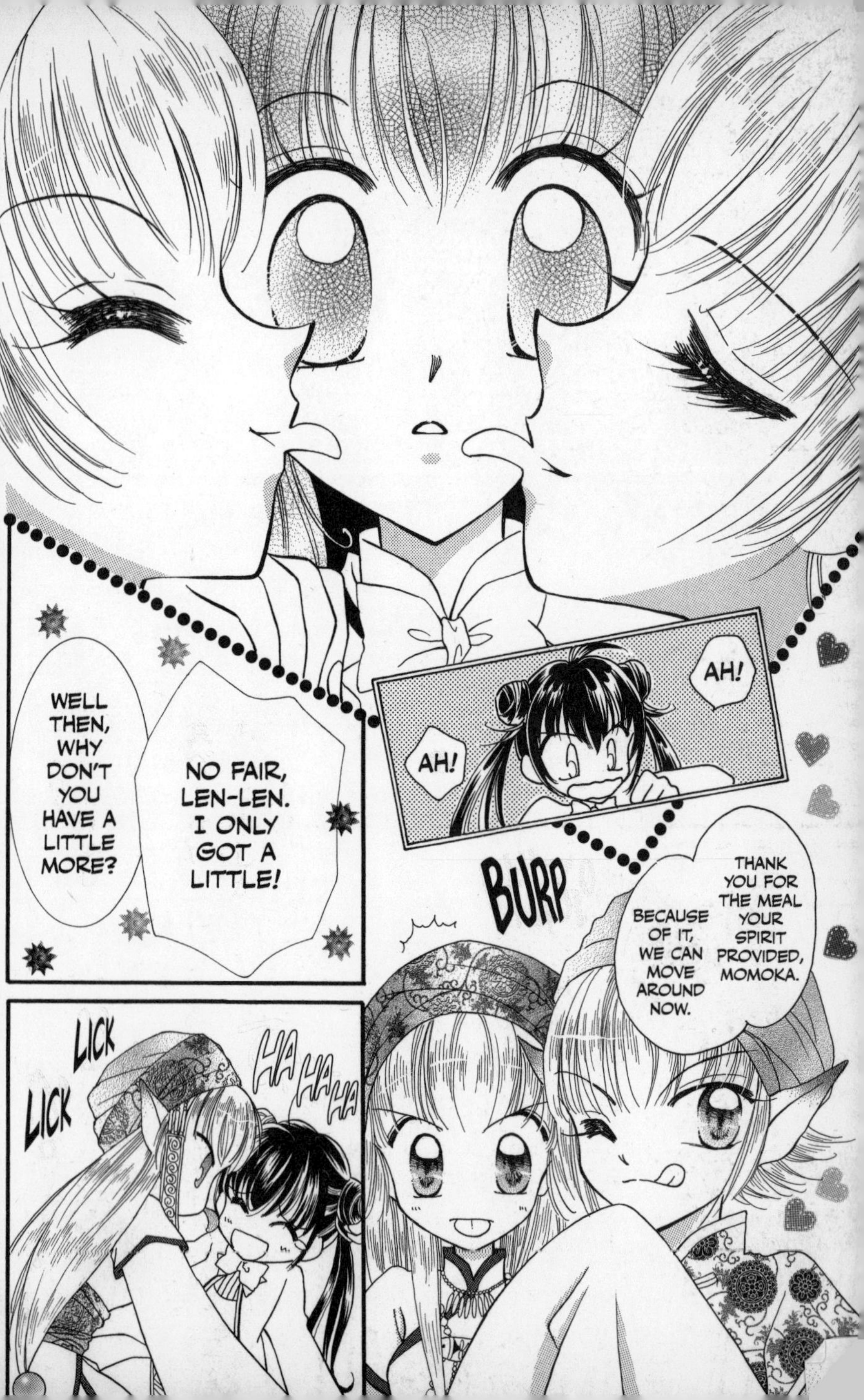
AH!
AH!
NO FAIR, LEN-LEN. I ONLY GOT A LITTLE!
WELL THEN, WHY DON'T YOU HAVE A LITTLE MORE?
BURP
THANK YOU FOR THE MEAL YOUR SPIRIT PROVIDED, MOMOKA.
BECAUSE OF IT, WE CAN MOVE AROUND NOW.
HA HA HA HA
LICK LICK

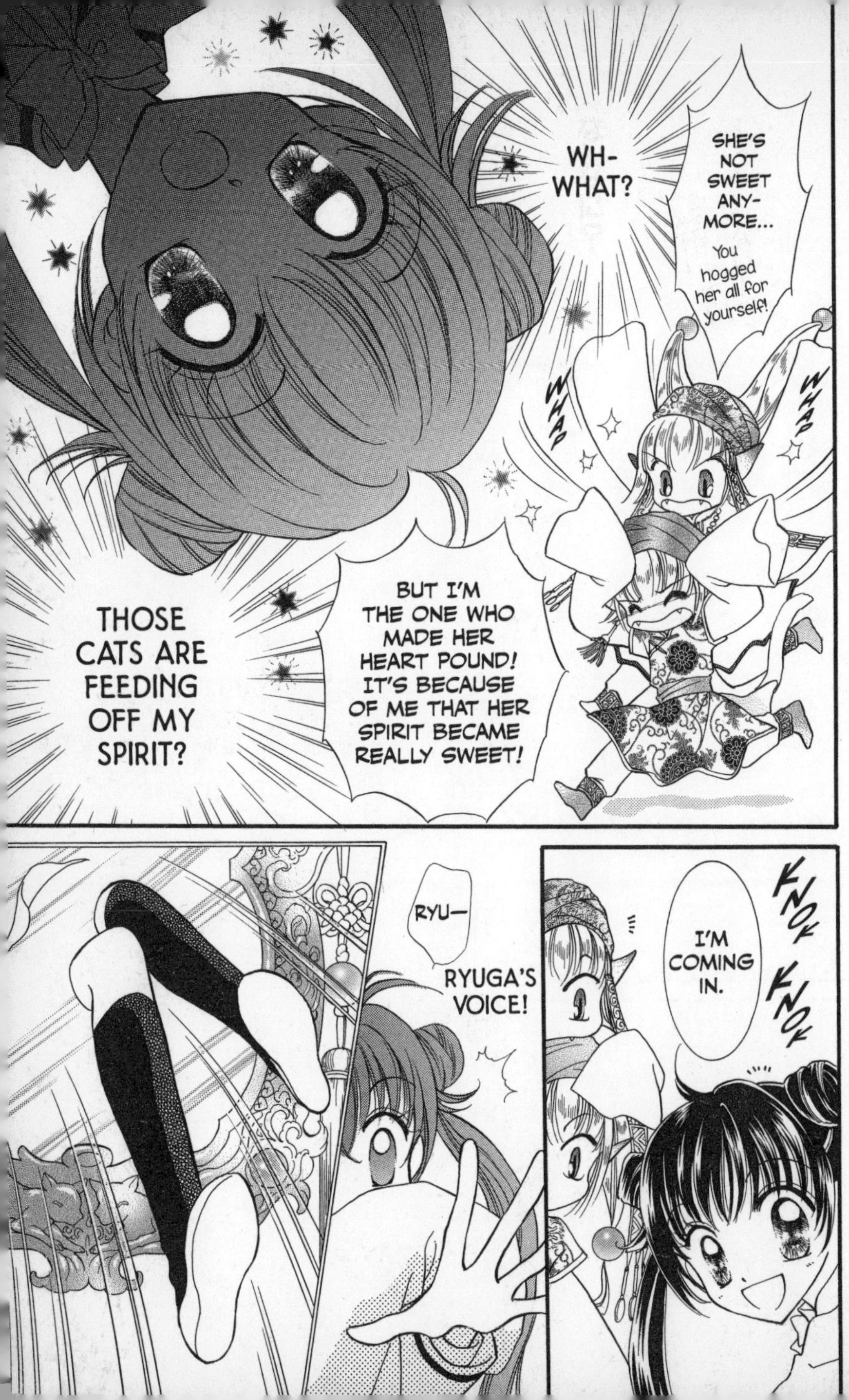
SHE'S NOT SWEET ANY-MORE...
You hogged her all for yourself!
WH-WHAT?
WHAP
WHAP
BUT I'M THE ONE WHO MADE HER HEART POUND! IT'S BECAUSE OF ME THAT HER SPIRIT BECAME REALLY SWEET!
THOSE CATS ARE FEEDING OFF MY SPIRIT?
KNOK KNOK
I'M COMING IN.
RYU—
RYUGA'S VOICE!

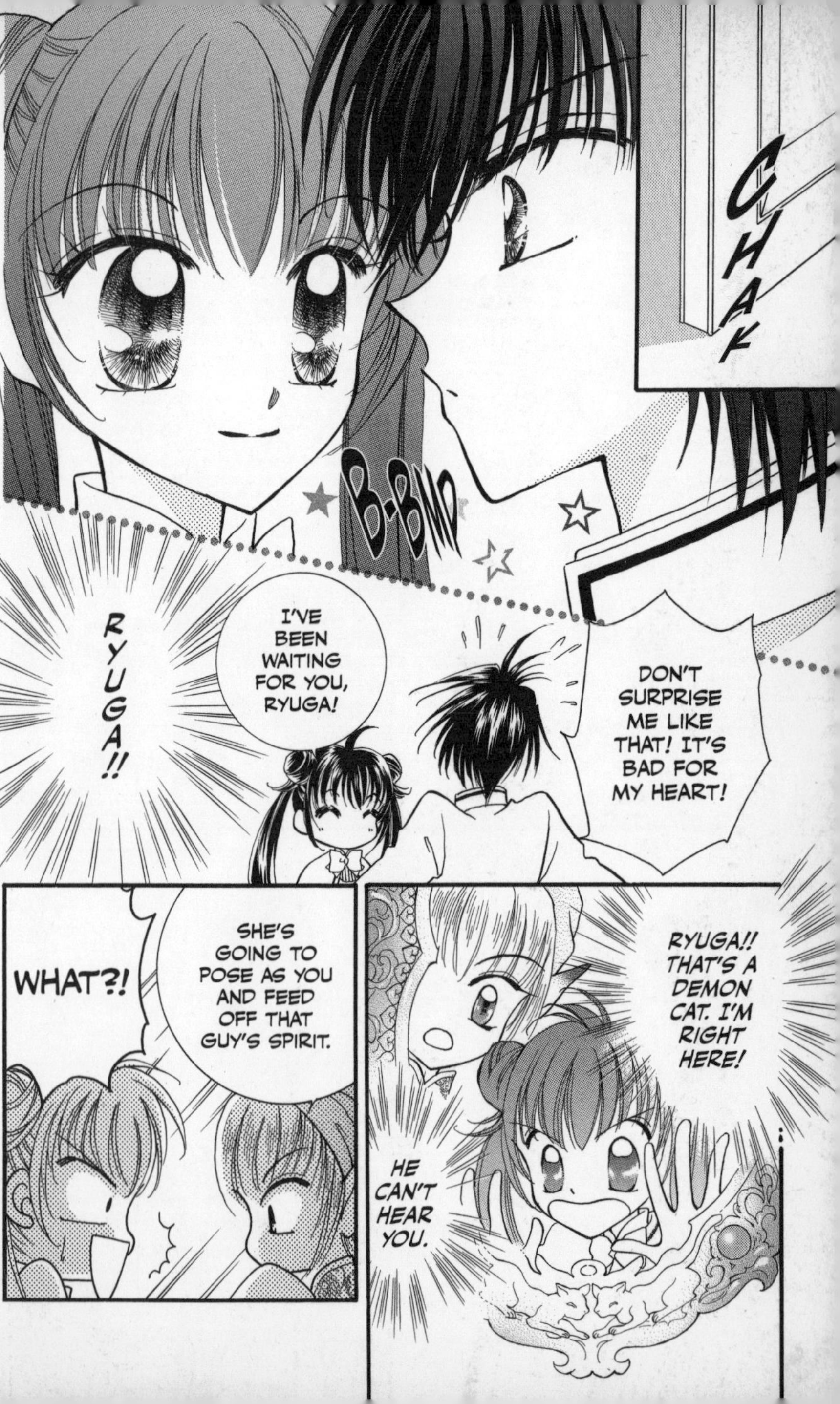
CHAK
B-BMP
DON'T SURPRISE ME LIKE THAT! IT'S BAD FOR MY HEART!
I'VE BEEN WAITING FOR YOU, RYUGA!
RYUGA!!
RYUGA!! THAT'S A DEMON CAT. I'M RIGHT HERE!
HE CAN'T HEAR YOU.
SHE'S GOING TO POSE AS YOU AND FEED OFF THAT GUY'S SPIRIT.
WHAT?!

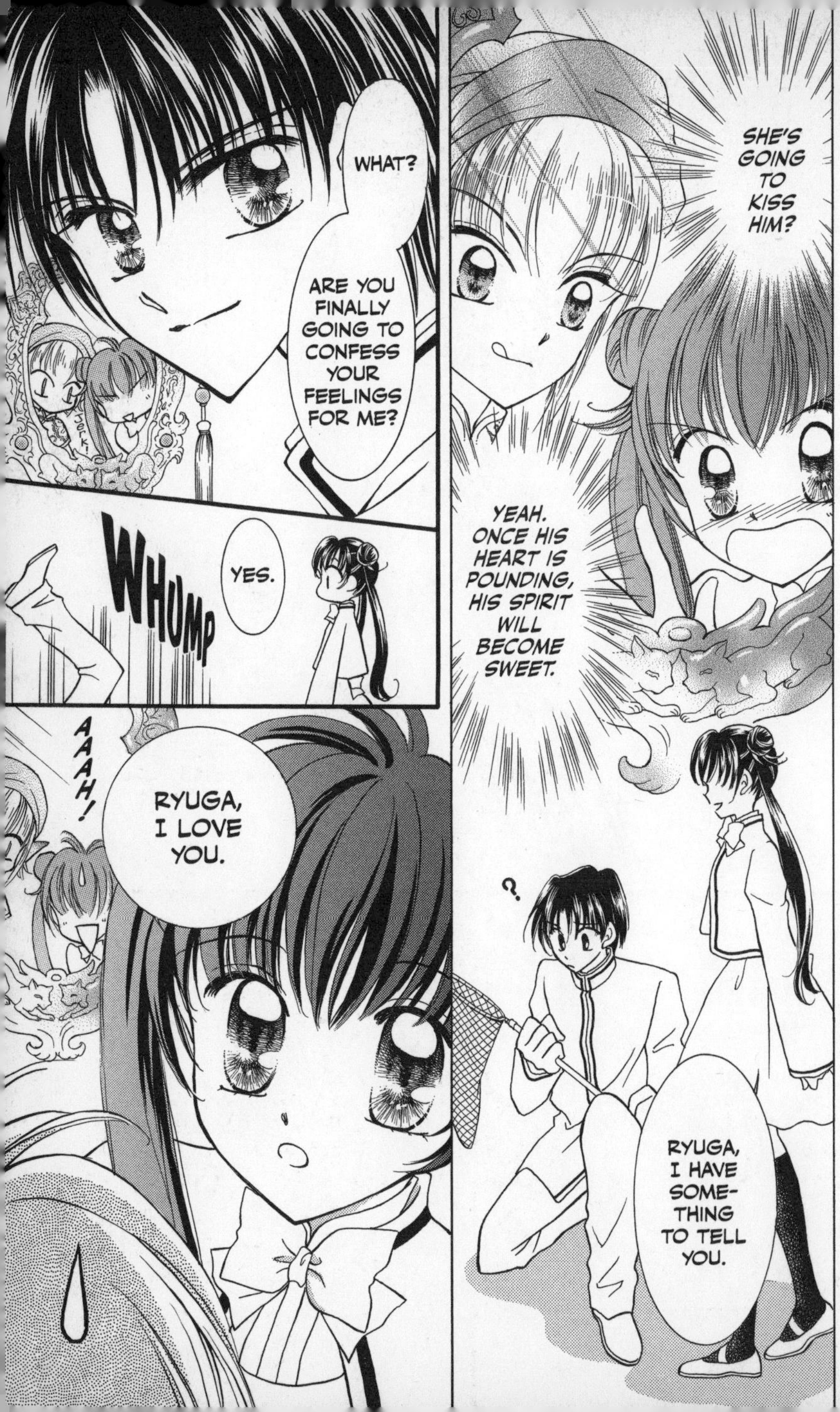
SHE'S GOING TO KISS HIM?
YEAH. ONCE HIS HEART IS POUNDING, HIS SPIRIT WILL BECOME SWEET.
?
RYUGA, I HAVE SOME-THING TO TELL YOU.
WHAT?
ARE YOU FINALLY GOING TO CONFESS YOUR FEELINGS FOR ME?
Jerk!
YES.
WHUMP
AAAH!
RYUGA, I LOVE YOU.

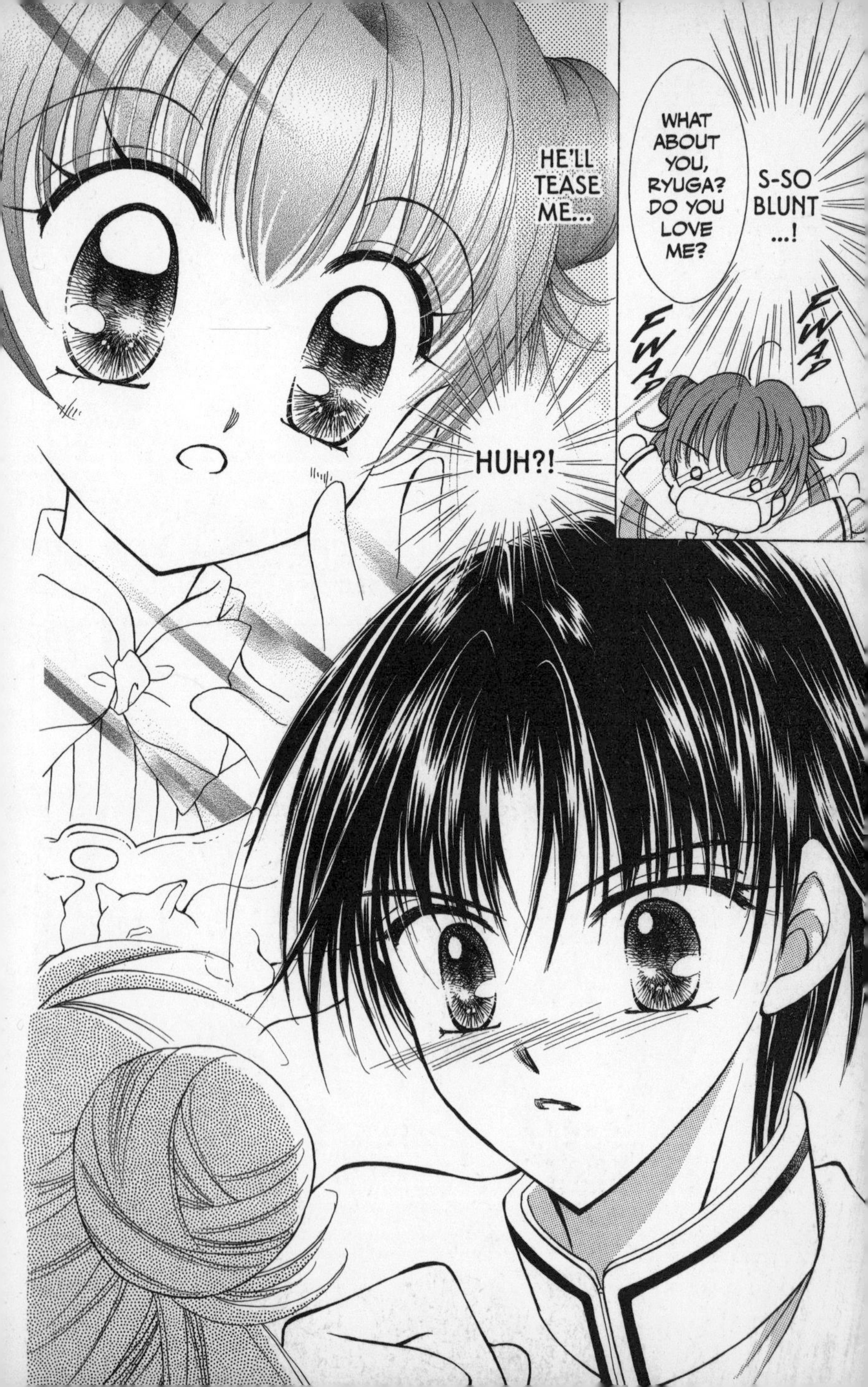
WHAT ABOUT YOU, RYUGA? DO YOU LOVE ME?
S-SO BLUNT ...!
FWAP
FWAP
HE'LL TEASE ME...
HUH?!

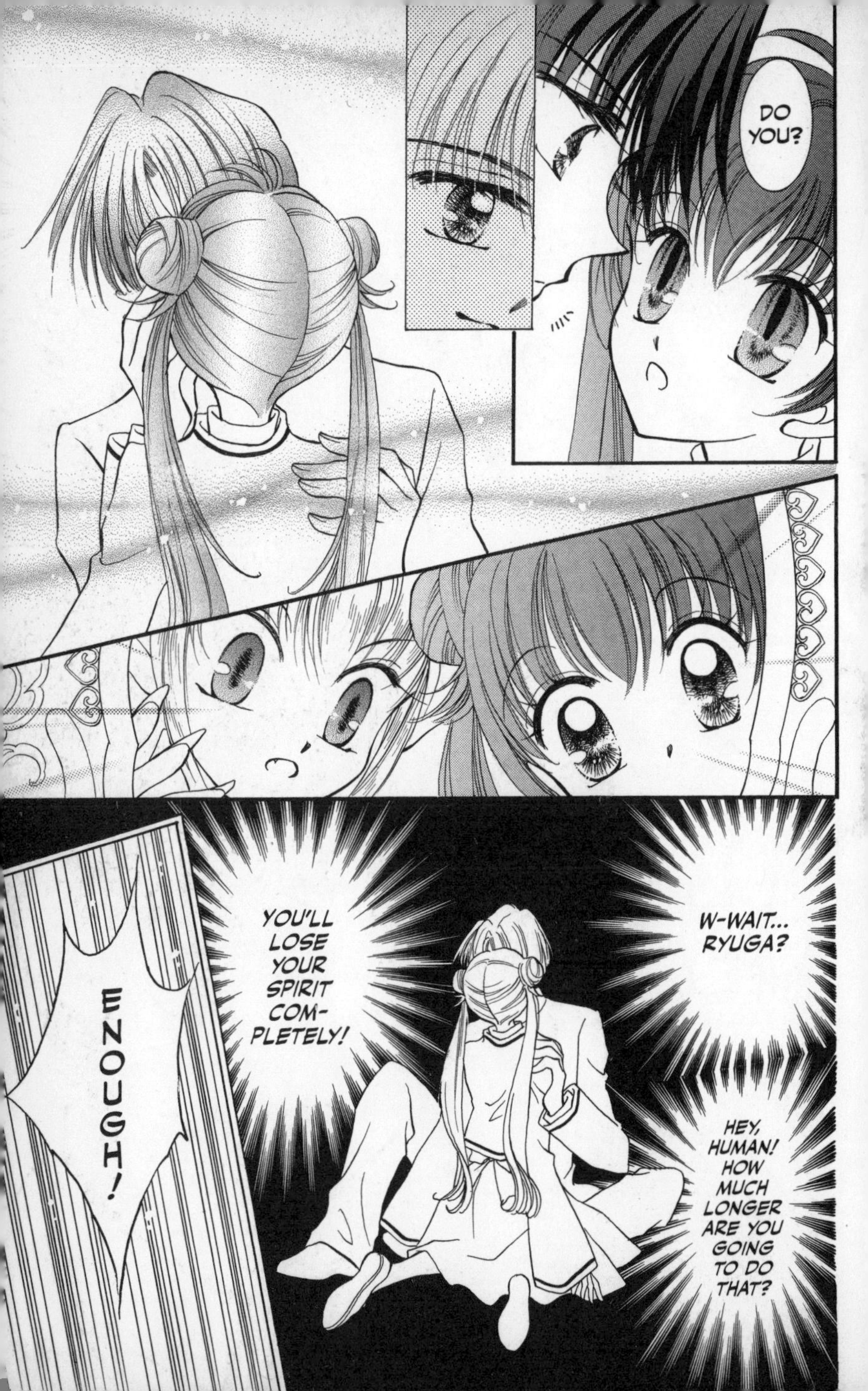
DO YOU?
W-WAIT... RYUGA?
HEY, HUMAN! HOW MUCH LONGER ARE YOU GOING TO DO THAT?
YOU'LL LOSE YOUR SPIRIT COM-PLETELY!
ENOUGH!

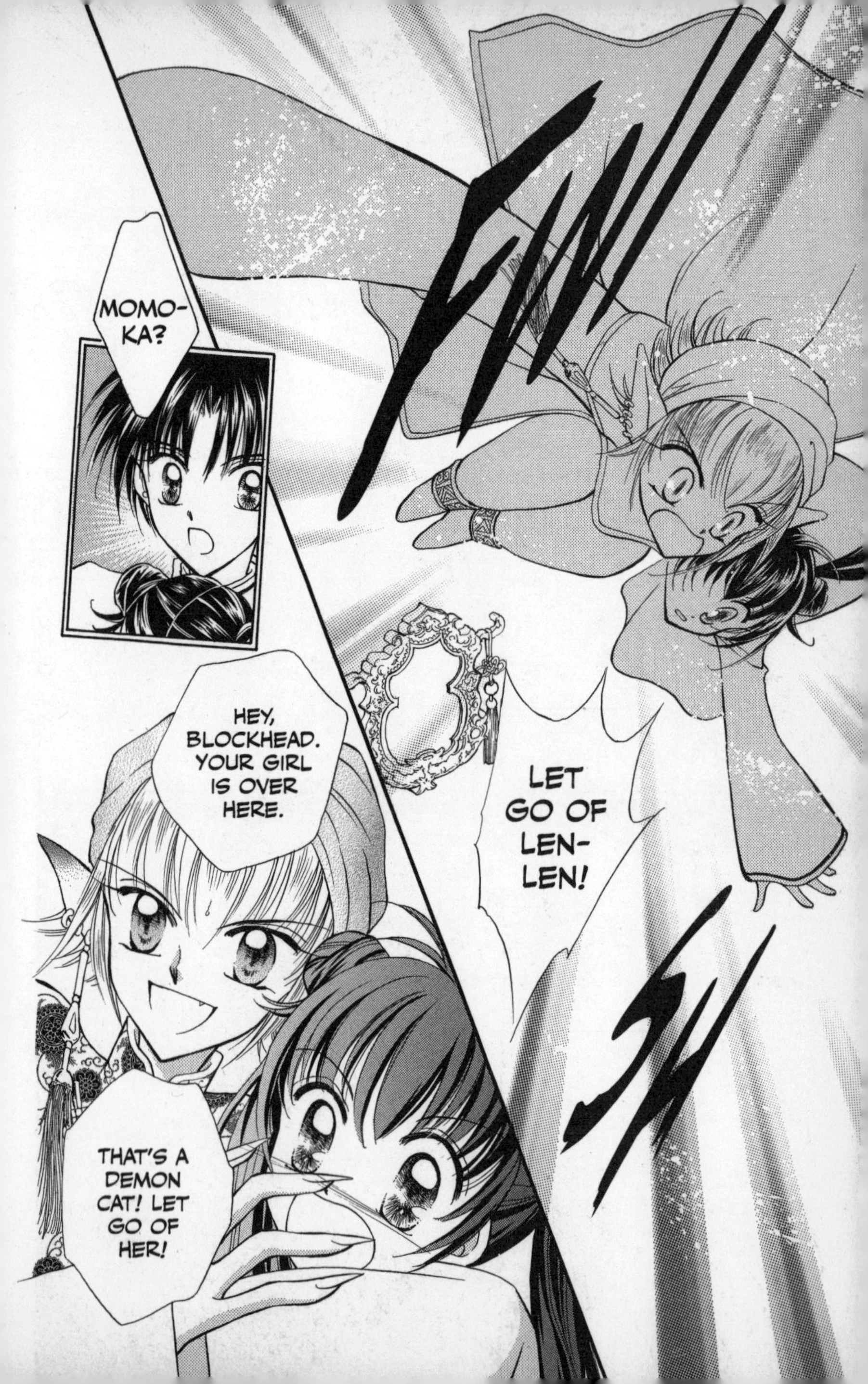
MOMO-KA?
LET GO OF LEN-LEN!
HEY, BLOCKHEAD. YOUR GIRL IS OVER HERE.
THAT'S A DEMON CAT! LET GO OF HER!

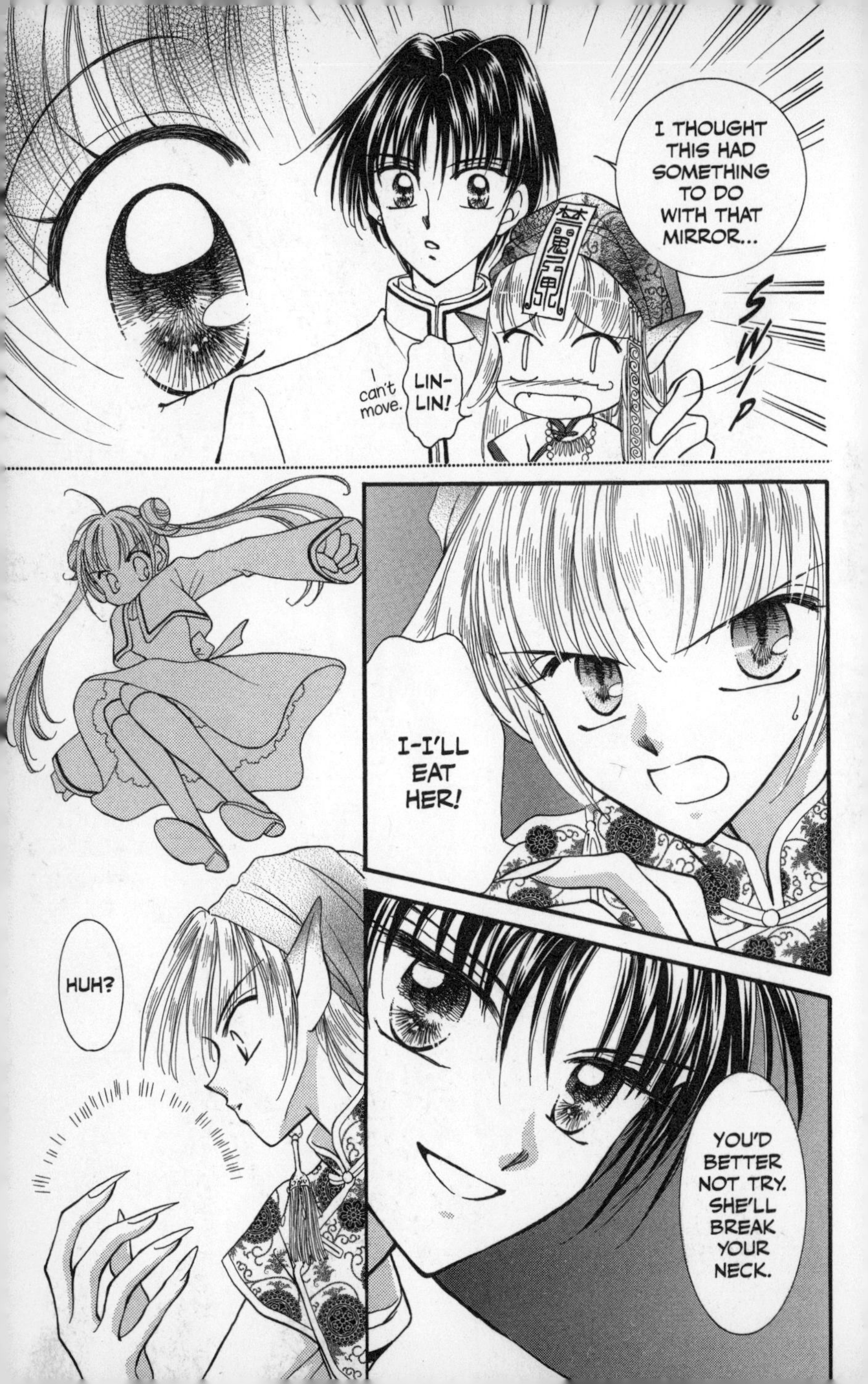
I THOUGHT THIS HAD SOMETHING TO DO WITH THAT MIRROR...
SWIP
LIN-LIN!
I can't move.
I-I'LL EAT HER!
YOU'D BETTER NOT TRY. SHE'LL BREAK YOUR NECK.
HUH?

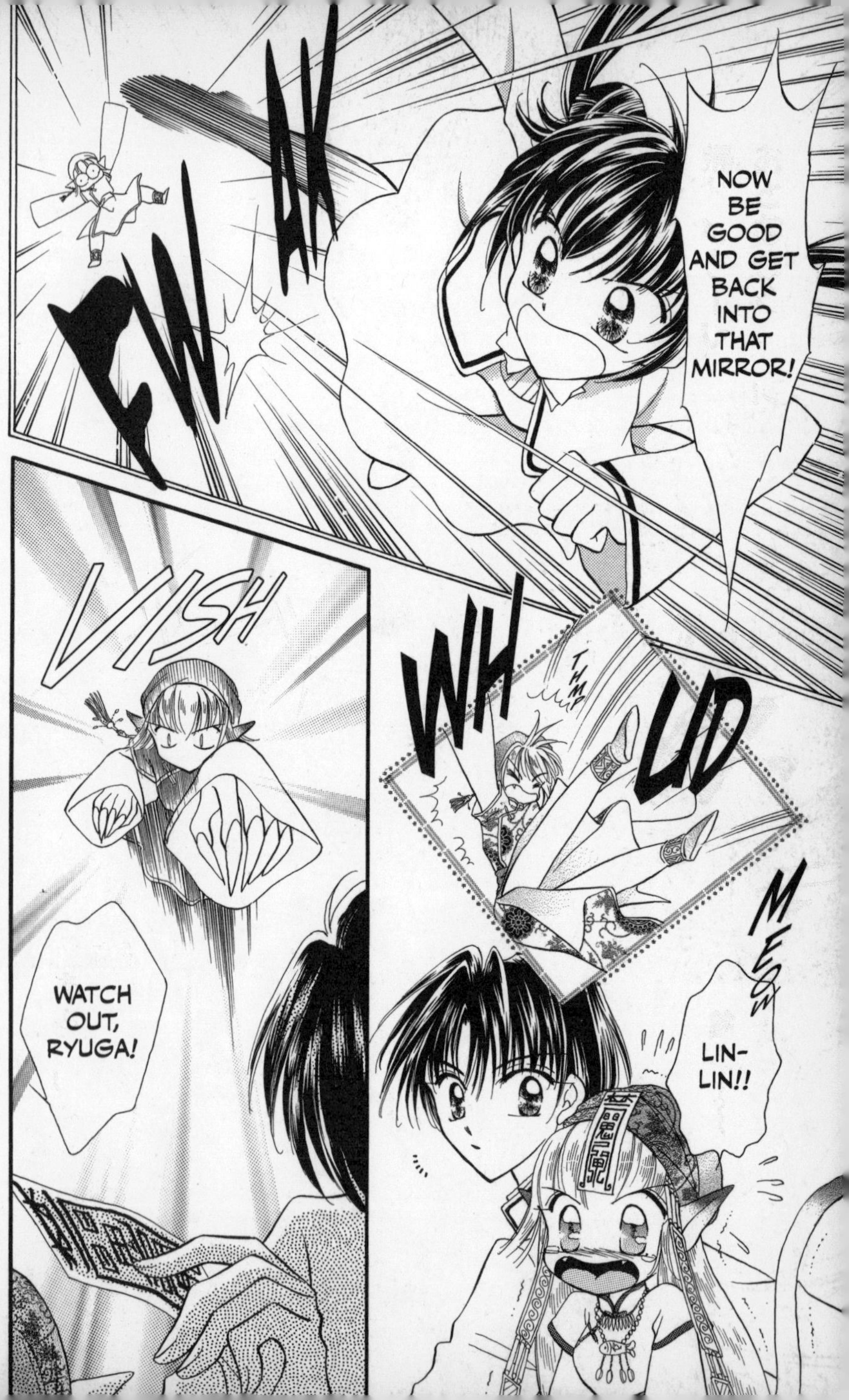
NOW BE GOOD AND GET BACK INTO THAT MIRROR!
FWAK
WHUD
THMP
MEOW
LIN-LIN!!
VISH
WATCH OUT, RYUGA!

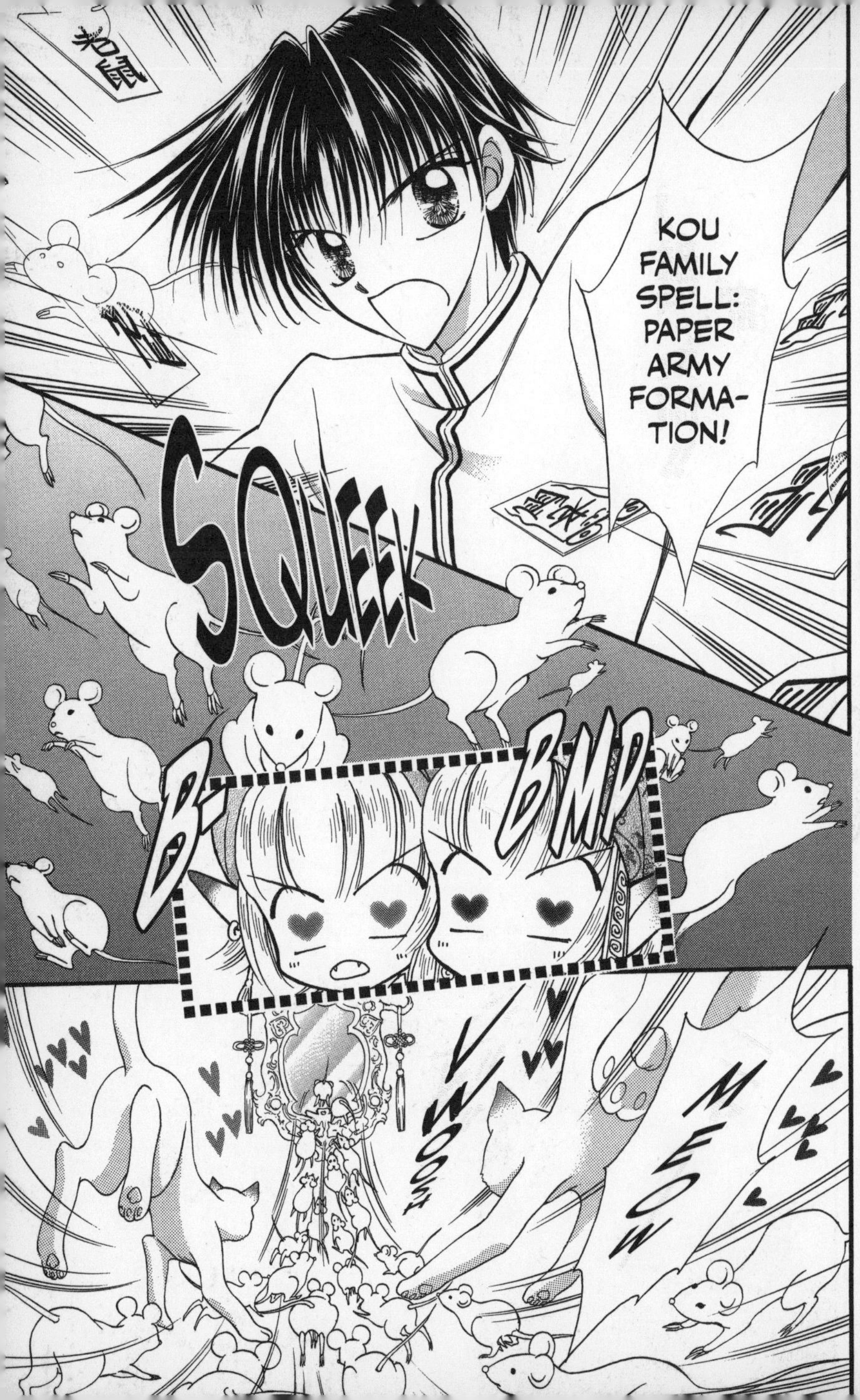
KOU FAMILY SPELL: PAPER ARMY FORMATION!
SQUEEK
B-BMP
MEOW
VWOOM!

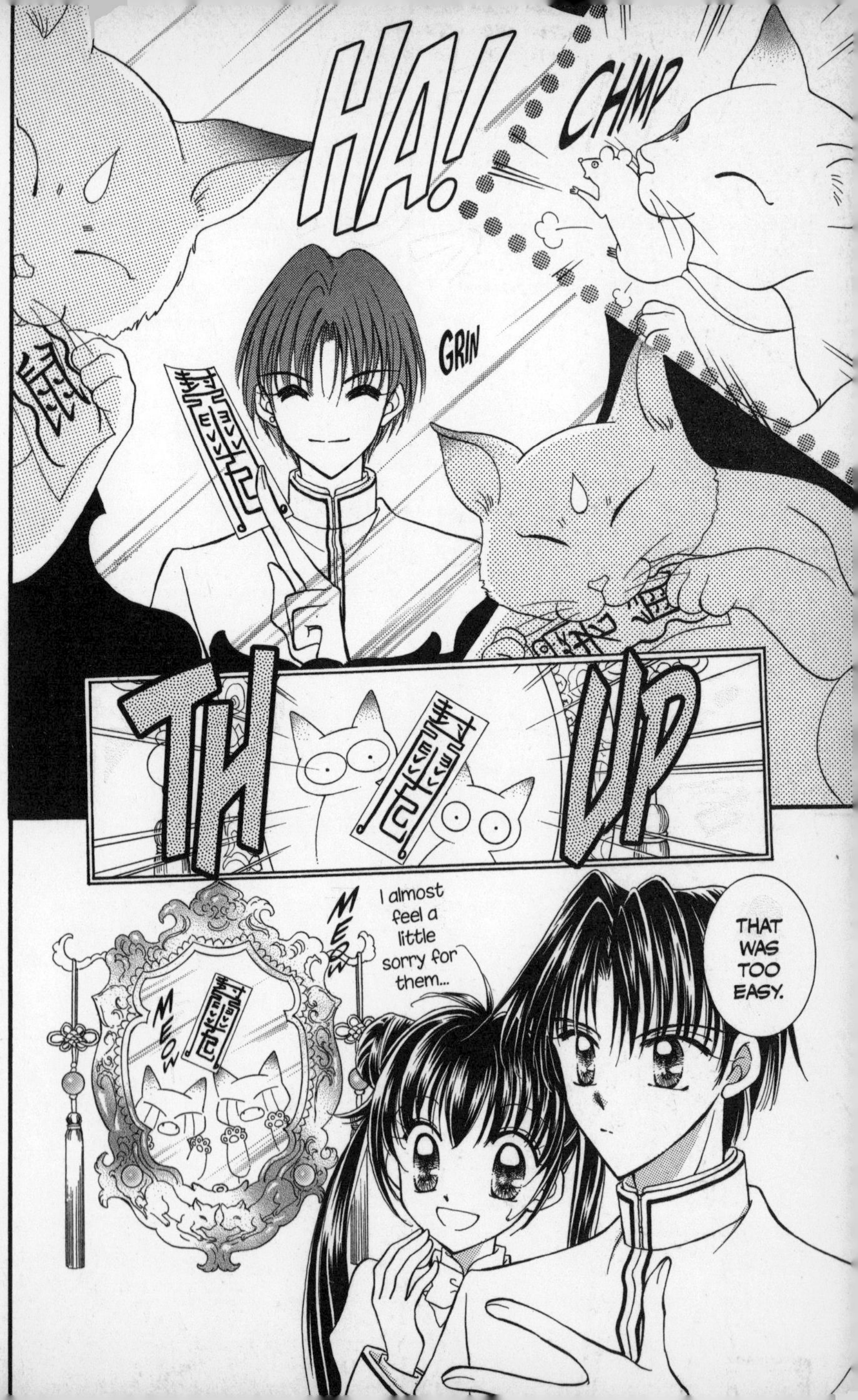
CHMP
HA!
GRIN
TH
UP
THAT WAS TOO EASY.
I almost feel a little sorry for them...
MEOW
MEOW

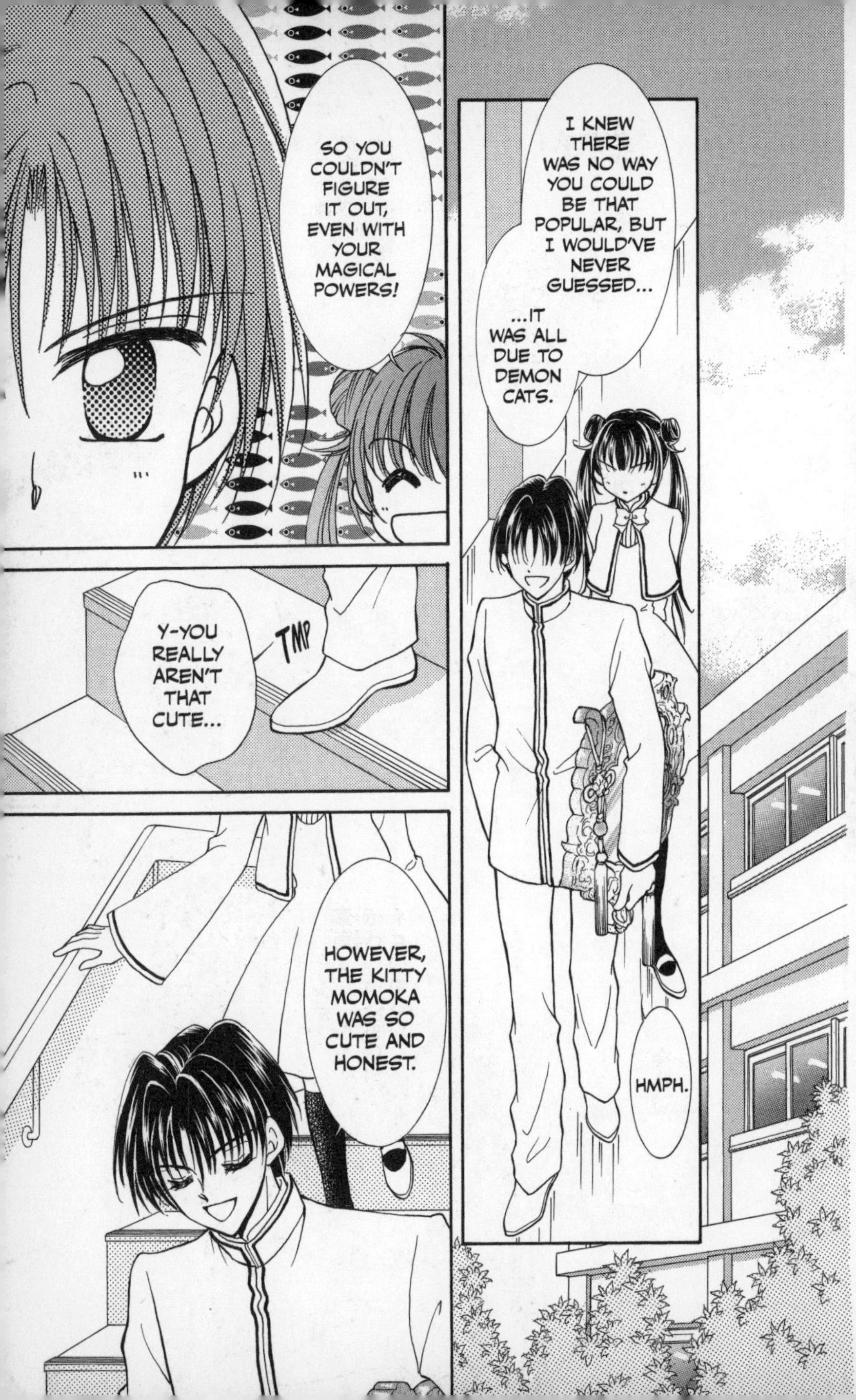
I KNEW THERE WAS NO WAY YOU COULD BE THAT POPULAR, BUT I WOULD'VE NEVER GUESSED...
...IT WAS ALL DUE TO DEMON CATS.
HMPH.
SO YOU COULDN'T FIGURE IT OUT, EVEN WITH YOUR MAGICAL POWERS!
...
Y-YOU REALLY AREN'T THAT CUTE...
TMP
HOWEVER, THE KITTY MOMOKA WAS SO CUTE AND HONEST.

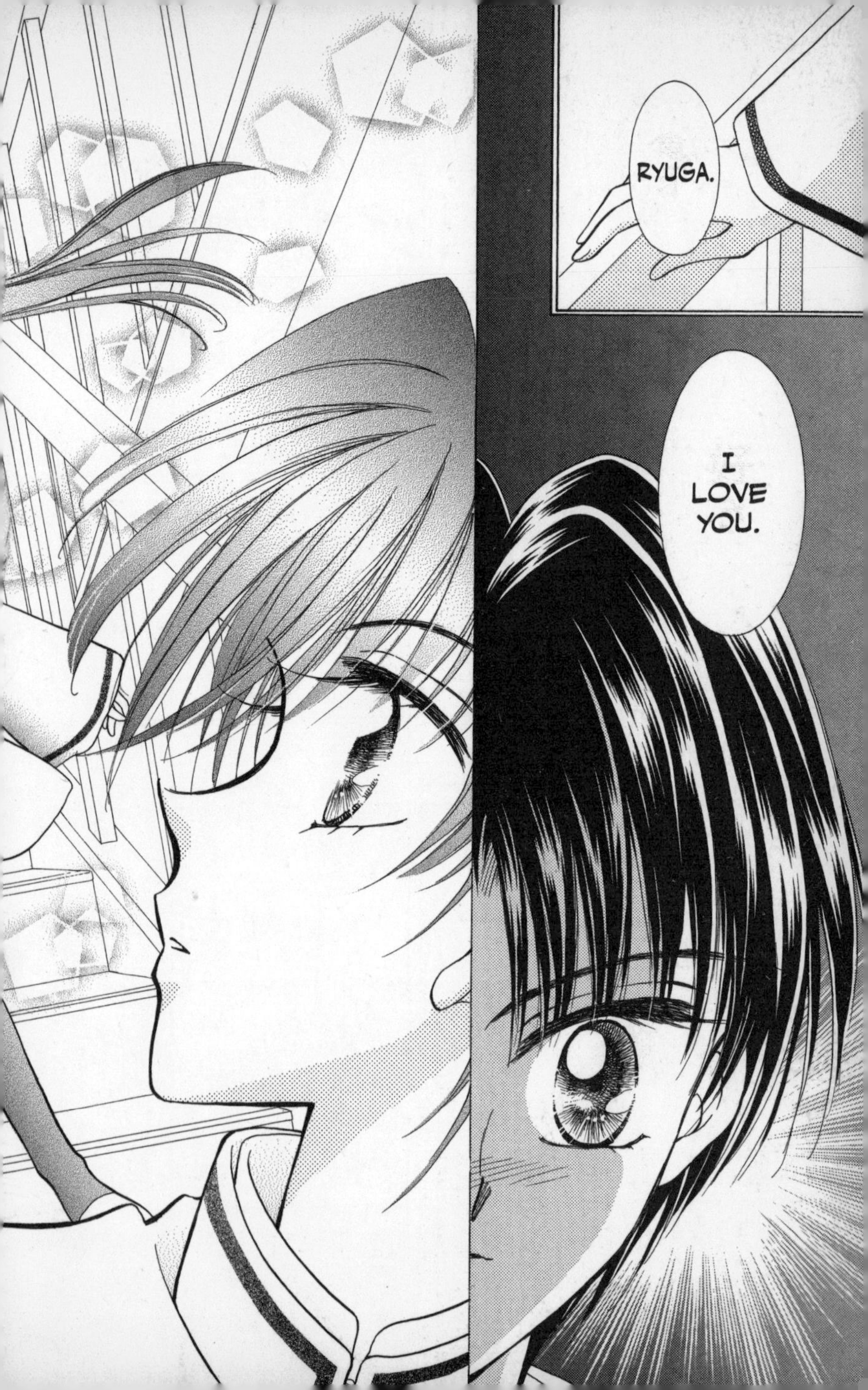
RYUGA.
I LOVE YOU.

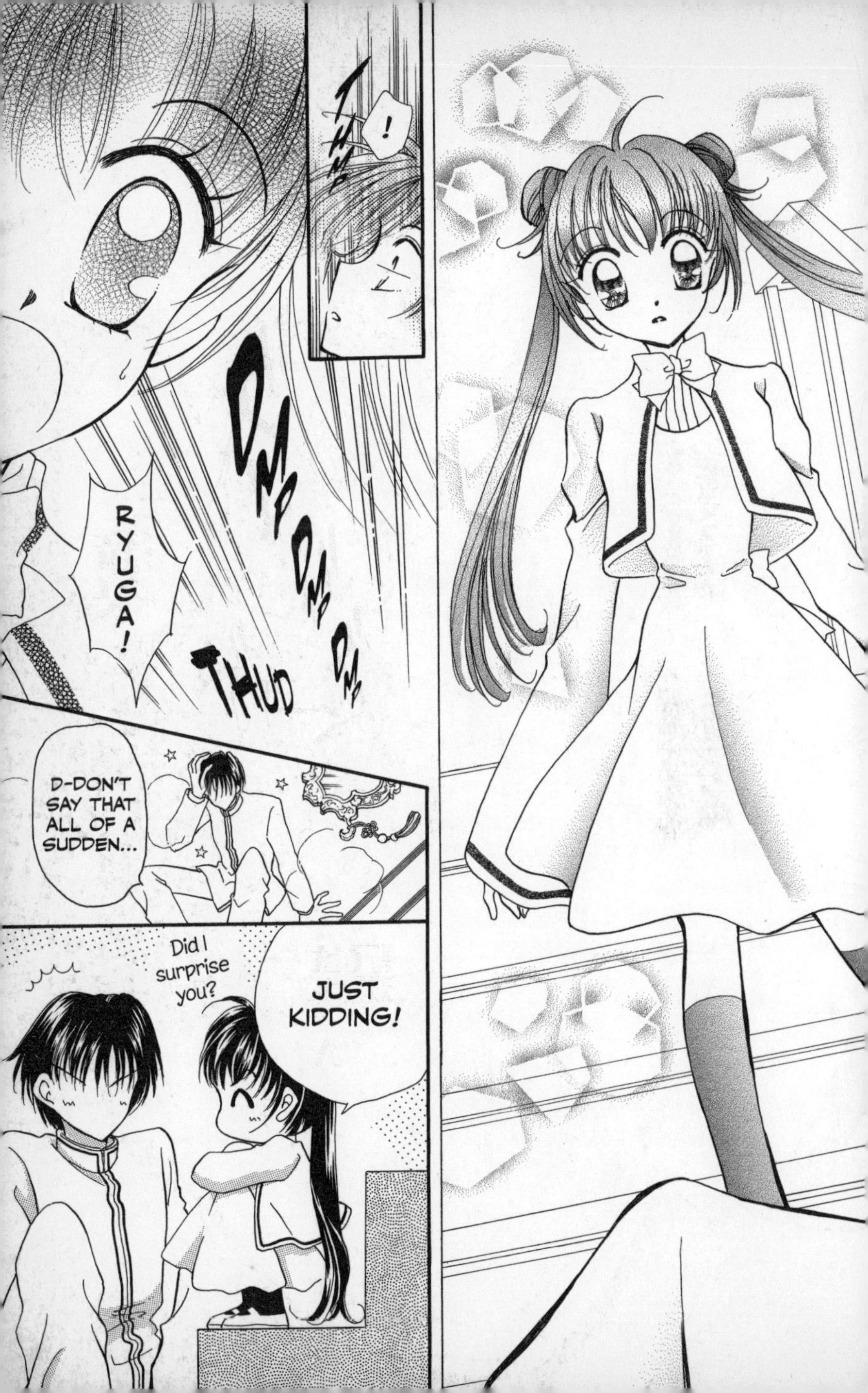
!
RYUGA!
DMP DMP DMP DMP
THUD
D-DON'T SAY THAT ALL OF A SUDDEN...
JUST KIDDING!
Did I surprise you?

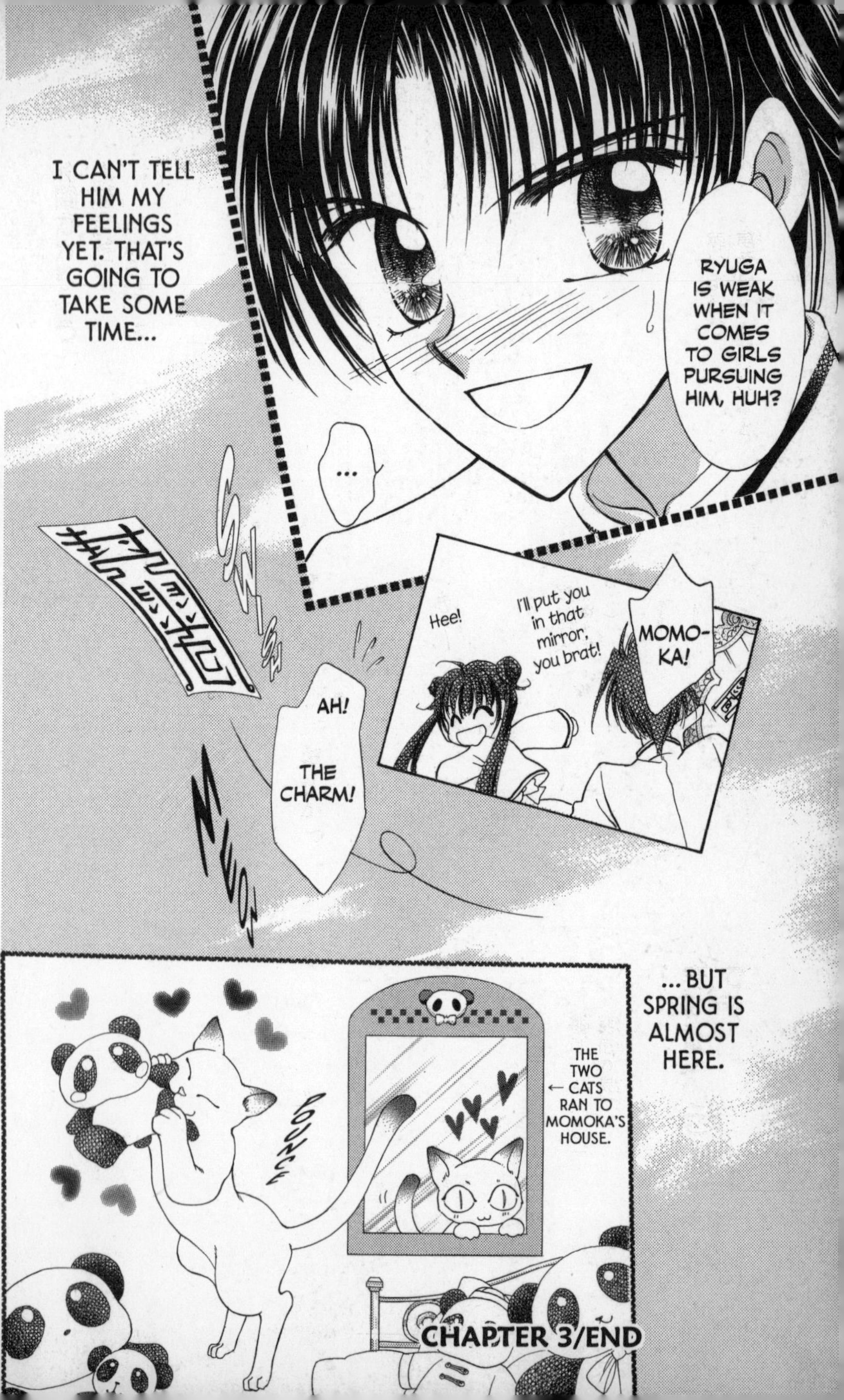
RYUGA IS WEAK WHEN IT COMES TO GIRLS PURSUING HIM, HUH?
...
I CAN'T TELL HIM MY FEELINGS YET. THAT'S GOING TO TAKE SOME TIME...
MOMO-KA!
I'll put you in that mirror, you brat!
Hee!
AH!
THE CHARM!
... BUT SPRING IS ALMOST HERE.
THE TWO ← CATS RAN TO MOMOKA'S HOUSE.
BOUNCE
CHAPTER 3/END

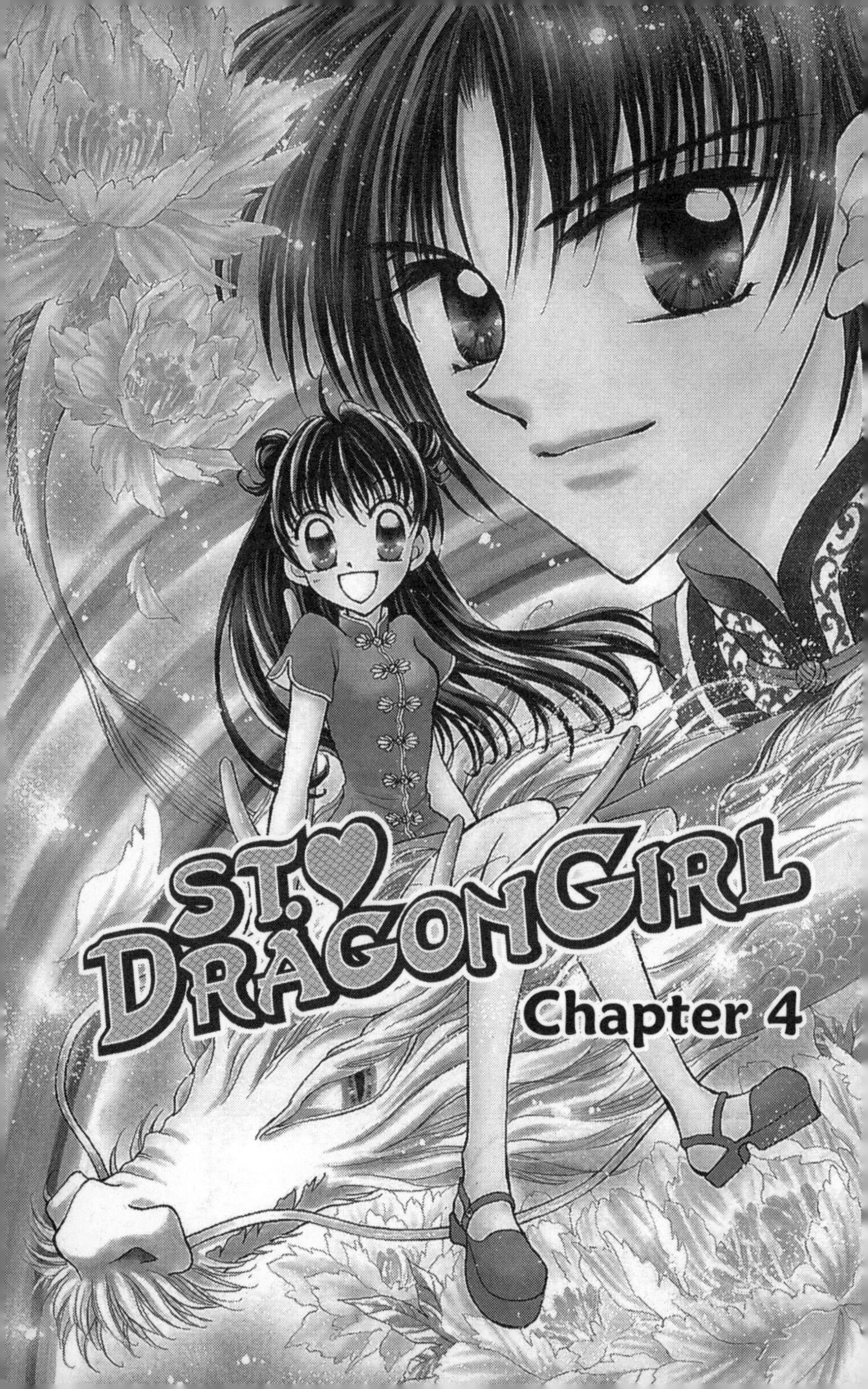
ST.♥ DRAGON GIRL
Chapter 4

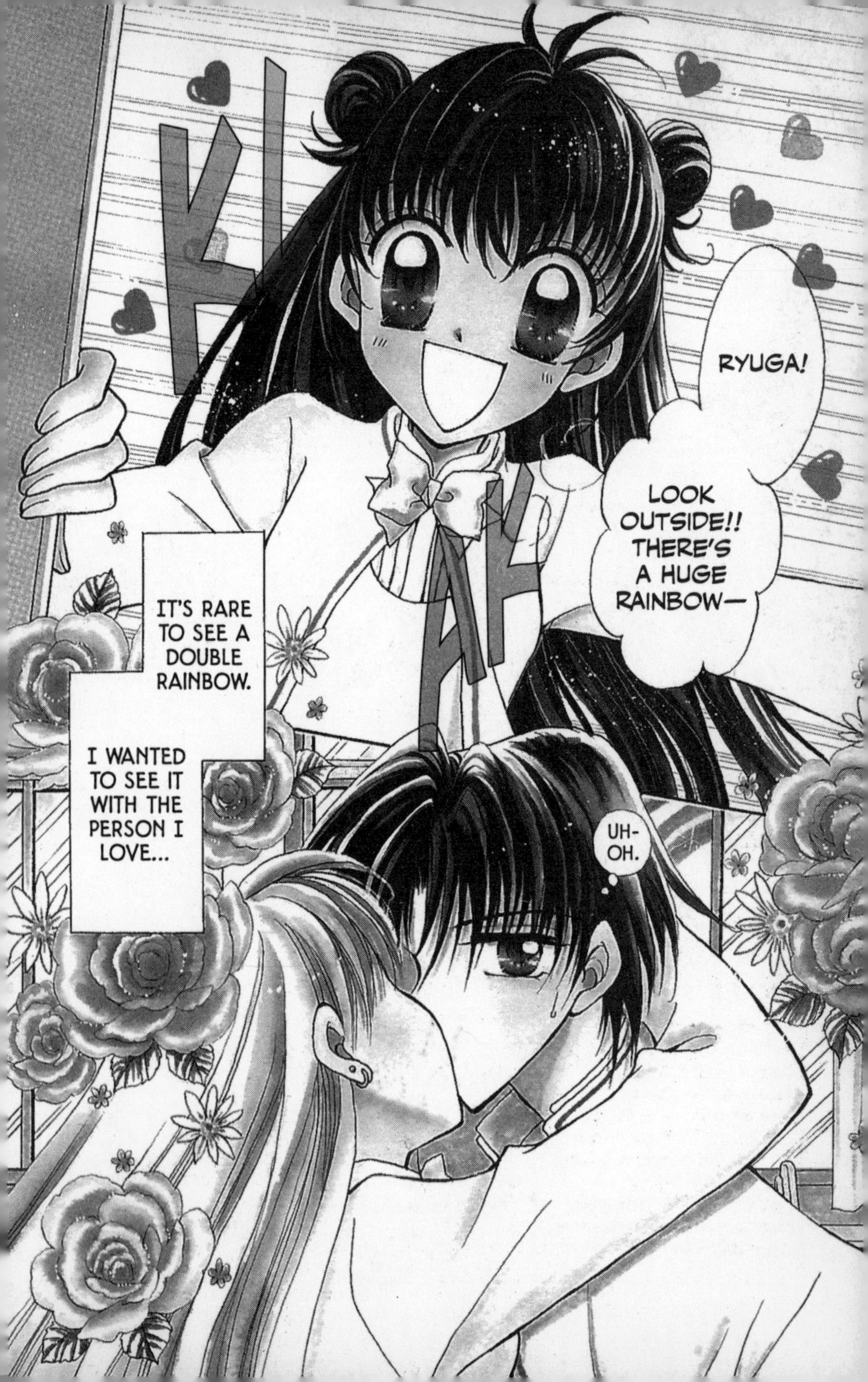
RYUGA!
LOOK OUTSIDE!! THERE'S A HUGE RAINBOW—
IT'S RARE TO SEE A DOUBLE RAINBOW.
I WANTED TO SEE IT WITH THE PERSON I LOVE...
UH-OH.

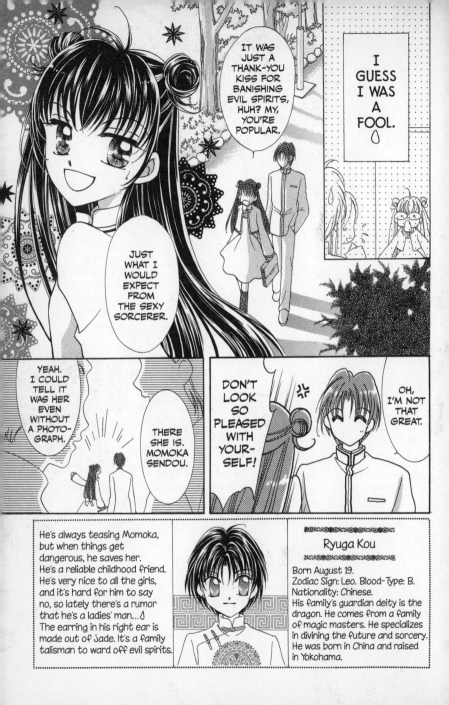

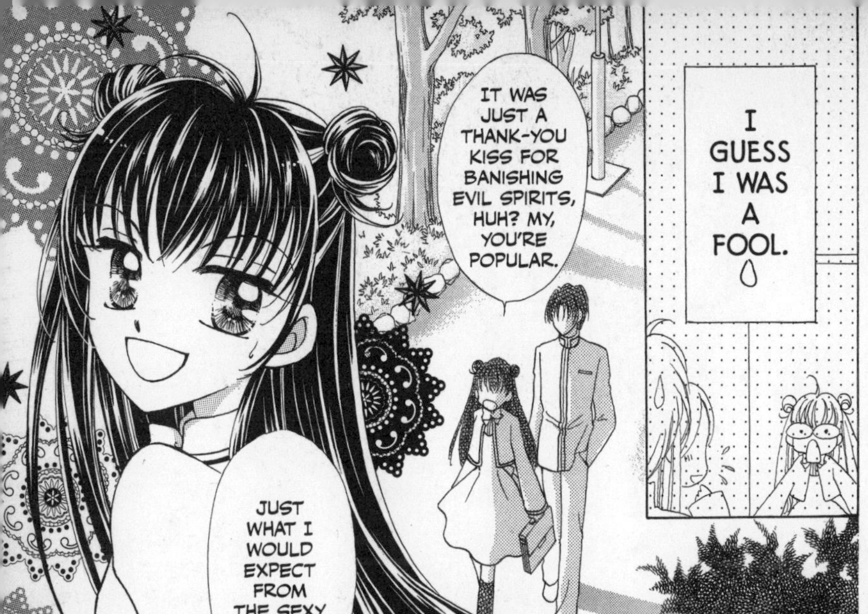
I GUESS I WAS A FOOL.
IT WAS JUST A THANK-YOU KISS FOR BANISHING EVIL SPIRITS, HUH? MY, YOU'RE POPULAR.
JUST WHAT I WOULD EXPECT FROM THE SEXY SORCERER.
OH, I'M NOT THAT GREAT.
DON'T LOOK SO PLEASED WITH YOUR-SELF!
THERE SHE IS. MOMOKA SENDOU.
YEAH. I COULD TELL IT WAS HER EVEN WITHOUT A PHOTO-GRAPH.

Ryuga Kou

Born August 19.
Zodiac Sign: Leo. Blood-Type: B.
Nationality: Chinese.
His family's guardian deity is the dragon. He comes from a family of magic masters. He specializes in divining the future and sorcery. He was born in China and raised in Yokohama.

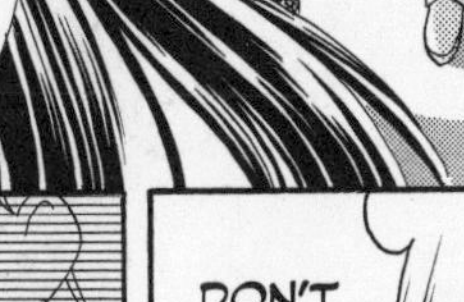

He's always teasing Momoka, but when things get dangerous, he saves her. He's a reliable childhood friend. He's very nice to all the girls, and it's hard for him to say no, so lately there's a rumor that he's a ladies' man... The earring in his right ear is made out of jade. It's a family talisman to ward off evil spirits.

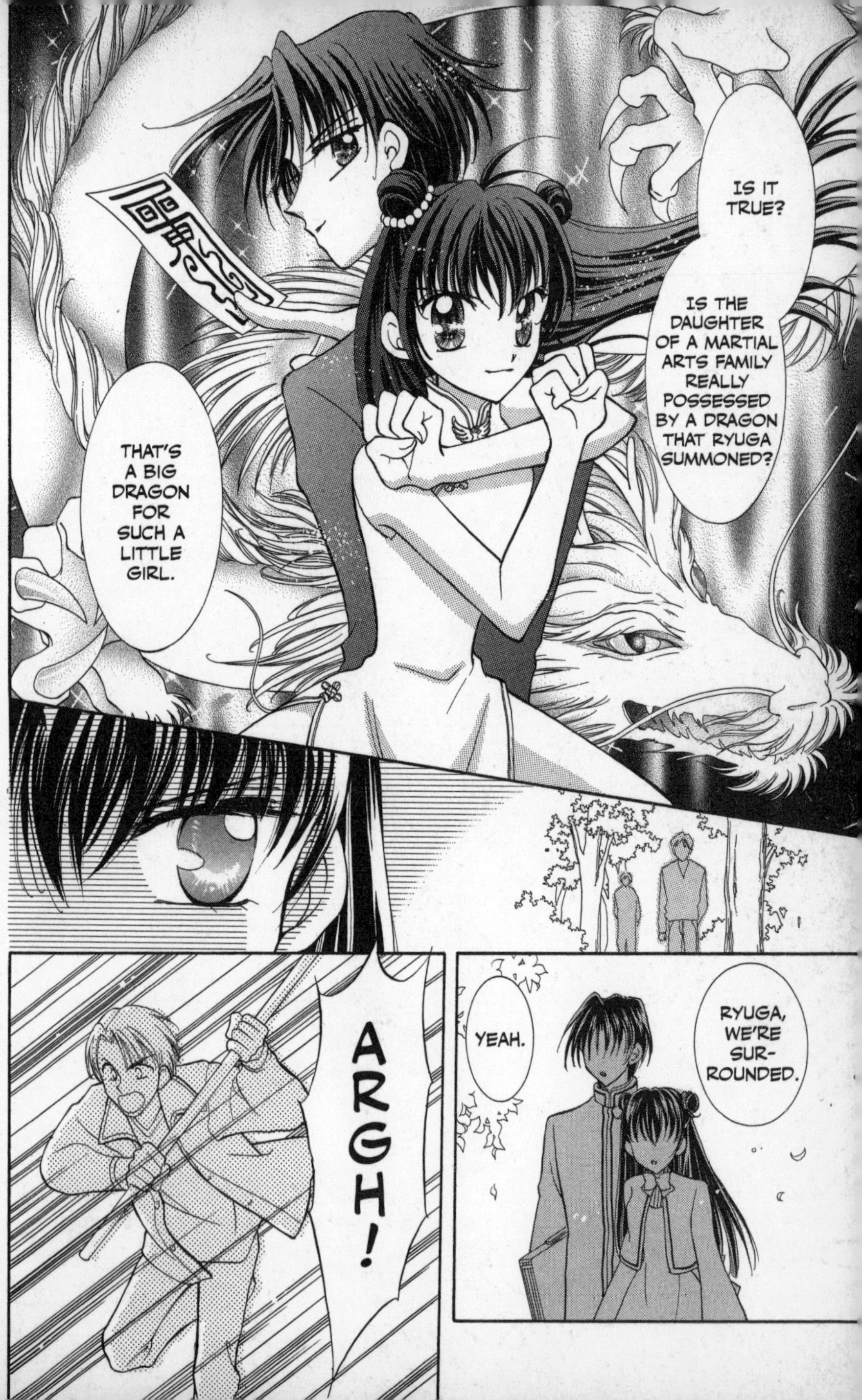
IS IT TRUE?
IS THE DAUGHTER OF A MARTIAL ARTS FAMILY REALLY POSSESSED BY A DRAGON THAT RYUGA SUMMONED?
THAT'S A BIG DRAGON FOR SUCH A LITTLE GIRL.
RYUGA, WE'RE SUR-ROUNDED.
YEAH.
ARGH!

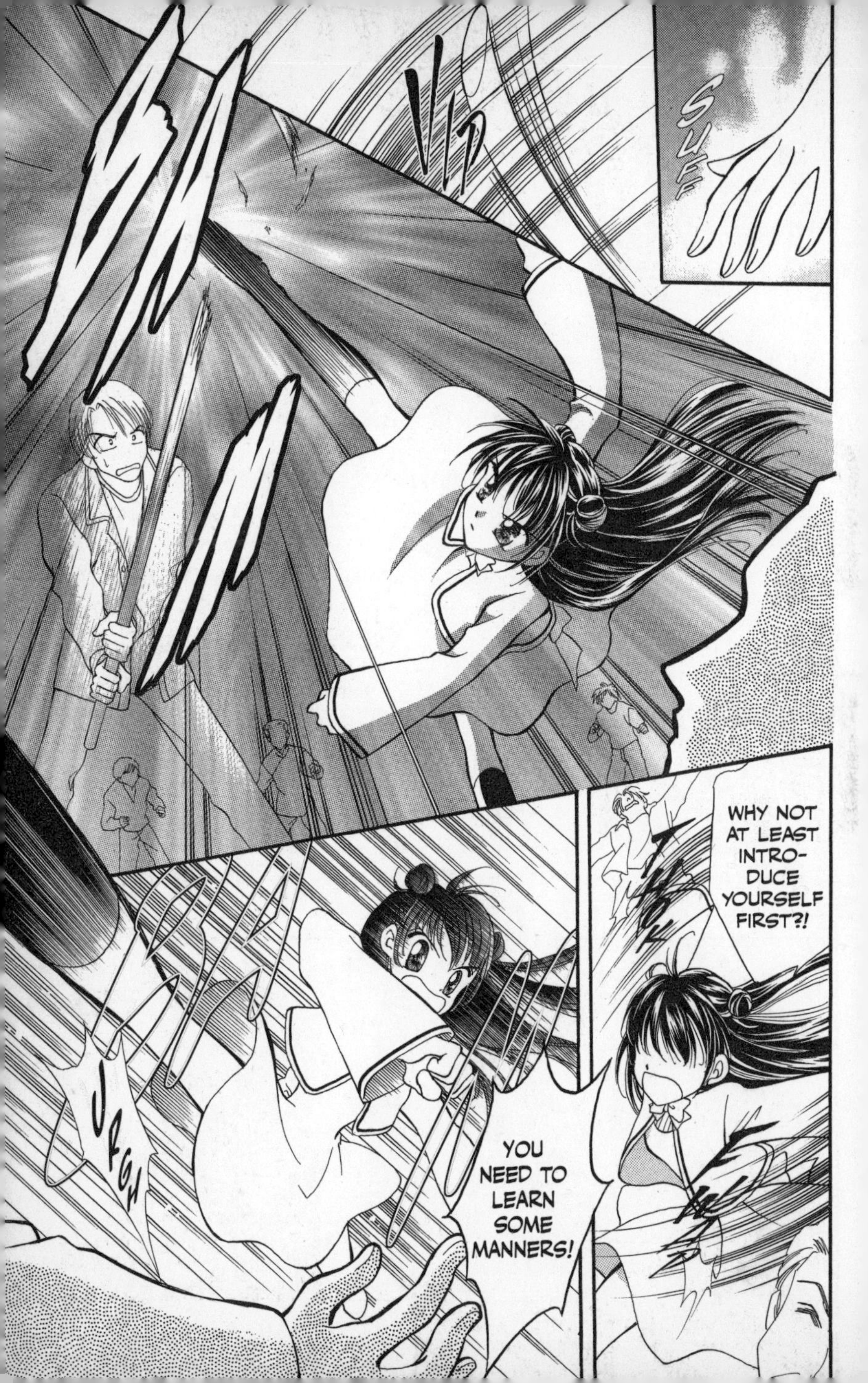
SUFF
VIP
WHY NOT AT LEAST INTRO-DUCE YOURSELF FIRST?!
YOU NEED TO LEARN SOME MANNERS!

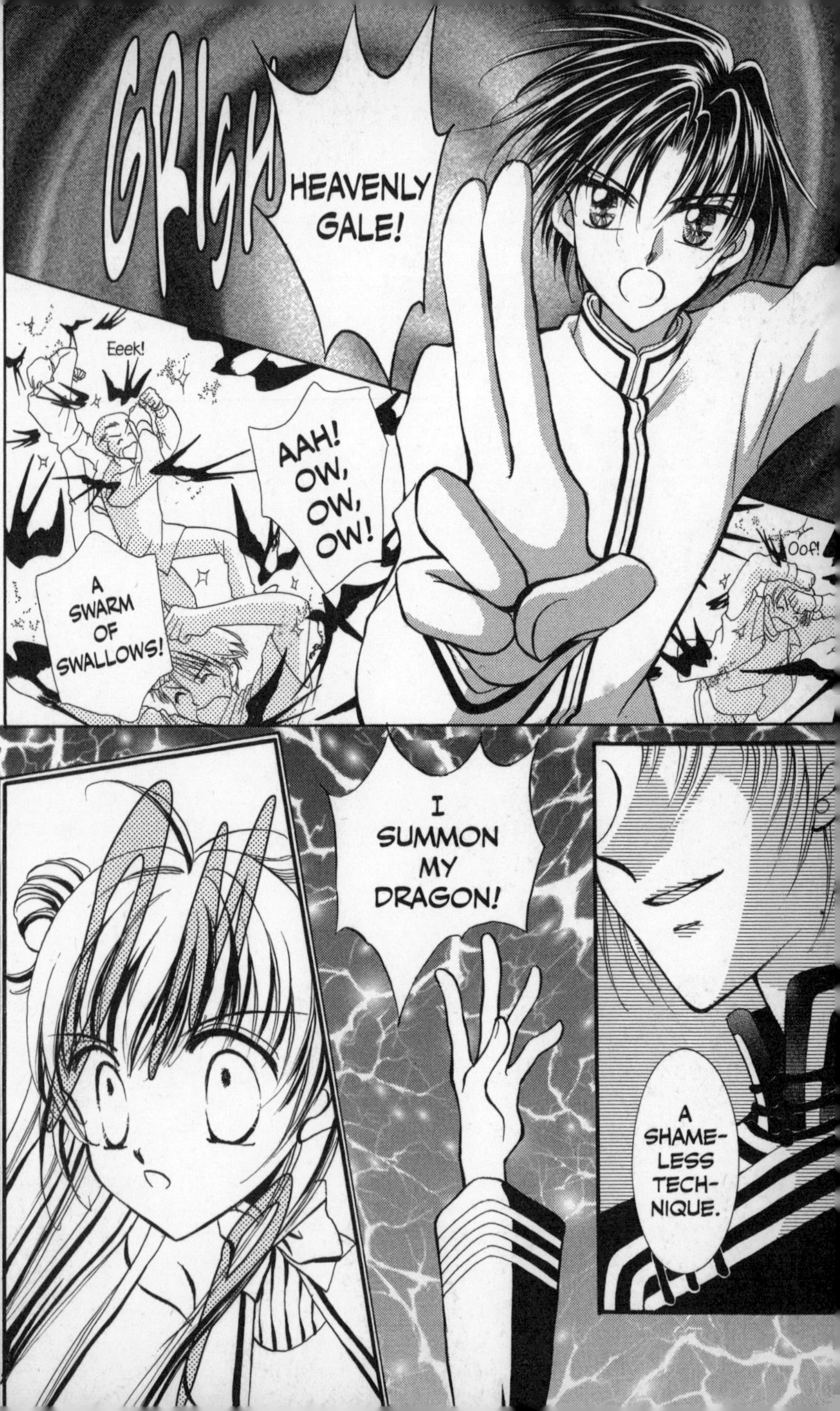
Oof!
CRISH
HEAVENLY GALE!
AAH! OW, OW, OW!
Eeek!
A SWARM OF SWALLOWS!
A SHAME-LESS TECH-NIQUE.
I SUMMON MY DRAGON!

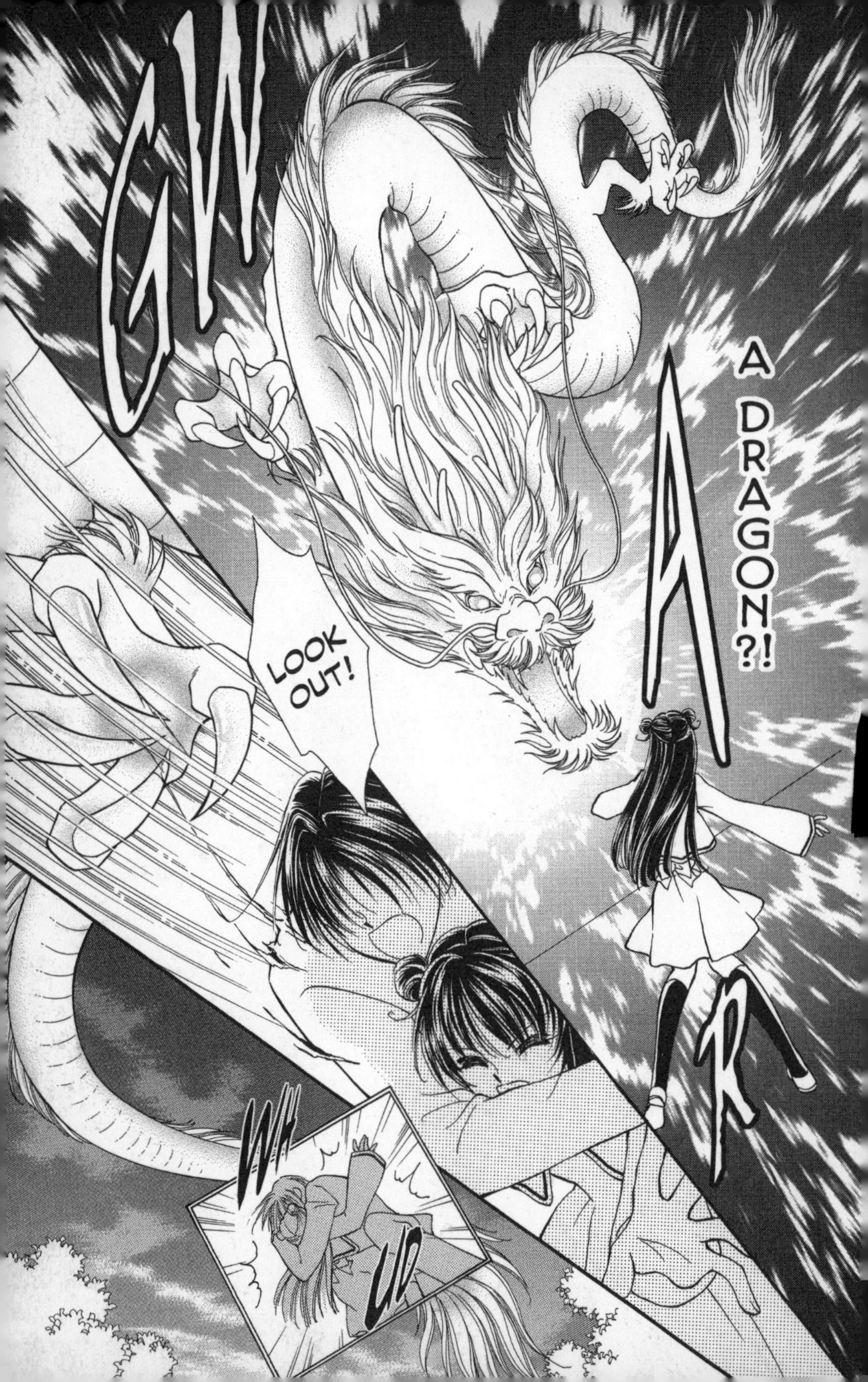
GW
A
A DRAGON?!
R
LOOK OUT!
WH
UD

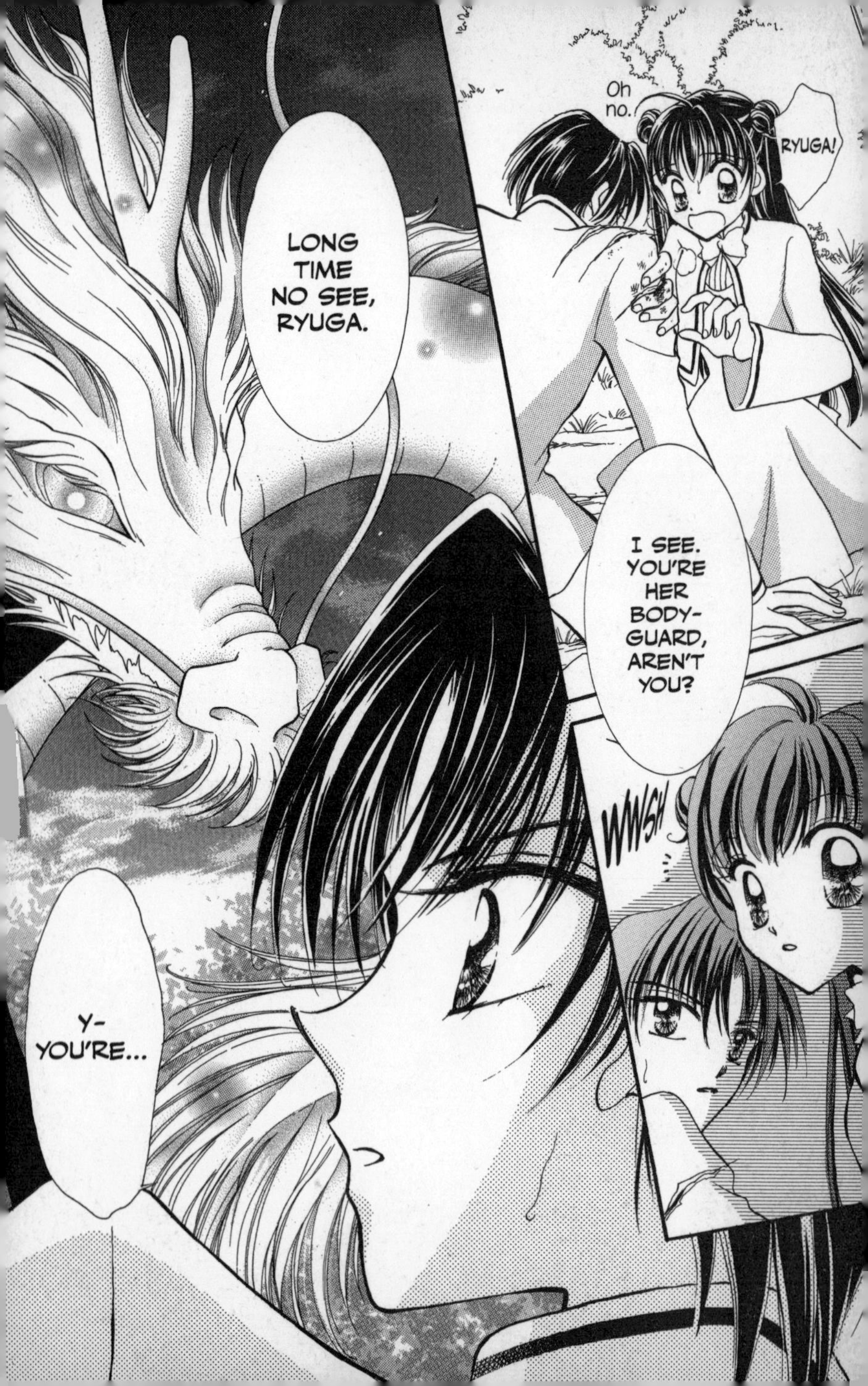

RYUGA!
Oh no.
LONG TIME NO SEE, RYUGA.
I SEE. YOU'RE HER BODYGUARD, AREN'T YOU?
WWSH
Y-YOU'RE...

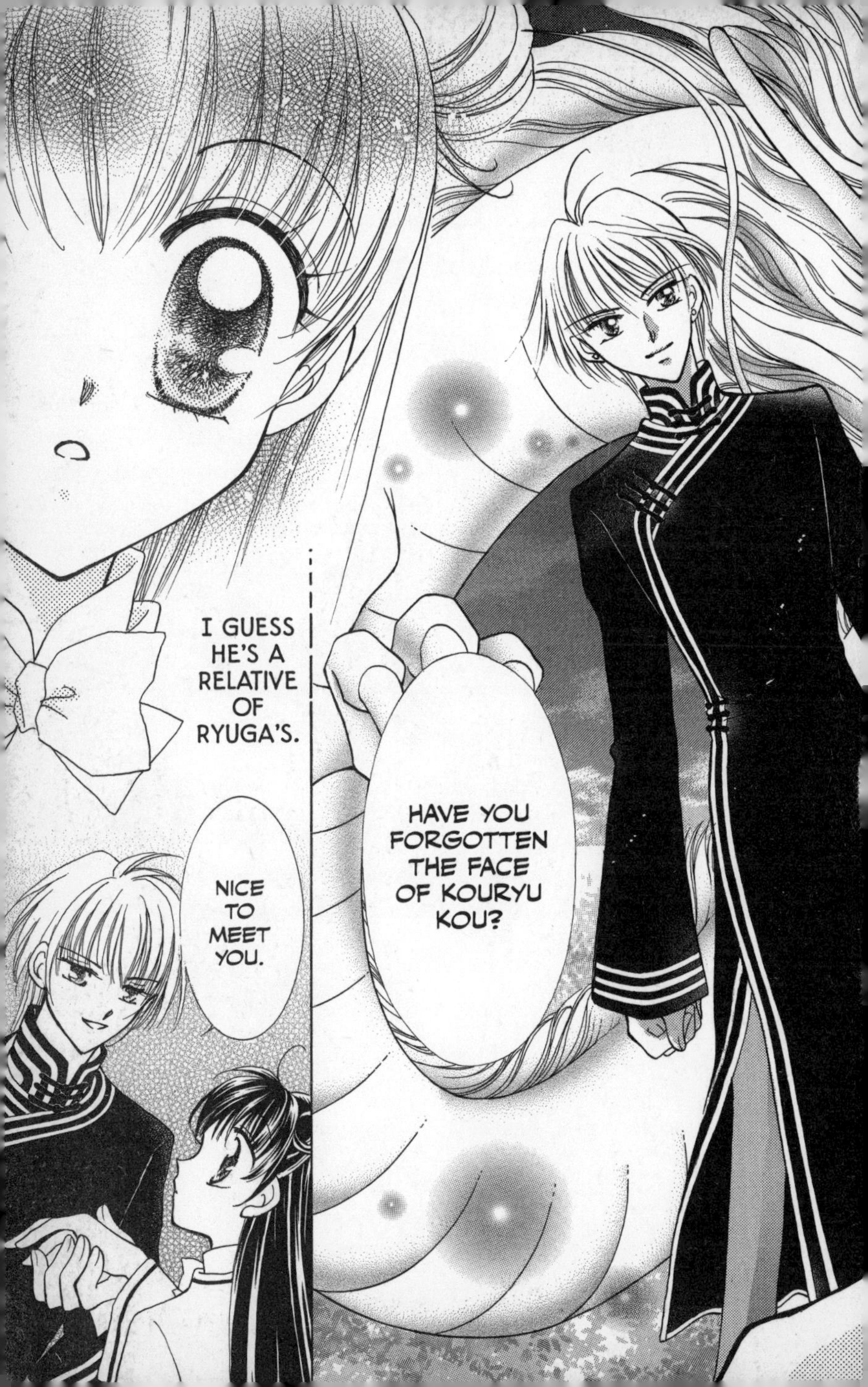
HAVE YOU FORGOTTEN THE FACE OF KOURYU KOU?
I GUESS HE'S A RELATIVE OF RYUGA'S.
NICE TO MEET YOU.

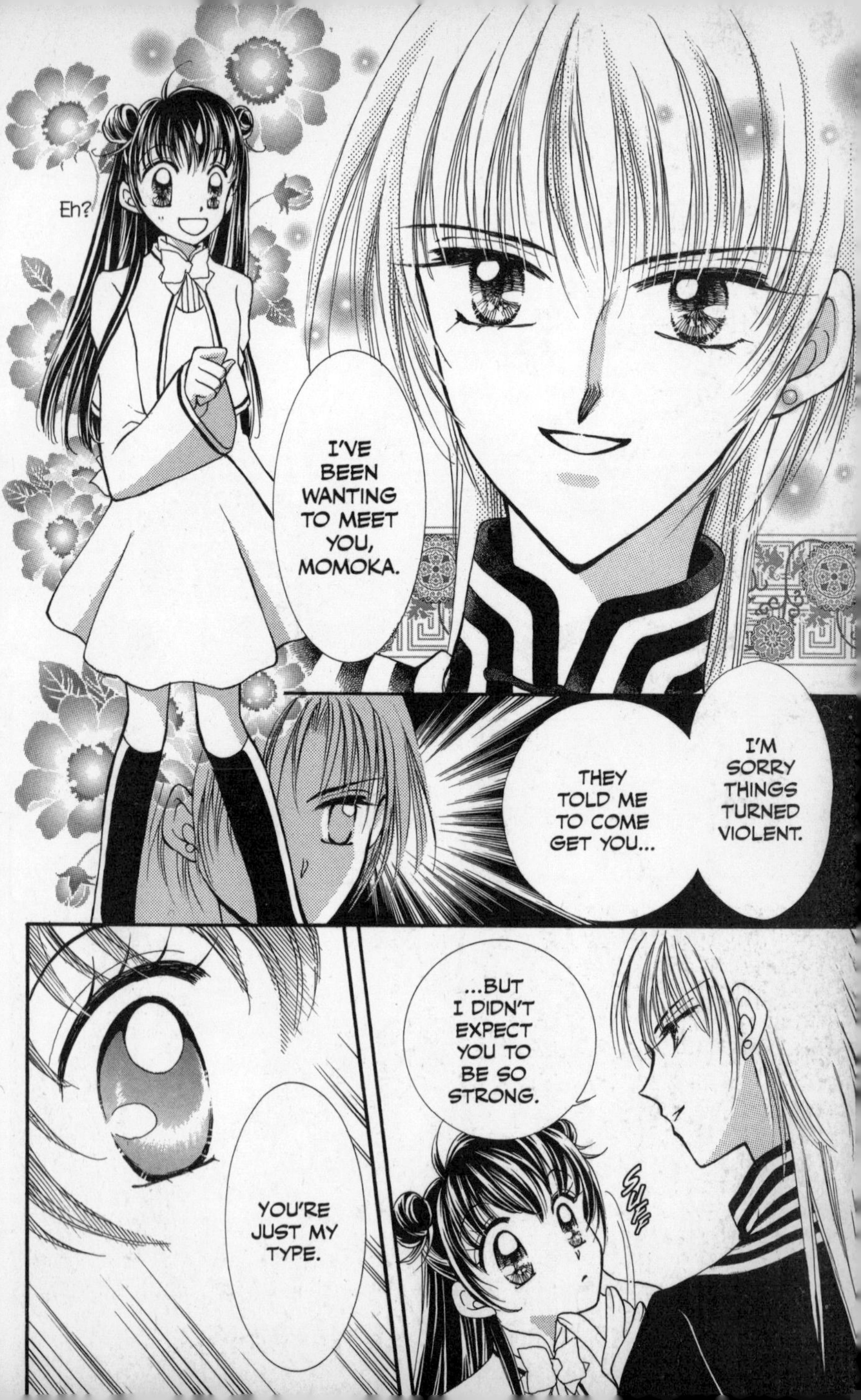
I'VE BEEN WANTING TO MEET YOU, MOMOKA.
I'M SORRY THINGS TURNED VIOLENT.
THEY TOLD ME TO COME GET YOU...
Eh?
...BUT I DIDN'T EXPECT YOU TO BE SO STRONG.
YOU'RE JUST MY TYPE.

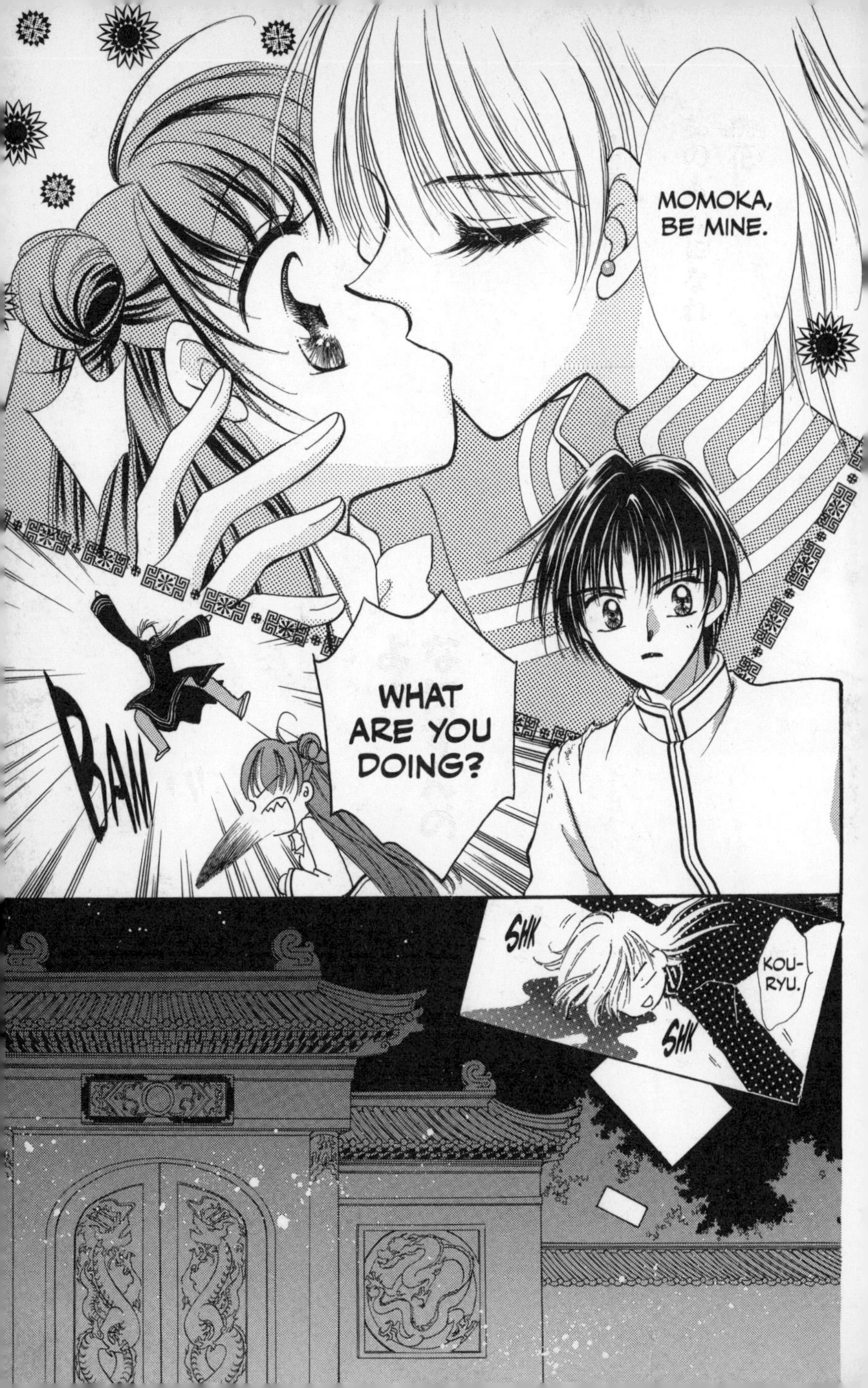
MOMOKA, BE MINE.
WHAT ARE YOU DOING?
BAM
KOU-RYU.
SHK
SHK

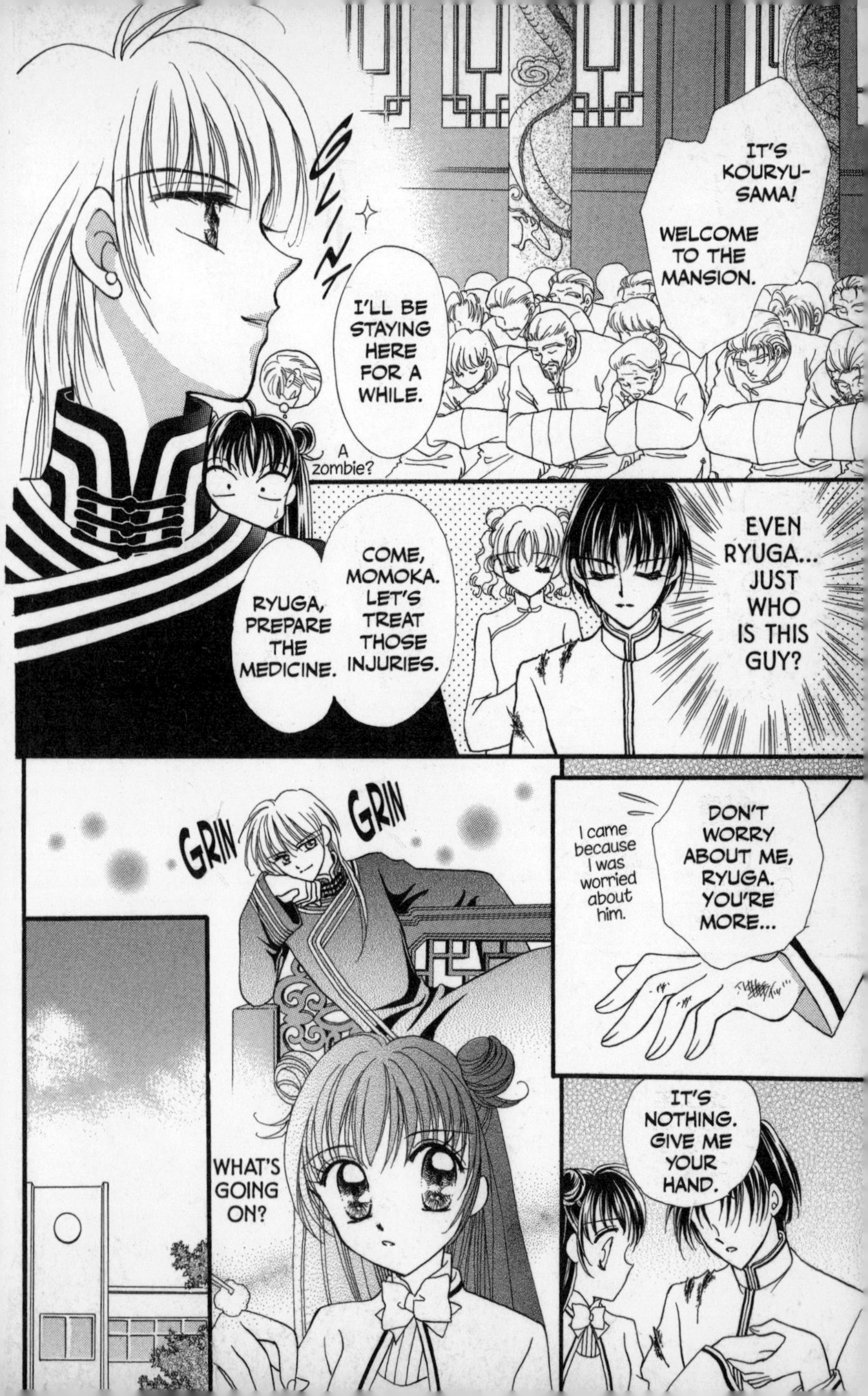
IT'S KOURYU-SAMA!
WELCOME TO THE MANSION.
GLINT
I'LL BE STAYING HERE FOR A WHILE.
A zombie?
EVEN RYUGA... JUST WHO IS THIS GUY?
COME, MOMOKA. LET'S TREAT THOSE INJURIES.
RYUGA, PREPARE THE MEDICINE.
DON'T WORRY ABOUT ME, RYUGA. YOU'RE MORE...
I came because I was worried about him.
IT'S NOTHING. GIVE ME YOUR HAND.
GRIN GRIN
WHAT'S GOING ON?

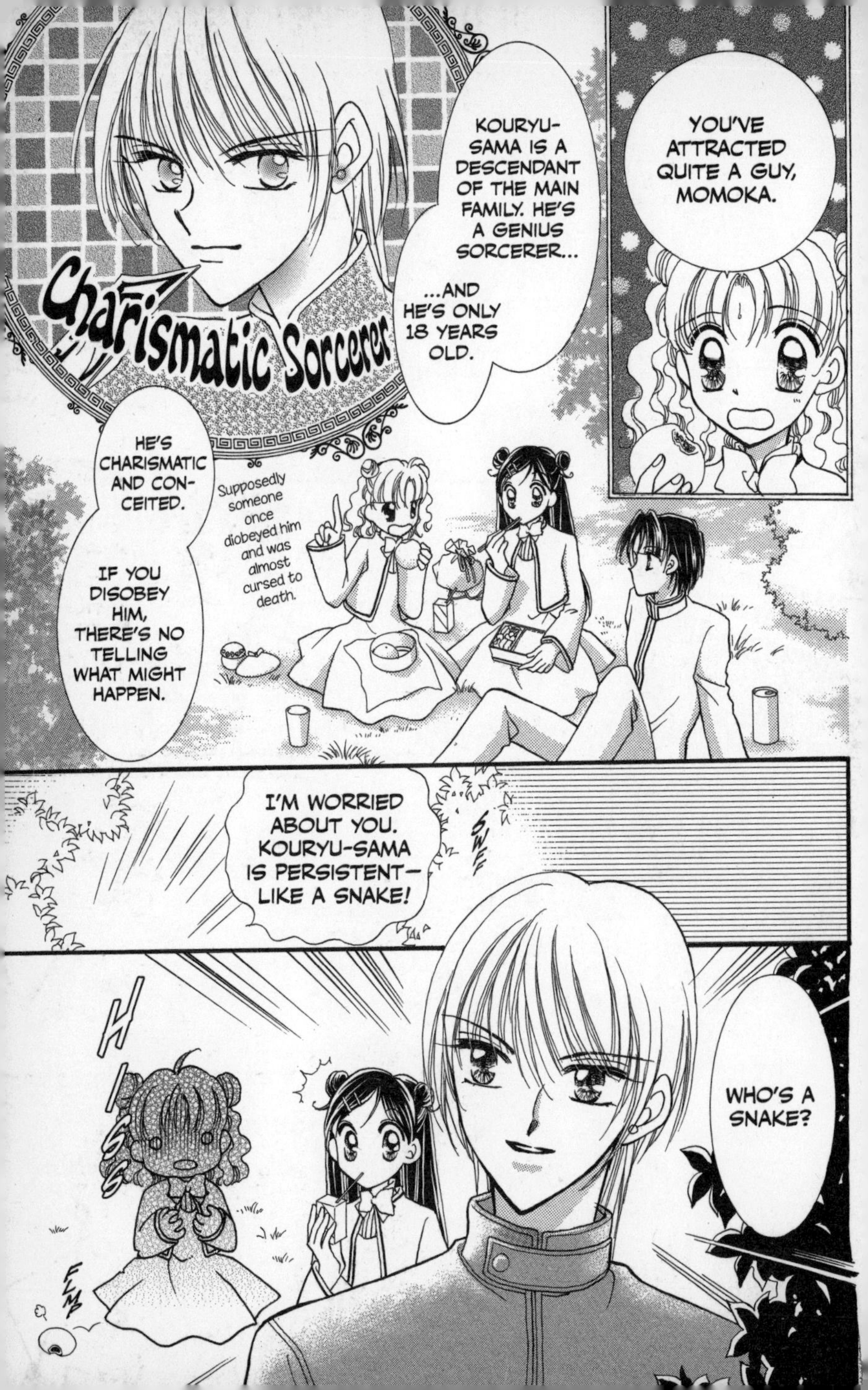
YOU'VE ATTRACTED QUITE A GUY, MOMOKA.
KOURYU-SAMA IS A DESCENDANT OF THE MAIN FAMILY. HE'S A GENIUS SORCERER...
...AND HE'S ONLY 18 YEARS OLD.
Charismatic Sorcerer
HE'S CHARISMATIC AND CONCEITED.
IF YOU DISOBEY HIM, THERE'S NO TELLING WHAT MIGHT HAPPEN.
Supposedly someone once diobeyed him and was almost cursed to death.
I'M WORRIED ABOUT YOU. KOURYU-SAMA IS PERSISTENT—LIKE A SNAKE!
WHO'S A SNAKE?

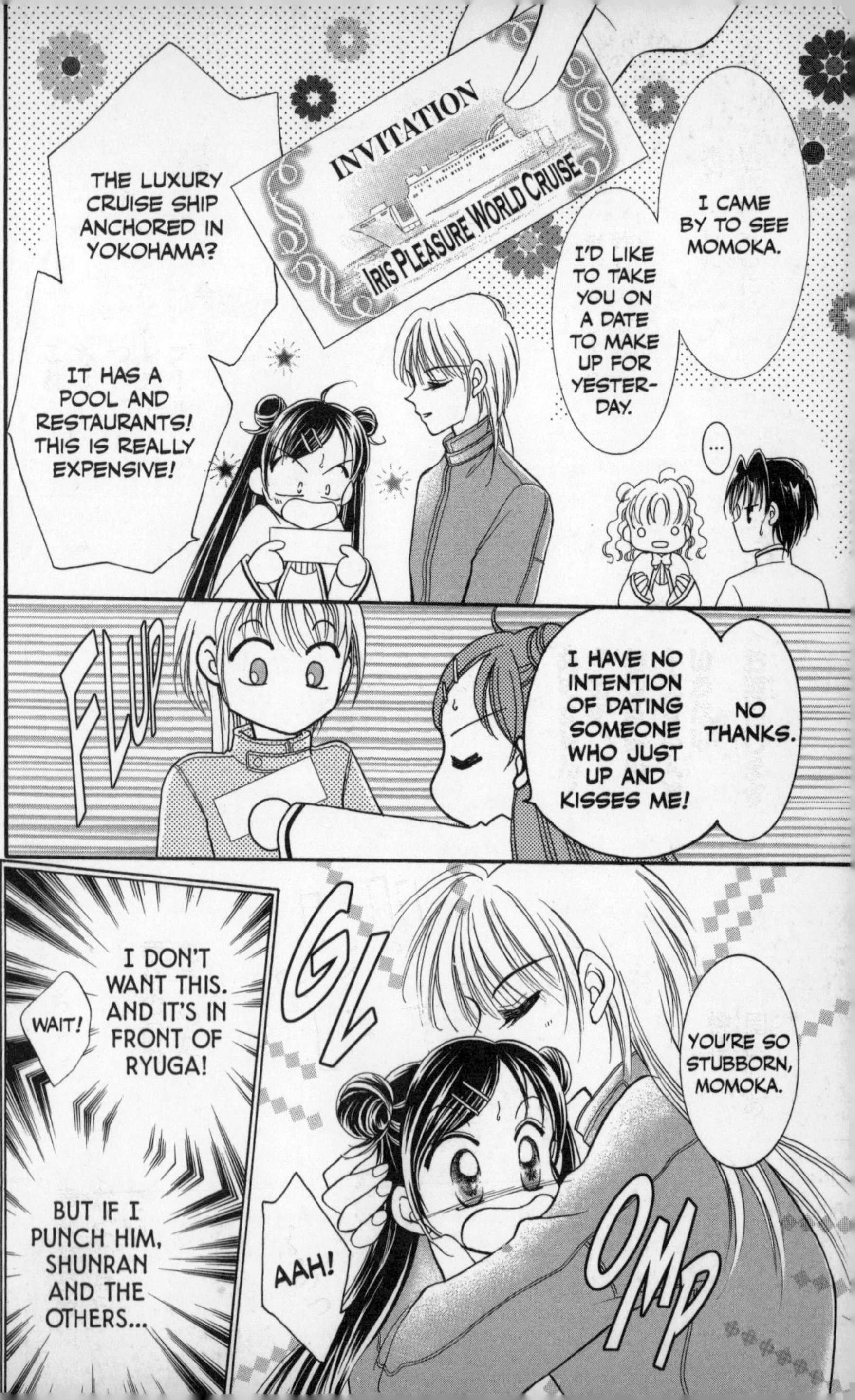
I CAME BY TO SEE MOMOKA.
I'D LIKE TO TAKE YOU ON A DATE TO MAKE UP FOR YESTER-DAY.
INVITATION
IRIS PLEASURE WORLD CRUISE
THE LUXURY CRUISE SHIP ANCHORED IN YOKOHAMA?
...
IT HAS A POOL AND RESTAURANTS! THIS IS REALLY EXPENSIVE!
NO THANKS.
I HAVE NO INTENTION OF DATING SOMEONE WHO JUST UP AND KISSES ME!
FLUP
YOU'RE SO STUBBORN, MOMOKA.
GL
OMP
I DON'T WANT THIS. AND IT'S IN FRONT OF RYUGA!
WAIT!
AAH!
BUT IF I PUNCH HIM, SHUNRAN AND THE OTHERS...

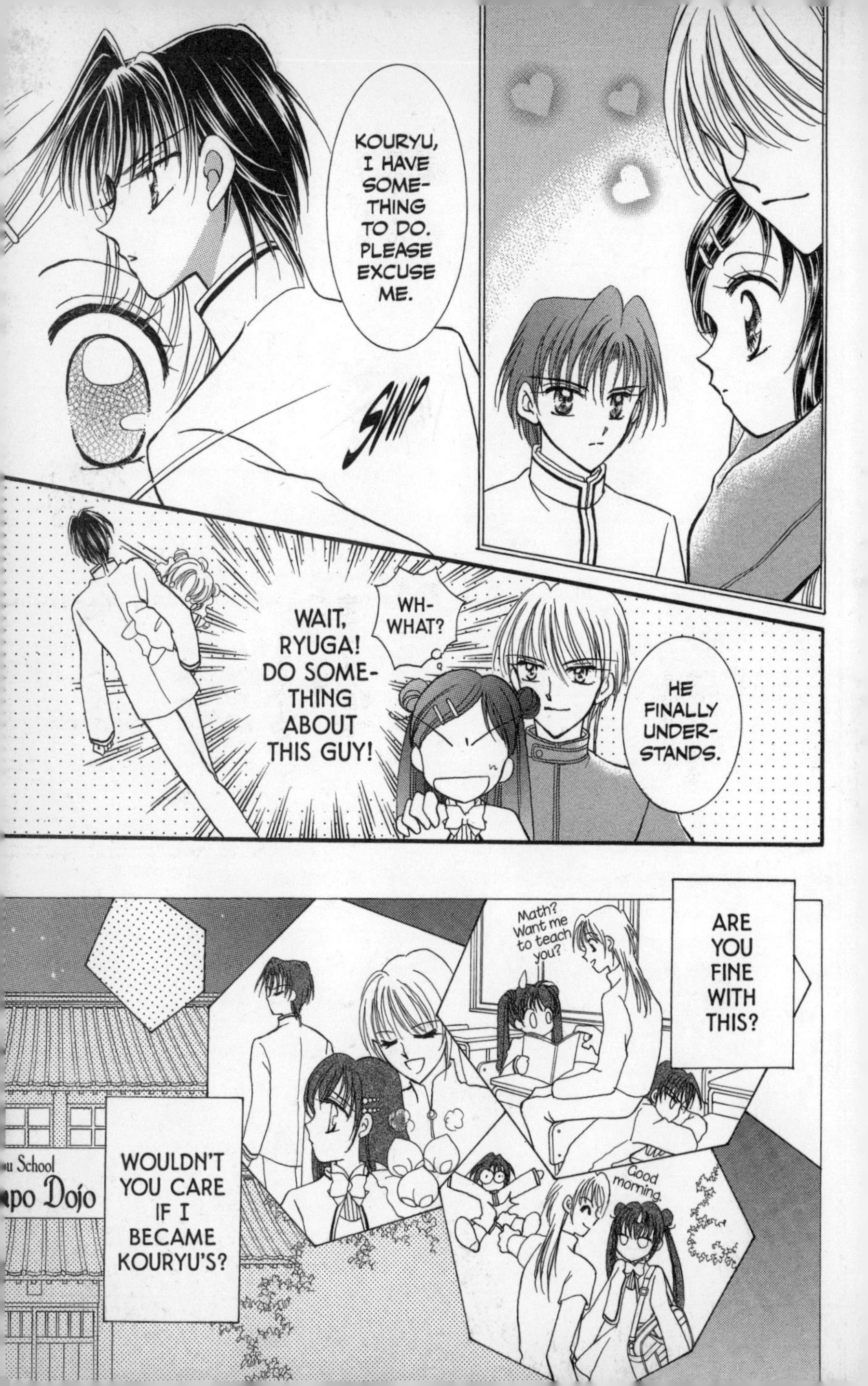
KOURYU, I HAVE SOME-THING TO DO. PLEASE EXCUSE ME.
SWIP
HE FINALLY UNDER-STANDS.
WH-WHAT?
WAIT, RYUGA! DO SOME-THING ABOUT THIS GUY!
ARE YOU FINE WITH THIS?
Math? Want me to teach you?
Good morning.
WOULDN'T YOU CARE IF I BECAME KOURYU'S?

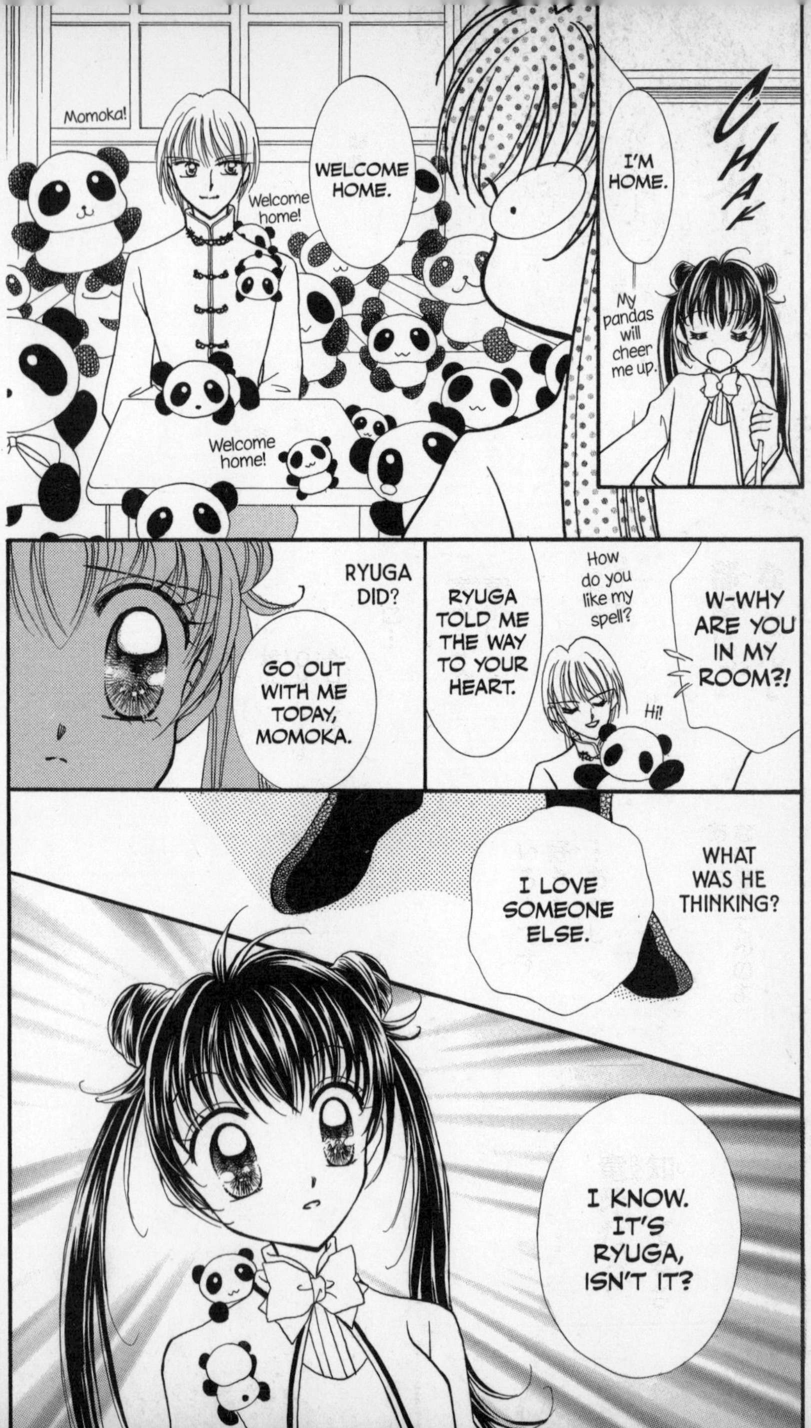
CHAK
I'M HOME.
My pandas will cheer me up.
WELCOME HOME.
Momoka!
Welcome home!
Welcome home!
W-WHY ARE YOU IN MY ROOM?!
Hi!
How do you like my spell?
RYUGA TOLD ME THE WAY TO YOUR HEART.
RYUGA DID?
GO OUT WITH ME TODAY, MOMOKA.
WHAT WAS HE THINKING?
I LOVE SOMEONE ELSE.
I KNOW. IT'S RYUGA, ISN'T IT?

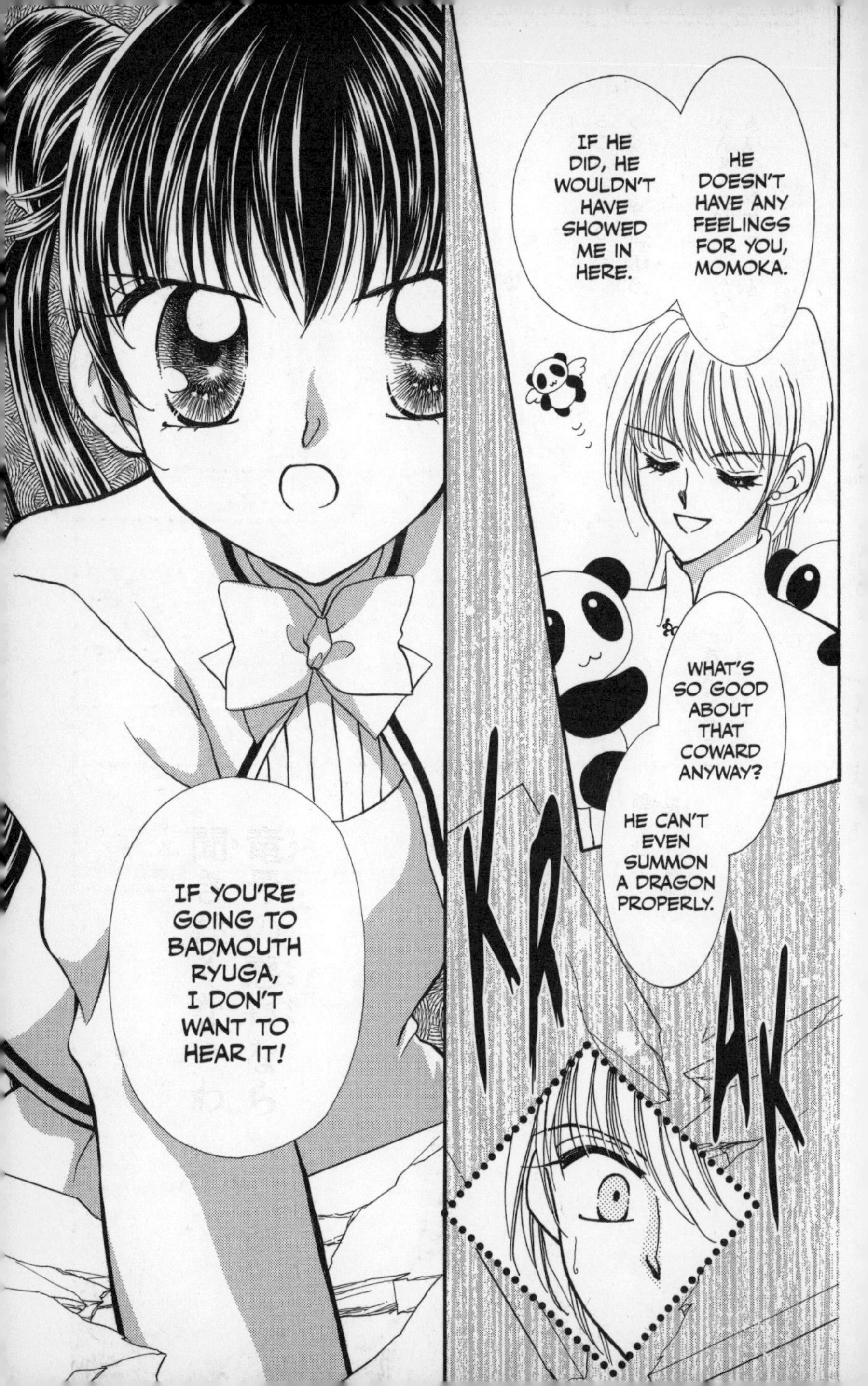
HE DOESN'T HAVE ANY FEELINGS FOR YOU, MOMOKA.
IF HE DID, HE WOULDN'T HAVE SHOWED ME IN HERE.
WHAT'S SO GOOD ABOUT THAT COWARD ANYWAY?
HE CAN'T EVEN SUMMON A DRAGON PROPERLY.
KRAK
IF YOU'RE GOING TO BADMOUTH RYUGA, I DON'T WANT TO HEAR IT!

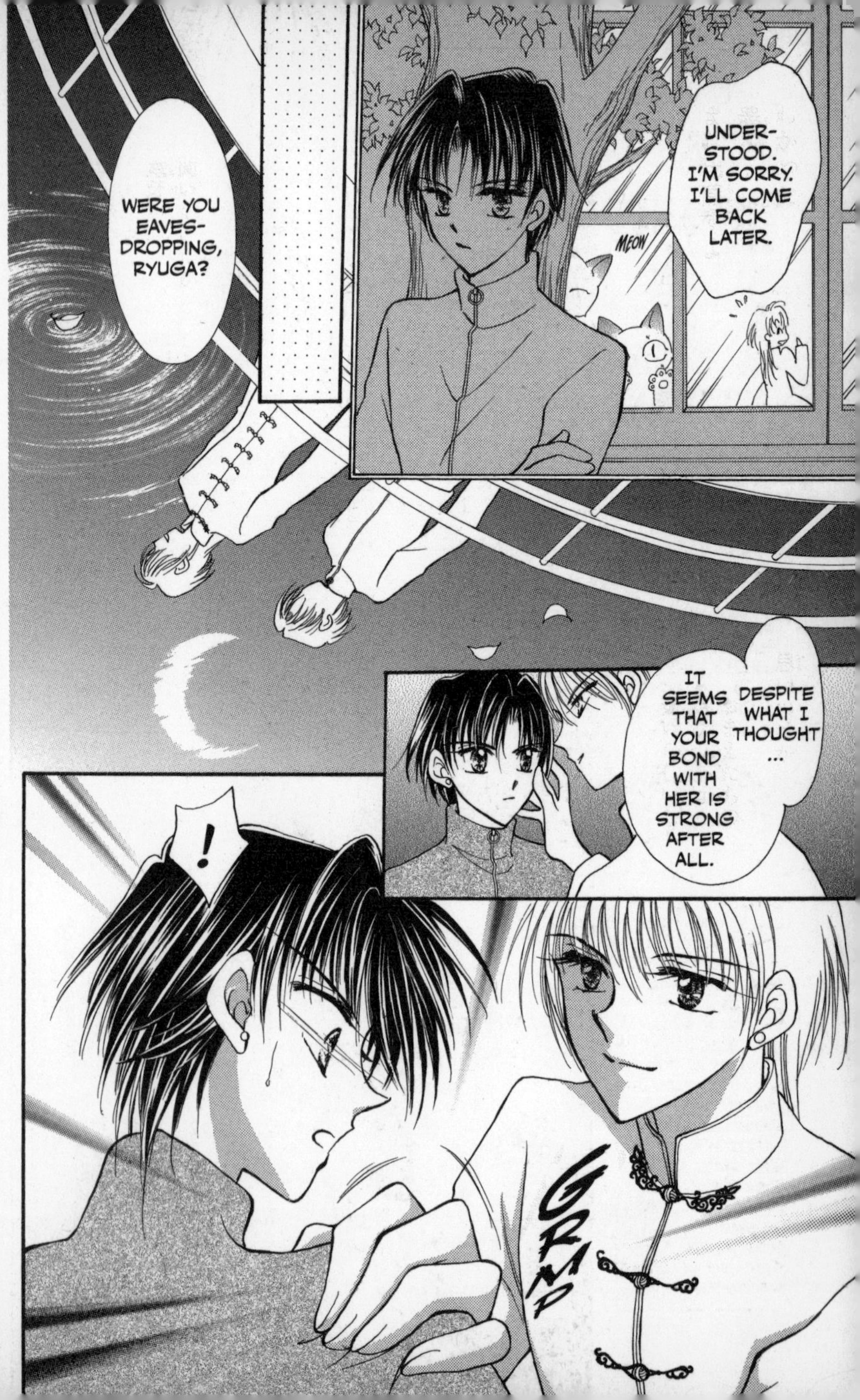
UNDER-STOOD. I'M SORRY. I'LL COME BACK LATER.
MEOW
WERE YOU EAVES-DROPPING, RYUGA?
DESPITE WHAT I THOUGHT ...
IT SEEMS THAT YOUR BOND WITH HER IS STRONG AFTER ALL.
!
GRMP

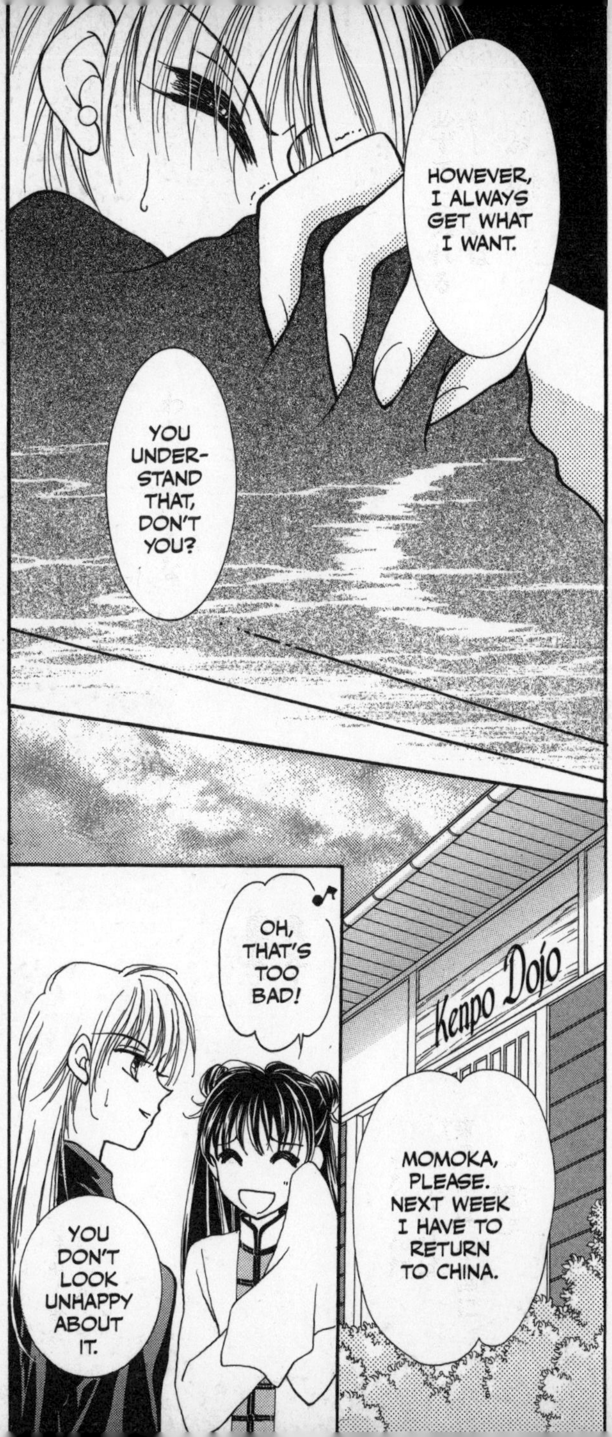
HOWEVER, I ALWAYS GET WHAT I WANT.
YOU UNDER-STAND THAT, DON'T YOU?
Kenpo Dojo
MOMOKA, PLEASE. NEXT WEEK I HAVE TO RETURN TO CHINA.
OH, THAT'S TOO BAD!
YOU DON'T LOOK UNHAPPY ABOUT IT.

6

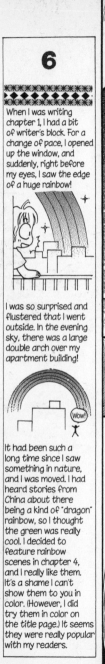

When I was writing chapter 1, I had a bit of writer's block. For a change of pace, I opened up the window, and suddenly, right before my eyes, I saw the edge of a huge rainbow!

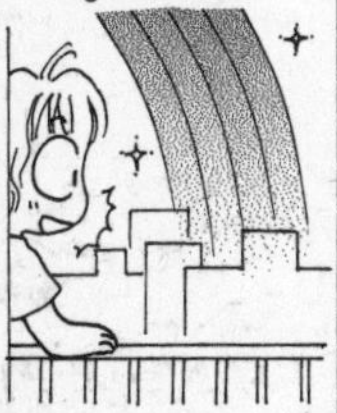

I was so surprised and flustered that I went outside. In the evening sky, there was a large double arch over my apartment building!

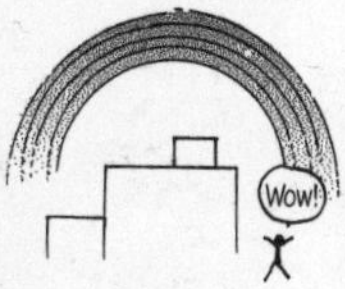
Wow!

It had been such a long time since I saw something in nature, and I was moved. I had heard stories from China about there being a kind of "dragon" rainbow, so I thought the green was really cool. I decided to feature rainbow scenes in chapter 4, and I really like them. It's a shame I can't show them to you in color. (However, I did try them in color on the title page.) It seems they were really popular with my readers.

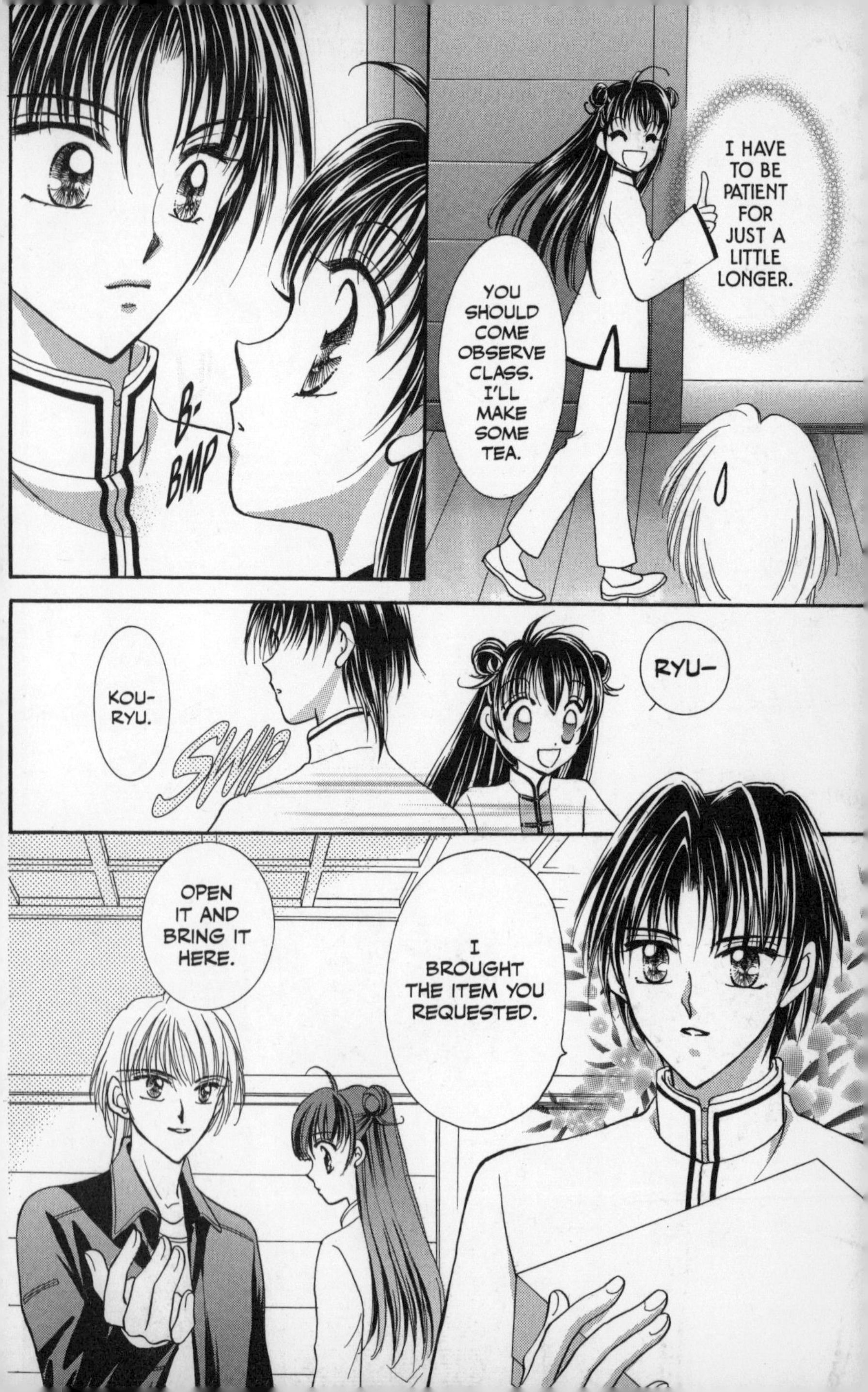
I HAVE TO BE PATIENT FOR JUST A LITTLE LONGER.
YOU SHOULD COME OBSERVE CLASS. I'LL MAKE SOME TEA.
B-BMP
RYU-
KOU-RYU.
SWIP
I BROUGHT THE ITEM YOU REQUESTED.
OPEN IT AND BRING IT HERE.

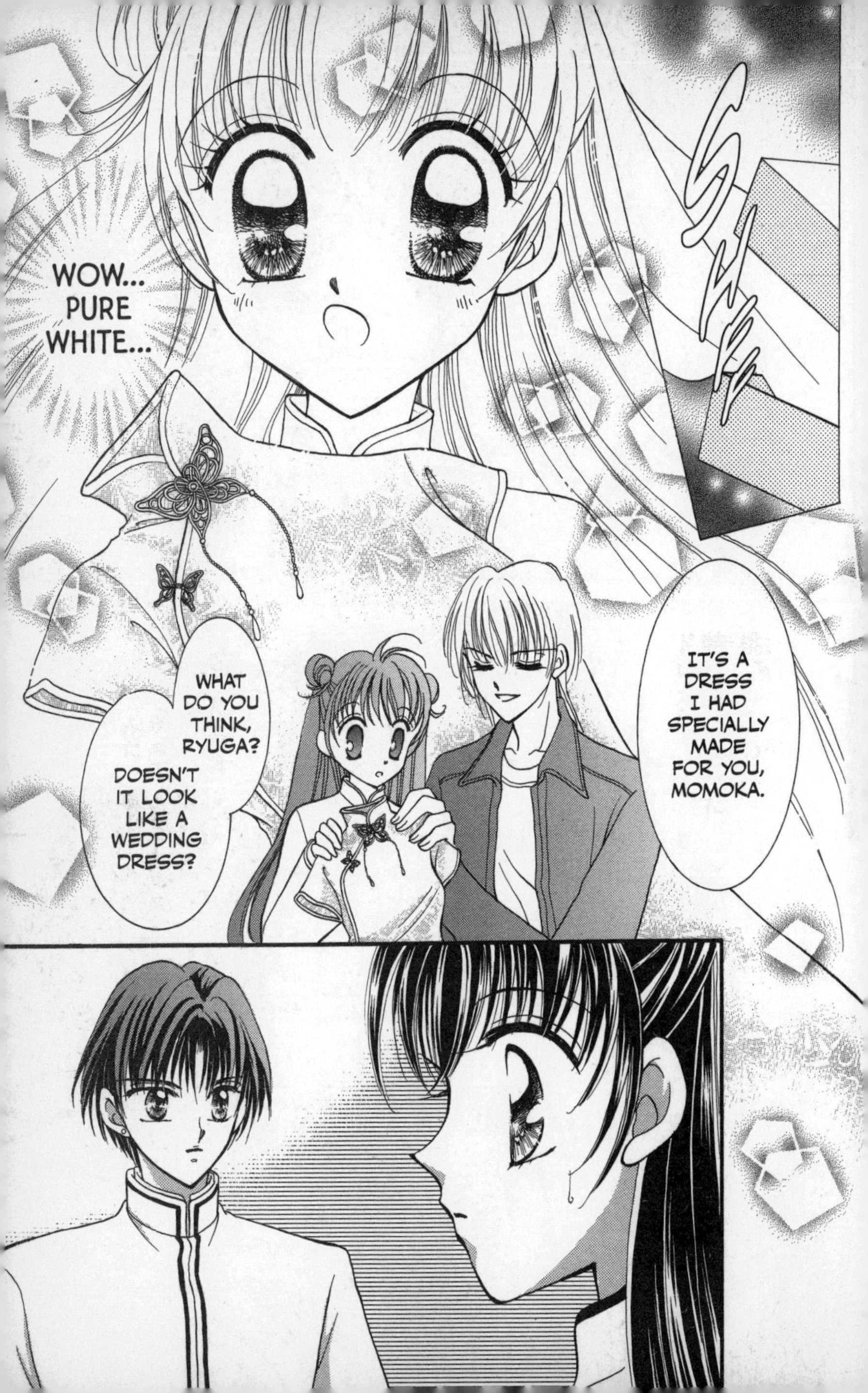
WOW... PURE WHITE...
IT'S A DRESS I HAD SPECIALLY MADE FOR YOU, MOMOKA.
WHAT DO YOU THINK, RYUGA? DOESN'T IT LOOK LIKE A WEDDING DRESS?

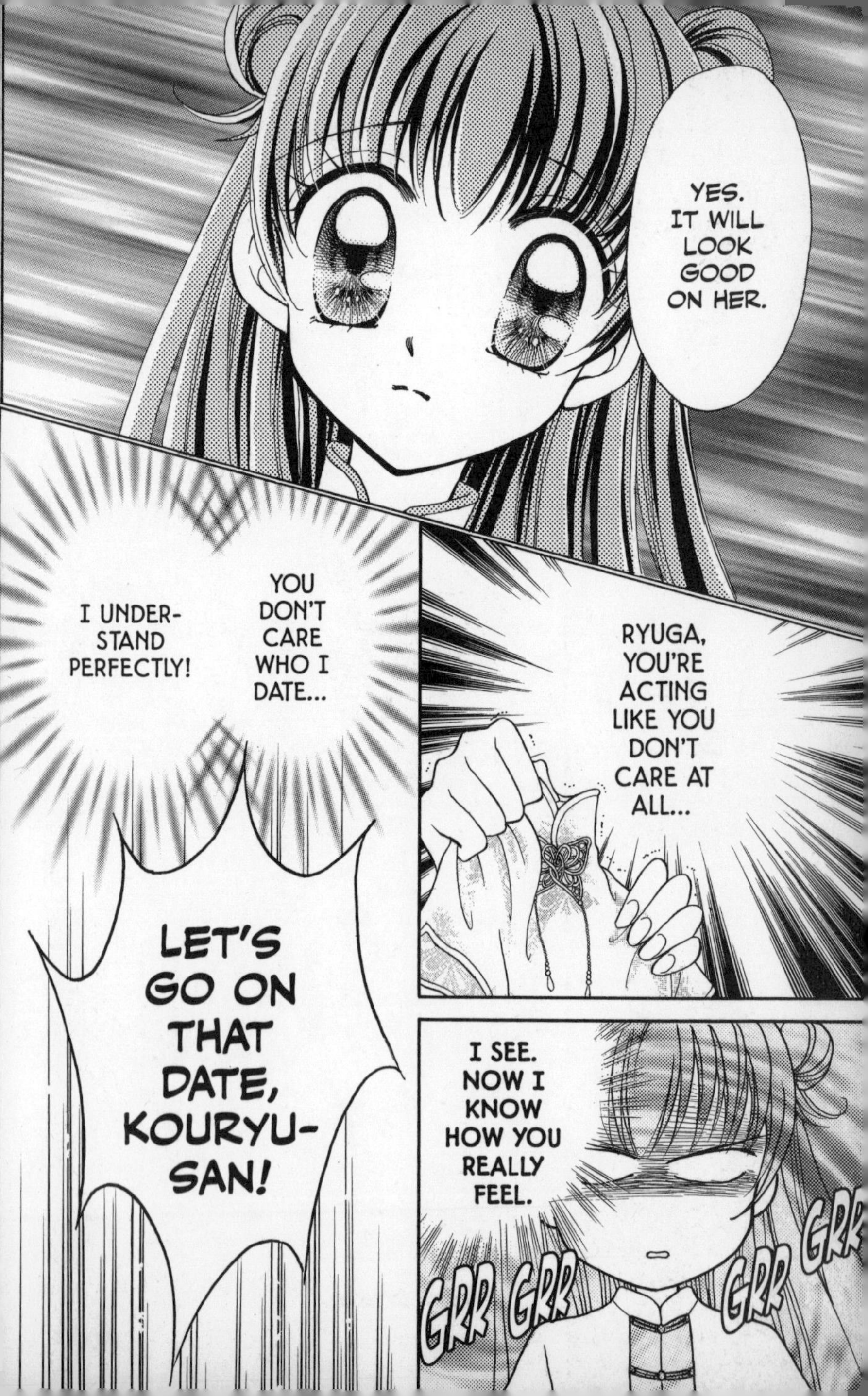
YES. IT WILL LOOK GOOD ON HER.
RYUGA, YOU'RE ACTING LIKE YOU DON'T CARE AT ALL...
I SEE. NOW I KNOW HOW YOU REALLY FEEL.
GRR GRR
GRR GRR
YOU DON'T CARE WHO I DATE...
I UNDER-STAND PERFECTLY!
LET'S GO ON THAT DATE, KOURYU-SAN!

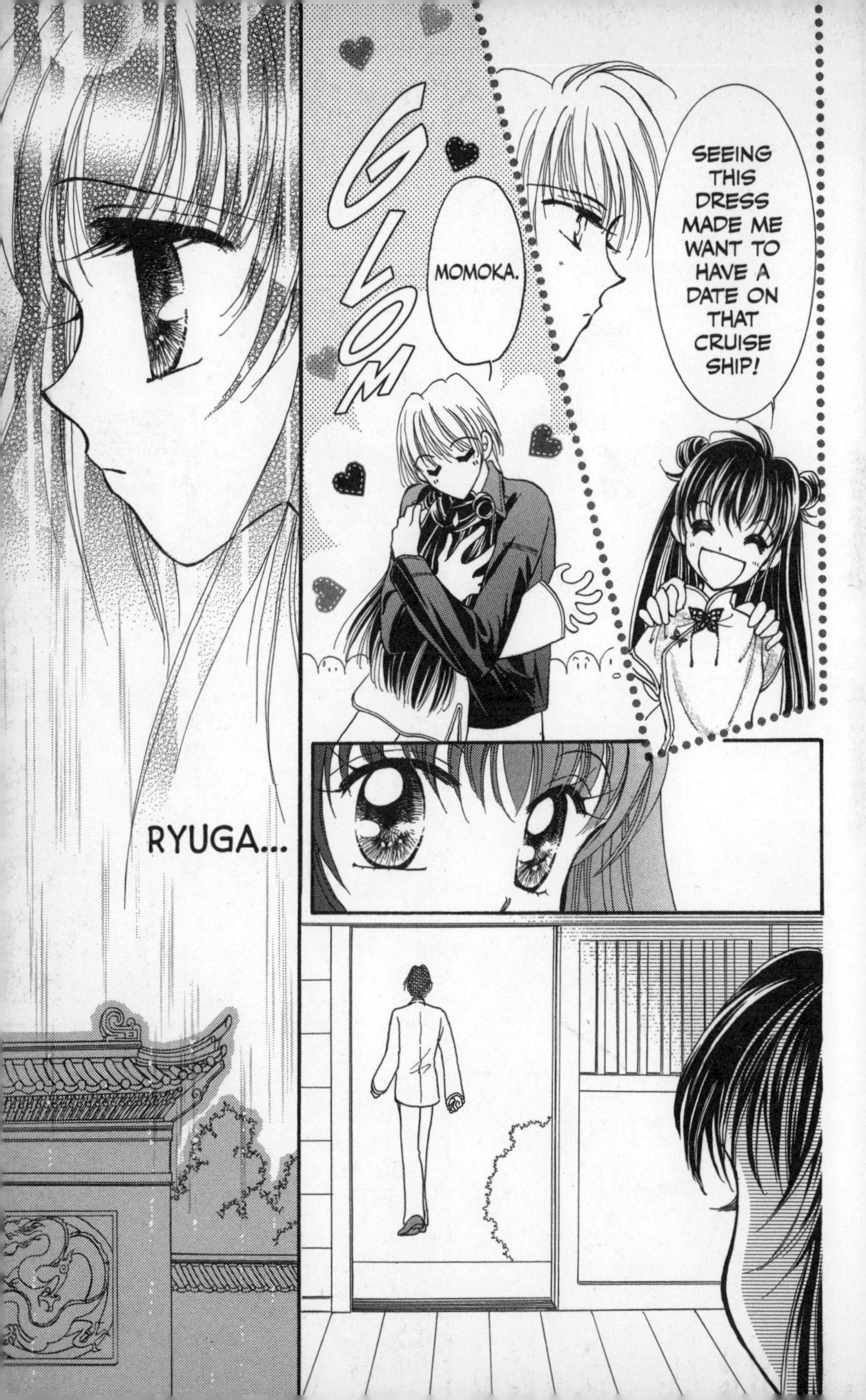
SEEING THIS DRESS MADE ME WANT TO HAVE A DATE ON THAT CRUISE SHIP!
MOMOKA.
GLOMP
RYUGA...

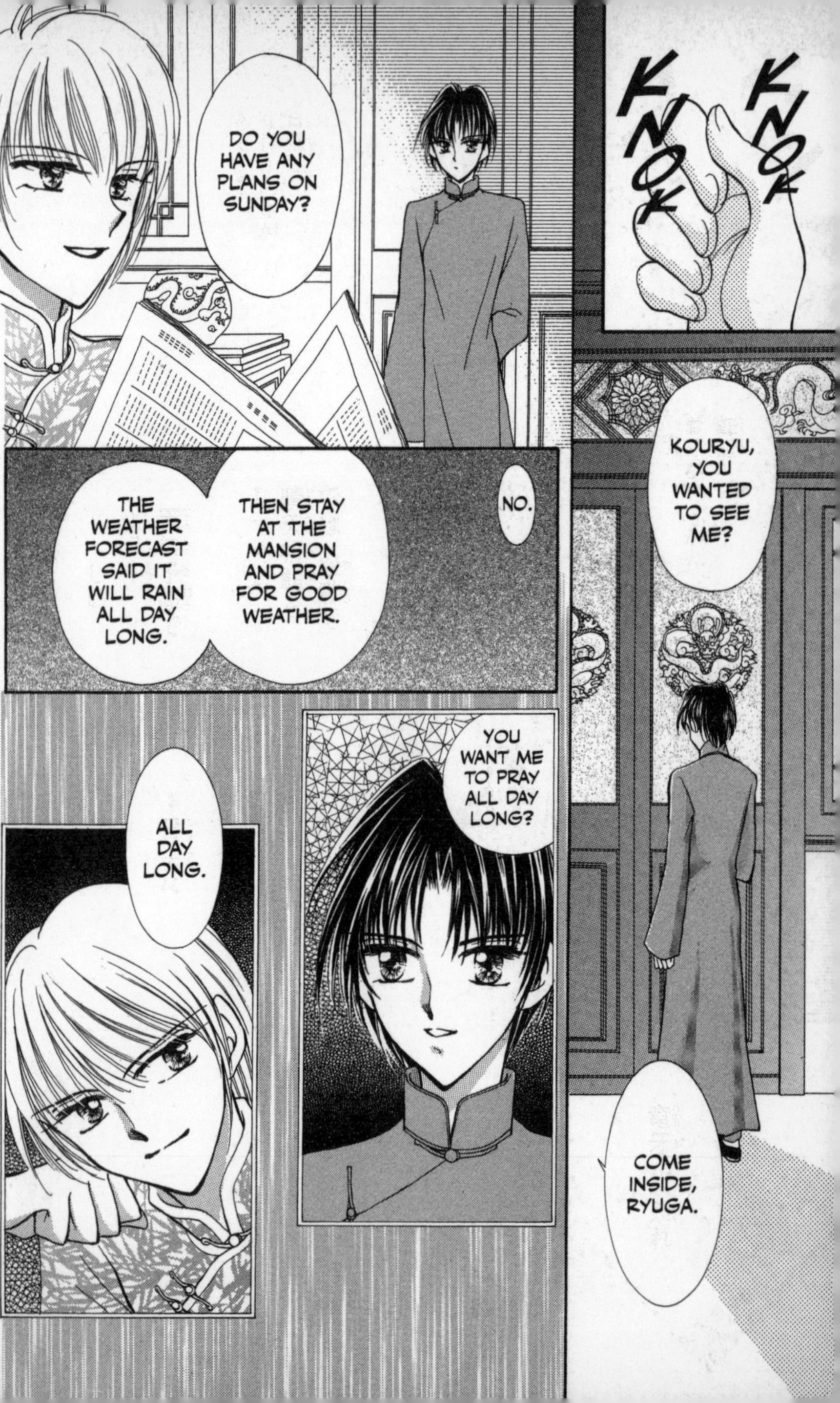
KNOK KNOK
KOURYU, YOU WANTED TO SEE ME?
COME INSIDE, RYUGA.
DO YOU HAVE ANY PLANS ON SUNDAY?
NO.
THEN STAY AT THE MANSION AND PRAY FOR GOOD WEATHER.
THE WEATHER FORECAST SAID IT WILL RAIN ALL DAY LONG.
YOU WANT ME TO PRAY ALL DAY LONG?
ALL DAY LONG.

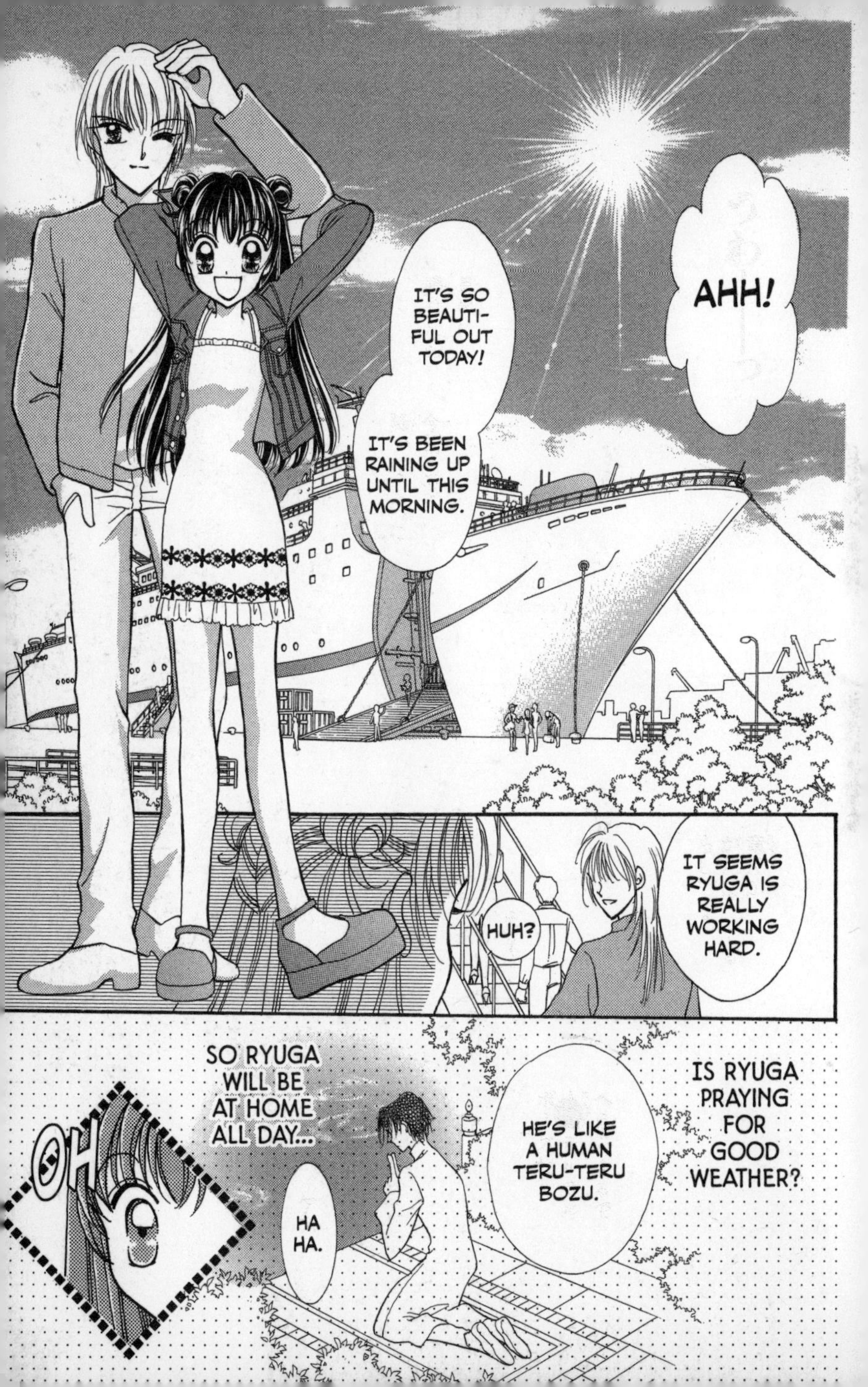
AHH!
IT'S SO BEAUTI-FUL OUT TODAY!
IT'S BEEN RAINING UP UNTIL THIS MORNING.
IT SEEMS RYUGA IS REALLY WORKING HARD.
HUH?
IS RYUGA PRAYING FOR GOOD WEATHER?
HE'S LIKE A HUMAN TERU-TERU BOZU.
HA HA.
SO RYUGA WILL BE AT HOME ALL DAY...
OH

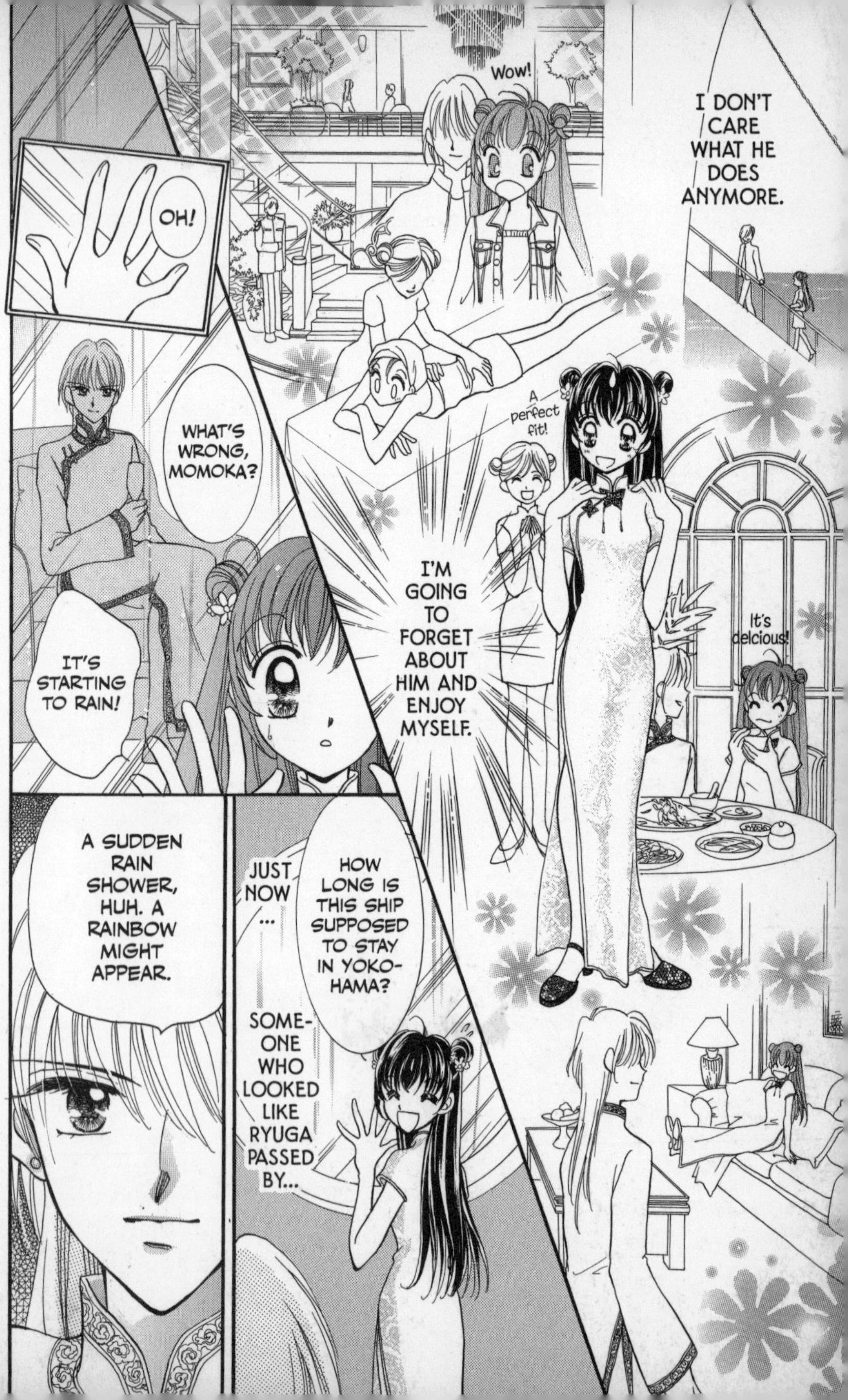
I DON'T CARE WHAT HE DOES ANYMORE.
Wow!
I'M GOING TO FORGET ABOUT HIM AND ENJOY MYSELF.
A perfect fit!
It's delcious!
OH!
WHAT'S WRONG, MOMOKA?
IT'S STARTING TO RAIN!
HOW LONG IS THIS SHIP SUPPOSED TO STAY IN YOKO-HAMA?
JUST NOW ...
SOME-ONE WHO LOOKED LIKE RYUGA PASSED BY...
A SUDDEN RAIN SHOWER, HUH. A RAINBOW MIGHT APPEAR.

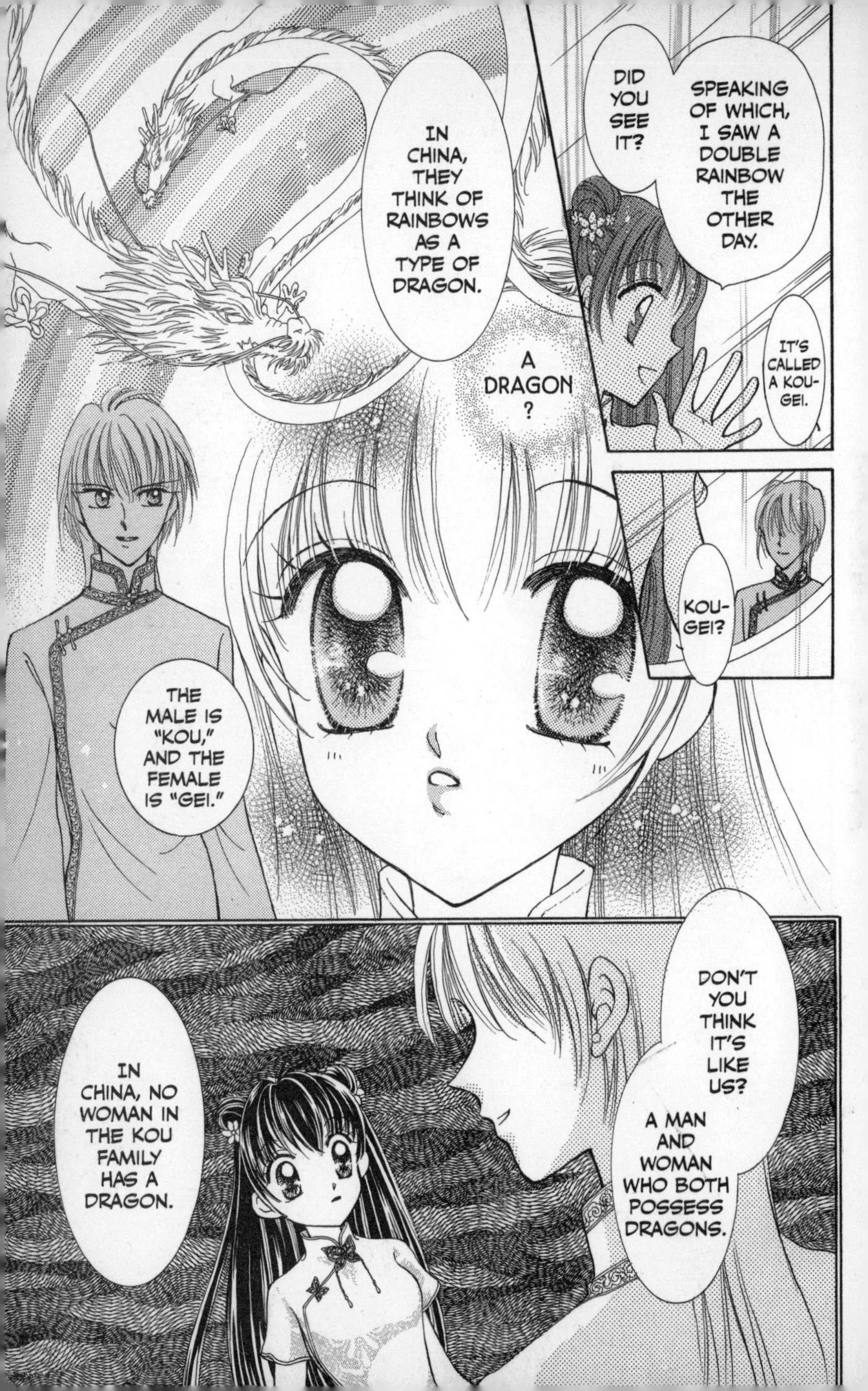
SPEAKING OF WHICH, I SAW A DOUBLE RAINBOW THE OTHER DAY.
DID YOU SEE IT?
IT'S CALLED A KOU-GEI.
KOU-GEI?
IN CHINA, THEY THINK OF RAINBOWS AS A TYPE OF DRAGON.
A DRAGON?
THE MALE IS "KOU," AND THE FEMALE IS "GEI."
DON'T YOU THINK IT'S LIKE US?
A MAN AND WOMAN WHO BOTH POSSESS DRAGONS.
IN CHINA, NO WOMAN IN THE KOU FAMILY HAS A DRAGON.

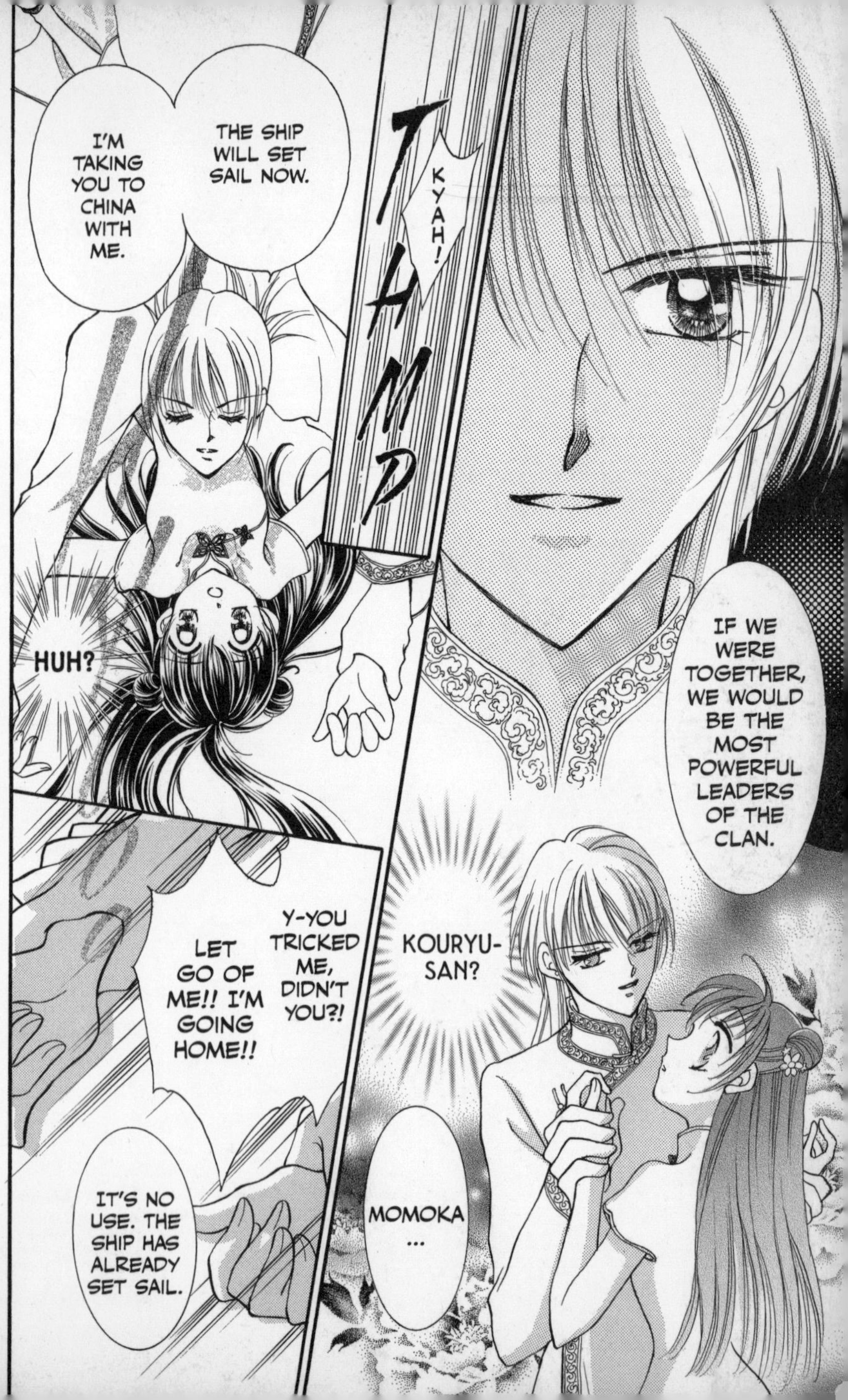
IF WE WERE TOGETHER, WE WOULD BE THE MOST POWERFUL LEADERS OF THE CLAN.
KOURYU-SAN?
MOMOKA ...
THMP
KYAH!
THE SHIP WILL SET SAIL NOW.
I'M TAKING YOU TO CHINA WITH ME.
HUH?
Y-YOU TRICKED ME, DIDN'T YOU?!
LET GO OF ME!! I'M GOING HOME!!
IT'S NO USE. THE SHIP HAS ALREADY SET SAIL.

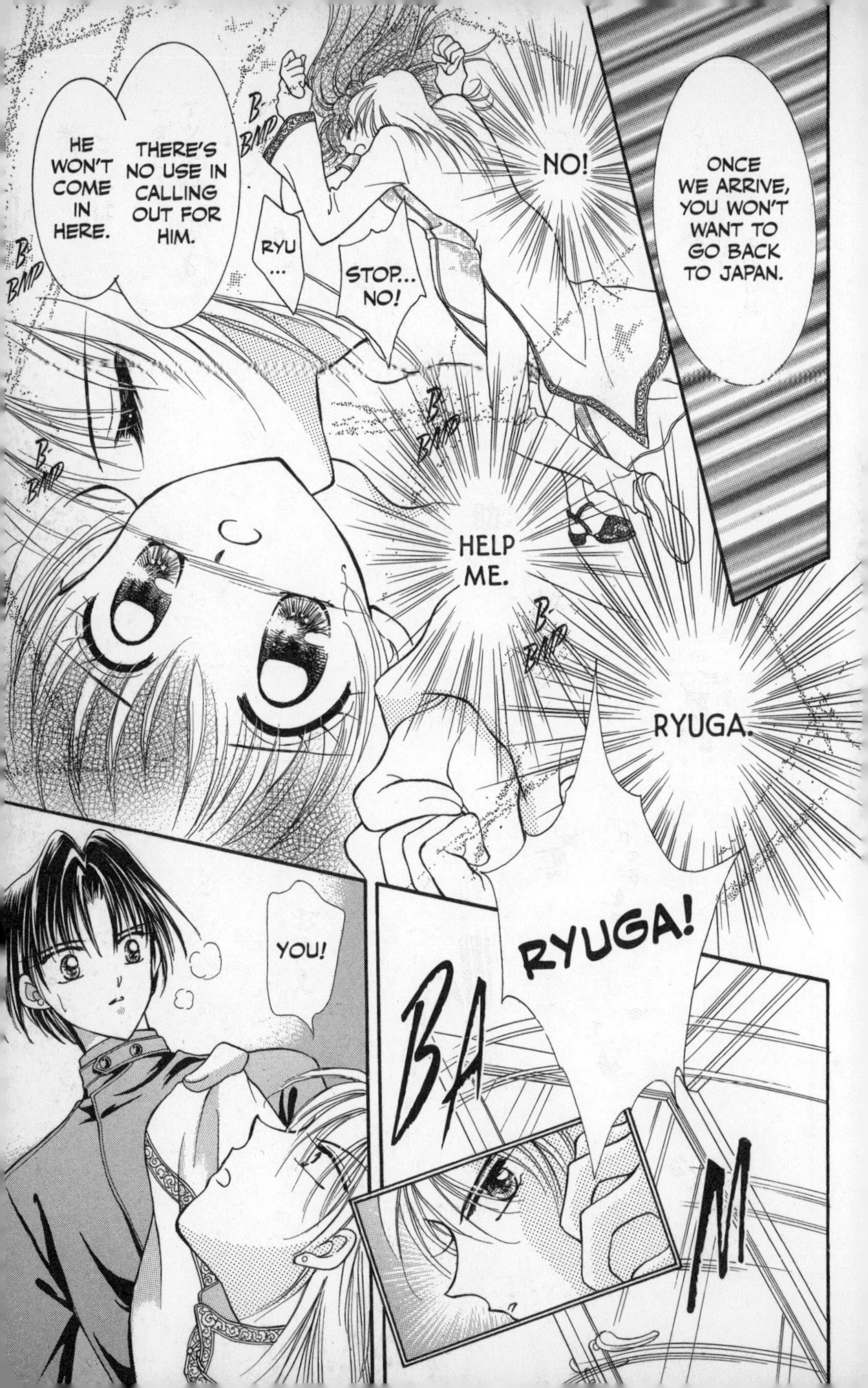
ONCE WE ARRIVE, YOU WON'T WANT TO GO BACK TO JAPAN.
NO!
THERE'S NO USE IN CALLING OUT FOR HIM.
HE WON'T COME IN HERE.
B-BMP
B-BMP
RYU ...
STOP... NO!
B-BMP
B-BMP
HELP ME.
B-BMP
RYUGA.
RYUGA!
BAM
YOU!

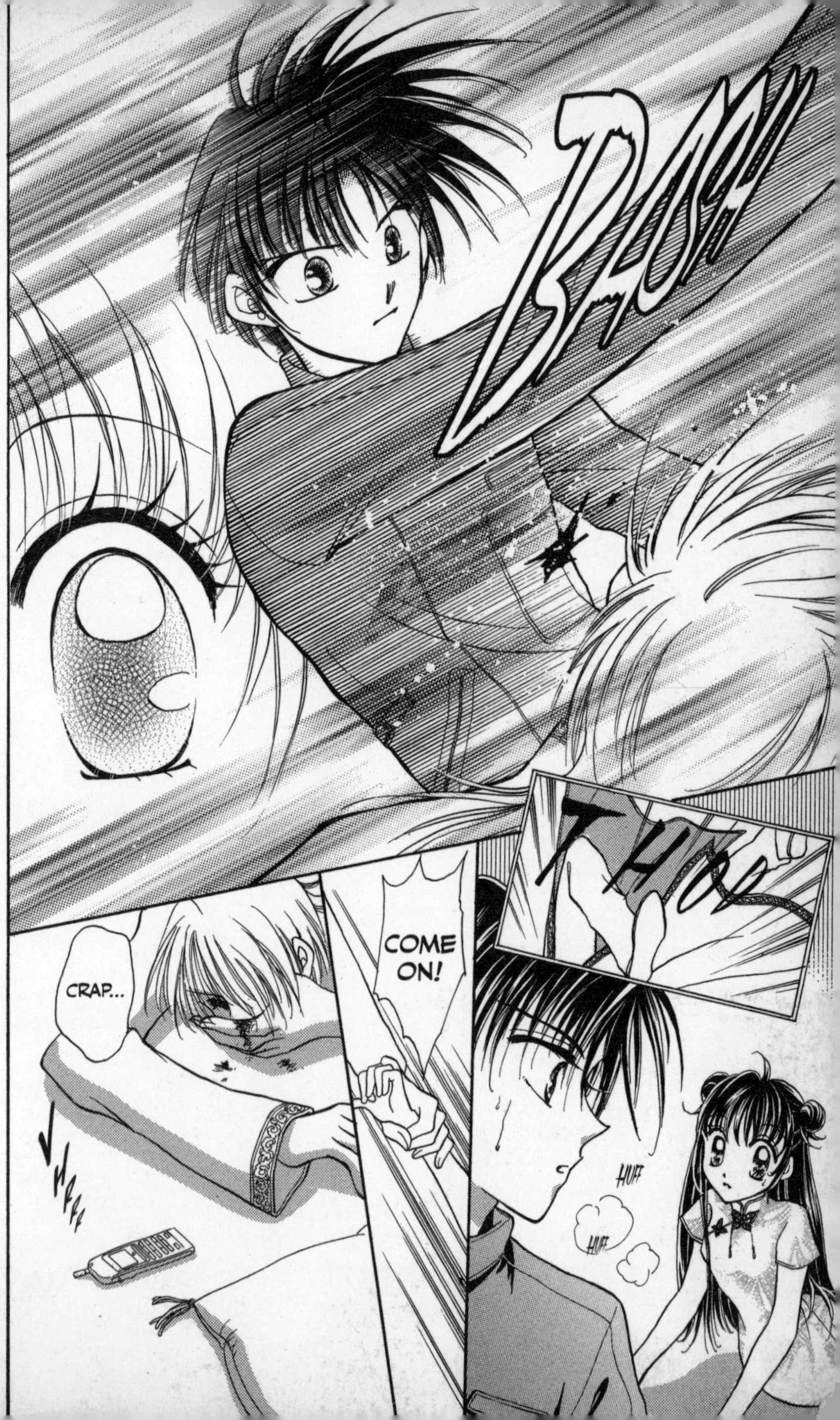
BASH
THUD
HUFF
HUFF
COME ON!
CRAP...

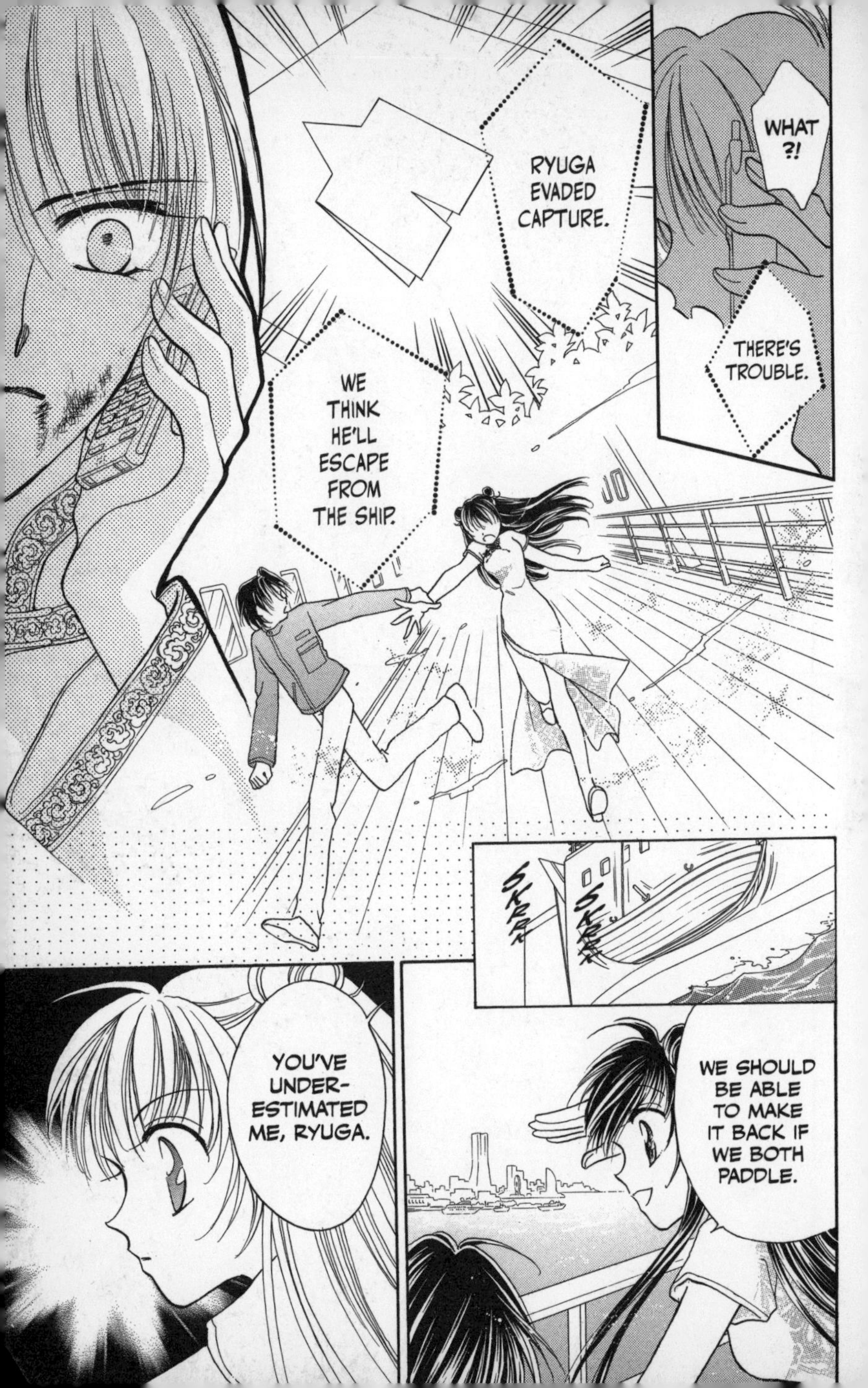
WHAT ?!
THERE'S TROUBLE.
RYUGA EVADED CAPTURE.
WE THINK HE'LL ESCAPE FROM THE SHIP.
SKRRR
SKRRR
WE SHOULD BE ABLE TO MAKE IT BACK IF WE BOTH PADDLE.
YOU'VE UNDER-ESTIMATED ME, RYUGA.

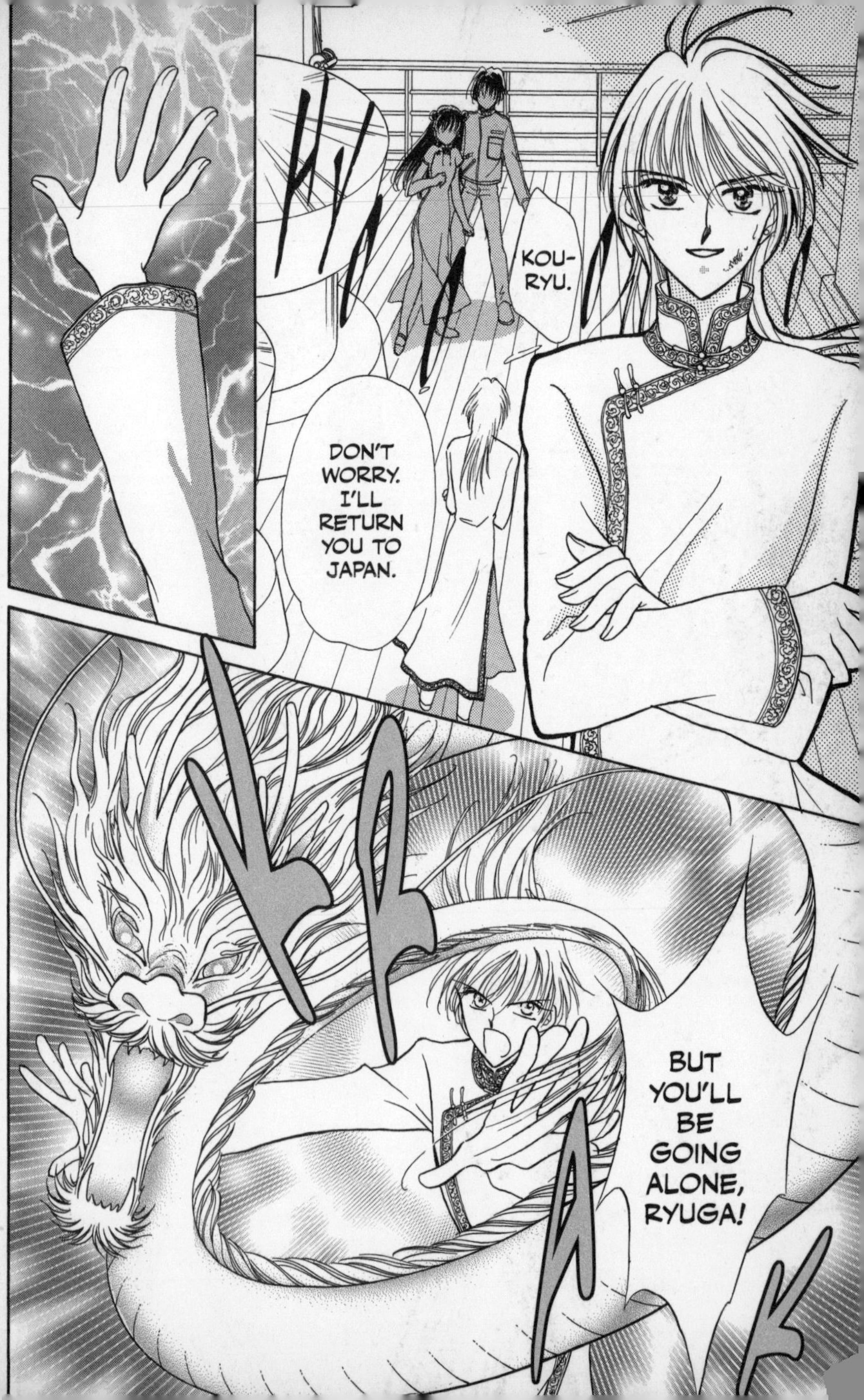
KOU-RYU.
DON'T WORRY. I'LL RETURN YOU TO JAPAN.
BUT YOU'LL BE GOING ALONE, RYUGA!

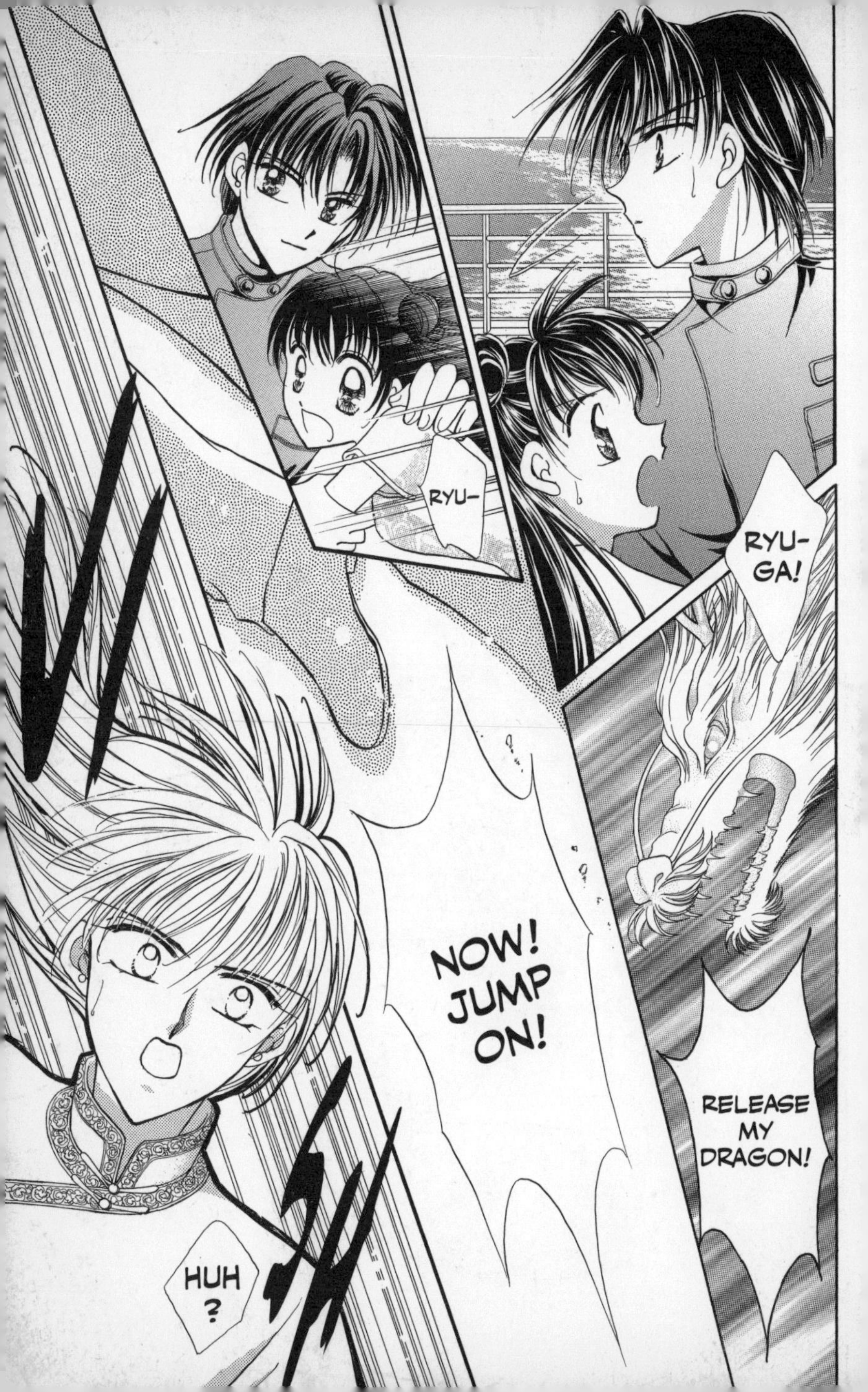
RYU-
RYU-GA!
RELEASE MY DRAGON!
NOW! JUMP ON!
HUH?

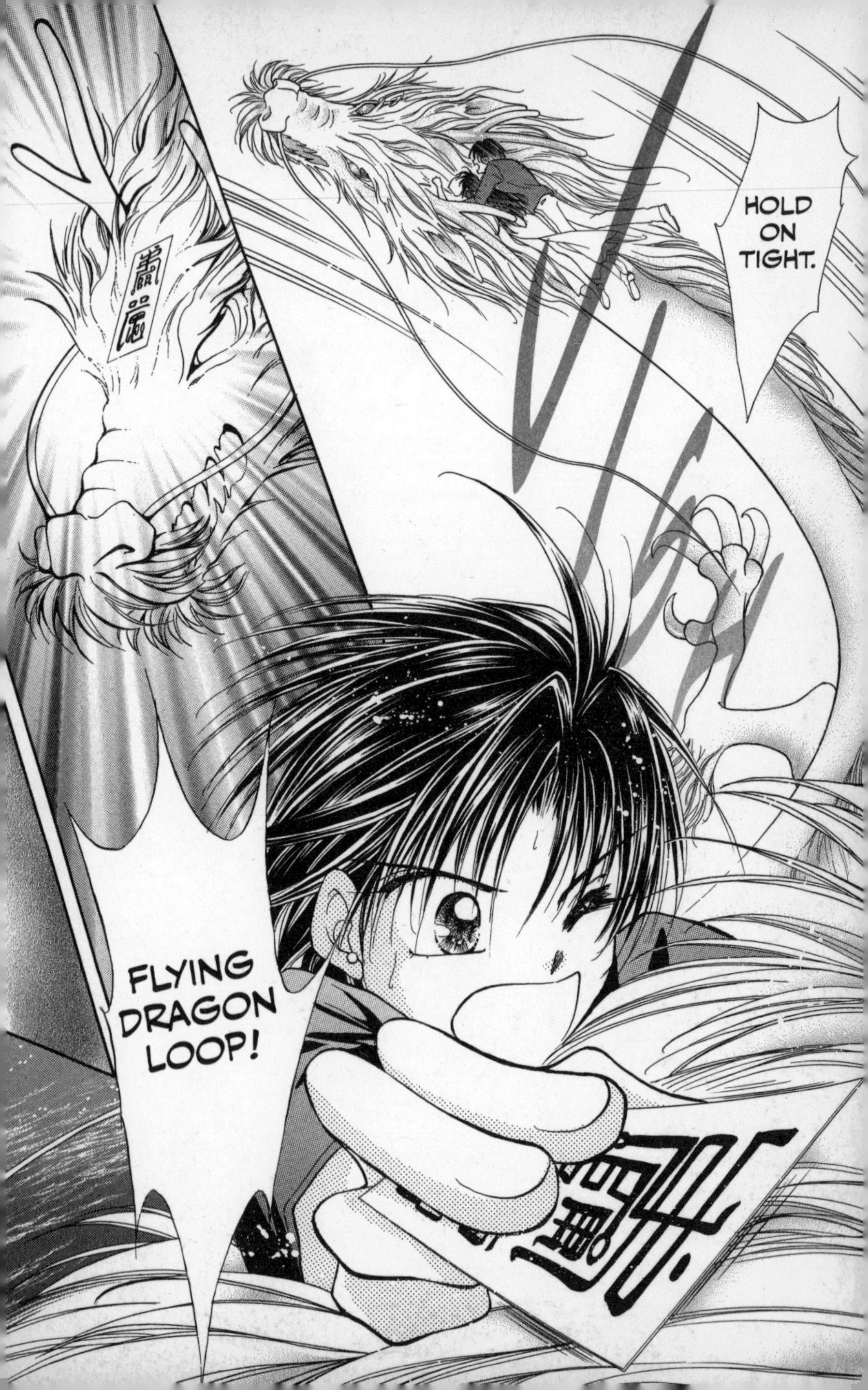
HOLD ON TIGHT.
FLYING DRAGON LOOP!

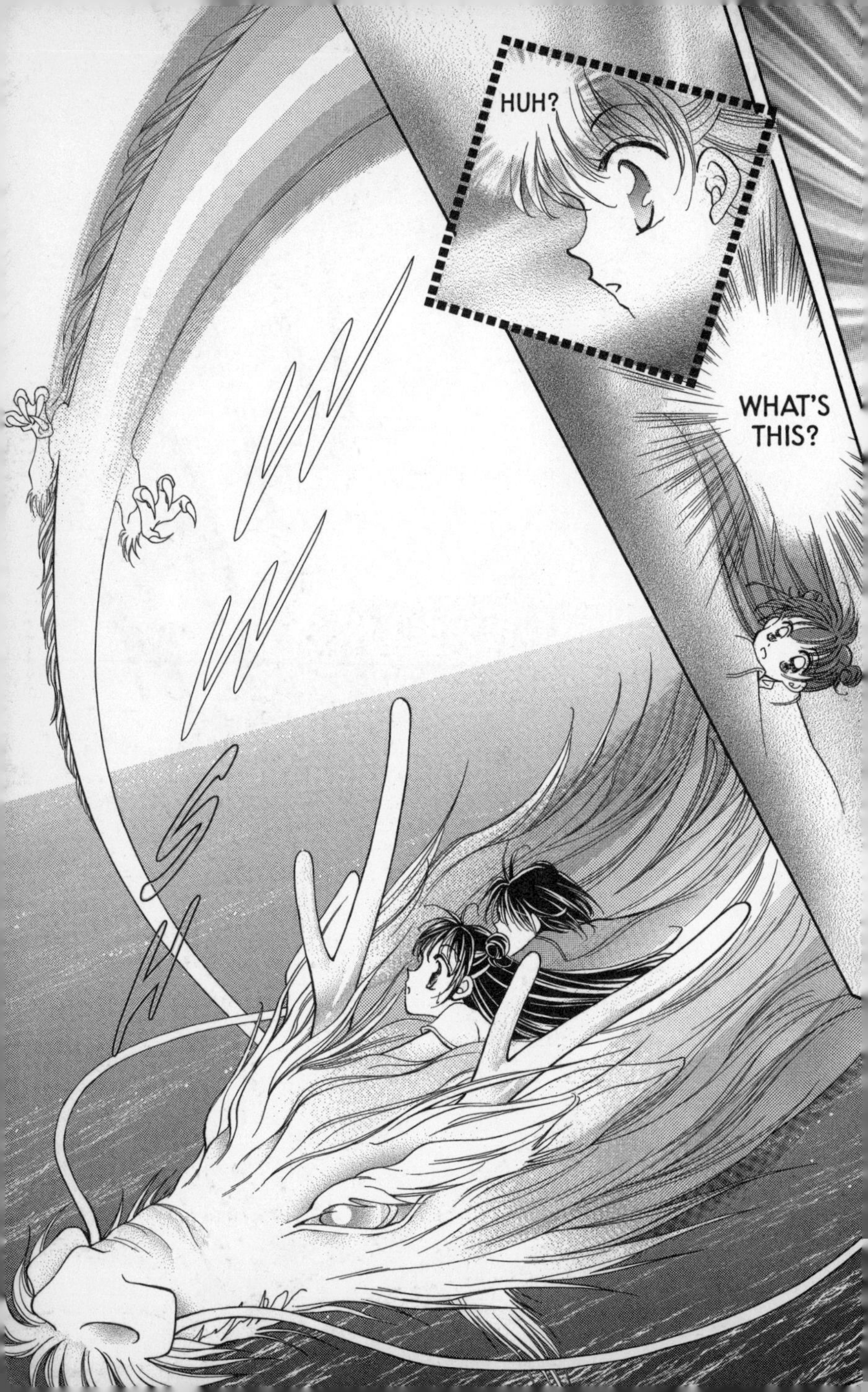
HUH?
WHAT'S THIS?

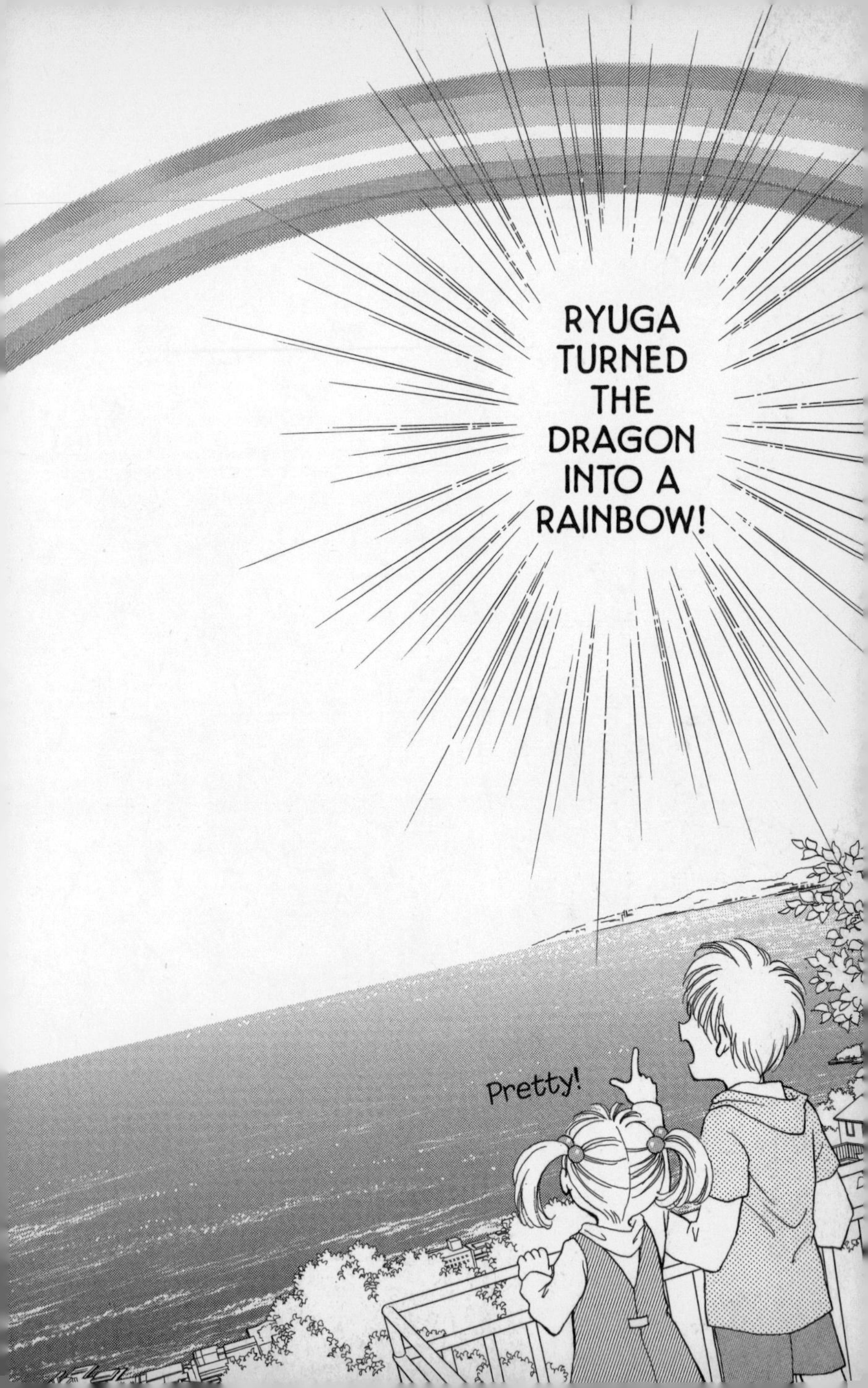
RYUGA TURNED THE DRAGON INTO A RAINBOW!
Pretty!

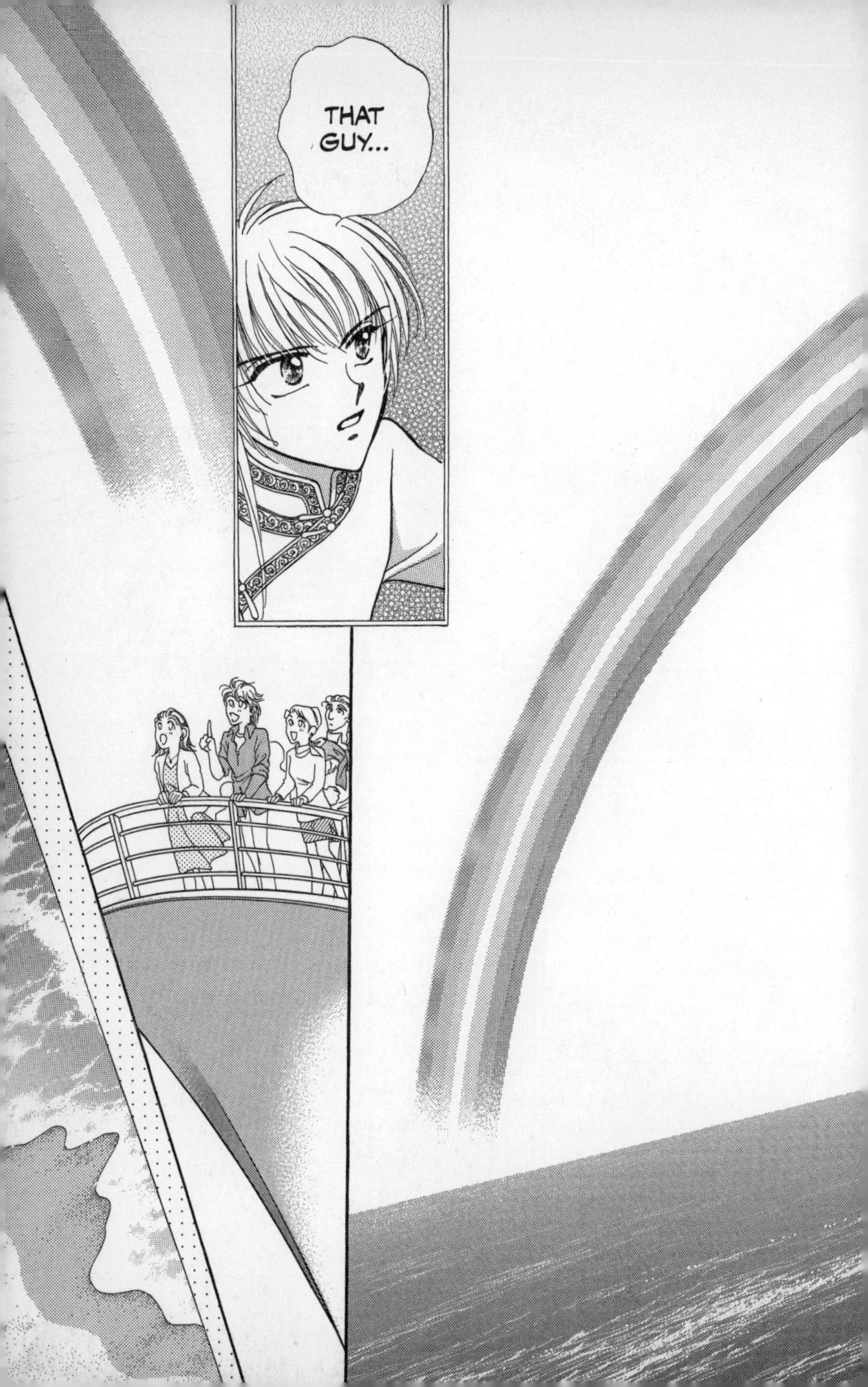
THAT GUY...

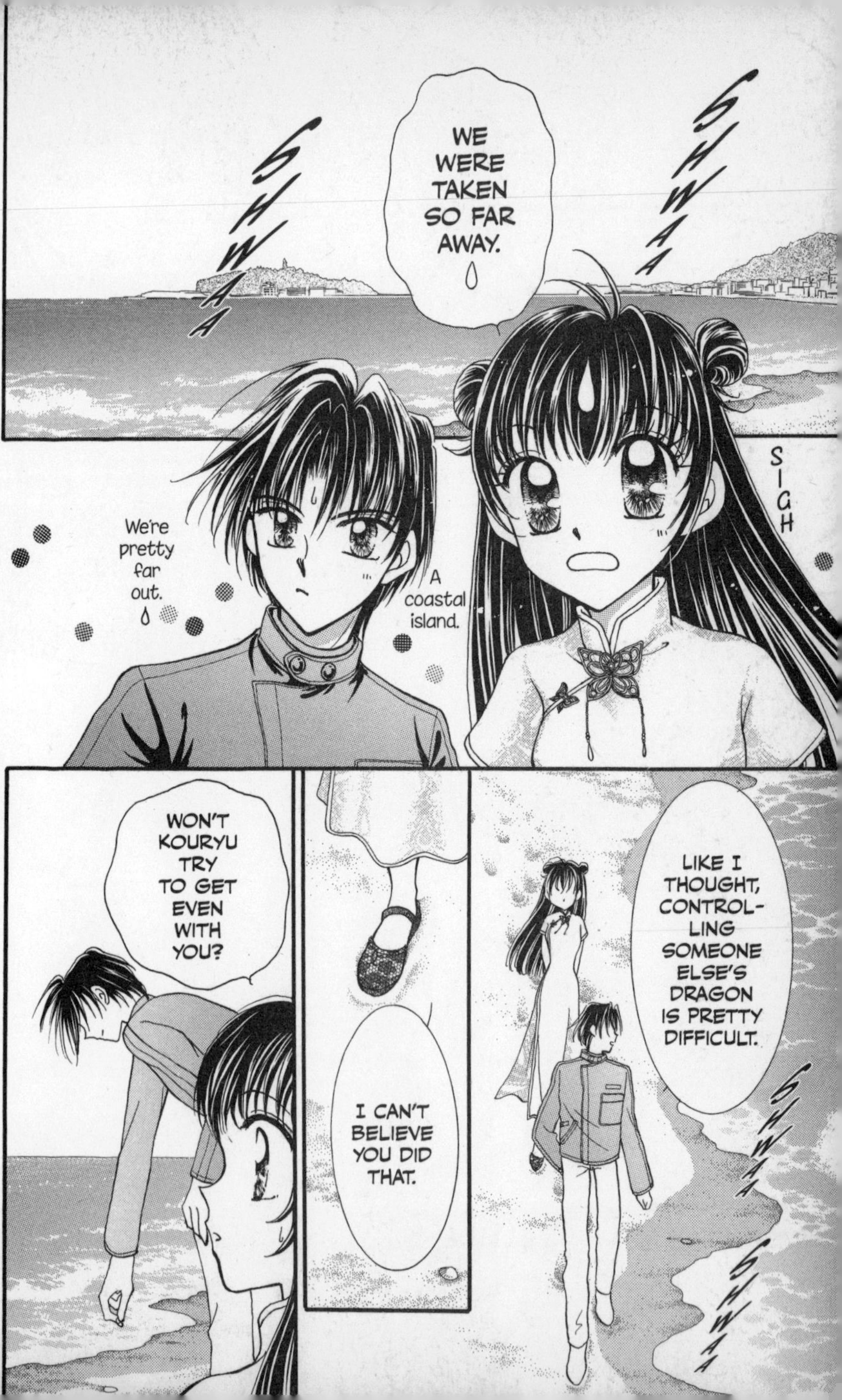
SHWAAA
WE WERE TAKEN SO FAR AWAY.
SHWAAA
SIGH
A coastal island.
We're pretty far out.
LIKE I THOUGHT, CONTROL-LING SOMEONE ELSE'S DRAGON IS PRETTY DIFFICULT.
SHWAAA
SHWAAA
I CAN'T BELIEVE YOU DID THAT.
WON'T KOURYU TRY TO GET EVEN WITH YOU?

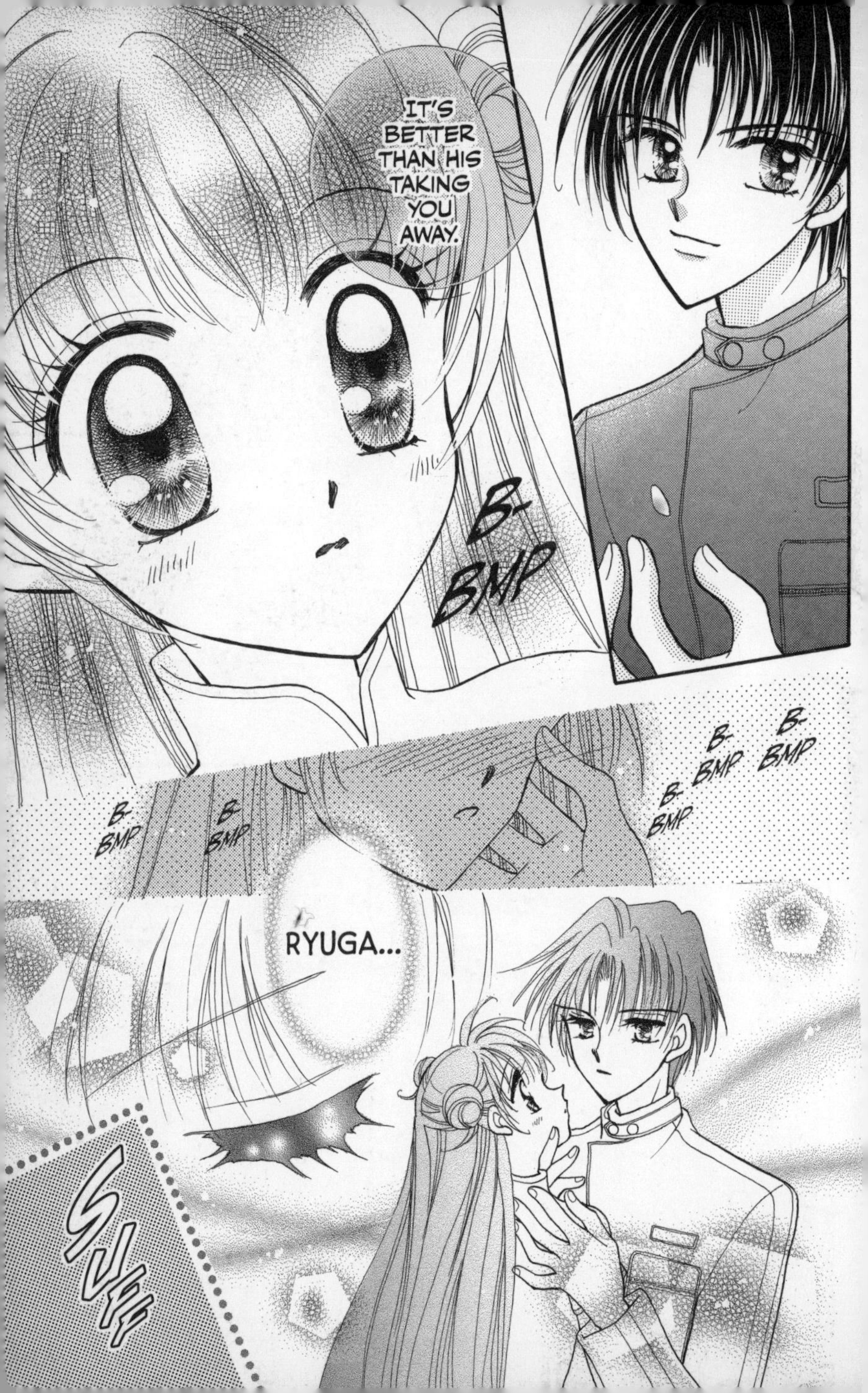
IT'S BETTER THAN HIS TAKING YOU AWAY.
B-BMP
B-BMP
B-BMP
B-BMP
B-BMP
B-BMP
RYUGA...

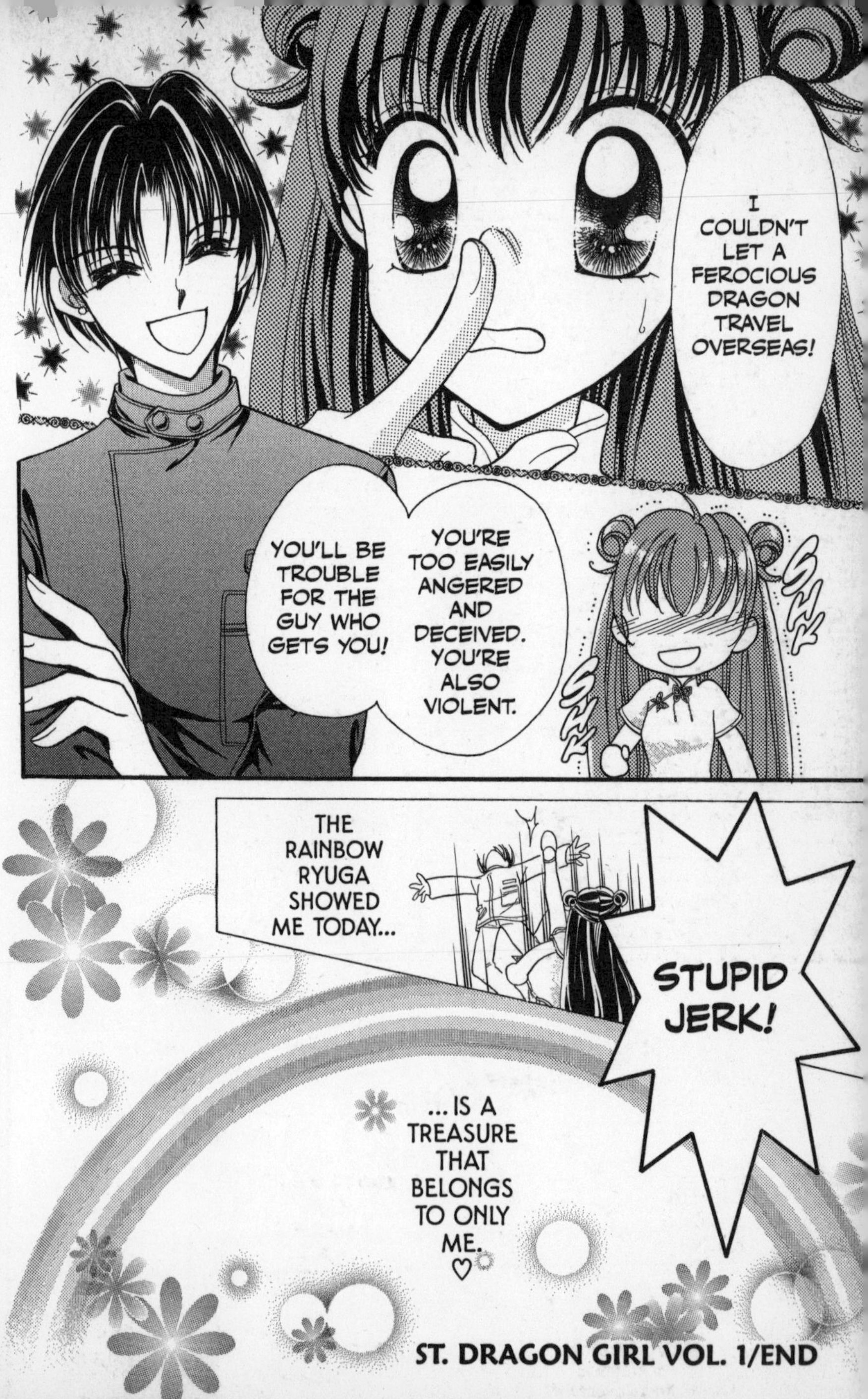
I COULDN'T LET A FEROCIOUS DRAGON TRAVEL OVERSEAS!
YOU'RE TOO EASILY ANGERED AND DECEIVED. YOU'RE ALSO VIOLENT.
YOU'LL BE TROUBLE FOR THE GUY WHO GETS YOU!
STUPID JERK!
THE RAINBOW RYUGA SHOWED ME TODAY...
...IS A TREASURE THAT BELONGS TO ONLY ME. ♡

ST. DRAGON GIRL VOL. 1/END

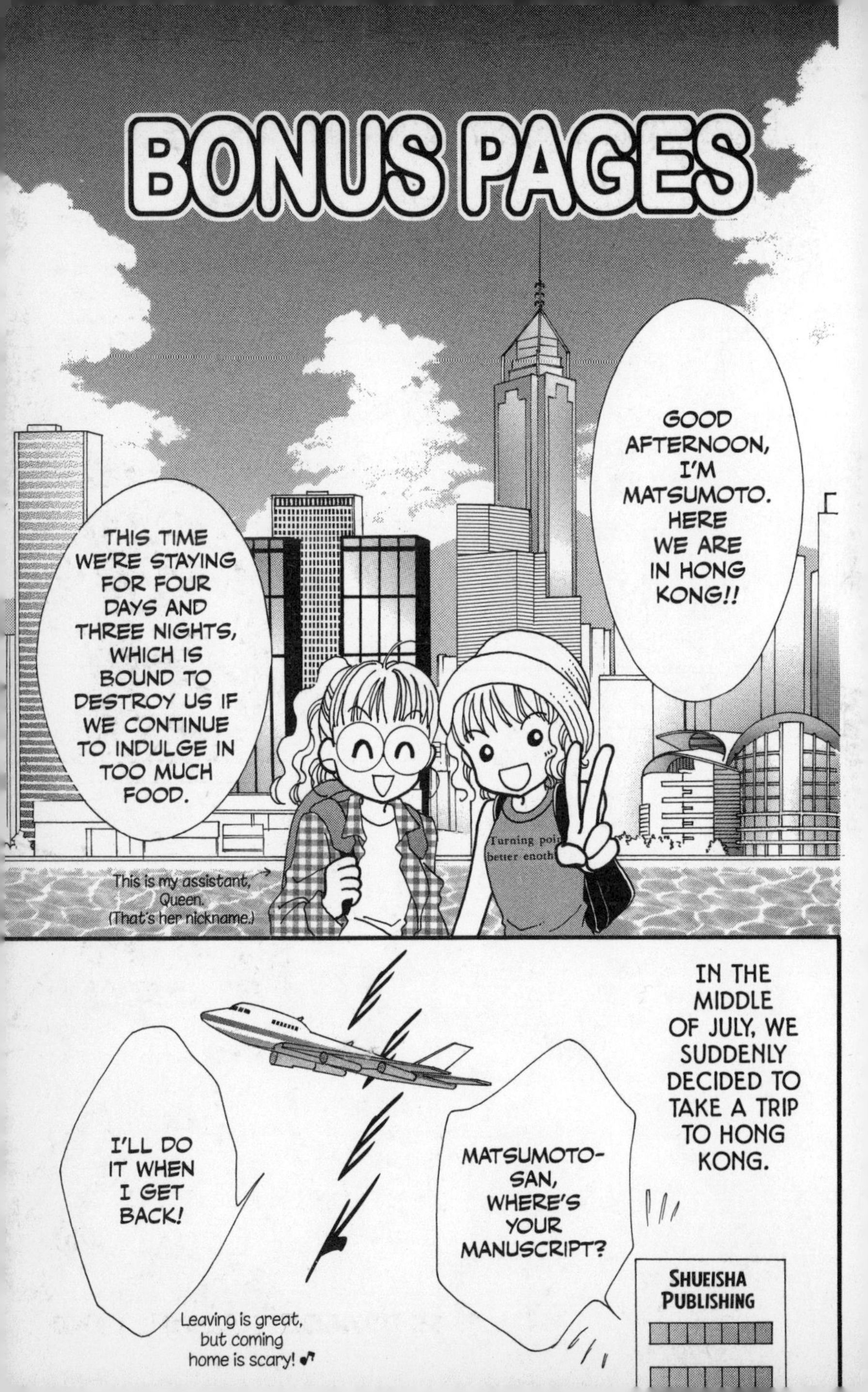
BONUS PAGES
GOOD AFTERNOON, I'M MATSUMOTO. HERE WE ARE IN HONG KONG!!
THIS TIME WE'RE STAYING FOR FOUR DAYS AND THREE NIGHTS, WHICH IS BOUND TO DESTROY US IF WE CONTINUE TO INDULGE IN TOO MUCH FOOD.
This is my assistant, Queen. (That's her nickname.)
IN THE MIDDLE OF JULY, WE SUDDENLY DECIDED TO TAKE A TRIP TO HONG KONG.
SHUEISHA PUBLISHING
MATSUMOTO-SAN, WHERE'S YOUR MANUSCRIPT?
I'LL DO IT WHEN I GET BACK!
Leaving is great, but coming home is scary! ♪

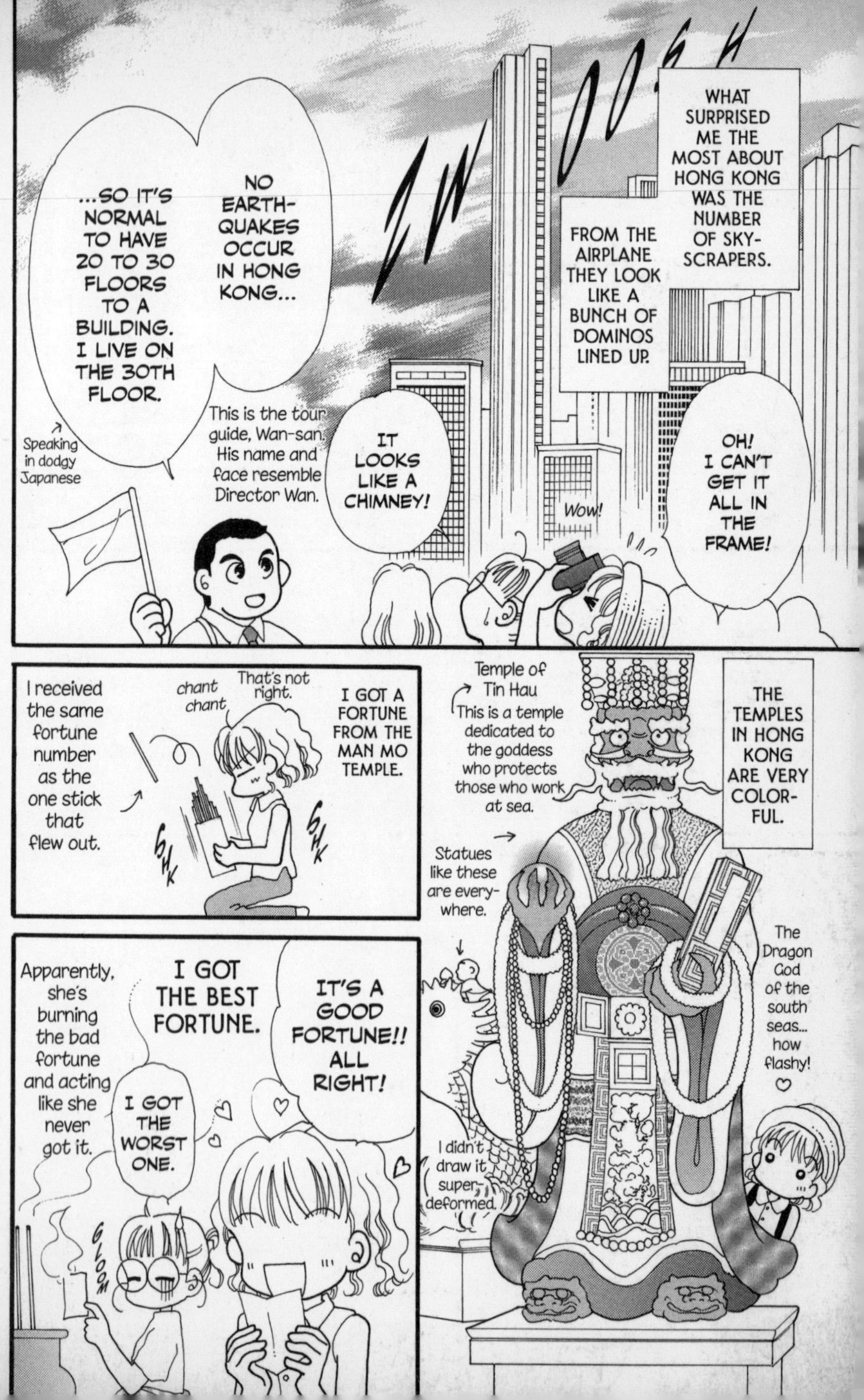
WHAT SURPRISED ME THE MOST ABOUT HONG KONG WAS THE NUMBER OF SKY-SCRAPERS.
FROM THE AIRPLANE THEY LOOK LIKE A BUNCH OF DOMINOS LINED UP.
ZWOOSH
OH! I CAN'T GET IT ALL IN THE FRAME!
Wow!
IT LOOKS LIKE A CHIMNEY!
This is the tour guide, Wan-san. His name and face resemble Director Wan.
NO EARTH-QUAKES OCCUR IN HONG KONG...
...SO IT'S NORMAL TO HAVE 20 TO 30 FLOORS TO A BUILDING. I LIVE ON THE 30TH FLOOR.
Speaking in dodgy Japanese
THE TEMPLES IN HONG KONG ARE VERY COLOR-FUL.
Temple of Tin Hau
This is a temple dedicated to the goddess who protects those who work at sea.
The Dragon God of the south seas... how flashy! ♡
Statues like these are every-where.
I didn't draw it super-deformed.
I GOT A FORTUNE FROM THE MAN MO TEMPLE.
That's not right.
chant chant
SHK
SHK
I received the same fortune number as the one stick that flew out.
IT'S A GOOD FORTUNE!! ALL RIGHT!
I GOT THE BEST FORTUNE.
I GOT THE WORST ONE.
Apparently, she's burning the bad fortune and acting like she never got it.
GLOOM

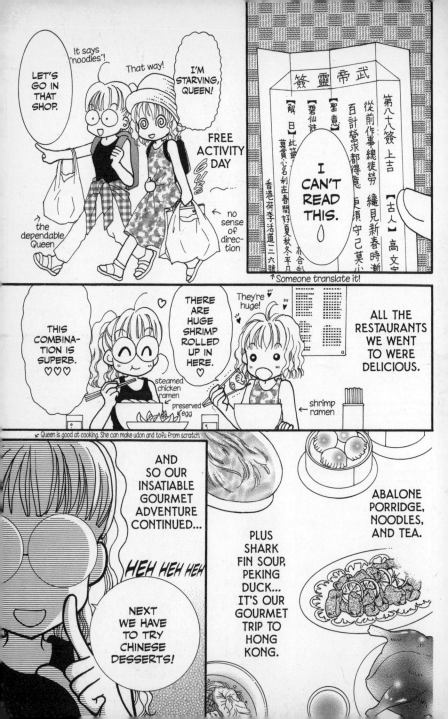

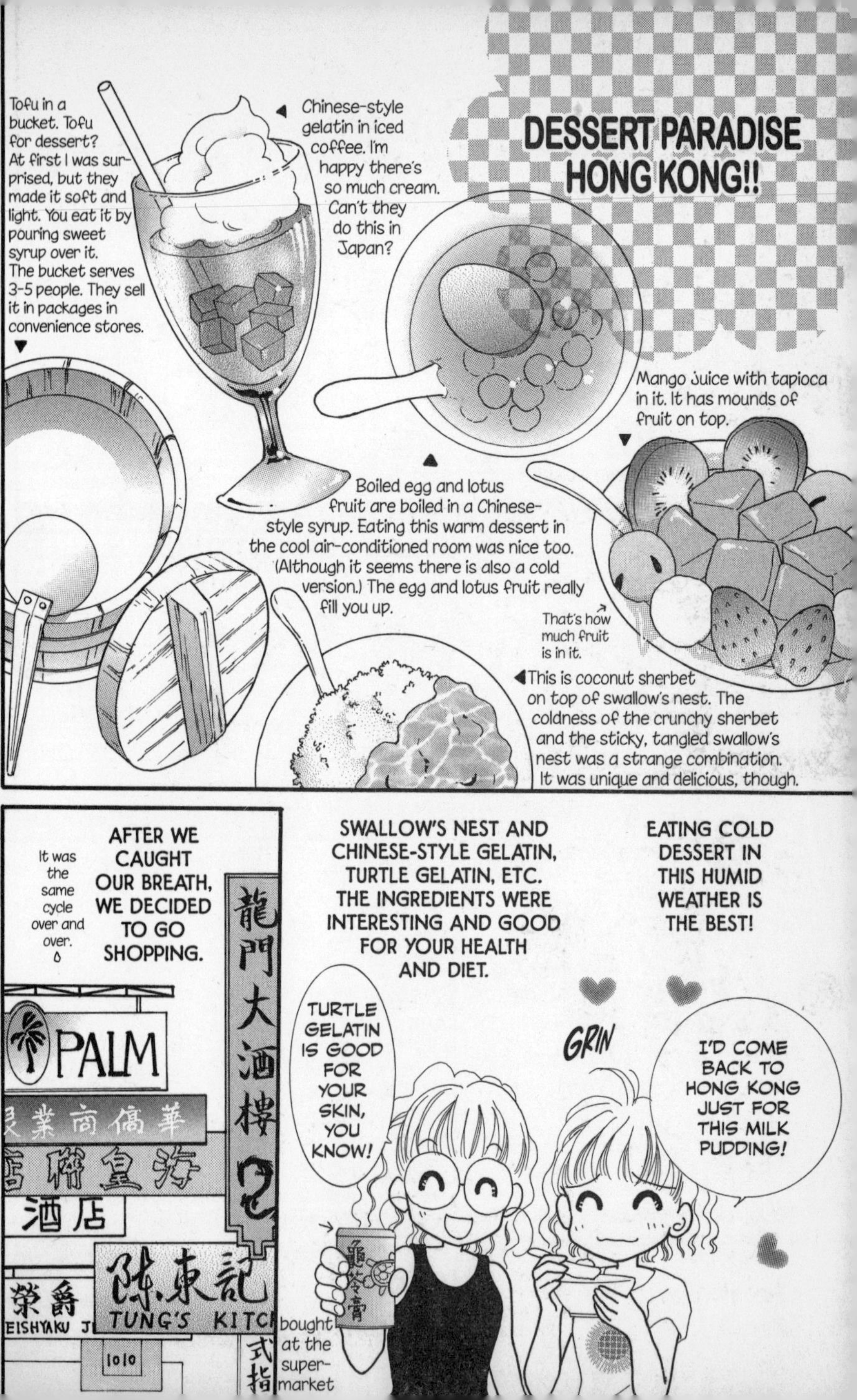
DESSERT PARADISE HONG KONG!!
Chinese-style gelatin in iced coffee. I'm happy there's so much cream. Can't they do this in Japan?
Tofu in a bucket. Tofu for dessert? At first I was surprised, but they made it soft and light. You eat it by pouring sweet syrup over it. The bucket serves 3-5 people. They sell it in packages in convenience stores.
Mango Juice with tapioca in it. It has mounds of fruit on top.
That's how much fruit is in it.
Boiled egg and lotus fruit are boiled in a Chinese-style syrup. Eating this warm dessert in the cool air-conditioned room was nice too. (Although it seems there is also a cold version.) The egg and lotus fruit really fill you up.
This is coconut sherbet on top of swallow's nest. The coldness of the crunchy sherbet and the sticky, tangled swallow's nest was a strange combination. It was unique and delicious, though.
EATING COLD DESSERT IN THIS HUMID WEATHER IS THE BEST!
SWALLOW'S NEST AND CHINESE-STYLE GELATIN, TURTLE GELATIN, ETC. THE INGREDIENTS WERE INTERESTING AND GOOD FOR YOUR HEALTH AND DIET.
GRIN
I'D COME BACK TO HONG KONG JUST FOR THIS MILK PUDDING!
TURTLE GELATIN IS GOOD FOR YOUR SKIN, YOU KNOW!
龜苓膏
bought at the super-market
AFTER WE CAUGHT OUR BREATH, WE DECIDED TO GO SHOPPING.
It was the same cycle over and over.
龍門大酒樓
PALM
酒店
陳東記
TUNG'S KITCH
1010

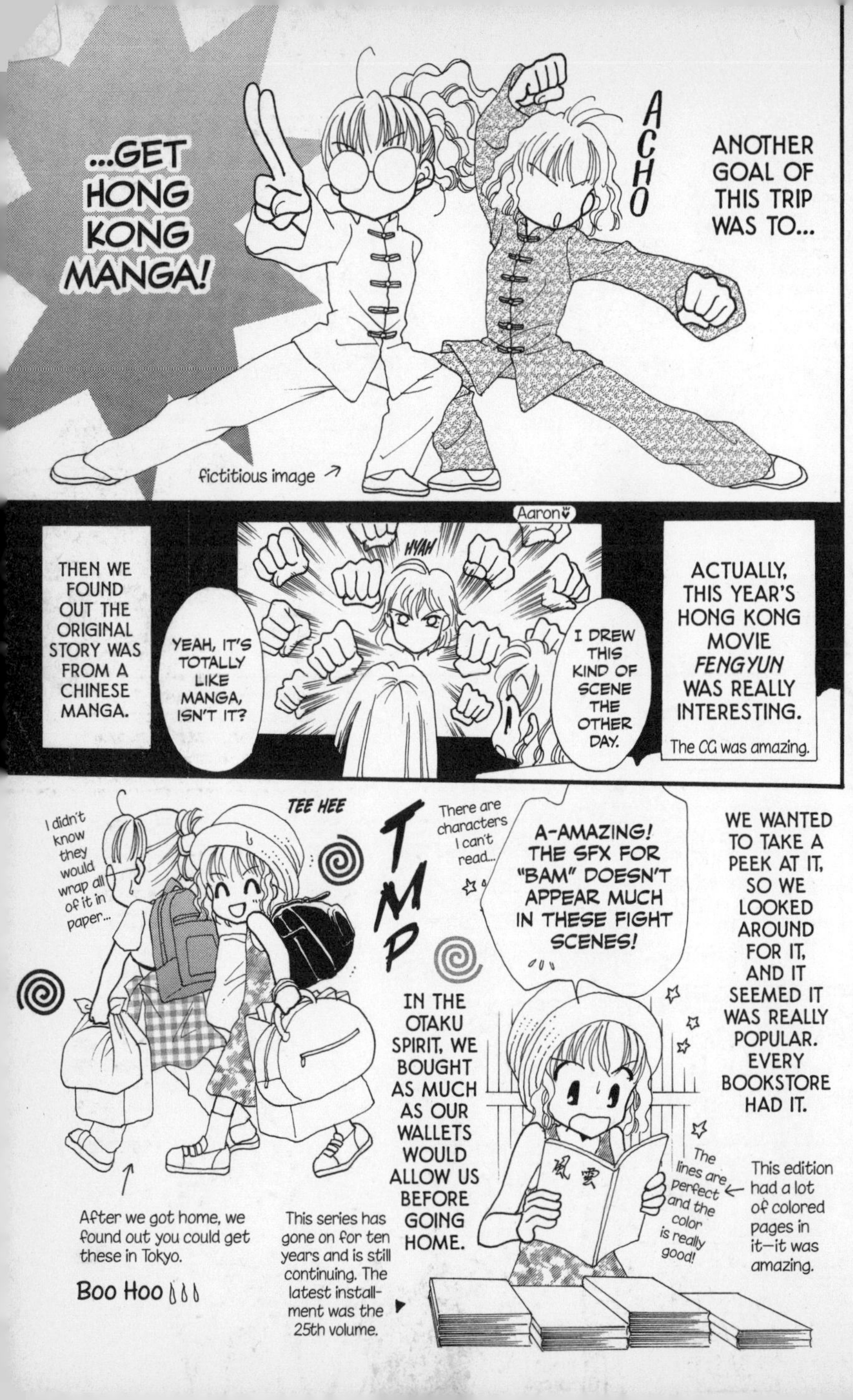
ANOTHER GOAL OF THIS TRIP WAS TO...
ACHO
...GET HONG KONG MANGA!
fictitious image
ACTUALLY, THIS YEAR'S HONG KONG MOVIE *FENGYUN* WAS REALLY INTERESTING.
The CG was amazing.
Aaron
HYAH
I DREW THIS KIND OF SCENE THE OTHER DAY.
YEAH, IT'S TOTALLY LIKE MANGA, ISN'T IT?
THEN WE FOUND OUT THE ORIGINAL STORY WAS FROM A CHINESE MANGA.
WE WANTED TO TAKE A PEEK AT IT, SO WE LOOKED AROUND FOR IT, AND IT SEEMED IT WAS REALLY POPULAR. EVERY BOOKSTORE HAD IT.
This edition had a lot of colored pages in it—it was amazing.
The lines are perfect and the color is really good!
A-AMAZING! THE SFX FOR "BAM" DOESN'T APPEAR MUCH IN THESE FIGHT SCENES!
There are characters I can't read...
IN THE OTAKU SPIRIT, WE BOUGHT AS MUCH AS OUR WALLETS WOULD ALLOW US BEFORE GOING HOME.
This series has gone on for ten years and is still continuing. The latest installment was the 25th volume.
TMP
TEE HEE
I didn't know they would wrap all of it in paper...
After we got home, we found out you could get these in Tokyo.
Boo Hoo

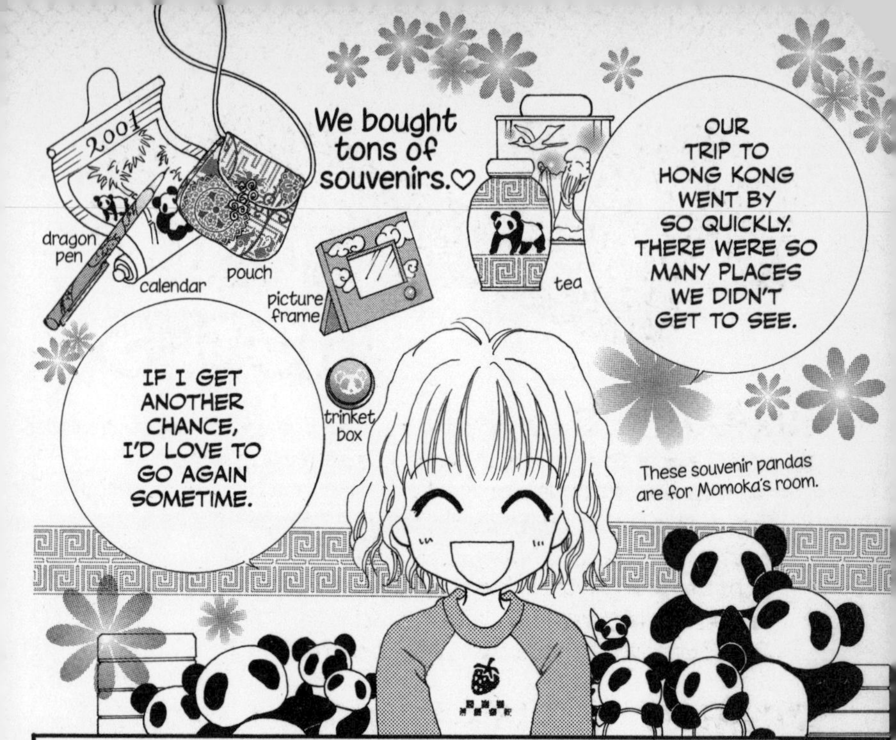
OUR TRIP TO HONG KONG WENT BY SO QUICKLY. THERE WERE SO MANY PLACES WE DIDN'T GET TO SEE.
We bought tons of souvenirs.♡
tea
picture frame
pouch
calendar
dragon pen
2001
trinket box
IF I GET ANOTHER CHANCE, I'D LOVE TO GO AGAIN SOMETIME.
These souvenir pandas are for Momoka's room.

IF YOU'D LIKE TO SEND A LETTER
TO NATSUMI MATSUMOTO,
PLEASE IT TO THE ADDRESS BELOW.

Natsumi Matsumoto
c/o Nancy Thistlethwaite, editor
VIZ Media
P.O. Box 77010
San Francisco, CA 94107

ALSO, PLEASE CHECK OUT
THE FAN ART REQUEST
AND RELEASE FORM ON
PAGES 192 AND 193.

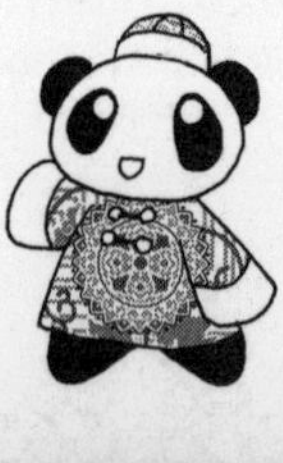

HONORIFICS

In Japan, people are usually addressed by their name followed by a suffix. The suffix shows familiarity or respect, depending on the relationship.

Male (familiar): first or last name + kun
Female (familiar): first or last name + chan
Adult (polite): last name + san
Upperclassman (polite): last name + senpai
Teacher or professional: last name + sensei
Close friends or lovers: first name only, no suffix

DRAGON WORDPLAY

The kanji for *ryu* in Ryuga's name means "dragon." That's why Ryuga tells Momoka, "The dragon who protects you should be me" on page 40. He's literally saying that he should be the *ryu* who protects her. Momoka comes back with a pun of her own when she says, "In that case, I want to be the dragon who protects you!" The literal is *Ryuga o mamoru. Ryu ga hoshii yo!* ("I'll protect Ryuga. I want the dragon!") But in Japanese, the second sentence also sounds like "I want Ryuga!" which is probably the cause of Ryuga's slight blush.

TERMS

Momoka means "peach flower."
Suijin means "water god."
Ni hao means "hello" in Chinese.
Kenpo means "the way of the fist."
A *kappa* is a mythical water sprite that resembles a turtle.
Tourin means "peach forest."
Giri chocolate is given out of duty rather than love.
Kouryu means "rainbow dragon."
Teru teru bozu is a doll that people make and hang up to bring clear weather.

ST. ♥ DRAGON GIRL

FAN ART SUBMISSIONS!

I'm looking for fan art to include in future volumes of the *St. ♥ Dragon Girl* manga.

Please fill out the form on the next page and send it in with your fan art to:

> Nancy Thistlethwaite, Editor
> VIZ Media
> P.O. Box 77010
> San Francisco, CA 94107

Guidelines:

- All fan art will be presented in black and white, but you can send color art if you want.
- Submissions should be no bigger than 8 1/2" by 11".
- All submissions must have a completed release form (see next page) for consideration.

Please be sure to include the following with your fan art.

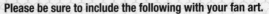

 FAN ART RELEASE

In exchange for allowing the artwork I submitted with this Fan Art Release ("Fan Art") to be considered for inclusion in the *St. ♥ Dragon Girl* manga series and/or other publications, I hereby irrevocably authorize and grant a non-exclusive, transferable, worldwide, perpetual license to VIZ Media, LLC and others authorized by it, to use, copy, print, publicly display, broadcast and edit the Fan Art and my name, in whole or in part, with or without my name identification, in any and all media now known or hereinafter developed without time, territory or other restrictions and to refrain from doing any or all of the foregoing. I release them all from any claims, liability, costs, losses or damages of any kind in connection therewith, including but not limited to copyright infringement, right of publicity/privacy, blurring or optical distortion. I agree that I have no right to approve any use of the Fan Art or my name as licensed above or the content thereof.

I represent and warrant that I am of the age of majority in my state or province of residence (or, if not, that a parent or legal guardian will sign on my behalf) and that this release does not in any way conflict with any existing commitments on my part. I represent that no other person, firm or entity claiming or deriving rights through me is entitled to grant the rights in the Fan Art I've granted to you (or granted by my parent or legal guardian on my behalf) and that I have the right to license it as outlined herein. I further represent and warrant that I have the full right to enter into this agreement without violating the legal or equitable rights of any third party and that no payments shall be due to me or any third party in conjunction with the use of the Fan Art or my name as outlined herein.

ACCEPTED AND AGREED TO:

Print Name: _____

Signature: _____

(Sign or have your Parent or Legal Guardian do so, if you are a minor)

Address: _____

Date: _____

"I want to write a manga that's as powerful and influential as a Hong Kong movie!" The "Dragon Girl" was born of those feelings I had. Drawing all the action scenes took a lot of work, but it was fun too. Out of all my heroines, Momoka is the liveliest and the strongest! (*laugh*) If her power gets across to you, I'll be really happy! ♥

—Natsumi Matsumoto

Natsumi Matsumoto debuted with the manga *Guuzen Janai Yo!* (No Coincidence!) in *Ribon Original* magazine. *St. ♥ Dragon Girl* was such a hit that it spawned a sequel, *St. ♥ Dragon Girl Miracle*. Her other series include *Angel Time* and *Alice kara Magic*. In her free time, Natsumi studies Chinese and practices tai chi. She also likes visiting aquariums and collecting the toy prizes that come with snack food in Japan.

St. ♥ Dragon Girl
Vol. 1
The Shojo Beat Manga Edition

STORY AND ART BY | **Natsumi Matsumoto**

English Adaptation | **Heidi Vivolo**
Translation | **Andria Cheng**
Touch-up Art & Lettering | **Gia Cam Luc**
Design | **Fawn Lau**
Editor | **Nancy Thistlethwaite**

Editor in Chief, Books | **Alvin Lu**
Editor in Chief, Magazines | **Marc Weidenbaum**
VP, Publishing Licensing | **Rika Inouye**
VP, Sales & Product Marketing | **Gonzalo Ferreyra**
VP, Creative | **Linda Espinosa**
Publisher | **Hyoe Narita**

SAINT DRAGON GIRL © 1999 by Natsumi Matsumoto. All rights reserved. First published in Japan in 1999 by SHUEISHA Inc., Tokyo. English translation rights arranged by SHUEISHA Inc. The stories, characters and incidents mentioned in this publication are entirely fictional.

Printed in Canada

Published by VIZ Media, LLC
P.O. Box 77010
San Francisco, CA 94107

Shojo Beat Manga Edition
10 9 8 7 6 5 4 3 2 1
First printing, December 2008

PARENTAL ADVISORY
ST. ♥ DRAGON GIRL is rated T for Teen and is recommended for ages 13 and up. This volume contains suggestive themes.
ratings.viz.com

store.viz.com

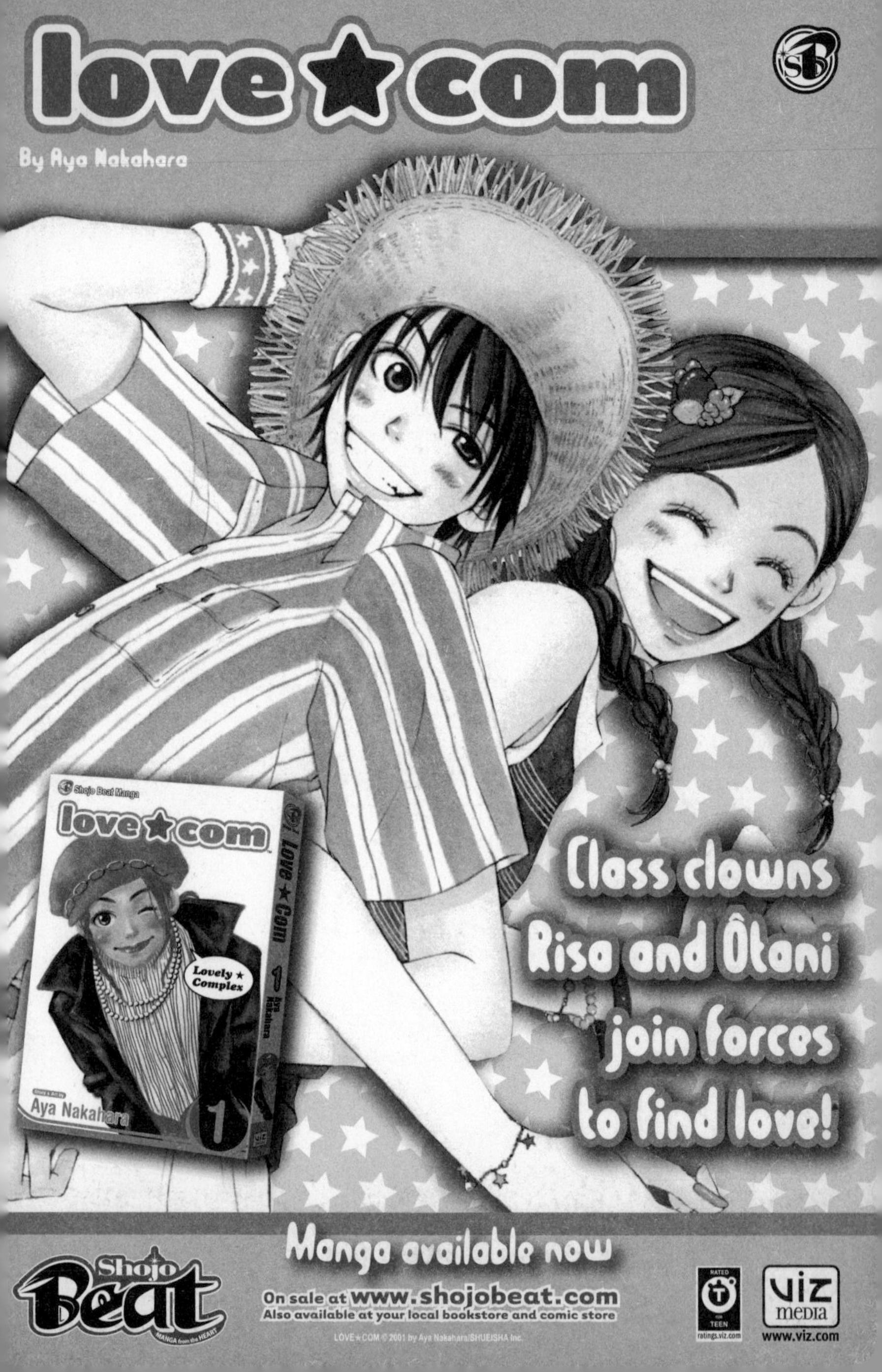

love★com
By Aya Nakahara
Shojo Beat Manga
love★com
Lovely ★ Complex
Story & Art by
Aya Nakahara
1
Class clowns Risa and Ôtani join forces to find love!
Manga available now
Shojo Beat
MANGA from the HEART
On sale at www.shojobeat.com
Also available at your local bookstore and comic store
LOVE★COM © 2001 by Aya Nakahara/SHUEISHA Inc.
RATED T FOR TEEN
ratings.viz.com
VIZ MEDIA
www.viz.com

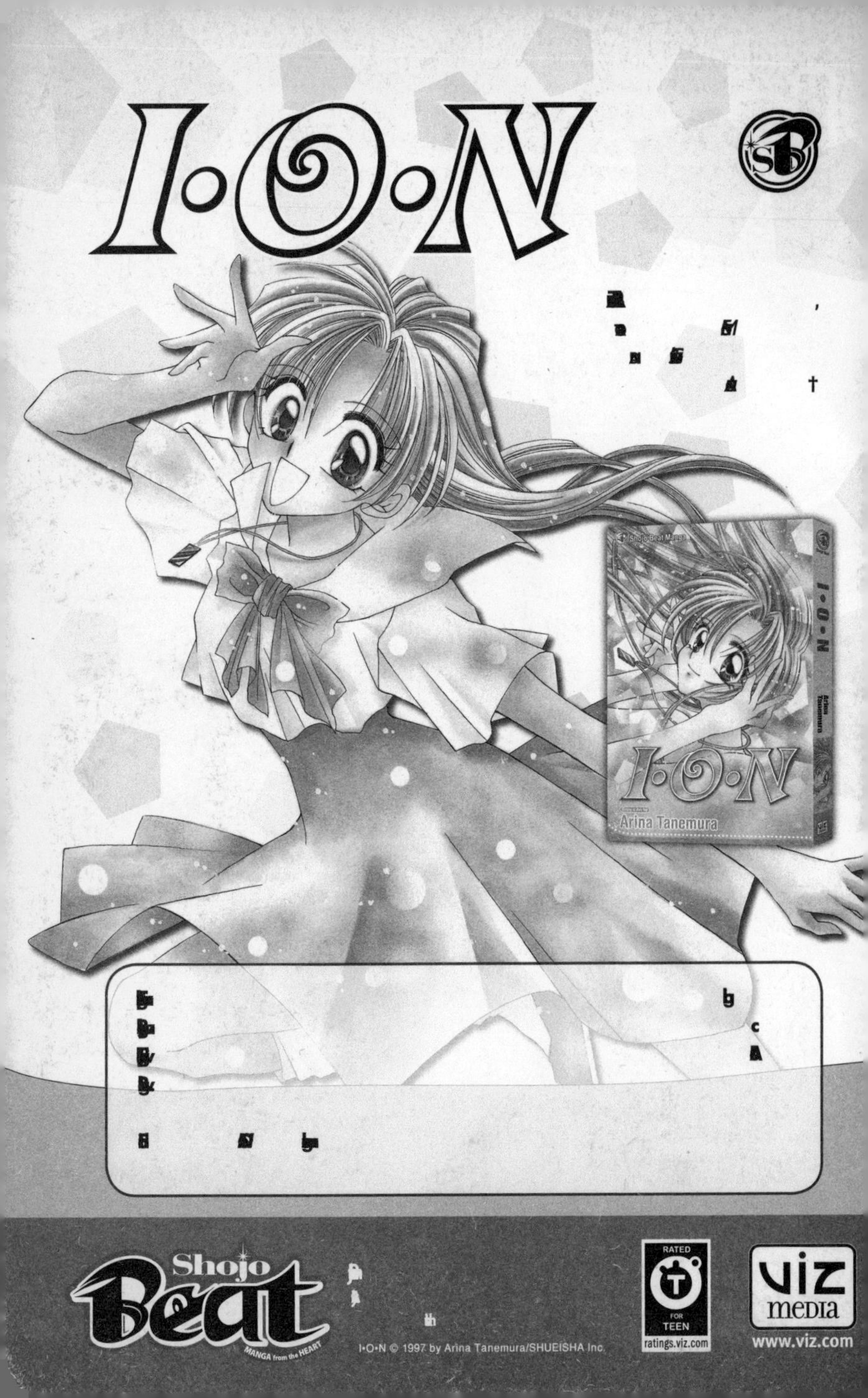

I•O•N
Shojo Beat Manga
I•O•N
Arina Tanemura
Arina Tanemura
Shojo Beat
MANGA from the HEART
I•O•N © 1997 by Arina Tanemura/SHUEISHA Inc.
RATED T FOR TEEN
ratings.viz.com
VIZ media
www.viz.com

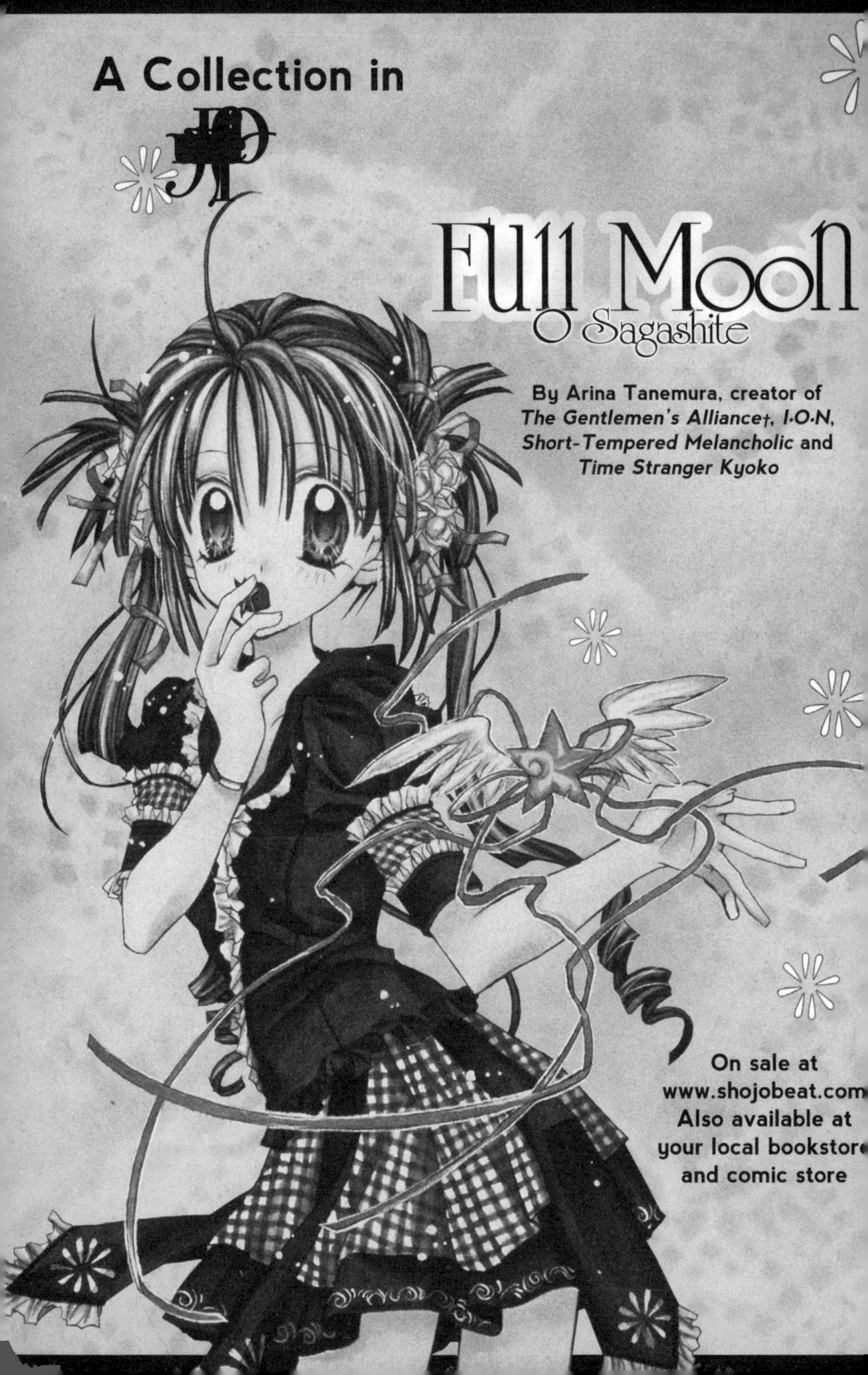
A Collection in
JP
Full Moon
O Sagashite
By Arina Tanemura, creator of
The Gentlemen's Alliance†, I·O·N,
Short-Tempered Melancholic and
Time Stranger Kyoko
On sale at
www.shojobeat.com
Also available at
your local bookstore
and comic store

Tell us what you think about Shojo Beat Manga!

Our survey is now available online. Go to:

shojobeat.com/mangasurvey

Help us make our product offerings better!